The Dolphin Writer, Book Three

The Dolphin Writer, Book Three

Crafting Essays

HOUGHTON MIFFLIN COMPANY   **Boston**   **New York**

Executive Publisher: Patricia Coryell
Editor-in-Chief: Carrie Brandon
Sponsoring Editor: Joann Kozyrev
Senior Marketing Manager: Tom Ziolkowski
Senior Development Editor: Judith Fifer
Project Editor: Shelley Dickerson
Art and Design Manager: Jill Haber
Cover Design Manager: Anne S. Katzeff
Senior Photo Editor: Jennifer Meyer Dare
Senior Composition Buyer: Chuck Dutton
New Title Project Manager: James Lonergan
Editorial Assistant: Daisuke Yasutake
Marketing Assistant: Bettina Chiu
Editorial Assistant: Anthony D'Aries

Cover image: Lisa Kreick—Ocean Eyes Photography; www.oceaneyesphotography.com

Printed in the U.S.A.

Library of Congress Control Number: 2007932616

Instructor's Annotated Edition ISBN 10: 0-618-37913-4
Instructor's Annotated Edition ISBN 13: 978-0-618-37913-2
For ordering, use student text ISBNs
Student Edition ISBN 10: 0-618-37910-X
Student Edition ISBN 13: 978-0-618-37910-1

1 2 3 4 5 6 7 8 9–DOC–11 10 09 08 07

Brief Contents

Table of Contents

Part II   THE WRITING PROCESS

Part IV   READING SELECTIONS

Each reading is followed by Mode and Skill Check questions and
Questions for Writing and Discussion.

Part V   HANDBOOK WITH EXERCISES   451

Parts of Speech   451
Nouns   451
Pronouns   453
Adjectives   455
Verbs   457
Adverbs   459
Prepositions   460
Conjunctions   462
Interjections   464

The Basic Sentence   464
Subjects   465
Other Elements of Simple Sentences   469
Verbs   476
Modifiers: Adjectives and Adverbs   491
Subject-Verb Agreement   504
Pronouns and Pronoun Agreement   512

Coordination   522
The Compound Sentence   522
Compound Elements   522
Three Kinds of Compound Sentences   523
Distinguishing Compound Elements from
  Compound Sentences   529
Avoiding Comma Splices and Run-ons in Compound Sentences   530

Preface

The Dolphin Writer

The Dolphin Writer is a three volume series that focuses on writing sentences to paragraphs (Book One), paragraphs to essays (Book Two), and essays (Book Three) in an easy-to-understand and affordable format. Each volume of the Dolphin Writer presents students with comprehensive yet approachable coverage of the writing process, from prewriting through peer evaluation through revision and preparation of the final paper. Book One includes complete coverage of sentence-to-paragraph issues such as grammar, mechanics, and usage, while Books Two and Three include a brief Handbook that contains this basic coverage. Each volume includes a readings section with ten level-appropriate readings.

The Dolphin Writer — Book Three

Key features of this volume include:

- the same topics and content as do other comparable textbooks, but for a price that is more than a third less than that of similar books

- careful step-by-step explanations of each part of the writing process along with many student models; each of the Writing Process chapters includes a "Student Demonstration" of the process, as well as many shorter student samples throughout the chapter

- a multitude of practice exercises that permit students to practice each new concept; half of the practice exercises are self-tests, with suggested answers listed in the back of the book

- carefully-selected photos and other illustrations that enhance student understanding of the text and help students learn to understand and interpret visuals

- a focus on student success in all areas of reading, writing, and studying, with Writing for Success boxes that suggest ways to organize, manage, or implement techniques, including how to use a computer to assist in the writing process

- Web Work boxes at the end of each chapter provide suggestions for sites that provide additional help, exercises, or suggestions for further exploration

- definitions of difficult words as well as allusions in many of the examples, exercises, and readings appear as footnotes so that students don't have to look them up

- chapter pedagogy supports students in anticipating, learning, and reviewing key concepts, as well as providing suggestions for discussion and writing practice

- an ESL appendix focuses on areas of difficulty for multilingual students or students who need additional practice in standard English

- a grammar handbook with practice exercises, to help students review grammar principles and obtain practice with problem areas

- a student website that includes grammar practice exercises and live links to additional information and practice sites

Organization of the Text

Part I of the text, **Writing, Reading, and Thinking,** helps students prepare for their experience in a writing course by introducing them to principles of critical thinking, and how active reading techniques like previewing and annotating the text can aid comprehension and stimulate the writing process. Chapter 1: Improving Writing and Thinking introduces broad issues of how students can develop and use critical thinking and writing abilities throughout their college courses and beyond.

Part II: The Writing Process covers all aspects of the writing process from prewriting, organizing, and outlining to writing, revising, editing, and preparing the final draft. Each chapter in this part includes a Writing for Success box that provides specific tips and ideas, as well as a student demonstration of the topics covered in the chapter.

Part III: Developing Essays with the Rhetorical Modes covers writing narration, description, process, illustration, classification, division, comparison/contrast, cause/effect, definition, and argument essays. Chapter 18 discusses how to combine modes of development, and Chapter 19 introduces the incorporation of source material into essays.

Part IV: Reading Selections includes ten high-interest reading selections from a diverse group of authors. The reading selections were carefully selected for reading level, relevance to students' lives, diversity of authorship and subject matter, and applicability to the modes and concepts introduced in this text.

Part V of this text provides a **Handbook** of basic grammar instruction, with exercises for additional practice in any given skill. (Additional practice exercises are also provided on the companion student website.)

The final sections at the back of the book include an appendix for multilingual writers that provides special focus and practice on concepts of concern for ESL writers, an Index, and a Rhetorical Index.

Ancillaries

For instructors

The instructor's website for this text provides sample syllabi, additional writing topic suggestions, and chapter quizzes.

WriteSpace for Developmental English, Houghton Mifflin's Blackboard-enabled classroom management system, allows instructors to create a customized course with additional online components for students, a customized gradebook, and HM Assess, a diagnostic tool that evaluates student problem areas and provides a customized study path for that student. Instructors can also utilize Re:Mark, for online paper review and marking, and Peer Re:Mark, which allows students to review and comment on each other's papers.

For students

A student website provides 650 interactive grammar exercises that generate instant feedback and direct students back to the appropriate text section for further study, and links to websites that provide further information and practice opportunities.

Acknowledgments

Special thanks are owed to the reviewers of this series:

Sydney Bartman of *Mount San Antonio College*

Kathleen Beauchene of *Community College of Rhode Island*

Dawn L. Brickey of *Charleston Southern University*

Carol Ann Britt of *San Antonio College*

James W. Cornish of *McLennan Community College*

Ned Cummings of *Bryant & Stratton College*

Joli J. Dusk of *Lurleen B. Wallace Community College*

Donna Eisenstat of *West Virginia University Institute of Technology*

Grushenka Engelbrecht-Castanon of *Northwest College*

Matt Fox of *Monroe Community College*

Hank Galmish of *Green River Community College*

Mary Gross of *MiraCosta College*

Aileen Gum of *San Diego Community College District*

Toni Holloway of *Mountain View College*

Teresa S. Irvin of *Columbus State University*

Lilia A. Joy of *Henderson Community College*

Patsy Krech of *The University of Memphis*

Steven Lacek of *Southern West Virginia Community and Technical College*

Jill A. Lahnstein of *Cape Fear Community College*

James Landers of *Community College of Philadelphia*

Catherine A. Lutz of *Texas A&M, Kingsville*

Patricia Maddox of *Amarillo College*

Teri Maddox of *Jackson State Community College*

Lisa Maggard of *Hazard Community & Technical College*

Patricia A. Malinowski of *Finger Lakes Community College*

Eugene Marino of *Monroe Community College*

Patricia McGraw of *Cape Cod Community College*

Carol Miter of *Riverside Community College, Norco Campus*

Theresa Mohamed of *Onondaga Community College*

Barbara E. Nixon of *Salem Community College*

Peggy Roche of *Community College of Allegheny County*

Sara Safdie of *Bellevue Community College*

James Scannell McCormick of *Rochester Community and Technical College*

Midge L. Shaw of *Rogue Community College*

Linda Spoelman of *Grand Rapids Community College*

Deborah Stallings of *Hinds Community College*

Karen Supak of *Western New Mexico University*

Linda Marianne Taylor of *Tri-County Technical College*

Dennielle True of *Manatee Community College*

Margaret Waguespcak of *Amarillo College*

Cody Yeager of *Central Oregon Community College*

Dana Zimbleman of *Jefferson College*

Improving Writing and Thinking

GOALS FOR CHAPTER 1

▶ Explain why it is important to develop good writing skills.

▶ Explain the three opportunities offered to you by this textbook, this course, your instructor, and your classmates.

▶ Explain how reading others' writing helps strengthen writing skills.

You have probably already written quite a few papers, letters, e-mail messages, and other documents. When you have to write something, do you enjoy it? Why or why not?

If you are like many people, you probably answered that you dislike writing. You might find writing distasteful because it is always so difficult, because you struggle with it, and/or because your previous efforts have been unrewarding in terms of grades or feedback from others.

Yet you know by now that you have to write. You will have to write papers like essays and research papers in your academic courses. You will have to write documents like reports, memorandums, and letters as part of your professional responsibilities. And you will have to write things like letters and notes in your personal life. Furthermore, your success in all of these areas will depend, in part, on your writing skills. As a matter of fact, there will be times in your life when others—such as your instructors, your supervisors, and your future customers or clients—will judge you and either reward you or hinder your progress based on your writing skills alone.

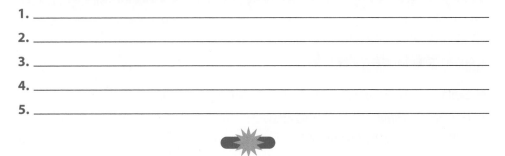

EXERCISE 1.1   **Considering the Benefits of Good Writing Skills**

On the blanks following, list all of the benefits you will gain now and in the future by improving your writing skills.

1. _____

2. _____

3. _____

4. _____

5. _____

Now that you have been reminded about how important good writing skills can be, you might be ready to commit to improving yours. So where do you begin? This book will cover various tools and techniques that are available to make both the writing process and your finished products better. Therefore, as you complete the activities and assignments in each chapter and share your results with your instructor and fellow students, you will be working on strengthening your writing skills. However, to get the most out of this course and this text, consider preparing yourself mentally to succeed by examining the many opportunities that lie before you.

Writing as Opportunity

Writing offers you several important opportunities: the opportunity to express yourself, the opportunity to expand your own understanding, and the opportunity to improve crucial thinking skills.

The Opportunity to Express Yourself

All humans like to express themselves. You probably like to discuss your ideas, beliefs, and feelings with friends or family members. You may like to express yourself creatively, perhaps by playing music, dancing, painting, or even writing poetry or stories. Writing is yet another tool for self-expression. Even the academic papers that you write give you a chance to share with others your thoughts about important subjects. So instead of viewing writing as a punishment, begin to look at it as another opportunity for telling others what you think and feel.

EXERCISE 1.2   **Writing to Express Yourself**

On the following blanks, write whatever comes into your head about something that inspires strong feelings in you. For instance, it could be the treatment of animals, your faith or spirituality, your favorite movie, or your educational goals. Take note of how freely your ideas and the words come when you write about something about which you feel passionately.

_____

_____

_____

_____

The Opportunity to Expand Your Own Understanding

Have you ever noticed that your thoughts and feelings always become clearer to you when you talk about them with others or write them down? That is because talking and writing require you to find words to express ideas that tend to be vague and half-formed before you try to communicate them. The act of finding language to share your thoughts helps you clarify in your own mind what you think and believe. Therefore, writing is a valuable tool for increasing your understanding of your own ideas.

Writing is also a valuable tool for learning. When you write, you must think extensively about your subject. This lengthier, deeper, and more intense thought often leads to new insights and discoveries about the topic; as a matter of fact, when you write, you are likely to make new connections that you may not have made if you had not written about the subject. Thus, writing leads you to expand your knowledge and understanding of your subject matter.

EXERCISE 1.3   **Writing to Expand Your Understanding**

On the following blanks, write down three subjects that you would like to learn more about. The next time an instructor gives you a choice of topics for a writing assignment, consider choosing one of the topics in this list. Or do not wait for an assignment. Begin writing about one or more of these topics in a journal.

1. _____

2. _____

3. _____

The Opportunity to Improve Crucial Thinking Skills

As mentioned previously, writing requires many different kinds of thinking skills, including logical reasoning, analysis, synthesis, creativity, and organization. These are the same thinking skills that you will need in many different areas of your academic, professional, and personal lives. Think of each new writing assignment as an opportunity to develop and strengthen the crucial thinking skills that will help you succeed in life.

EXERCISE 1.4   **Writing to Improve Thinking Skills**

On the following blanks, list two writing assignments that you have to complete in the near future. They could be academic, professional, or personal writing tasks. Beside each assignment, write down what you believe you will need to do in order to complete it.

1. _____

_____

2. _____

_____

The Opportunities Before You Now

Now that you have begun to think of the process of writing itself as an opportunity, consider next the opportunities that now lie before you as you begin this course. Specifically, this course, this textbook, this instructor, and these classmates offer you a number of valuable opportunities to develop your writing skills.

The Opportunity to Increase Your Knowledge About Writing

If writing has always been difficult or unrewarding for you, then you probably need to increase your knowledge about the process of writing and the essential features of a successful finished product. This course, this book, and your instructor's expertise can help you learn more about what you need to do to become a better writer, so view this course as an opportunity to expand valuable knowledge.

The goal of this text is to help you improve your writing skills by increasing your understanding of *what* you are doing and *how* you are doing it. Thus, Part II covers the writing process, describing steps you can follow and techniques you can use to discover, organize, and find the right words to express your ideas. Part III will show you different methods that you can use to develop your ideas so that you will communicate more effectively with your readers. Part IV will provide you with reading selections to study and learn from, and Part V offers a handy grammar handbook to answer your questions about the mechanics of writing.

EXERCISE 1.5　Setting Goals for Improvement

Place a check mark on the blank beside every aspect of your writing that you would like to improve. Then, for each checked item, fill in the chapter number(s) or part of this book that contains information about those topics. Use this book's table of contents and index to help you identify chapter and part numbers.

____ Overcoming writer's block (Chapter ____)

____ Finding topics and ideas to write about (Chapter ____)

____ Figuring out how to organize or determine the right order for ideas (Chapter ____)

____ Writing clear sentences (Part ____)

____ Spelling words correctly (Part ____)

____ Making sentences grammatically correct (Part ____)

____ Knowing where to put commas, semicolons, and other punctuation marks (Part ____)

____ Developing, or explaining ideas (Chapters ____)

____ Knowing where to find information, or research (Chapter ____)

____ Other: _____ (Chapter(s) ____)

The Opportunity to Practice and Gain Valuable Feedback

In addition to increasing your knowledge about the processes and features of good writing, you must also practice writing if you are going to improve your writing skills. This textbook includes numerous writing assignments, and this course offers valuable opportunities to get feedback on what you write from your instructor and perhaps even from your classmates. The comments and suggestions that you get from others will help you identify your strengths as a writer along with areas that need improvement. Thus, you will have many chances to discover what works and what does not work and to make adjustments accordingly the next time you write.

So get in the habit of carefully considering the feedback you get from your instructor and from your peers. Instead of putting a graded paper away right after you receive it, spend some time really trying to understand the instructor's suggestions for improvement. For those weak areas he or she identifies, formulate a plan for improving them so that you will not repeat the same mistakes in your next paper. For example, if your paper contains apostrophe errors, resolve to study the rules for apostrophes. If your instructor points out organizational problems, review the chapter about organizing ideas. If you do not understand a teacher's comments or suggestions, make an appointment with him or her to ask questions and get some advice about how you can improve the next time.

EXERCISE 1.6   **Considering Feedback**

The following paper was written by a student who was assigned to argue in favor of something. This student wrote the paper and submitted it, and then his instructor graded the paper, adding comments and suggestions in red ink. Read over this graded paper and the teacher's comments and answer the questions that follow.

Americans Should Own Hybrid Cars

By Lana Browning

Use a technique to interest the reader

Hybrid gasoline-electric cars hit the American market in the 1990s. As they run, they draw power alternately from either their gasoline engines, or their electric generators, so they use a lot less gas. But unlike the old 1970s

Good background info

versions, they charge themselves, and do not

need to be plugged in every night. They're also just like regular cars, so they go just as fast and as far as a car with a gasoline engine. But they're much more fuel-efficient, and that is what's important today. Each American would *pronoun agreement*   *pronoun agreement* sleep better at night, if (they) traded in (their) gasoline-engine cars for a hybrid car.

One good reason to switch is for your own personal savings. It will *details?* cost you less to own and operate a hybrid car, because you'll need *details?* a lot less gas. Today's hybrid cars get 50 to *comma splice* 60 miles per gallon, that is more than double the gas mileage of regular cars.

Research to find specific details

While you're saving money, you can be more environmentally conscious. The vehicles Americans drive are starting to cause serious problems. Vehicles *details?* contribute significantly to air pollution, especially in larger cities like Los Angeles, which is a growing concern for all citizens. Global warming, which is caused by burning fossil fuels like gasoline, may begin to *explain* cause big problems for our planet. So, if you continue to drive a gasoline-only car, you're contributing to environmental problems that are only going to get worse unless we all make a change.

Add a transi-
tion and clear
topic sentence

Vehicles, especially huge sport-utility vehi-

cles / that guzzle gas, are keeping us in need of

how much?   *comma splice*

huge quantities of oil for <u>fuel, this</u> makes our

effective sup-
porting points

country depend on foreign sources for that oil.

how? why?

We all know that America would be <u>better off</u> if

we could be independent. If we used less oil, we

might be able to furnish our own needs with

supplies found in our own country. Therefore,

buying a hybrid car is a patriotic duty.

So these are three good reasons for every-

one to switch to a hybrid car. They're not that

much more expensive than a regular car, and

besides, you end up saving a lot of money on

usage

gas anyway. So the next time (your) shopping

for a car, consider a hybrid. You'll be making

good
conclusion

the right choice.

1. What is one thing the instructor praised about this paper?

_____

2. What grammatical concept does the writer need to learn more about?

_____

_____

3. What is the instructor's advice about all three of the writer's body paragraphs?

_____

_____

4. Where in this book could this student go for more instruction in each of the
following? Write the chapter number(s) on the blanks provided.

Developing ideas with specific details (Chapters _____)
Researching a topic (Chapter _____)

Using transitions (Chapters _____)
Comma splices (Part _____)
Pronoun agreement (Part _____)
Commas (Part _____)

 EXERCISE 1.7 **Considering Current Strengths and Areas for Improvement**

Find one of your graded papers from another class you took. Read the instructor's comments and suggestions. Then fill in the following blanks.

Three of my strengths seem to be

   1. _____

   2. _____

   3. _____

Three areas where I need to improve are

   1. _____

   2. _____

   3. _____

Comments or suggestions that I do not understand are

_____

_____

The Opportunity to Learn from Others' Writings

So far, you have learned that improving writing skills involves increasing your knowledge about writing, practicing, and learning from the feedback you get. A third way to improve your writing skills is to read and study the writing of others. This text includes both professional selections and student writing as examples and as the basis of exercises. These selections will help you by giving you helpful models of writing concepts in action. They will also provide you with ideas for your own compositions. They will give you information you can use to support your ideas. Finally, they will encourage you to strengthen your critical thinking skills.

Reading to Improve Writing Skills. One important benefit of reading is the opportunity to study the writing of others and get models of successful essays that can help you when you create your own documents. Thus, the more you read—especially if you try to read the writings of capable and talented authors—the more exposure you will get to the different ways to organize and develop a topic.

EXERCISE 1.8   **Reading to Improve Writing Skills**

Read the next essay and answer the questions that follow by writing your answers on the blanks provided.

The Learning Curve

1   The patient needed a central line. "Here's your chance," S., the chief resident, said. I had never done one before. "Get set up and then page me when you're ready to start."

2   It was my fourth week in surgical training. The pockets of my short white coat bulged with patient printouts, laminated cards with instructions for doing CPR and reading EKGs and using the dictation system, two surgical handbooks, a stethoscope, wound-dressing supplies, meal tickets, a penlight, scissors, and about a dollar in loose change. As I headed up the stairs to the patient's floor, I rattled.

3   This will be good, I tried to tell myself: my first real procedure. The patient—fiftyish, stout, taciturn[1]—was recovering from abdominal surgery he'd had about a week earlier. His bowel function hadn't yet returned, and he was unable to eat. I explained to him that he needed intravenous[2] nutrition and that this required a "special line" that would go into his chest. I said that I would put the line in him while he was in his bed, and that it would involve my numbing a spot on his chest with a local anesthetic, and then threading the line in. I did not say that the line was eight inches long and would go into his vena cava, the main blood vessel to his heart. Nor did I say how tricky the procedure could be. There were "slight risks" involved, I said, such as bleeding and lung collapse; in experienced hands, complications of this sort occur in fewer than one case in a hundred.

4   But, of course, mine were not experienced hands. And the disasters I knew about weighed on my mind: the woman who had died within minutes from massive bleeding when a resident lacerated[3] her vena cava; the man whose chest had to be opened because a resident lost hold of a wire inside the line, which then floated down to the patient's heart; the man who had a cardiac arrest when

1. **taciturn:** reserved; cold or aloof
2. **intravenous:** used in administering fluids or medicines into the veins

3. **lacerated:** torn or cut; shredded

the procedure put him into ventricular fibrillation[1]. I said nothing of such things, naturally, when I asked the patient's permission to do his line. He said, "O.K."

5   I had seen S. do two central lines; one was the day before, and I'd attended to every step. I watched how she set out her instruments and laid her patient down and put a rolled towel between his shoulder blades to make his chest arch out. I watched how she swabbed his chest with antiseptic, injected lidocaine, which is a local anesthetic, and then, in full sterile garb, punctured his chest near his clavicle[2] with a fat three-inch needle on a syringe. The patient hadn't even flinched. She told me how to avoid hitting the lung ("Go in at a steep angle," she'd said. "Stay right under the clavicle"), and how to find the subclavian vein, a branch to the vena cava lying atop the lung near its apex[3].

6   She pushed the needle in almost all the way. She drew back on the syringe. And she was in. You knew because the syringe filled with maroon blood. ("If it's bright red, you've hit an artery," she said. "That's not good.") Once you have the tip of this needle poking in the vein, you somehow have to widen the hole in the vein wall, fit the catheter[4] in, and snake it in the right direction—down to the heart, rather than up to the brain—all without tearing through vessels, lung, or anything else.

7   To do this, S. explained, you start by getting a guide wire in place. She pulled the syringe off, leaving the needle in. Blood flowed out. She picked up a two-foot-long twenty-gauge wire that looked like the steel D string of an electric guitar, and passed nearly its full length through the needle's bore, into the vein, and onward toward the vena cava. "Never force it in," she warned, "and never, ever let go of it." A string of rapid heartbeats fired off on the cardiac monitor, and she quickly pulled the wire back an inch. It had poked into the heart, causing momentary fibrillation. "Guess we're in the right place," she said to me quietly. Then to the patient: "You're doing great. Only a few minutes now." She pulled the needle out over the wire and replaced it with a bullet of thick, stiff plastic, which she pushed in tight to widen the vein opening. She then removed this dilator[5] and threaded the central line—a spaghetti-thick, flexible yellow plastic tube—over the wire until it was all the way in. Now she could remove the wire. She flushed the line with a heparin solution and sutured[6] it to the patient's chest. And that was it.

8   Today, it was my turn to try. First, I had to gather supplies—a central-line kit, gloves, gown, cap, mask, lidocaine—which took me forever. When I finally

1. **fibrillation:** rapid irregular heartbeat
2. **clavicle:** bone at the front of the human shoulder
3. **apex:** peak; summit
4. **catheter:** thin tube used in medicine

5. **dilator:** something that makes something else wider or larger; used in medicine
6. **sutured:** sewed up, usually with stitches or medical staples

had the stuff together, I stopped for a minute outside the patient's door, trying to recall the steps. They remained frustratingly hazy. But I couldn't put it off any longer. I had a page-long list of other things to get done: Mrs. A needed to be discharged; Mr. B needed an abdominal ultrasound arranged; Mrs. C needed her skin staples removed. And every fifteen minutes or so I was getting paged with more tasks: Mr. X was nauseated and needed to be seen; Miss Y's family was here and needed "someone" to talk to them; Mr. Z needed a laxative. I took a deep breath, put on my best don't-worry-I-know-what-I'm-doing look, and went in.

9   I placed the supplies on a bedside table, untied the patient's gown, and laid him down flat on the mattress, with his chest bare and his arms at his sides. I flipped on a fluorescent overhead light and raised his bed to my height. I paged S. I put on my gown and gloves and, on a sterile tray, laid out the central line, the guide wire, and other materials from the kit. I drew up five cc's of lidocaine in a syringe, soaked two sponge sticks in the yellow-brown Betadine, and opened up the suture packaging.

10   S. arrived. "What's his platelet[1] count?"

11   My stomach knotted. I hadn't checked. That was bad: too low and he could have a serious bleed from the procedure. She went to check a computer. The count was acceptable.

12   Chastened[2], I started swabbing his chest with the sponge sticks. "Got the shoulder roll underneath him?" S. asked. Well, no, I had forgotten that, too. The patient gave me a look. S., saying nothing, got a towel, rolled it up, and slipped it under his back for me. I finished applying the antiseptic and then draped him so that only his right upper chest was exposed. He squirmed a bit beneath the drapes. S. now inspected my tray. I girded[3] myself.

13   "Where's the extra syringe for flushing the line when it's in?" Damn. She went out and got it.

14   I felt for my landmarks. Here? I asked with my eyes, not wanting to undermine the patient's confidence any further. She nodded. I numbed the spot with lidocaine. ("You'll feel a stick and a burn now, sir.") Next, I took the three-inch needle in hand and poked it through the skin. I advanced it slowly and uncertainly, a few millimetres at a time. This is a big goddam needle, I kept thinking. I couldn't believe I was sticking it into someone's chest. I concentrated on maintaining a steep angle of entry, but kept spearing his clavicle instead of slipping beneath it.

15   "Ow!" he shouted.

16   "Sorry," I said. S. signalled with a kind of surfing hand gesture to go underneath the clavicle. This time, it went in. I drew back on the syringe. Nothing.

---

1. **platelet:** blood particles involved in clotting

2. **chastened:** subjected to discipline
3. **girded:** got ready

She pointed deeper. I went in deeper. Nothing. I withdrew the needle, flushed out some bits of tissue clogging it, and tried again.

17   "Ow!"

18   Too steep again. I found my way underneath the clavicle once more. I drew the syringe back. Still nothing. He's too obese, I thought. S. slipped on gloves and a gown. "How about I have a look?" she said. I handed her the needle and stepped aside. She plunged the needle in, drew back on the syringe, and, just like that, she was in. "We'll be done shortly," she told the patient.

19   She let me continue with the next steps, which I bumbled through. I didn't realize how long and floppy the guide wire was until I pulled the coil out of its plastic sleeve, and, putting one end of it into the patient, I very nearly contaminated the other. I forgot about the dilating step until she reminded me. Then, when I put in the dilator, I didn't push quite hard enough, and it was really S. who pushed it all the way in. Finally, we got the line in, flushed it, and sutured it in place.

20   Outside the room, S. said that I could be less tentative the next time, but that I shouldn't worry too much about how things had gone. "You'll get it," she said. "It just takes practice." I wasn't so sure. The procedure remained wholly mysterious to me. And I could not get over the idea of jabbing a needle into someone's chest so deeply and so blindly. I awaited the X-ray afterward with trepidation[1]. But it came back fine: I had not injured the lung and the line was in the right place.

21   Not everyone appreciates the attractions of surgery. When you are a medical student in the operating room for the first time, and you see the surgeon press the scalpel to someone's body and open it like a piece of fruit, you either shudder in horror or gape in awe. I gaped[2]. It was not just the blood and guts that enthralled[3] me. It was also the idea that a person, a mere mortal, would have the confidence to wield that scalpel in the first place.

22   There is a saying about surgeons: "Sometimes wrong; never in doubt." This is meant as a reproof[4], but to me it seemed their strength. Every day, surgeons are faced with uncertainties. Information is inadequate; the science is ambiguous[5]; one's knowledge and abilities are never perfect. Even with the simplest operation, it cannot be taken for granted that a patient will come through better off—or even alive. Standing at the operating table, I wondered how the surgeon knew that all the steps would go as planned, that bleeding would be controlled and infection would not set in and organs would not be injured. He didn't, of course. But he cut anyway.

23   Later, while still a student, I was allowed to make an incision myself. The surgeon drew a six-inch dotted line with a marking pen across an anesthetized

---

1. **trepidation:** fear or hesitation
2. **gaped:** stared with mouth open; opened a gap
3. **enthralled:** captivated; fascinated
4. **reproof:** criticism; scolding
5. **ambiguous:** vague or unclear

patient's abdomen and then, to my surprise, had the nurse hand me the knife. It was still warm from the autoclave[1]. The surgeon had me stretch the skin taut with the thumb and forefinger of my free hand. He told me to make one smooth slice down to the fat. I put the belly of the blade to the skin and cut. The experience was odd and addictive, mixing exhilaration from the calculated violence of the act, anxiety about getting it right, and a righteous faith that it was somehow for the person's good. There was also the slightly nauseating feeling of finding that it took more force than I'd realized. (Skin is thick and springy, and on my first pass I did not go nearly deep enough; I had to cut twice to get through.) The moment made me want to be a surgeon—not an amateur handed the knife for a brief moment but someone with the confidence and ability to proceed as if it were routine.

24   A resident begins, however, with none of this air of mastery—only an overpowering instinct against doing anything like pressing a knife against flesh or jabbing a needle into someone's chest. On my first day as a surgical resident, I was assigned to the emergency room. Among my first patients was a skinny, dark-haired woman in her late twenties who hobbled in, teeth gritted, with a two-foot-long wooden chair leg somehow nailed to the bottom of her foot. She explained that a kitchen chair had collapsed under her and, as she leaped up to keep from falling, her bare foot had stomped down on a three-inch screw sticking out of one of the chair legs. I tried very hard to look like someone who had not got his medical diploma just the week before. Instead, I was determined to be nonchalant[2], the kind of guy who had seen this sort of thing a hundred times before. I inspected her foot, and could see that the screw was embedded in the bone at the base of her big toe. There was no bleeding and, as far as I could feel, no fracture.

25   "Wow, that must hurt," I blurted out, idiotically.

26   The obvious thing to do was give her a tetanus shot and pull out the screw. I ordered the tetanus shot, but I began to have doubts about pulling out the screw. Suppose she bled? Or suppose I fractured her foot? Or something worse? I excused myself and tracked down Dr. W., the senior surgeon on duty. I found him tending to a car-crash victim. The patient was a mess, and the floor was covered with blood. People were shouting. It was not a good time to ask questions.

27   I ordered an X-ray. I figured it would buy time and let me check my amateur impression that she didn't have a fracture. Sure enough, getting the X-ray took about an hour, and it showed no fracture—just a common screw embedded, the radiologist said, "in the head of the first metatarsal[3]." I showed the patient the X-ray. "You see, the screw's embedded in the head of the first metatarsal," I said. And the plan? she wanted to know. Ah, yes, the plan.

---

1. **autoclave:** sterilization equipment   3. **metatarsal:** foot bone
2. **nonchalant:** casual; offhand

28   I went to find Dr. W. He was still busy with the crash victim, but I was able to interrupt to show him the X-ray. He chuckled at the sight of it and asked me what I wanted to do. "Pull the screw out?" I ventured. "Yes," he said, by which he meant "Duh." He made sure I'd given the patient a tetanus shot and then shooed me away.

29   Back in the examining room, I told her that I would pull the screw out, prepared for her to say something like "You?" Instead she said, "O.K., Doctor." At first, I had her sitting on the exam table, dangling her leg off the side. But that didn't look as if it would work. Eventually, I had her lie with her foot jutting off the table end, the board poking out into the air. With every move, her pain increased. I injected a local anesthetic where the screw had gone in and that helped a little. Now I grabbed her foot in one hand, the board in the other, and for a moment I froze. Could I really do this? Who was I to presume?

30   Finally, I gave her a one-two-three and pulled, gingerly at first and then hard. She groaned. The screw wasn't budging. I twisted, and abruptly it came free. There was no bleeding. I washed the wound out, and she found she could walk. I warned her of the risks of infection and the signs to look for. Her gratitude was immense and flattering, like the lion's for the mouse—and that night I went home elated.

31   In surgery, as in anything else, skill, judgment, and confidence are learned through experience, haltingly and humiliatingly. Like the tennis player and the oboist[1] and the guy who fixes hard drives, we need practice to get good at what we do. There is one difference in medicine, though: we practice on people.*

1. What was your favorite part of this essay? Why? What did the author do that made this part especially powerful or interesting to you?

_____

_____

_____

2. Which paragraph seems especially descriptive to you? What details does the author include that help you picture in your mind what he is describing?

_____

_____

_____

1. **oboist:** woodwind instrument player

Source: "The Learning Curve" as it appeared in *The New Yorker,* January 28, 2002 and published in a slightly different version in *Complications: A Surgeon's Notes on an Imperfect Science* as "Education of a Knife" by Atul Gawande. Copyright 2002 by Atul Gawande. Reprinted by permission of Henry Holt and Company, LLC.

3. How does the author build suspense as he narrates each story?

_____

_____

_____

4. What specific emotions did you experience as you read this essay?

_____

_____

_____

Reading for Ideas. Where will your ideas for compositions come from? Sometimes they will arise from your own experiences in life, from television or films, or from talking to other people. Often, though, they will come to you as you read the writing of others. Reading can provide a springboard of ideas for your own compositions.

For example, read the following essay entitled "The Sacred Table." As you read, try to think of possible essay topics, and write your ideas in the margin or on a separate sheet of paper.

The Sacred Table

1 In Italy, where I come from, we have a special name for family mealtime: *sacro desco*. It means "sacred table" because we honor it as a sacred time each day when we come together to share home-cooked meals, to talk and learn about each other as a family.

2 Eating together has always been very important to me and my own family. We have always looked forward to it because it's a time when we feel close and our lives integrate with one another; it brings constancy and stability to our life and a connection with our culture and traditions.

3 I never cooked until I got married at age twenty-eight. I tried to reproduce all of my mother's Italian dishes, and Victor, my husband, was so flattering: When he liked what I cooked, he'd jump up from his chair to come kiss me and tell me how talented I was. That's how I learned to cook.

4 Before I got into food professionally, I was a biologist, working long hours in a laboratory. When I came home from work, I headed straight to the kitchen. After I had my son, Guiliano, he was in there with me so I could see what he was doing. I'd let him play with the pots and pans and tear the lettuce for the salads, and I would hold him up to stir sauces and risotto. He loved the aromas.

5   Now he's handing down his love of good food and of eating to his daughter, Gabriella. At age three, she loves to be held up, like her father was, to stir the risotto with her special spoon, to mimic her pappa, saying, "It's not done!" And she loves vegetables, from artichokes to string beans. That's the starting point— to set cooking up as a pleasurable, memorable experience. If children eat at the same table, at the same time, they see what others are eating and they start to enjoy all types of food and look forward to mealtime.

6   I'm saddened because there isn't much that brings families together these days. But we all have to eat to stay alive, so why not eat food that's healthful, tastes good, and that we can enjoy as a family? It worries me that in America, family mealtime is falling by the wayside because people believe they are too busy.

7   The problem is really not time, because we can make simple and healthful meals that taste good in less time than it takes to prepare convenience food or drive to fast-food restaurants. It's more a matter of priorities. We make time to talk on the phone, play tennis, get manicures, even to wait in line at restaurants, but we don't want to take the time to cook and eat together in the privacy of our own homes.

8   Maybe it's because we live in an age where cooking is defined as "gourmet" and has to be elaborate, take a lot of time, use hard-to-find ingredients and end up in a fancy presentation. I'm continually fighting this concept because it threatens cooking's most important benefits—to eat fresh, healthy food that's prepared, as Victor says, by someone who has warmth and love for you. It's a hug and a kiss. That's the kind of food that is life for our families.

9   I don't think it's a good idea to even attempt complicated dishes in the home because when we bring our children or our spouse to the table, they don't want to take pictures of the food; they want to eat good-tasting, satisfying dishes. All we really need is to cook simply, like putting a veal chop under the broiler, making a simple pasta with a fresh salad, or drizzling a little olive oil on a piece of fish or pork and throwing it on the barbecue.

10   I would love to see people fall in love with home cooking again. There are so many simple yet wonderful things we can do at home, like the pasta sauce my family loves—not because it's easy, but because it's delicious. I just empty a good can of tomatoes into a pot, peel an onion and put it in the center, add a piece of butter, turn the fire on low, and go do other things. That's all there is to it.

11   I'm appealing to mothers and fathers to bring back family mealtime as a sacred time of the day. Get a cookbook—one that's easy. Tell your spouse and children that at a certain hour you'll sit down and eat together. Let them help in some way—peel potatoes, snap beans—for if everyone contributes to the dinner, it will have more of a family feel.

12   Make it a special time . . . a time that's all about sharing something we enjoy with the people we love.*

*Source: Janis Frawley-Holler writes more about life's simple pleasures in *Island Wise: Lessons in Living from the Islands of the World* (Broadwire Books). www.islandwisebook.com

Here is a list of topic ideas generated by one student:

> My family's dinners
> Food traditions in different countries
> Fast food
> Benefits of home cooking
> Healthy eating
> "Simple" cooking
> Eating at home versus eating out at a restaurant
> Benefits of family mealtimes

You probably have additional ideas on your own list. As you can see, this one brief essay was the springboard for many topic ideas.

EXERCISE 1.9   **Generating Essay Topic Ideas from Reading**

Read the following essay. Then, on the blanks provided, write down possible essay topics that occurred to you as you read.

Cheating Wends[1] Way from Youth Sports to Business

1   At a Florida speedway not long ago, during a night of racing for the increasingly popular quarter-midget cars, an official pointed out a crew chief notorious for slipping a banned additive into his fuel tank. The cars look like Indy car skeletons and can go thirty miles per hour. The performance-enhancing chemical apparently worked. His car was a consistent winner.

2   Puzzled, I asked why he didn't bust the cheater. The official sighed. That would lead to a fuss, he said, maybe litigation, possibly the disruption of the race season. He said that the other competitors also preferred to let nature take its course; soon enough, the crew chief's driver—his son—would turn eight and move up to a higher race classification. Let someone else deal with the problem.

3   "But what about the other fathers and sons?" I asked. "What lessons were they learning? Wasn't sports supposed to be that one fair place where the white lines defined the boundaries of what was right and what was wrong?"

4   The beleaguered[2] official, half my age, gave me one of those "grow up" looks and said, "Don't blame us. Look at society."

5   But this is where it starts, I said. A Little League pitcher lies about his age. A teenage basketball star fibs about his address so he can join a high school team

---

1. **wends:** travels along a route   2. **beleaguered:** bothered; annoyed

out of his district. Grades and test scores are altered for a promising college football recruit. Kids see grown-ups shrug or wink, if not pull the strings behind the scenes. By the time we hear about a major leaguer corking his bat or an Olympian on steroids, it's hard to be shocked. Sometimes it seems like part of the game. Then we blame the celebrity athlete for being a bad role model and "society" for creating a win-at-all-costs culture.

6   Maybe if the cheating stayed in the game, it wouldn't matter as much as it does. After all, the final score of an athletic contest is rarely earthshaking. But haven't we been led to believe that sports are where many of us learn life's lessons? What happens when those twelve-year-olds become politicians, police officers and stockbrokers? At a time when the two-year anniversary of the Enron scandal[1] is being observed and former Tyco executive Dennis Kozlowski is on trial on charges of looting his company, are there dots to be connected between that first little lie to win a peewee game and the complex webs of deceit spun to win on Wall Street and in Washington?

7   "A case could be made that what Enron officials did isn't significantly different from what can happen in a sporting event," says Stanford University's Jim Thompson, founder of the Positive Coaching Alliance. "The auditors weren't paying attention, so they decided they could push the envelope and see what they could get away with."

8   Brenda Light Bredemeier, a psychologist who co-directs the University of Notre Dame's Mendelson Center for Sports, Character and Community, agrees, adding: "First of all, there's no question that within sports is the great opportunity to teach moral values. The greatest predictor of moral behavior is the child's perception of how his or her coach and peers define success. That becomes the norm for the child. And athletes take that norm off the playing field and out onto the street."

9   Thompson and Bredemeier were among several dozen coaches, academics and journalists who met last month in upstate New York at the National Institute for Sports Reform's inaugural conference. They spent little time bewailing sports' current sex and drug scandals. Those were merely late-stage symptoms, they agreed, of a malady[2] contracted in childhood from parents and coaches bending the rules.

10   "I'm very concerned that at even younger ages than ever before, our children are learning how the rules do not really matter unless you get caught breaking them, and if you do, the penalties are not really bad," said Bill Cushing, a coach and regional youth sports director in the Albany, N.Y., area.

---

1. **Enron scandal:** a major corporate scandal in the United States in which executives at the Enron corporation were involved in financial trickery for their own gain

2. **malady:** illness; problem

"Players are coached how to get away with fouls and how to get an unfair advantage as part of the game. Many parents are against this, but they are afraid of being humiliated by coaches if they complain. . . . Kids develop their own values based on what they see happening around them. The lessons learned in sports are carried through life and cause things like Enron, plagiarism[1], hazing[2], academic cheating, the 'Superman' mentality when it comes to drugs, drinking and driving, abusive sex."

11   While the conferees tended to agree with Cushing, there was no consensus on remedies. The group's founder, Bruce Svare, a professor of psychology and neuroscience and a kids' team coach, would solve the problem by banning college athletic scholarships, which he called "the root of all evil."

12   Thompson disagreed. His solution would be to re-educate coaches to win while honoring the rules: "Character education on the playing field is immediate, intense and in-your-face. Wouldn't it be great if we have athletes saying, 'I wouldn't dare do something bad because I want my coach and team to be proud of me'?"

13   Cushing's solution is the best and most difficult. He says parents have to stand up. If doing it individually is too daunting[3], get a group to face down the parent who breaks the rules, or the coach who brushes you off. If you wait for time to do the job, the next problem could be a lot bigger than a game or an auto race. That crew chief needs to be grounded before his seven-year-old son is on track to drive a corporation.*

Topic ideas:

_____

_____

_____

_____

_____

_____

_____

1. **plagiarism:** copying another's work and passing it off as one's own
2. **hazing:** initiating someone into an organization by torturing or humiliating him or her
3. **daunting:** intimidating; off putting

*Source: Robert Lipsyte, "Cheating Wends Way from Youth Sports to Business," USA Today, December 10, 2003, p. 23A. Reprinted with permission.

EXERCISE 1.10   Generating Ideas from a Photograph

Study the following photograph. Then, on the blanks provided, write down possible essay topics that occur to you as you look at the image.

ThinkstockRF/Jupiter Images

_____

_____

_____

_____

_____

Reading for Learning and Critical Thinking. In addition to giving us topic ideas, reading also provides us with information we can include in our own compositions. From our reading, we glean facts, examples, direct quotations, and other kinds of information that helps us develop and support our own thoughts about a subject.

Furthermore, reading exposes us to others' thoughts about important topics and leads us to reflect more upon those topics. As a result, reading helps us form or confirm our own thoughts and beliefs. In other words, reading encourages us to think critically by holding what we know up to scrutiny and then deciding if our opinions are still valid.

You do not have to agree with everything you read. Critical thinking involves considering what a writer has to say and then applying your own powers of logic and observation to decide if those ideas are valid.

⭐ **EXERCISE 1.11**   **Reading for Learning and Critical Thinking**

Read the next essay and then answer the questions that follow by writing your answers on the blanks provided.

Bridezilla's Revenge

People love oohing and aahing over a bride—almost as much as they enjoy tsk-tsking about her wedding plans. And there are enough over-the-top, outlandish or just plain quirky weddings in modern America to provide plenty of opportunities for griping. During one recent talk show focusing on the bizarre wedding of TV personality Star Jones—who had a 49-person bridal party and wore a dress with a 27-foot crystal-studded train—scores of listeners called in to complain about wedding travesties[1] that they had themselves endured. The callers recounted tedious vows, painfully off-key songs warbled by bride and groom, the inclusion of the groom's dog in the ceremony. They exchanged horror stories about controlling brides-to-be who obsessed over the trim on bridesmaids' dresses and got into screaming fights about appetizers.

There is a reason why weddings bring out the worst in some young couples: A profound social shift has transformed marriage, and today's wedding ceremonies reflect this change. Marriage is now based on the love of two partners who have an equal say in determining how their commitment will work. As a result, constructing a marriage is now a more personal undertaking—but it is also more precarious[2].

The contemporary romanticization of marriage would be unrecognizable to the majority of people in the past. Through most of human history, marriage has been a practical economic and political institution over which the betrothed had little control. From the early Middle Ages to the 18th century, marriages for upper-class Europeans were the way that families raised funds, sealed political alliances and made sure that no former lovers or illegitimate children could make claims on their wealth. Elite weddings were extravagant affairs that involved expensive negotiations and festivities, often carried out over a period of months. But these elaborate weddings were not about the personal relationship between bride and groom, who might have never met—and might actually have been in love with someone else.

In the middle classes, marriage was predominantly a business proposition. It was one of the main ways that men raised capital, and the only way that women established economic security. Right up through the 1700s, the dowry[3]

---

1. **travesties:** distortions; monstrosities
2. **precarious:** uncertain
3. **dowry:** money or property brought by a bride to her husband at marriage

a wife brought to marriage was often the biggest infusion of cash and property a man would ever acquire—and endowing a daughter placed a much heavier strain on a woman's family than any modern wedding.

Even in the lower classes, marriage had more to do with practical needs than individual love. Most farms and businesses required both a man and a woman to run them, so partners were chosen with an eye toward their value as workers. Because neighbors depended on each other for loans, labor and joint village activities such as building fences, these matches were matters of intense public interest.

Throughout medieval Europe, whole villages actively took part in courting rituals and wedding festivities, to an extent that would shock us today. Suitors who were frowned upon might be pelted with rotten food and stones, and the hapless[1] couple who went ahead with an unpopular match might be treated to catcalls[2] as they left the church or greeted by young men wearing horns to suggest that the wife would be unfaithful. When a community approved the match, the couple got even less privacy. After the wedding festivities, neighbors would escort the couple to bed, to the accompaniment of loud music and ribald[3] jokes. Early the next morning, they returned to awaken the couple with more music and revelry.

By the second half of the 18th century, leading sectors of European society were beginning to toy with the radical idea that marriage should be based on the love and free choice of both partners. Marriage was more often seen as the union of soul mates in the 19th century, but wedding rituals remained highly formulaic[4]. Fathers walked their daughters down the aisle to represent a woman's transfer from her father's to her husband's protection. Brides wore white to symbolize their purity. Wedding vows emphasized the man's duty to provide and protect, and usually included the wife's promise to obey.

Fast-forward a century, and ritualized ceremonies have become ubiquitous[5]. In the 1950s, the growing emphasis on romance merged with the postwar consumer economy to create a major wedding industry. This was the golden age of what most people now think of as the "traditional" marriage, although in truth the emphasis on love was fairly new. Many modern Americans now contrast today's ostentatious[6] celebrations with the supposedly more modest weddings of that era. But this is a misconception: An average wedding now costs roughly $22,000, but that represents a smaller proportion of household income than in 1960, when the typical formal wedding cost two-thirds of the median family's yearly income!

What is really new about weddings today is not the price tag but the preoccupation with creating a personalized ceremony. In the 1950s and 1960s,

1. **hapless:** unfortunate
2. **catcalls:** disapproving taunts
3. **ribald:** vulgar; obscene
4. **formulaic:** always the same
5. **ubiquitous:** present everywhere
6. **ostentatious:** flashy; flamboyant

marriage came off the rack, so to speak. Nearly everyone married, almost always at an early age. Idealization of love notwithstanding, marriage was as much a union of two gender roles as of two individuals. The "rules" were clear-cut: Wives were to be homemakers. Husbands must be breadwinners. As a result, most 1950s weddings were as conventional as the unions they initiated. From the vows to the music to the cake decorations, weddings were variations on the same theme, depending on how much money was available.

Today, each partner brings independent habits, tastes, resources and skills that must be consciously adapted to the new relationship. Men and women now expect to negotiate a marriage that meets the individual needs of both partners. For most people, these changes are extremely liberating, and marriages that succeed can be much more rewarding and fulfilling than those of the past.

But marriage is also less stable. Couples are no longer held together by pressures from in-laws or society; women can support themselves, and men are no longer ostracized[1] if they do not marry or are divorced. Few couples before in history have had to make so many conscious choices about the kind of relationship they will have. And these decisions can be very stressful.

So perhaps we should cut anxious brides and grooms some slack. Tasteful or garish, simple or ostentatious, weddings today are the first chance a couple gets to announce to the world their chosen joint identity. Couples are preoccupied with getting each detail right because they are struggling to reflect the uniqueness of their relationship—and the hope that it will be strengthened, rather than undermined, by their individual identities and ambitions. The hope is powerful, but so is the fear that they might not get it right. Still, with plenty of time to work out the specifics, the bride and groom might want to let go of all the worrying. After all, marital bliss can't be found in the color of a bridesmaid's taffeta dress.*

1. List two pieces of information that you learned by reading this essay:

a. _____

b. _____

2. Do you agree with the author's explanation of the reason why weddings bring out the worst in some couples? Why or why not? In your opinion, are there other reasons why many people obsess over the details of their weddings? What are they? Are any or all of these reasons valid?

_____

_____

_____

1. **ostracized:** excluded; shunned

*Source: "Bridezilla's Revenge" by Stehanie Coontz, reprinted with permission from *Psychology Today Magazine*, copyright © 2005 Sussex Publishers, LLC.

3. Do you agree that "Men and women now expect to negotiate a marriage that meets the individual needs of both partners"? Explain your answer.

_____

_____

_____

4. Do you agree with the author's statement that "couples are preoccupied with getting each detail [of their wedding] right because they are struggling to reflect the uniqueness of their relationship—and the hope that it will be strengthened, rather than undermined, by their individual identities and ambitions"? Why or why not?

_____

_____

_____

5. Do your own personal experiences with weddings (your own or others') support or refute the author's opinions? Explain your answer.

_____

_____

_____

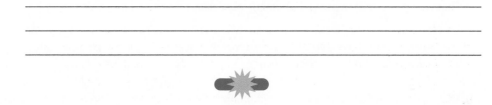

CHAPTER 1 REVIEW

To review the main points in this chapter, write a brief response to each of the following questions.

1. Why is it important to have good writing skills?

2. Writing offers three important opportunities. What are they?

3. Why is it important to express yourself through writing?

4. How does writing offer you the opportunity to expand your understanding of topics and your thoughts about these topics?

5. What thinking skills does writing offer you the opportunity to improve?

6. How do you think this text will help you improve your writing skills?

7. Take a finished piece of writing that you have and share it with a classmate or your instructor. Ask him or her for feedback.

8. How can reading and studying the writing of others help you improve your writing?

Access the *Writer's Digest* Web site at **www.writersdigest.com.** Search or click on a link for personal writing and explore the information available about writing a journal. Also, take a look at the "How to Journal" portion of Oprah Winfrey's Web site at **http://www.oprah.com/journal/journal_howto.jhtml.** Then answer the following questions.

1. According to these Web sites, what are some of the benefits of personal writing, such as writing in a journal?

2. What are some of the different kinds of journals you could create?

3. Look through the journal writing prompts offered on one or both Web sites. What are two or three of them that would be especially interesting for you to write about?

4. What experience have you had with journal or diary writing in the past? Do you think that recording your thoughts in a journal could help you now? How?

Online Study Center   For more information and exercises, go to the Online Study Center that accompanies this textbook, at **http://www.college .hmco.com/pic/dolphinwriterthree.**

More on the Reading/ Writing Connection

GOALS FOR CHAPTER 2

▶ Actively read a passage.

▶ Read a passage critically.

▶ Write reading journal entries.

▶ Read photographs and graphs critically.

In Chapter 1, you explored ways that reading the writing of others helps you strengthen your own writing skills. When you read, you get ideas about *what* to write and *how* to write it. In addition, carefully considering what you read helps you improve the thinking skills that are essential to good writing. In this chapter, you will focus on how to get more from your reading so that what you read helps you become a better writer.

Active Reading

How can you get the most out of your reading to make sure that you will reap all of its benefits for your writing skills? First of all, you must learn to become an active reader. **Active reading** is the process of interacting with a text in ways that improve comprehension and retention of the information. What do active readers do?

- Active readers do more than just run their eyes over the text in front of them; they interact with the text and think as they read.

- Active readers read with a pen or pencil in their hand, marking key words or ideas or jotting notes in the margins.

- Active readers reread the text if necessary and consciously try to connect the text's information to their own experiences and beliefs.

The techniques that active readers use are essential to understanding and remembering ideas and information, especially those in more challenging reading selections. In the next four sections of this chapter, you will learn about some tried-and-true techniques of the active reader.

Preview the Text

The first step in reading any selection involves previewing, or surveying, the text. To *preview* means to obtain a preliminary sample of something. When you preview a reading selection, you skim, or glance, over it to try to get a sense of the piece's content and organization. You are not looking for specific details or information; instead, you skim a reading selection to get an idea of the author's subject, main point, overall focus, or purpose.

Here are some tips for previewing a text:

- To get this sense of the selection's "big picture," you should read the title of the selection, which will usually state the subject and sometimes even indicate the main point.

- Then try to find the thesis statement, or main point, of the selection. The thesis, which is the idea the author wants you to know or to believe by the time you have finished reading, usually appears somewhere near the beginning of the selection, often in the first paragraph.

- Also, glance over the headings in the selection, which function as "mini-titles" for the different sections. If there are no headings to guide you, read the first sentences of the paragraphs to get some idea of the topics they will address.

- Read the titles of any visual aids, such as graphs or charts, that are included with the text.

- Read over any introductory material—such as a brief summary paragraph—which may offer clues about the selection's main point.

Your goal in previewing the text is to get an overview of the text's topics, main idea, and overall organization. This overview will allow you to assemble a rough mental framework of the whole selection. Then, as you read more thoroughly later on, you will be able to fit the specific ideas and information into this framework as you go. You will have a better understanding of how the specific details relate to one another. As a result, your comprehension while reading will increase.

Formulate Questions and Read for Answers

A second proven active reading technique involves formulating questions and then reading for the answers to these questions. Completing this step helps to keep readers focused on finding certain kinds of information in a text, so it often improves concentration and, therefore, comprehension.

To formulate questions, simply turn the title, headings, or topic sentences of a selection into questions before you read the text. For example, if the title of a selection is "The Benefits of Exercise," you could turn it into *What are* the benefits of exercise?" Then, as you read, you can search for the answers to that question. If the heading is "Walking versus Jogging," you could turn it into "How are jogging and walking alike and different?" or "Which is better: walking or jogging?" If you own the text you are reading, actually write your questions in the margins. If you have borrowed the text and cannot write in it, consider making a photocopy of it and then writing your questions in the margins of that photocopy. Or you can take notes on a separate sheet of paper by writing your questions and leaving a blank space for each of the answers, which you will fill in later as you read.

Underline and Highlight Key Words and Phrases

A third tried-and-true technique for active reading is underlining and/or highlighting key words and phrases in a text with your pen or highlighter marker. This method is valuable for two reasons. First, it encourages you to look for important information while you are reading, which helps to keep you focused on the main points or information. Second, it makes a review of the information more efficient because you can scan the important words you have already identified rather than reread the entire text.

What do you highlight or underline in a text? The following is a list of information that is usually worth marking:

- Any words or phrases in distinctive typeface. If an author has put key terms in bold print or color, highlight them to make them stand out even more.

- The answers to the questions you formulated from headings or topic sentences. Read with the question in mind, and every time you discover an answer (or part of the answer), highlight it.

- Words or phrases referring to major details that develop the idea stated in each paragraph's topic sentence. Look for and underline or highlight the main reasons, examples, or other kinds of the details provided to explain the topic sentence's point.

The key to effective highlighting is to avoid overdoing it. Highlighting whole sentences or paragraphs is pointless, for the major ideas will not stand out when you go back to the text again later. Instead, you will end up unnecessarily rereading long sections of the text. Also, highlighting whole passages will not help you focus on finding the most essential information. Therefore, concentrate on marking only those words that will help you quickly piece together the general gist, or essence, of the text when you are reviewing it later.

Take Notes on the Text

One final effective active reading technique involves taking notes. Taking notes means recording in writing the major information and ideas in a text. You might choose to take these notes in the margins of the text itself (which is called *annotating*), in a notebook, or on separate sheets of paper.

Regardless of where you write them, notes offer two important benefits. First of all, good notes often increase your comprehension of the text. Taking notes requires you to think more about what you are reading, so you wind up understanding it better. Secondly, writing down information and ideas helps you remember them better. For many people, taking the extra time to hand-write the main points helps implant the points in their memory more securely.

Good notes always begin with highlighting or underlining main ideas or key terms. When you write notes, they might take one or more of the following forms:

- **A list of the main ideas in all of the paragraphs.** Put them in your own words and condense them whenever possible. Do not try to include all of the details, just the most important points.

- **A summary of the chapter or article.** In your own words, write a paragraph or two to tell about the main ideas of the selection.

- **An outline.** Outlines not only list the major and minor details of a reading selection; they also reveal the relationships among those details. You can use a Roman numeral outline, but the notes are usually for your eyes only, so you could also adopt or create a more informal system. No matter what kind of outline you use, though, make sure that it clearly demonstrates the general and specific relationships among the ideas.

The passage that follows is the first part of an article entitled "Shop 'til We Drop?" Notice how the reader has used many of the active reading techniques.

Shop 'til We Drop?

1   We *shop,* therefore we are. This is not exactly the American ⟨credo⟩, but it comes   *System of* close to being the American pastime. Even infants and toddlers quickly absorb   *belief* the consumer spirit through television and trips to the supermarket ("I want that" is a common refrain). As we age, consumption becomes an engine of envy,   *Consumption* because in America the idea is that everyone should have everything—which   *is a way of life* means that hardly anyone ever has enough. The notion that wants and needs   *in America* have reached a limit of material and environmental absurdity, though preached fervently by some social activists and intellectuals, barely influences ordinary Americans. They continue to flock to shopping malls, automobile dealers, cruise ships, and health clubs. There are always, it seems, new wants and needs to be satisfied.

2   Although consumerism now defines all wealthy societies, it's still practiced most religiously in its country of origin. Indeed, Americans have rarely so indulged the urge to splurge as in the past decade. Look at the numbers. In 2002,   *Consumer* consumer spending accounted for 70 percent of U.S. national income (gross do-   *spending is* mestic product), which is a modern American record, and a much higher figure   *higher in* than in any other advanced nation. In Japan and France, consumer spending in   *America than* 2002 was only 55 percent of GDP; in Italy and Spain, it was 60 percent. These   *in other* rates are typical elsewhere. Even in the United States, consumer spending was   *countries* only 67 percent of GDP as recently as 1994. Three added percentage points of GDP may seem trivial, but in today's dollars they amount to an extra $325 billion annually.

What are **The Effects of Spending** *?*

3   This spending spree has, in some ways, been a godsend. Without it, the U.S. and world economies would recently have fared much worse. During the 1997–98 Asian financial crisis, the irrepressible buying of American consumers cushioned   ① the shock to countries that, suddenly unable to borrow abroad, had to curb their   *Positive effect:* domestic spending. Roughly half of U.S. imports consist of consumer goods,   *it helps other* automobiles, and food (oil, other raw materials, and industrial goods make up   *countries* the balance). By selling Americans more shoes, toys, clothes, and electronic gadgets, Asian countries partially contained higher unemployment. U.S. trade deficits exploded. From 1996 to 2000, the deficit of the current account (a broad measure of trade) grew from $177 billion to $411 billion.

4   Later, the buying binge sustained the U.S. economy despite an onslaught of   ② bad news that, by all logic, should have been devastating: the popping of the   *Positive effect:* stock market "bubble" of the 1990s; rising unemployment (as dot-com firms   *it helps our* went bankrupt and business investment—led by telecommunications spending—   *economy* declined); 9/11; and a string of corporate scandals (Enron, WorldCom, Tyco).

But American consumers barely paused, and responded to falling interest rates by prolonging their binge. Car and light-truck sales of 17.1 million units in 2001 gave the <u>automobile industry its second-best year ever,</u> after 2000. The fourth- and fifth-best years were 2002 (16.8 million units) and 2003 (an estimated 16.6 million units). <u>Strong home sales</u> buoyed appliance, furniture, and carpet production.

Why Americans Spend So Much *Do* *?*

5   To some extent, the consumption boom is old hat. <u>Acquisitiveness is deeply embedded in American culture.</u> Describing the United States in the 1830s, Alexis de Tocqueville marveled over the widespread "taste for physical gratification." Still, the ferocity of the latest consumption outburst poses some interesting questions: Why do Americans spend so much more of their incomes than other peoples? How can we afford to do that? After all, economic theory holds that societies become wealthier only by sacrificing some present consumption to invest in the future. And if we aren't saving enough, can the consumer boom continue?

Americans have always wanted more

6   Let's start with why Americans spend so much. <u>One reason is that our political and cultural traditions differ from those of other nations.</u> We do some things in the private market that other societies do through government. <u>Health care, education,</u> and <u>social welfare</u> are good examples. Most middle-class Americans under 65 pay for their own health care, either directly or through employer-provided health insurance (which reduces their take-home pay). That counts as private consumption. In countries with government-run health care systems, similar medical costs are classified as government spending. The same thing is true of education. Although U.S. public schools involve government spending, college tuition (or tuition for private school or pre-school) counts as personal consumption. Abroad, governments often pay more of total educational costs.

⑦

These things are counted toward the personal consumption percentage

7   It's also true that <u>the United States saves and invests less than other nations</u>— investment here meaning money that, though initially channeled into stocks, bonds, or bank deposits, ultimately goes into new factories, machinery, computers, and office buildings. Low U.S. saving and investment rates have often inspired alarm about America's future. In 1990, for instance, Japan's national savings rate was 34 percent of GDP, more than double the U.S. rate of 16 percent. By outinvesting us, Japan (it was said) would become the world's wealthiest nation. That hasn't happened, in part because what matters is not only how much countries invest but how well they invest it. And Americans generally are better investors than others.

②

We invest less, but we invest wisely

8   Of course, there's waste. The hundreds of billions of dollars invested in unneeded dot-com and telecom networks in the late 1990s are simply the latest re-

minder of that. But <u>the American business system corrects its blunders fairly quickly.</u> If projects don't show signs of becoming profitable, they usually don't get more capital. Wall Street's obsession with profits—though sometimes deplored as discouraging long-term investment—compels companies to cut costs and improve productivity. If bankrupt firms (Kmart and United Airlines are recent examples) can't improve efficiency, their assets (stores, planes) are sold to others who hope to do better. American banks, unlike Japanese banks, don't rescue floundering companies; neither (usually) does the government, unlike governments in Europe. Getting more bang from our investment buck, we can afford to invest less and consume more.

Companies profit or quickly die

9   <u>Our privileged position in the world economy reinforces the effect.</u> Since the 1970s, we've run trade deficits that have allowed us to have our cake and eat it too: All those imports permit adequate investment rates without crimping consumption. We send others dollars; they send us cars, clothes, and computer chips. It's a good deal as long as we're near full employment (when we're not, high imports add to unemployment). The trade gap—now about five percent of GDP—persists in part because the dollar serves as the major global currency. Foreigners—companies and individuals—want dollars so they can conduct trade and make international investments. Some governments hoard dollars because they'd rather export than import. The strong demand for dollars props up the exchange rate, making our imports less expensive and our exports more expensive. Continuous trade deficits result.

③
strong demand for dollars helps us continue to spend money on imported products

10   All this suggests that the <u>consumer boom could go on forever,</u> because Americans always feel the need to outdo the Joneses—or at least to stay even with them. <u>No level of consumption ever suffices,</u> because the <u>social competition is constant.</u> The surge in prosperity after World War II briefly fostered the illusion that the competition was ebbing because so many things that had once been restricted (homes, cars, televisions) became so widely available. "If everyone could enjoy the good things of life—as defined by mass merchandisers—the meanness of class distinctions would disappear," Vance Packard wrote in his 1959 classic *The Status Seekers.* Instead, he found, Americans had developed new distinctions, including bigger homes and flashier clothes.*

Social competition continues to fuel the consumption

Homes, cars, electronics just keep getting bigger, more luxurious, and more expensive

*Source: Adapted from Robert J. Samuelson, "Shop 'til We Drop?" *The Wilson Quarterly,* Winter 2004, pp. 22–29. Robert J. Samuelson is a columnist for *The Washington Post* and *Newsweek.*

Actively read the remainder of the article "Shop 'til We Drop?"

The "Consumption Treadmill"

11 Four decades later, little has changed. Americans constantly pursue new markers of success and status. In 2002, the median size of a new home was 20 percent larger than in 1987, even though families had gotten smaller. Luxury car sales have soared. According to the marketing research firm of J. D. Power and Associates, in 1980 luxury brands—mainly Cadillacs and Lincolns, along with some Mercedes—accounted for only 4.5 percent of new-vehicle sales. By 2003, luxury brands—a category that now includes Lexus, Infinity, and Acura, along with Hummers and more BMWs and Mercedes—exceeded 10 percent of sales. Second homes are another way that people separate themselves from the crowd. Perhaps 100,000 to 125,000 such homes are built annually, says economist Gopal Ahluwalia of the National Association of Homebuilders. In the 1990s, comparable figures were between 75,000 and 100,000.

12   To critics, this "consumption treadmill" is self-defeating, as Cornell University economist Robert H. Frank put it in his 1999 book *Luxury Fever: Money and Happiness in an Era of Excess*. People compete to demonstrate their superiority, but most are frustrated because others continually catch up. Meanwhile, over-consumption—homes that are too big, cars that are too glitzy—actually detracts from people's happiness and society's well-being, Frank argued. Striving to maximize their incomes, workers sacrifice time with family and friends—time that, according to surveys, they would prize highly. And society's reluctance to take money out of consumers' pockets through taxation means too little is spent to solve collective problems such as poverty and pollution.

13   As a cure, Frank proposed a progressive consumption tax. People would be taxed only on what they spent, at rates rising to 70 percent above $500,000. Savings (put, for example, into stocks, bonds, and bank deposits) would be exempt. The tax would deter extravagant spending and encourage saving, Frank contended. Total consumption spending would be lower, government spending could be higher, and the competition for status would simply occur at lower levels of foolishness. The "erstwhile Ferrari driver . . . might turn instead to [a] Porsche," he wrote. Whatever their merits, proposals such as this lack political support. Indeed, they do not differ dramatically—except for high tax rates—from the present income tax, which allows generous deductions for savings, through vehicles such as 401(k) plans and individual retirement accounts.

14   Still, America's consumption boom could falter, because it faces three powerful threats: debt, demographics, and the dollar.

The Democratization of Credit

15 Over six decades, we've gone from being a society uneasy with credit to a society that rejoices in it. In 1946, household debt was 22 percent of personal disposable income. Now, it's roughly 110 percent. Both business and government have promoted more debt. In 1950, Diners Club introduced the modern credit card, which could be used at multiple restaurants and stores. (Some department stores and oil companies were already offering cards restricted to their outlets.) New laws—the Fair Housing Act of 1968, the Equal Credit Opportunity Act of 1974—prohibited discriminatory lending. One result was the invention of credit-scoring formulas that evaluate potential borrowers on their past payment of bills, thereby reducing bias against women, the poor, and minorities. Similarly, the federal government encourages home mortgages through Fannie Mae and Freddie Mac, government-created companies that buy mortgages.

16   This "democratization of credit" has enabled consumer spending to grow slightly faster than consumer income. People simply borrow more. Economist Thomas Durkin of the Federal Reserve notes the following: In 1951, 20 percent of U.S. households had a mortgage, compared with 44 percent in 2001; in 1970, only 16 percent of households had a bank credit card, compared with 73 percent in 2001. The trouble is that this accumulation of debt can't continue forever. Sooner or later, Americans will decide that they've got as much as they can handle. Or lenders will discover that they've exhausted good and even mediocre credit risks. No one knows when that will happen, but once it occurs, consumer spending may rise only as fast as consumer income—and slower still if borrowers collectively repay debts.

The Role of Demographics

17 What could hasten the turning point is the baby boom. We're now on the edge of a momentous generational shift. The oldest baby boomers (born in 1946) will be 58 in 2004; the youngest (born in 1964) will be 40. For most Americans, peak spending occurs between the ages of 35 and 54, when household consumption is about 20 percent above average, according to Susan Sterne, an economist with Economic Analysis Associates. Then it gradually declines. People don't buy new sofas or refrigerators. They pay off debts. For 15 years or so, the economy has benefited from baby boomers' feverish buying. It may soon begin to suffer from their decreased spending.

The Dollar

18 Finally, there's the dollar. Should foreign demand for U.S. investments wane—or should American politicians, worried about jobs, press other countries to stop

accumulating U.S. Treasury securities—the dollar would decline on foreign exchange markets. There would simply be less demand, as foreigners sold dollars for other currencies. Then our imports could become more expensive while our exports could become cheaper. Domestic supplies might tighten. Price pressures on consumer goods—cars, electronics, clothes—could intensify. This might cause Americans to buy a little less. But if they continued buying as before, the long-heralded collision between consumption and investment might materialize. (As this article goes to press, the dollar has dropped from its recent highs. The ultimate effects remain to be seen.)

19   Little is preordained. Sterne thinks retired baby boomers may defy history and become spendthrifts. "They don't care about leaving anything to their kids," she says. "There's no reluctance to go into debt." Their chosen instrument would be the "reverse mortgage," which unlocks home equity. (Under a reverse mortgage, a homeowner receives a payment from the lender up to some percentage of the home's value; upon the owner's death, the loan is repaid, usually through sale of the house.) Maybe. But maybe the post–World War II consumption boom has reached its peak. If the retreat occurs gently, the consequences, at least on paper, should be painless and imperceptible. We'll spend a little less of our incomes and save a little more. We'll import a little less and export a little more. These modest changes shouldn't hurt, but they might. The U.S. and world economies have grown so accustomed to being stimulated by the ravenous appetite of ordinary Americans that you can't help but wonder what will happen if that appetite disappears.

Table 2.1 Big Spenders (Consumer Spending as a Percentage of GDP, 2002)

France	55%
Japan	55%
Germany	57%
Italy	60%
Spain	60%
United Kingdom	68%
United States	70%

Source: Organization for Economic Cooperation and Development.

Table 2.2 Where the Consumer Dollar Goes

	1959	2000
Durable goods	13.4%	12.1%
Motor vehicles	5.9%	5.0%
Furniture & household equipment (including computers)	5.7%	4.6%
Other (including books, sporting equipment)	1.8%	2.5%
Non-durable goods	46.7%	29.7%
Food	25.4%	14.1%
Clothing & shoes	8.3%	4.9%
Energy (including gasoline)	4.8%	2.7%
Other (including drugs, tobacco products, toys)	8.2%	8.1%
Services	39.9%	58.1%
Housing	14.2%	14.2%
Household operation (utilities & maintenance)	5.9%	5.7%
Transportation (including car maintenance & repair, mass transit, airlines)	3.3%	4.0%
Health care	5.2%	14.8%
Recreation (including sports events, movies, cable TV, Internet services, video rentals)	2.0%	3.9%
Other (including financial services, personal care, higher education & private schools, legal services)	9.3%	15.6%

Source: Bureau of Economic Analysis, U.S. Department of Commerce.

Critical Reading

In addition to reading actively, you will also need to read critically in order to get the most out of what you read. Critical reading does not mean reading to criticize or find fault with a text. Instead, **critical reading** is the process of determining whether or not a text is valid and then deciding whether or not you agree with the ideas presented.

The ultimate goal of critical reading is critical thinking, an important skill in all areas of life, not just your academic courses. Critical thinkers do not believe everything they hear or read. Instead, they approach new ideas and information with a healthy skepticism. They have learned how to analyze texts and ideas not only to understand them better but also to decide whether they should accept those ideas, reject them, or think about them further. College students, in particular, are expected to read critically. Professors assign textbook chapters, journal articles, and other readings not just to have you memorize facts but also to encourage you to think about the texts so that you can expand and refine your ideas.

Critical reading, of course, begins with active reading. In order to evaluate an author's ideas or information, you need to completely understand them, and practicing the active reading techniques will increase your comprehension of the material. After actively reading a text, a critical reader thinks in depth about what he or she has read. Thinking critically about a reading selection involves all of the following:

- Evaluating the evidence given in support of the thesis and main idea. Does it seem to be adequate? Does it seem to be accurate?

- Scrutinizing the author's conclusions. Do they arise logically from the evidence presented? Does the author exhibit any bias—in other words, does he or she obviously have certain opinions or prejudices?

- Comparing the ideas and information with your own experiences and observations

- Agreeing or disagreeing with the author after doing all of the above

To assist critical reading and thinking, you can engage in several activities:

- As you read, you can **annotate, or write brief comments in the margin of the text.** These comments can include your reactions to specific points or details and your questions about those points and details. They can take the form of words or phrases (such as *true, seems exaggerated,* and so on) or even symbols (such as writing an exclamation point next to a sentence that surprises you or writing a question mark in the margin when you are confused). Annotation is a valuable skill for critical thinking because it can become a kind of dialogue between you and the author as the author tries to convince you to accept his or her ideas.

- You can also **answer the questions** that may follow a text. In textbooks, in particular, authors provide a list of questions that help you focus on the most important information or even begin to apply the information to your own life. Even if your instructor does not assign these questions, think about how you would answer them.

- Finally, you can **discuss the text with others.** Participate in class discussions about reading selections and suggest to your classmates that you discuss texts more informally as well. By talking about what you read with others, you will confirm your understanding of the text. Also, you will get the opportunity to compare your reactions with those of other critical readers. These conversations will help all of you decide if the text is valid.

The following passage has been annotated to show how one writer responded to a text.

The Demise of Writing

1   It may seem curious at a time when Amazon.com has a market value approximately that of New Zealand [that] books as we know them are a dying breed. Indeed, there are unmistakable signs that text will atrophy[1] by the end of the next century; it will be used mainly for instructional purposes and be <u>accessible</u>   *Why?*
<u>only to the technological elite.</u>

2   It may seem inconceivable that text will have mostly disappeared within the lifetime of anyone alive today, but remember, the <u>rate of change is accelerating</u>.   *Hasn't the rate* If the World Wide Web can go from an obscure geekish curiosity to the driving   *of change* economic force of the developed world in about five years, what will 50 or 70 or   *begun to slow* 100 years bring?   *down?*

3   We're not seeing profound changes yet; what can be seen today, if you know where to look, are indications around the edges of our experience. The pattern they form points clearly in one direction: the end of text.

4   Moveable type is already gone, replaced by the digital font. Ink on paper will be next, replaced by the electronic tablet. Already, commercial versions of the <u>digital book</u> are available: thin LCD panels with text stored in RAM. The   *But this tech-* Rocket eBook has a 4 1/2" by 3" screen, weighs about a pound and a half, and   *nology is still* can store 4,000 pages of text and graphics. Today's typical novel can be down-   *too expensive* loaded in about three minutes from a transportable medium (like CD-ROM) or   *for many* downloaded from a computer or the Internet. The "textport" will become the   *people* checkout desk of the virtual library of 2010.

5   Currently, the technology is clunky (bulky batteries that last only four to nine hours), inelegant (the text is hard to read unless conditions are perfect), and expensive (about $500 for the eBook, plus $20 per book). However, all that will change very soon. <u>By 2005, the bookpad will cost about $20</u>, weigh no more   *Is this now* than six ounces, reproduce text with greater clarity than ink-on-paper, and be   *true?* able to store an encyclopedia (or 500 novels) on a single chip. Of particular appeal to an aging population, the type size will be variable—you'll make it as large as your eyesight requires.

6   But that's the short-term, mechanical aspect. Over the longer term, <u>the</u>   *Seems hard to* <u>printed word will vanish as a medium of expression</u>. By 2070, the only people   *believe* using text as literature (as opposed to information transmission) will be an elite

1. **atrophy:** weaken; wither away

Thesis

and mostly very elderly priesthood, for whom it will be an arcane[1] art form—sort of like the sonnet or haiku[2] today. The demise of text for literature will result from several developments.

Increasing Illiteracy

Is illiteracy growing, declining, or holding steady? If it's not growing, this argument may not apply.

7   Even in the United States, at a time when technological "progress" makes reading a survival skill, one-fifth of the population is functionally illiterate. A small percentage of these are older people with little formal education. A much larger percentage are youths—high-school and even college graduates, who, despite their degrees, can't fill out a simple employment form. And this is functional illiteracy. The percentage who can fill out the employment form but not understand Tom Wolfe[3] (let alone Shakespeare) is vastly larger.

May not be true—each generation pursues higher education

8   From our current perspective this seems strange. Yet we are fooled by thinking that our time represents the way things always were and always will be. When it comes to reading, today's 80% literacy rate is an anomaly[4], the result of dramatically higher education levels. Remember, the baby-boomer cohort[5] is not only the best educated cohort in history—it's likely the best educated that ever will be.

9   This is why the most recent version of Microsoft's Word program includes not just spelling checkers but subroutines that suggest and correct syntax[6], grammar, and even paragraph structure. And clearly these functions are needed.

Increasing Use of Pictures and Sound

Are graphic novels as popular as traditional novels?

10   Today, expressive and instructional communications are increasingly transmitted either orally or visually. An example is the so-called "graphic novel," a fusion of comicbook illustration and serious prose. The cartoon strip that preceded it was an attempt to circumvent[7] illiteracy during the first half of this century, and it became firmly established in the United States during the low-education days of the Depression.

TV has done more to diminish text than graphic novels have.

11   Comic strips became so popular with those who otherwise had great difficulty reading newspapers that a week's worth were bundled into one place, and the comic book was born. Its current transmogrification[8] into the graphic novel (for example, *Maus* by Art Spiegelman or *Tantrum* by Jules Feiffer) further diminishes text.

---

1. **arcane:** hidden; unknowable
2. **sonnet, haiku:** types of poems
3. **Tom Wolfe:** modern American author; author of such works as *The Right Stuff* and *Bonfire of the Vanities*
4. **anomaly:** irregularity; glitch
5. **cohort:** group
6. **syntax:** sentence structure
7. **circumvent:** go around; take pains to avoid
8. **transmogrification:** changing form or appearance in a bizarre way

12   If the graphic novel works as ink-on-paper, imagine how much better it will work on an <u>eBook</u>. The images, which are cartoonlike stills now, will be <u>digital photo images and moving 3-D holograms</u>[1] by 2010. And machine gun fire won't be written out as "Braaaaaakkk!" on paper; we'll hear it from a sound chip and built-in speakers.

sounds like TV and DVDs

13   The proliferation[2] of aural and visual expression will continue to be driven by technological advances, specifically voice-recognition capability and the removal of bandwidth[3] limitations on full-motion video.

Voice Recognition

14   Microprocessors' ability to understand and respond to verbal instructions and communicate via voice output is poised on the edge of a great leap forward, one that will finally fulfill the promise of the microchip as an indispensable tool and helpmate of the masses. <u>Voice chips</u> are going to change our world sooner than we expect. No longer will we interact with devices via text and keyboard; we'll talk to them, perhaps even giving them names:

Not everyone will be able to afford such a sophisticated computer

15   "Sven," we'll say to our computer, "make reservations for me to fly to Denver today. I want to arrive about 7 p.m. and stay at the Brown Palace. Charge it to my business Visa."

16   "VCR, record the World Cup satellite feed from Brazil this afternoon and the Pavarotti concert tomorrow night, and remind me about them when I get home from Denver."

17   "Toaster, a little bit darker on the next piece, please."

18   And even as Microsoft gets into the business of telling us how to write, it's hedging its bet by preparing to bring the Audible, Inc., audiobook technology to Windows CE devices. Dick I. Brass, Microsoft vice president for technology development, says in *Forbes,* "You're going to be able to play a book on every platform Microsoft makes."

Realistic Video

19   "A picture is worth a thousand words" isn't just a saying. <u>The cerebral cortex</u>[4] <u>can process 1,000 times as much information, 1,000 times faster visually than verbally</u>. The reason is that the optic nerve has a bandwidth—or data-transmission rate—a trillion times larger than a standard telephone line, so sending moving images over phone lines is insufferably[5] slow.

Interesting!

---

1. **holograms:** three-dimensional photographic images
2. **proliferation:** increase in; rise of
3. **bandwidth:** range of radio frequencies
4. **cerebral cortex:** outer layer in front of brain
5. **insufferably:** unbearably; intolerably

20   Why? Because the slowest speed that even approximates full-motion video is 20 frames per second. Movies operate at 24. TV flickers at 30. Traditionally, every pixel—or picture element—must be repainted every frame. So a standard 720 by 480 pixel television screen has to be repainted a minimum of 20 times a second. That's 720 by 480 multiplied 20 times each second, multiplied by 60 for one minute of motion, which is a lot of pixels per minute and a lot of information whether you transmit it in digital or analog[1] form. A coaxial cable[2] can handle this amount of data, but not a phone line. That's why picture phones have never worked: Compression algorithms[3] can cut the transmission flow somewhat, but not enough for anything better than a freeze-frame image every 10 seconds or so.

But we will still need to keep records of communications and transactions for future reference

21   But the bandwidth barrier is about to be broken. The nature of the technology that will ultimately do it doesn't matter—it could be satellite transmission or fiber or something totally new. Bandwidth limitations are too critical not to be overcome, and, as soon as they are, text will take another giant leap backwards. Why spend a lot of time typing in a memo when you can simply speak it and send it? You'll be able to communicate 1,000 times more information visually and verbally than with text alone.

What about different learning styles? Some people learn better through reading than through listening to spoken language.

22   For the receiver, the information will be much easier to assimilate[4] and the impact many times greater. Already we see how hard it is to use traditional methods to teach kids who have been raised in the fastpaced, visual world of MTV—lecturing doesn't begin to cut it, let alone a textbook.

23   And as for the sender, after a decade or two with this vastly enhanced visual capability, who will bother to learn how to write well? We write to communicate linear[5] thinking, which does extraordinarily well in part because it causes linear thinking—the way we express thought impacts the way we think. And as we increasingly communicate with multilayered, asynchronous[6] images, our thinking will become increasingly nonlinear as well.

Interesting analogy

24   Baseball versus football provides a simple but instructive example. Baseball—linear and sequential, ordered, one-thing-at-a-time—was our national pastime until the advent of television. Television is images, multilayered, where instant replay can even (momentarily) reverse the arrow of time. This is a medium made for football, where many things happen at once—and it's a medium that helps make football the new national pastime, as the 30-frame-per-second image begins to transform our past mode of linear, sequential one-batter-at-a-time thinking.

1. **analog:** represented in measurable physical quantities, such as length, width, or voltage
2. **coaxial cable:** high-speed transmission cable
3. **compression algorithms:** ways of encoding computer information in a shortened form
4. **assimilate:** incorporate; become part of
5. **linear:** in a straight line
6. **asynchronous:** occurring at different times

25   The implications of this are profound. As the image replaces text as the main form of communication, our collective thought processes will move from being linear and single and sequential to simultaneous and multilayered and holistic[1]. Society will become less "left-brained" and analytical and more "right-brained" and intuitive. The more we think nonlinearly the less we will communicate with text, which will cause even more nonlinear thinking, which will lead to less text, and so forth in a continuously self-reinforcing cycle.

seems like a far-fetched generalization

26   When you put all these trends together, you may begin to see how 50 years from now books, newspapers, and magazines will be but quaint relics of the past. In 100 years, few people will want to read at all, and fewer still will know how to write. Text will be outmoded, except for instruction booklets and the aptly named textbooks containing technical information.

I disagree— many people will always enjoy books and reading

27   In Gen-X speak, "Text is toast." Communication, both factual and expressive, will be through sound and pictures. We will have returned to the troubadour, the cave painter, the oral tradition, come full circle back to the age of Homer[2].*

EXERCISE 2.2   **Reading Critically**

Actively read the next passage and then answer the questions that follow by writing your answers on the blanks provided.

Marriage, Not Children, Is a Family's Center

1 A journalist recently asked: "When they become adults, what will be the biggest problem facing today's kids?"

2   I answered: "That many if not most of them, even those growing up in two-parent homes, are not developing a functional sense of what is truly meant by 'marriage' and, therefore, 'family.'"

3   How's that? Today's all-too-typical child is prevented from learning what marriage is all about by well-intentioned parents who rarely act from within the roles of husband and wife; rather, they act almost exclusively from within the roles of mother and father. This is, after all, the new American ideal, based in large part on the nefarious[3] modern notion that the more attention you pay to, the more involved you are with, and the more you do for your child, the better a parent you are.

1. **holistic:** relating to a whole; including or involving all of something related to a person in the treatment of illness
2. **Homer:** Greek playwright
3. **nefarious:** wicked or evil

*Source: Geoffrey Meredith, "The Demise of Writing," originally published in the October 1999 issue of *The Futurist*. Used with the permission of the World Future Society.

4   I am a member of the last generation of American children to grow up in families where the marriage, irrespective of its imperfections, occupied center-stage. Your mother was a housewife, not a stay-at-home mom who was in perpetual orbit around her kids. Even if she worked outside the home, as mine did, the '50s mother did not arrive home from work bearing a load of guilt, which she attempted to discharge by dancing as fast as she could in her children's lives through the evening until they finally consented to go to bed.

5   Likewise your father, when he came home from work, had no intention of romping with his children all evening, "re-bonding" with them. He came home looking forward to spending a quiet evening with his wife, his intended partner for life.

6   After dinner, Mom and Dad retired to coffee and conversation in the living room, and the kids, well, they found things of their own to do (including their homework, which they did on their own as well). They did not slink off into the Land of Unwanted Children.

7   There were exceptions to this general rule, of course, but there are two living generations (mine and my parents') who remember that once upon a time in America, the husband-wife relationship was stronger than the parent-child relationship, as it should be.

8   "Come on now, John," someone is saying. "You don't actually mean stronger. You mean as strong as."

9   No, I most definitely mean stronger. Unlike today's mom, the mom of the 1950s and before was not married to her child; she was married to her husband.

10   And unlike today's dad, the dad of bygone days was a husband first, a father second, and he was most definitely not his child's buddy (the new ideal in American fatherhood). Under no other circumstances can children learn what marriage truly means and involves, and make no mistake about it, that learning is far more important than being an honor student or a star athlete—infinitely more important, in fact.

11   If you want more proof of why the husband-wife relationship should trump[1] that of parent and child, consider this unarguable proposition: Nothing makes a child feel more insecure than the feeling that his parents' relationship is shaky, that it might come undone at any moment. It follows that nothing makes a child feel more secure than knowing his parents' relationship, while not perfect, is strong enough to endure any hardship, any disagreement.

12   The primacy of the husband-wife relationship gives a child full permission to begin preparing for his emancipation[2]. The fact that he is not essential to his parents' well-being—that their well-being is contained within their marriage—gives him full, unfettered[3] permission to leave and venture out into a life of his

1. **trump:** defeat someone or outdo somebody

2. **emancipation:** freeing of someone or a group of people

3. **unfettered:** released; liberated or unchained

own. A child's leaving home should be cause for celebration, exciting and full of promise for all concerned.

13   When the parent-child relationship is foremost, however, emancipation is difficult for all concerned. Sometimes, the child is able to leave physically, but not emotionally. At other times, emancipation takes the form of a painful "divorce" from which it is difficult for any of the parties involved to ever fully recover.

14   The greatest gift one can give a child upon his emancipation is not the keys to a new car or condominium, but the security of knowing that in the truest sense, he can always come home again—not to live, mind you, but to visit. I have spoken to many young emancipated adults who tell me that the greatest pain in their lives involves the turmoil they go through when trying to decide how to split up "visit time" between Mom's house and Dad's house.

15   Sometimes, our own children tell Willie and me how "lucky" they are that we are still together and to know that we always will be. It's actually a slip of the tongue, because they both know that luck has nothing to do with it. It was, and is, a matter of keeping the natural order of things in their natural order.*

1. What is the main point of this selection? Express this idea in your own words.

2. Does the author provide adequate and accurate support for his main point? List the evidence that the author includes and decide whether it is adequate and accurate.

3. Do you agree with the author that a child should be aware that "he is not essential to his parents' well-being"? Is the author's argument in support of this opinion convincing?

4. Do you agree or disagree with the author's assertions about today's families? Why?

*Source: John Rosemond, "Marriage, Not Children, Is a Family's Center," © Knight-Ridder/Tribune Media Information Services. All rights reserved. Reprinted with permission.

5. Compare the author's ideas and information about today's families with your own experiences.

_____

_____

_____

Reading Visuals Critically

When sharpening your critical reading skills, do not forget about visuals. In our multimedia world, we get as much information from visual sources as we do from verbal or written sources. Photographs, drawings, cartoons, and graphs often say as much as text does. Effective readers know how to interpret and respond critically to these kinds of visuals.

Interpreting Photographs

Photographs, which appear in everything from magazine articles to advertisements, often convey a certain point about the subject. Look, for example, at the following photo. Would you say that the photographer is making a statement? What is it?

Getty Images

First of all, look at the man in the center of the photograph. He is sitting on the ground, wrapped in a sleeping bag. Is he camping out? Probably not. Because he is on what appears to be a sidewalk or city street and because he is wearing a grim look on his face, we are supposed to understand that he's homeless. Now, what do the other elements of the photograph tell you? Two people are walking past the man on the ground. The blurred quality of their legs suggests that they are moving briskly. We see them only from the waist down, but we can assume that they are ignoring the man on the ground. Thus, we can conclude that the photographer wanted to make the point that people ignore the problem of home-lessness and do not do anything about it.

Photographs can also attempt to persuade the viewer to think a certain way about their subject. For example, look at this public service announcement from an animal rights organization:

Courtesy PETA.org

When we look at this public service announcement, our eyes are drawn immediately to the image of the tiger cub. Does it look content? No, it appears to be cry-ing or suffering. Because it is chewing on the bars of the cage, it looks as though it wants to escape. The animal rights organization chose this photograph to help convince viewers that the circus is cruel to animals.

When you encounter a photograph, try to answer the following questions:

1. What emotions do you feel when you look at the photograph? Do you think that the photographer is trying to influence you by stirring these emotions?

2. What is the photographer's purpose and/or message?
3. Do you agree with the photographer's point?

EXERCISE 2.3   **Interpreting a Photograph**

Study the next photograph and then answer the questions that follow.

Georges Tourdjman/Getty Images

1. What emotions do you feel when you look at the photograph? Do you think that the photographer is trying to influence you by stirring these emotions?

_____

2. What is the photographer's purpose and/or message?

_____

3. Do you agree with the photographer's point?

_____

Reading Graphs and Charts Critically

You will often encounter graphs and charts as you read, and you should get in the habit of studying the information that they present. A **graph** is a visual aid composed of lines or bars that correspond to numbers or facts arranged along a vertical axis and a horizontal axis. **Line graphs** show trends over time, and **bar**

graphs show comparisons of figures. A **chart,** or table, lists information or data in rows or columns so that readers can find a specific fact quickly or compare information. For two examples of charts, see pages 36–37.

Authors will often state the main point of a graph or chart. Sometimes, however, they let readers draw their own conclusions. For example, what statement does the following graph make?

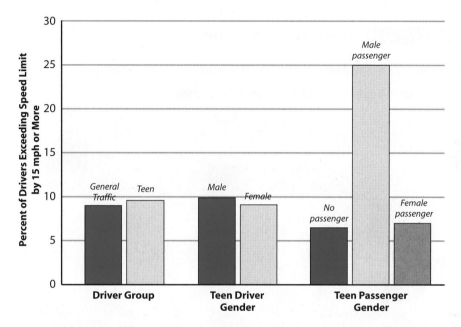

Source: "The Observed Effects of Teenage Passengers on the Risky Driving Behavior of Teenage Drivers" (published online in *Accident Analysis and Prevention*).

To understand the point of this graph, you must look at each comparison. First, note what is being compared and what the bars correspond to. Different kinds of drivers are being compared. The vertical axis indicates that the bars correspond to the percentage of each group that exceeds the speed limit by fifteen miles per hour or more. Therefore, the graph is about who is most likely to speed. Now, note the comparisons. The first pair of bars compares general traffic with teenager drivers. As a group, teenagers are only slightly more likely to speed than all other drivers. The second set of bars indicates that slightly more male than female teenage drivers exceed the speed limit. Finally, look at the third set of bars. What happens to the rate of speeding when teenagers have passengers in the car? Well, if they have no passenger or a female passenger, they are less likely than usual to speed. However, if they have a male passenger, their speeding rate more than doubles. The point of this graph, then, is that more speeding among teenagers takes place when the vehicle contains a male passenger.

Get in the habit of asking yourself these questions when reading a graph:

1. To what do the horizontal and vertical axes correspond?
2. What groups or amounts are being compared?
3. What trends do you notice in the information?
4. What conclusions can you draw from the comparisons or trends?

EXERCISE 2.4   **Reading a Graph Critically**

Study the next graph and then answer the questions that follow.

Recent Trends in Wealth Ownership, 1983–1998

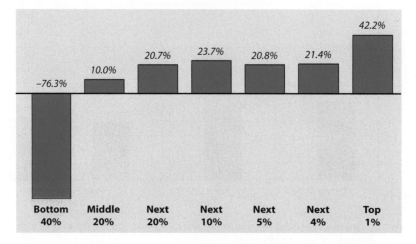

Source: Edward N. Wolff, "Recent Trends in Wealth Ownership, 1983–1998," April 2000. Table 3.

1. What do the groups along the graph's horizontal axis represent?

_____

_____

2. To what do the percentages correspond?

_____

_____

3. How is one of these groups unlike all of the others?

_____

_____

4. In which two groups was the rate of change the greatest?

_____

_____

5. State the main point of this graph.

_____

_____

Keeping a Reading Journal

A reading journal is a notebook in which you record your responses to what you read. This can be a very valuable tool for improving reading comprehension, for stimulating critical thinking, and for generating ideas for your own papers. Responding in writing also helps to clarify what you have learned about the topic and to identify what you still need to find out. Often, you do not really know exactly what you think about a topic until you sit down and try to put your ideas into words. The act of finding language for your thoughts helps you understand what you know and what you believe about the topic, especially those with which you are unfamiliar.

A reading journal can contain a number of different kinds of reactions, but the following are all particularly effective:

- a summary of what you learned

- your feelings about the ideas or information

- the reasons why you agree or disagree with the author

- an explanation of how your own experiences either support or disprove the information

- questions you have about the information

- a comparison of the information with other authors' writings on the topic

As an example, read the following passage and then read one student's reading journal entry about it.

When Doodling Turns Deadly . . .

1 Apparently, none of the adults at Mellon Middle School have ever heard of art therapy. Becca Johnson, a sixth grader, certainly has: "That's my way of saying I'm angry," she said Tuesday, after the 11-year-old was suspended from her suburban Pittsburgh school for doodling two hangman-style stick figures with arrows stuck through their heads. The names of a teacher and a substitute were scrawled beneath the drawings, and Becca's school contends the sketches represent "a terrorist threat."

2   It seems that Johnson, an honor student, was really ticked off about getting a D on her vocabulary test. So she made a couple of drawings on the back of the test, expressing her feelings . . . creatively, if you will. That's what she was told to do by her parents, who are understandably miffed[1] about the whole incident. "We've always told her that you can't take your feelings out on your teacher," says Barbara Johnson, Becca's mom, "so write about it or draw it, as a catharsis[2]."

3   And that would have been that if it hadn't been for one of Becca's classmates, who spotted the drawing and freaked out. Teachers were told, administrators were called in. Suddenly, the normal frustrations of a high-achieving student were hauled out and stuffed under a microscope. Meanwhile, of course, what really bears close examination is the paranoia that leads to this kind of overreaction.

4   I shudder to think what might have happened to me if anyone had seen some of the doodles I came up with during my time in school. Chemistry class: Doodle of chemistry teacher with little beakers[3] coming out of his head like horns; exploding Bunsen burners[4] in the background. French class: Doodle of French teacher with large baguette[5] in her derriere[6]. Calculus class: Trust me, you don't want to know.

5   The point is, I channeled my grouchiness over being bored, being worried about [the] prom—heck, about being a teenager—into very bad, not particularly creative art. The drawings weren't very nice, certainly, but they weren't threatening. I never, ever would have dreamed of acting on any of them. (And besides, I didn't know enough about chemistry to successfully blow anything up.)

6   Granted, I was in school long before Columbine[7]—and while things were not perfect back then, they were a lot simpler, in many ways. Teachers were more worried about students skipping classes than about any one of us whipping out a semi-automatic weapon and gunning down our classmates. Most of the time, just showing up was good enough, and whether you spent the interim[8] time doodling was kind of beside the point.

7   And really, I don't think things are so different in the post-Columbine world. Kids haven't changed much in the last ten years, even though the bad eggs seem to get their hands on guns more often. Middle and high school students are no more villainous now than they were back in the 1980s—and they have much better hair now, too.

8   I know that teachers and principals have a very tough job. And of course they should be on the lookout for signs of violent behavior. But let's keep our

1. **miffed:** annoyed
2. **catharsis:** emotional release
3. **beakers:** cups or glass containers used in chemistry
4. **Bunsen burners:** flames used in chemistry class to heat up chemicals
5. **baguette:** long French bread

6. **derriere:** French word for behind or backside of a person
7. **Columbine:** incident in Colorado in which two students at Columbine High School shot and killed or wounded several students and teachers in 1999
8. **interim:** temporary; provisional

hysteria to a dull roar, shall we? Becca Johnson shouldn't be punished for doodling. If anything she should be rewarded for showcasing her pent-up annoyance in such a peaceful and non-destructive manner. Rather than suspend Becca, let's take a moment to give her a round of applause. And it sounds to me like she could also use an art class.*

Here is one student's response to this article:

> Jessica Reaves' essay "When Doodling Turns Deadly . . ." describes an incident in which a sixth grader was suspended for drawing pictures of two teachers with arrows stuck in their heads. She says that "paranoia" caused teachers and school administrators to overreact, and she argues that doodling like this provides a harmless outlet for teenagers' emotions and frustrations. She describes her own doodles, which weren't nice but weren't threatening either. But the doodles of others might be, especially nowadays.
>
> Jessica Reaves doesn't think that kids have changed all that much, but she herself points out that not very long ago, two Columbine High School students killed thirteen people in a shooting spree on the school's campus. Maybe most kids aren't more "villainous" now than kids in the 1980s were, but there's no doubt that a few kids are much more dangerous. I don't know if we should blame violent TV shows and video games, easier access to guns, or some other cause of the problem. Whatever the reason, no one can deny that there have been some terrible incidents of violence among young people since the 1990s. After all, the 2007 shooting rampage at Virginia Tech was the deadliest in U.S. history. I agree with Jessica Reaves that we shouldn't get hysterical, but I don't think you can blame teachers for getting worried when they see violent drawings of themselves. Jessica Reaves thinks that the sixth-grade doodler should be rewarded for dealing with her frustration in a peaceful and non-destructive manner. Yet the author would probably also want teachers and school officials to remain vigilant in order to stop violence before it starts. She would probably want to know why no one did anything if this particular student did turn out to be a ticking time bomb who finally did something awful. So it seems to me that the answer is at neither one extreme (suspending the sixth-grade doodler) or the other (rewarding her), but somewhere in the middle.

When you write, you continue to think, which leads to new insights. As a result, compositions are a common college assignment, for instructors know that writing helps students learn more. Use the power of writing, then, to get more out of what you read.

Source: Jessica Reaves, "When Doodling Turns Deadly . . . ," *Time,* May 2, 2002, © 2002 Time Inc. Reprinted with permission.

 **EXERCISE 2.5**   **Writing Reading Journal Entries**

On your own paper, write a reading journal entry for each of the following reading selections in Chapters 1–2:

"The Learning Curve" (pages 10–15)
"Cheating Wends Way from Youth Sports to Business" (pages 18–20)
"Bridezilla's Revenge" (pages 22–24)
"Shop 'til We Drop?" (pages 31–36)

In Chapters 8–18, you will be examining the different modes for arranging ideas in paragraphs and essays. Each of these chapters will include readings that will give you ideas for compositions of your own and stimulate your critical thinking. Part IV of this text, too, includes a variety of longer reading selections that will provide you with more topic ideas.

Writing Opportunities

1. Compare and contrast the eating or dinner rituals that you had as a family growing up with the ones that you have now. Do you still eat as a family or with a new set of people, for example, roommates or dormmates? How is this different from the way that you grew up?

2. Have we become anesthetized to cheaters and cheating? Think about some of the recent scandals that have been reported in the newspapers—Enron, the steroid use scandal in baseball, and so on. Have people's reactions been the same as they would have been twenty years ago? Why or why not?

3. What is your idea of the perfect wedding? Where would it be, what would it include, and who would participate in or witness the event?

4. Write a cause/effect essay discussing whether or not we are experiencing "the end of text."

5. Would you agree with Robert Samuelson that Americans are on a "consumption treadmill"? Give examples of people you know who would illustrate Samuelson's point.

CHAPTER 2 REVIEW

To review the main points in this chapter, write a brief response to each of the following questions.

1. What are active readers, and how will being an active reader help you with your reading and writing?

2. Why is previewing important?

3. What should you do when you formulate questions about a reading? How is this helpful in approaching a reading task?

4. What is the benefit of underlining and/or highlighting key words or phrases in a text?

5. What is the definition of *taking notes*, and how will taking notes be helpful to you?

6. What is critical reading?

7. What kinds of questions should you ask yourself to interpret a photograph? a graph?

8. What is a reading journal, and how will keeping one be helpful to you?

WebWork

Go to the Library of Congress "American Memory" Web site at **http://memory .loc.gov/ammem/.** Browse through the photographs in the collection and find one that interests you. Then answer the following questions about the photograph you have selected:

> What emotions do you feel when you look at the photograph? Do you think that the photographer is trying to influence you by stirring these emotions?
>
> What is the photographer's purpose and/or message?
>
> Do you agree with the photographer's point?

Write a reading journal entry about your photograph. Does the photograph give you ideas you could write about? What are those ideas?

Online Study Center   For more information and exercises, go to the Online Study Center that accompanies this textbook, at **http://www.college.hmco.com/pic/ dolphinwriterthree.**

3 Prewriting

▶ List the five steps of the writing process and describe the major task of each one.

▶ Use various prewriting techniques to generate ideas.

▶ Define the term *thesis* and list the two components of a main idea.

▶ Explain the two characteristics of an effective thesis.

▶ Explain how audience and purpose affect the thesis.

The Writing Process

In Chapter 1 of this book, you learned that writing is complex because it requires a variety of different mental skills. Fortunately, though, these different kinds of thinking tasks do not have to be performed at the same time. Instead, you can separate them into different steps or stages of a larger process. As a matter of fact, writing can be viewed as a series of five main steps, each of which focuses on a particular kind of thinking:

Step 1: Prewriting. Discover your topic and generate ideas about it.

Step 2: Organizing and Outlining. Use logic to determine the order in which you should present ideas, and create a plan for your paper.

Step 3: Writing. Using your outline as a guide, write the sentences and paragraphs that clearly state and develop your ideas.

Step 4: Revising. Reevaluate your paper's organization and development of ideas and make the necessary improvements.

Step 5: Editing and Preparing the Final Draft. Correct grammatical and spelling errors, and generate a final copy that is ready to submit.

Chances are good that as you write, you are already completing all or most of these steps to some extent. However, you may not be devoting enough time and effort to each one, or you may be trying to complete two or more of the steps at the same time. For example, you might be attempting to think of and to organize your thoughts *as* you are actually writing a draft, or you may be trying to write, revise, and edit simultaneously.

If you are neglecting or combining the steps, though, you are probably making the writing process more difficult, more time-consuming, and less rewarding for yourself. Because each of the steps requires a different kind of thinking, eliminating a step (such as organizing) or trying to complete it along with another step makes the whole process more difficult. When you are completing the various mental challenges simultaneously, you also slow yourself down, so the whole process takes more time. What is more, you reduce the overall quality of your writing when you do not give adequate attention to each separate stage.

Therefore, to make the writing process easier, faster, and more rewarding, always complete all of the five stages and complete each one of them separately. While you work, return to previous stages as necessary. For example, if you realize during the revision stage that you have not fully developed one of your points, return to the prewriting stage to generate more ideas. If during the revision stage you think of another great point that you left out, go back to the organization stage to decide where to insert it. Then go back to the writing stage to actually compose the additional paragraphs.

The remainder of this chapter will focus on prewriting, the first stage in the writing process. Chapter 4 will cover organizing and outlining. Chapter 5 will show you how to make the paper's actual composition go more smoothly. Chapter 6 will focus on revising, and Chapter 7 will discuss the procedures to follow to edit and prepare the final draft.

Prewriting

In Chapter 1 of this book, you were reminded that everyone has important ideas, thoughts, feelings, and beliefs about the world we live in. In other words, everyone has something significant to say. You may not agree, of course, if you tend to experience "writer's block," the state of being unable to think of ideas whenever you sit down to write. It is indeed frustrating to be faced with a blank sheet of paper or a blank computer screen and be unable to think of anything to say. You can use certain techniques to help yourself get started and to begin coaxing those ideas out from where they are hiding. These techniques are known as **prewriting,** and this chapter will introduce you to several of them.

First, consider all of the benefits of prewriting. Prewriting is an important tool for writers because it has four uses:

1. **Prewriting can help you find a topic to write about.** On those occasions when you can write your paper about a topic of your own choice, prewriting can help you think of one.

2. **Prewriting can help you narrow a topic or find some interesting aspect of it.** When your topic is assigned, as it often is in academic courses, you may need to narrow it down. Even in a longer research paper, you could not do justice to a big subject like "The Civil War" or "abnormal psychology." You need to find a more specific aspect on which to focus, and prewriting can help you narrow, or limit, your topic to one that is more manageable for the assignment. In addition, prewriting can help you discover an aspect of the topic that is interesting to you. When you write about a topic that interests you, you will be more enthusiastic about the paper. As a result, you are more likely to write a better paper.

3. **Prewriting can help you remember or discover what you already know about a topic.** Not only can you prewrite to discover a topic, but you can also prewrite to find out what you know about a topic. You probably have some knowledge or beliefs about most topics, and prewriting can help you unlock this information from where it is stored in your mind. At the same time, prewriting allows you to get a better understanding of what you *do not* know about a topic. Then you can determine what you will need to find out—through reading and research—before you begin to write.

4. **Prewriting can help you decide what you want to say about your topic.** Once you have decided on a topic and explored what you know about it, you can use prewriting techniques to help you formulate the idea or opinion that you want to express about that topic. In addition, you can use prewriting as a tool to help you begin to sort through your thoughts about the topic so that you can determine which of those thoughts you want to include in your paper.

As you can see, prewriting is a valuable step in the writing process. It breaks through writer's block, getting the ideas flowing and helping you find a starting point. As a result, it reduces the anxiety and frustration that you might have felt in the past as you began writing.

The next section of this chapter covers five effective prewriting techniques that you can use to help yourself get started.

Talking

Have you ever noticed that after you have talked about a subject with someone for the first time, you understand more clearly what you yourself think about that topic? Even if you have given a considerable amount of thought to a subject, your ideas about it can tend to remain vague and half-formed until you try to find the words to express them. The act of putting your ideas and feelings into language helps to make them clearer. Remember, when you discuss a subject with someone else (which requires using language), you understand it better.

The next time you need to generate ideas for a paper, try having an oral or written conversation (in person, via e-mail, or in an Internet chat room) with a fellow student, friend, relative, or coworker. Tell the other person what you know or what you think about the topic, and use the discussion as an opportunity to learn more. Afterward, you might want to jot your ideas down on paper using one of the other prewriting techniques discussed in this chapter.

EXERCISE 3.1   **Using Talk to Generate Ideas**

With one of your classmates, have a five- to ten-minute conversation about a current event or story in the news that neither of you has ever discussed or written about previously. Then write your answers to the following questions on the blanks provided.

1. What topic did you and your classmate discuss?

_____

_____

_____

2. During this conversation, what did you realize that you know or believe about the topic?

_____

_____

_____

3. What did you learn about the topic from your partner?

_____

_____

_____

Freewriting

A second effective prewriting technique is **freewriting.** The goal of freewriting is to generate ideas by recording, as quickly as you can, the flow of thoughts going through your mind. You simply consider the topic and then write down what you are thinking about that topic. At this stage, though, you do not censor or reject any thoughts, nor do you try to organize them. You do not bother to cross out or correct anything—that comes later. You also do not pause to think about where to place a comma or to determine what is exactly the right word. In fact, you do not pause at all; instead, you write nonstop, and if you run out of ideas, you continue writing something like "my mind is blank my mind is blank my mind is blank . . . " until another thought comes to mind. Then you record that thought. Do not worry about neatness because freewriting is for your eyes only; it is a tool for the writer to get some ideas flowing, and readers do not see it.

When one student considered the topic "obesity," she generated the following freewriting:

Obesity

News reports say that more and more people are getting overweight or obese. Can't remember definition of obese, but I remember reading that about a third of Americans need to slim down. Its hard to do though. I weigh 10 pounds more than I should. A few of my friends are at least a little chubby. Food is everywhere, portion sizes in resturants are huge, fast food is delicious but loaded with fat and calories. People are busy and have a hard time finding time for exercise or make nutritious meals. So we end up eating a lot of junk food on the run. Junk food tastes better than healthy food. Staying at your ideal weight takes a lot of willpower. Then there's the psychological problems that factor in to being overweight. Its an uphill battle for a lot of people.

You probably noticed as you read this freewriting that it contains errors like misspellings and missing punctuation. That is fine, however, because the point of freewriting is to explore thoughts without worrying about the mechanics of writing. By completing this freewriting about obesity, this student touched on several different causes of the problem, and she is well on her way to creating an essay that will examine the reasons why obesity is becoming so prevalent.

Freewriting is also useful for finding a topic to write about and for narrowing a topic. If you are in search of a topic to write about, you can freewrite about "things that anger me" or "topics that interest me." Once you have generated several topic possibilities, pick one or two of the most promising and freewrite about each of them. Similarly, if you need to narrow a broad topic, freewrite about different aspects of it in order to find one that interests you.

When you freewrite, you may want to time yourself. In other words, set a timer for ten minutes, and do not stop writing until the timer goes off. Doing this will encourage you to write longer than you might ordinarily write, helping you generate more ideas.

EXERCISE 3.2   Using Freewriting to Generate Ideas

Choose one of the topics from the following list and freewrite about that topic for at least ten minutes.

College	A mistake
Stress	Wealth
Food	Taking risks

EXERCISE 3.3   Using a Photograph for Freewriting

Study the following photograph. Then freewrite about this image for five to ten minutes.

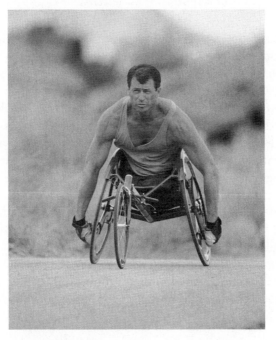

RubberballRF/Jupiter Images

Brainstorming

While freewriting involves recording ideas in the form of sentences, **brainstorming** involves writing down just the words and phrases that spring to mind when you think about a subject. You can write these words and phrases in rows and columns, or you can just write them all over the page. For example, when one student was asked to brainstorm about the topic "taking tests," here is what he wrote:

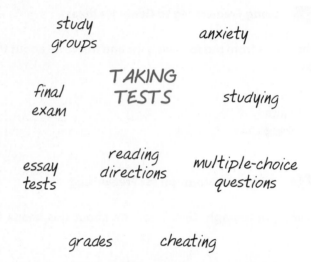

Like freewriting, brainstorming is most effective when you decide to spend a certain minimum amount of time—such as ten minutes—generating all the ideas you can. Do not pause to evaluate the worth of an idea, and do not censor any ideas. Later, you will go back and reconsider the value of each idea, but while you brainstorm, you simply write them all down. Just focus on the topic and record everything that pops into your head as quickly as possible. Because brainstorming is a tool for only you, the writer, do not worry about spelling, organization, or neat penmanship, for no one else needs to see it.

Brainstorming can be useful for finding a subject to write about. For example, you could write down "things that make me angry" in the middle of a piece of paper and then fill up the page with your pet peeves. In addition, brainstorming is an effective tool for narrowing a subject. Write down your broad subject and then record all of the specific aspects that occur to you. If you already have a topic, you can use brainstorming to generate ideas about it. For instance, you might write down "reasons why people do things they know are bad for them" and then fill up the page with all of the reasons you can think of.

EXERCISE 3.4   **Using Brainstorming to Generate Ideas**

Select one of the topics from the following list and brainstorm for at least ten minutes about that topic.

Fame   A great career
Parents   A difficult task

Clustering

Clustering is like brainstorming in that you write down words or phrases that occur to you when you think about a topic. However, when you cluster, you loosely group ideas as chains of thought, recording them on the page in the order in which they occur to you. Clustering is based upon the idea that one thought leads to another. If you were to create a cluster of ideas about the Fourth of July holiday, you might begin by jotting down one particular train of thought:

JULY 4th

fireworks

explosions of colored
light in the night sky

people sitting on blankets
on the grass to watch

sounds of crowd gasping,
applauding

Then you would add another thought chain:

You exhaust one train of thought before beginning another one, continuing to add new clusters branching out from the main topic until you cannot think of any more ideas.

Clustering can be especially useful for generating descriptive details about a subject. You can guide yourself toward coming up with information related to each of the five different senses by focusing each train of thought on a particular kind of detail:

You would complete this cluster by continuing to add more details in the chain for each sense.

EXERCISE 3.5   **Using Clustering to Generate Ideas**

Select one of the topics from the following list and create a cluster of ideas that contains at least six different branches.

A memorable trip   My favorite restaurant
An object I could not live without   A person whom I admire

Asking Questions

A fifth way to generate ideas is by asking—and then finding answers to—questions about your topic. The best place to start is by posing the six questions (*Who? What? When? Where? Why?* and *How?*) that journalists ask when they are collecting information for a news story. These questions will help you narrow a broad topic. For example, a student who was assigned to write a paper about the presidency in the United States wrote the following questions:

The Presidency

Who have been our best and worst presidents?
Who has been our greatest president?
What is a president's typical day like?
What are the president's responsibilities?
When has a president made a serious mistake?
When has a president saved the nation from disaster?
Where does the president live and work?
Why is the president's role an important one?
How has the presidency changed over time?
How does presidential security work?

These questions allowed the student to see many different aspects of the topic on which she could focus, and they helped her discover that she was most interested in concentrating on how the presidency has changed over time. Therefore, she created a new round of questions about that more specific topic:

WRITING FOR SUCCESS

More Prewriting Techniques

This chapter covers several common, tried-and-true prewriting techniques. But there are others. In fact, you yourself might already use a technique that was not covered in this chapter. If that is true, consider sharing information about your technique with your instructor and classmates.

The following list briefly describes some other techniques that you might want to try:

- **Draw.** If you are going to describe something, draw a picture of it to retrieve details from your memory.
- **Meditate.** Clear your mind and focus all of your attention on your topic.
- **Create a dialogue.** Pretend that you are having a conversation with someone about your topic. Have your imaginary partner ask you questions about the topic and then give the answers.
- **Use the cubing technique.** Cubing prompts you to explore your topic from different angles. Imagine six different activities as though they were each on one side of a cube, like the

die used in board games. Here are six typical activities for a cubing exercise:

1. **Describe your topic.** What do you see?
2. **Compare and/or contrast your topic with something else.** What is similar to it? What is different from it?
3. **Associate your topic.** What associations or thoughts come to mind when you think about it?
4. **Analyze your topic.** What are its parts or ingredients?
5. **Apply your topic.** What can you do with it?
6. **Argue for or against your topic.** Take a stand and give reasons to support your position.

You should feel free to come up with the idea-generation method that works best for you. Experiment, explore, and feel free to alter existing techniques to make them more productive for you.

Changes in the Presidency

Who are people who have affected the president's roles and responsibilities?
What are some of these specific changes?
When did these changes begin to occur?
Why did these changes occur?
How do today's presidents differ from earlier presidents?

The student can now choose the questions that interest her most and then use one of the other prewriting techniques—such as freewriting or brainstorming—to generate more ideas and to discover areas that she will need to research for more information.

EXERCISE 3.6   **Asking Questions to Generate Ideas**

Select one of the topics from the following list and generate *Who? What? When? Where? Why?* and *How?* questions for that topic.

Hunting
Space travel
Museums
A historic event, such as a war or movement
Fashion
Daycare centers
Violence in schools
Reality television shows
The Super Bowl
Recycling

Now that you have practiced five different prewriting techniques, you may have found that one of the methods seems particularly effective for you. You should definitely use that method to generate ideas for your papers. However, be aware that different techniques can be suited to different kinds of topics. For example, if your paper will be in the form of a personal story from your experience, freewriting might be the best way to begin to remember the details, whereas the question method might yield more ideas for a paper about a World War I battle. Therefore, you might want to consider using at least two different prewriting techniques each time you need to generate ideas. Using a combination of methods may yield the best, most comprehensive results.

Topic to Thesis

At the beginning of this chapter, you learned that one use for prewriting is to discover what you want to say about a topic. After you decide on a topic and explore your ideas about that topic, the next step in the process is determining your **thesis,** the main idea or point that you want to make. In order to write a coherent essay, you must begin with a very clear understanding of your thesis, so it is important to spend some time working on it until it expresses exactly what you want to communicate.

A thesis has two main components. It includes, first of all, your topic. Usually your thesis will begin with this topic. Then the thesis goes on to state the point that you want to make about the topic. Here are some examples:

Topic	*Point*
Professional athletes	are not always the best role models.
Topic	*Point*
Dating	is much different now than it was when my grandparents were young.
Topic	*Point*
Preparation for a job interview	should include three important steps.

Remember that a topic alone cannot be a thesis. The thesis includes both the topic and what you want to say about that topic:

Topic: A happy marriage
Thesis: A happy marriage has three main ingredients: good communication, trust, and mutual respect.

Topic: Legalizing marijuana
Thesis: Legalizing marijuana is a bad idea.

Topic: Tips for saving money
Thesis: Some money-saving tips may help you increase the size of your bank account.

EXERCISE 3.7   **Writing the Thesis**

In the following list, complete each thesis by adding a point about each topic.

1. Owning a pet _____.

2. Divorce _____.

3. Today's teenagers _____.

4. A good leader _____.

5. Earning a college degree _____.

6. The clothes we wear _____.

7. Eating out in restaurants _____.

8. Computers _____.

9. Men and women _____.

10. Cell phones _____.

Considering Your Topic, Audience, and Purpose

As you are determining your thesis, you need to consider not only *what* you want to say but also *why* and *to whom* you want to say it. Therefore, in addition to the topic, there are two other factors—audience and purpose—that will affect your thesis.

First of all, who is going to read your paper? The readers you have in mind affect what you say and how you say it. To illustrate, let us say that you are planning to write about an exercise you enjoy, yoga. That is a big topic, and there is a lot to say about it. Considering one specific audience will help you narrow it down to a more manageable size. Possible readers include current yoga students, fitness buffs who have never tried yoga, and people who do not exercise at all. Each of these three groups has different needs and desires, and you would want to consider them as you decide what point to make about the subject. Notice in the following examples how the thesis might change for each of these different groups:

Audience	*Thesis*
Current yoga students	If you are doing only Hatha yoga, you ought to try some of the other styles.
Fitness buffs	Adding yoga to an exercise routine enhances and speeds up the results of a regular workout.
People who do not exercise	You should try yoga if you need to relieve stress, reduce your blood pressure, or lose weight.

The second factor to take into consideration is your purpose. Why do you want to write about your topic for the audience you have chosen? For academic papers, your purpose will always be either to inform or to persuade. An **informative thesis** states something that you want readers to know about the topic. The thesis for fitness buffs, for example, indicates that the purpose of the paper will be to help readers learn more about the subject. A **persuasive thesis,** on the other hand, indicates that you want to convince your readers to change a particular opinion, a belief, or a behavior. Words like *should, must,* or *ought to* usually indicate their persuasive purpose. Note that the thesis for current yoga students and the thesis for people who do not exercise are both persuasive.

As another example, consider the thesis "Volunteer work offers many health benefits for the volunteer." The writer intends to explain to people who do not know much about volunteering how volunteers are physically affected by their work. This thesis is informative. But notice how the purpose of this next statement differs: "Retired people should do volunteer work." This thesis is persuasive because the writer wants to convince the reader to do something. To achieve that purpose, the writer may include some of the same information that he or she would have included in a paper with the informative thesis. However, other kinds of information may also be appropriate.

EXERCISE 3.8   **Considering Topic, Audience, and Purpose**

For each thesis, identify a possible audience and purpose. Then rewrite the thesis to suit a different audience AND a different purpose. Identify the audience and purpose you have in mind for the revised thesis.

1. Tanning in a tanning bed can have negative consequences.

Audience: _____ Purpose: _____

Revised thesis: _____

Audience: _____ Purpose: _____

2. Recycling should be mandatory for all of our town's residents.

Audience: _____ Purpose: _____

Revised thesis: _____

Audience: _____ Purpose: _____

3. Community colleges and universities are both similar and different.

Audience: _____ Purpose: _____

Revised thesis: _____

Audience: _____ Purpose: _____

4. Public schools need to emphasize science much more than they do now.

Audience: _____ Purpose: _____

Revised thesis: _____

Audience: _____ Purpose: _____

5. The Google search engine works differently than other Internet search engines do.

Audience: _____ Purpose: _____

Revised thesis: _____

Audience: _____ Purpose: _____

Prewriting to Thesis: A Student Demonstration

For a demonstration of the writing process, you will follow the process that a student named Juan went through in order to write an essay for his English class. In this chapter, you will see how Juan began with prewriting, generated ideas, and decided on his thesis. Chapters 4 through 7 explain the process he went through to complete each of the other four steps.

Juan's instructor assigned the class the task of writing an essay about something everyone should learn to do. Juan decided to brainstorm about the topic first. He came up with the following ideas:

Something Everyone Should Learn to Do

computers	write well
good manners	CPR
speak a foreign language	change a flat tire
e-mail	communication
managing money	cook
safe driving	get organized
Internet research	

Juan looked over his brainstorming and decided that he was most interested in writing about learning to speak a foreign language. He himself was bilingual, so he thought he might be able to share with readers some ideas about speaking more than one language. He decided to prewrite again, this time using freewriting to generate more ideas:

I think that everybody should know how to speak at least two languages. America is a multicultural society many citizens speak languages other then english. My family and me speak spanish and english. One of my sisters is learning how to speak French too. She wants to visit France one day. Knowing two languages means I can

communicate easily with more people. This helps me at work especially.
I can talk to Spanish-speaking customers, which is an asset. I can
travel more easily because I can speak to the people who live in many
other countries. I want to learn how to speak other languages to increase my opportunities no matter where I go. And I can help others
by translating. One time I was in the emergency room with my son, he
had the flu. I helped a family from Mexico communicate with the
nurses to get there son treated for a cut finger.

On the basis of this freewriting, Juan realized that being bilingual has several
benefits. He wrote down this thesis:

Being bilingual helps you in life.

Then he realized that he could write a more specific thesis:

Being bilingual benefits you in different ways.

In Chapter 4, you will see how Juan organized and outlined his ideas for his essay.

EXERCISE 3.9   **Prewriting for an Essay**

In this chapter, you will begin to write an essay, and you will continue to work on this
essay in stages as you study the chapters on the writing process. In this chapter, you
will complete prewriting about your topic and formulate a thesis. As part of your
work for Chapters 4 through 7, you will organize your ideas, write the essay, revise it,
and then edit and prepare it for submission to your instructor.

   To get started, choose a topic that seems interesting to you from the following list:

   A significant decision that I made
   Television
   A time when I surprised myself
   Men versus women
   An unfair law
   A solution to a problem

Next, use at least two different prewriting methods to generate ideas about this
topic. If you use the talking method of prewriting, write down what you learned or
what became clearer to you during your conversation.

   Finally, write a thesis that would be suitable for an essay.

To review the main points in this chapter, write a brief response to each of the following questions.

1. Write a short summary discussing the five steps of the writing process and explaining why these steps will help you with your writing tasks.

2. Why is it detrimental to eliminate or try to combine the steps of the writing process?

3. Discuss why prewriting is an important step in the writing process.

4. What are the benefits of talking about a topic with another person? Discuss this question with a classmate.

5. Define the following words: *freewriting, brainstorming,* and *clustering.*

6. How can asking questions help you generate ideas for writing?

7. What is a thesis, and what makes a thesis effective?

8. What are three factors that help shape a thesis?

 **Web**Work

Try the Thesis Generator at **http://mciu.org/~spjvweb/thesisgenerator.html** for writing or refining your own thesis. Consider the thesis that you produced for Exercise 3.9 or a thesis that you wrote for Exercise 3.7 or Exercise 3.8. How many ways can you improve that thesis by following the Thesis Generator's advice?

Online Study Center For more information and exercises, go to the Online Study Center that accompanies this book, at **http://www.college .hmco.com/pic/dolphinwriterthree**.

4 Organizing and Outlining

▶ Explain why organizing ideas before writing is an important step.

▶ Follow a three-step process to group and order relevant ideas.

▶ Explain the difference between natural and logical organization.

▶ Complete informal and formal outlines.

▶ Create an informal or formal outline.

In Chapter 3, you learned how to use prewriting to generate ideas. The next step of the writing process is to organize those ideas and prepare an outline to follow as you write.

Organizing

When you are generating ideas, those ideas will rarely occur to you in an organized manner. Nor should they. When you prewrite, you want to free your creative mind to let the ideas flow without your worrying about their order. Before you write, you must bring some organization to these thoughts. When you read something, you expect the author to have grouped ideas together, divided them into paragraphs, and linked thoughts together so that you can follow them. Likewise, the readers of your writing will expect you to have done the same. If you offer your readers a collection of disorderly, random thoughts, they are likely to become confused about what you are trying to say. They are also likely to miss important connections that you want them to make.

Determining the right order for ideas can be a challenging task because there are often several different ways to arrange your thoughts. To find the most effective pattern, you might have to think of several different possibilities before you can decide which one is best. It is important to devote some time and attention to examining all of the pieces and figuring out how to fit them together, for your organization (or lack of it) can make or break your paper. This chapter will show you some techniques that you can use to organize your ideas.

Determining a Framework

In Chapter 3, you learned that prewriting helps you discover your topic and what you want to say about that topic. Prewriting should include the creation of a thesis that will keep your writing focused on just one point. Next, you will need to determine the best framework for arranging your ideas about your main point. You begin to create this framework when you examine your thesis and your prewriting (your brainstorming, freewriting, clustering, or whatever other type you used) and go through a three-step process to decide on what to include and how to order that information:

Step 1: Circle ideas and information that match your thesis, and ignore or cross out ideas that seem irrelevant.

Step 2: Group similar ideas and information together.

Step 3: Decide on the best way to put these groups of ideas in order.

In step 1, you look at the ideas that you collected during prewriting with your thesis in mind. You evaluate each thought or piece of information, asking yourself if it relates to or supports the point in your thesis. Then you circle, highlight, or otherwise mark these relevant ideas. At the same time, you either ignore or cross out the ideas and information that do not relate to the point in your thesis. Do not erase these ideas; you might decide later that one or two really are useful, so you should not eliminate them for good. But develop a system for marking the ideas that will be useful. For example, one student was asked to write an essay on the topic of an athlete who is a good role model. The student decided to freewrite about bicycle racer Lance Armstrong, and she came up with the following thesis:

Lance Armstrong is a good role model for today's youth.

When she looked over her freewriting for ideas that matched this point, she circled some key words and phrases:

We hear a lot in the news about athletes who behave badly or get arrested for breaking laws. We do not hear as much about athletes who are doing good things. But I think Lance Armstrong is one of those people. He was a great (champion) then he got cancer. He was not expected to live, but he (would not give up) Instead, he (battled the disease with courage and strength) He went through a really difficult period of cancer treatments. Amazingly, he then went right back to training, (determined to work harder) then he ever had before. He became an even better racer, and kept on winning. His achievements have made many (young athletes want to follow in his footsteps) He (refused to give up) And that is what makes him a hero. The (Lance Armstrong Foundation) funds cancer research, and Lance (inspires cancer patients to persevere) His (humanitarian projects) include writing (a book about his experiences) He has (won the Tour de France seven times) because he is a (fierce competitor) He is divorced with three kids.

What this student looked for were reasons why Lance Armstrong is a good role model. She circled these reasons, and she ignored the sentences that did not focus on Lance Armstrong's admirable qualities and actions.

Another student, given the same assignment, chose to brainstorm about golfer Tiger Woods. He generated this thesis:

Tiger Woods is one athlete who is a very good role model.

When this student examined his brainstorming, he looked for ideas that relate to Tiger Woods's admirable qualities. In addition, he crossed out those ideas that seemed unrelated. Notice that some of the ideas are neither circled nor crossed out, for this student was not yet sure whether they would be useful.

Tiger Woods

(stays focused)	(always strives to improve his game)
~~wealthy~~	~~married a model~~
(Tiger Woods Foundation)	(determined)
(helps disadvantaged kids)	~~product endorsements~~
(long practices)	started very young
won Master's four times	youngest Master's champion
~~famous celebrity~~	(concentration)

As you complete this first step of the organizing process, you will need to honestly evaluate the quantity of your ideas. Did you generate enough ideas in your prewriting, or did you come up with only a few? If the number of ideas you have generated seems skimpy, go back to the prewriting stage, perhaps selecting another technique, and try to think of more.

EXERCISE 4.1   **Evaluating the Relevancy of Ideas**

Examine the following thesis and the cluster provided. In the cluster, circle words or phrases that match the thesis. Either ignore or cross out words and phrases that do not relate to the thesis.

Thesis: When choosing the right pet to fit your lifestyle, you should take several things into consideration.

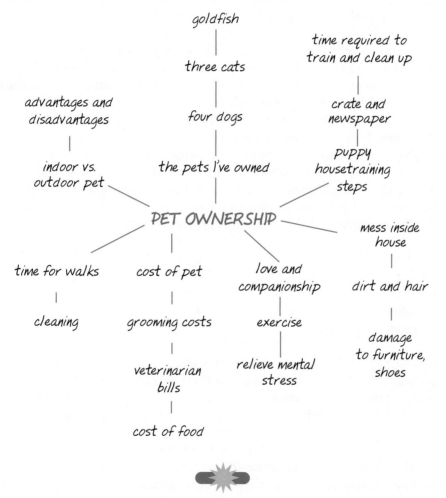

After you have identified relevant ideas in step 1, you are ready to go on to step 2, which involves grouping similar things together. Before you see how to do this with prewriting, consider how you would go about doing it with common household items. Let us say you are going to organize your kitchen cabinets by putting like things together in the same place. You have the following items on your kitchen table:

three cans of soup	forks	plastic containers
dish detergent	salt and pepper	glass bowls
plates	drinking glasses	boxes of macaroni and cheese
knives	scouring powder	a ladle
a box of cereal	sponges	tea bags

If you mix up all of these items, it might be more difficult to locate something when you need to find it. Therefore, you want to group them together logically. How would you go about doing it? You could group the soup, cereal, macaroni and cheese, and tea bags together because they are all food items. The salt and pepper could go in this group, too. You might put the silverware and utensils (forks, knives, ladle) together in another group and put the dishware (plates, bowls, glasses) in yet another. The cleaning items (dish detergent, scouring powder, and sponges) probably belong in a different group, and so on. This is not the only method for grouping these items, but it is probably the most common one because it makes the most sense to the most people.

However, how would you group this next set of items?

paper clips	a watch	a napkin
the sun	a football field	leaves
a pencil	a ring	a dollar bill
a mailbox	a radio	green beans
a basket	a dime	cake

Different groupings are possible for this set of items. For example, you could group them according to shape (some of these things are round, and some are square or rectangular), function (some of these things relate to food or eating, for example), color (several of these things are green), material (some of these things are made of metal), or some other criterion. As you can see, these things can be grouped in a number of different ways. Such will be the case when you look at the ideas that you generate for writing. Sometimes the right grouping will be immediately apparent to you. At other times, you may have to experiment with different ways to group thoughts together.

Now let us apply this same procedure to ideas generated in a prewriting exercise. When you were circling key words and phrases in step 1, you probably circled some things that actually go together or say the same thing in different words. For example, look back at the student's freewriting about Lance Armstrong on pages 75–76. Which of the circled phrases seem to belong together? Several of the phrases relate to Lance Armstrong's achievements:

champion
young athletes want to follow in his footsteps
Lance Armstrong Foundation
inspires cancer patients to persevere
humanitarian projects
book about his experiences
won Tour de France seven times

If you examine this list further, though, you might realize that some of the achievements are athletic, and some of them are humanitarian:

Athletic achievements
champion
won Tour de France seven times

Humanitarian efforts
young athletes want to follow in his footsteps
Lance Armstrong Foundation
inspires cancer patients to persevere
humanitarian projects
book about his experiences

Other circled words and phrases in the freewriting relate to Lance Armstrong's attitude and personal qualities:

Attitude/personal qualities
would not give up
battled the disease with courage and strength
determined to work harder
refused to give up
fierce competitor

When you sort the items into groups, you can see three different aspects of Lance Armstrong that are admirable: his athletic achievements, his humanitarian efforts, and his attitude and personal qualities.

Of course, this is not the only way to group these thoughts. You could, for instance, group them according to the different people—young athletes and cancer patients, in particular—who have been especially inspired by Lance Armstrong's accomplishments. There may be other possibilities as well.

Now look back at the brainstorming on Tiger Woods on page 76. How would you group those ideas together? You could group them together according to the same categories used for the essay about Lance Armstrong. Or you could examine the specific personal qualities that make him a good role model. Here is another possibility:

Admirable mental characteristics
stays focused
determined
concentration

Dedication to hard work and improvement
long practices
always strives to improve his game

Generosity
Tiger Woods Foundation
helps disadvantaged kids

EXERCISE 4.2   **Sorting Items into Groups**

Group each of the following sets of items according to how they are alike. On the blank provided, write down any item that does not belong with the others.

1. kitchen   stove   door   dishwasher   bathroom   refrigerator   dining room

Group 1: _____

Group 2: _____

Item that does not belong: _____

2. basketballs   baseballs   skis   hockey   pucks   cycling   wheel   skating

Group 1: _____

Group 2: _____

Item that does not belong: _____

3. *Time   Newsweek   People   Us Weekly   the Washington Post
the New York Times   Entertainment Weekly   the Miami Herald
Alice in Wonderland*

Group 1: _____

Group 2: _____

Item that does not belong: _____

4. Boston   Cleveland   Massachusetts   Texas   Los Angeles   Las Vegas
   Idaho   Lake Erie

Group 1: _____

Group 2: _____

Item that does not belong: _____

5. Northwestern   Islamic   Jewish   French   Italian   Catholic   Norwegian
   Jamaican

Group 1: _____

Group 2: _____

Item that does not belong: _____

EXERCISE 4.3   **Grouping Ideas from a Prewriting**

Go back to Exercise 4.1 and examine the items that you circled. How would you
group the relevant items in this cluster? List your groups in the space provided.

_____

_____

_____

After you have determined possible groupings for relevant items, step 3 involves deciding on the order in which you should present these groups to your reader. Sometimes the groups will naturally organize themselves, as you will see in the next section. For those topics that do not naturally order themselves, you will have to use logic, letting the relationships among the groups suggest the best arrangement.

Natural Versus Logical Organization

When you are deciding on the best order for your ideas, you will have to decide whether to use natural organization or logical organization. Some topics organize themselves, so they are arranged with **natural organization.** When you tell a story, for instance, or write a set of directions to explain how to do something, you will give your readers the events or the steps chronologically, in the order in which they occur.

However, many more topics do *not* naturally organize themselves. For these topics, you will have to use **logical organization.** In other words, you will have to evaluate the groups you created and apply logic to decide if they are related to each other in some way. These relationships may indicate a certain order for presenting the groups. For example, the items in one of the groups may actually be the cause of the items in another of the groups. Recall, for example, the three groups of reasons why Lance Armstrong is a good role model: his athletic achievements, his humanitarian efforts, and his attitudes and personal qualities. Does one of these things cause another? You could say that his attitudes and personal qualities lead him to act in certain ways. As a result, you might want to discuss those first. But then should you discuss his athletic achievements or his humanitarian efforts next? You would have to determine if it matters whether you should present the discussion of one before the other.

This is not the only way to arrange these groups. You might decide, for instance, that Lance Armstrong is a role model first and foremost because of his athletic achievements. If so, you would discuss that point first. Then you would have to apply logic to determine which of the other reasons should be presented next.

When you examine your groups, you might decide that some are more important than others. Order of importance may affect how you arrange your ideas. Sometimes it is best to present the most important information first, and sometimes it is best to save it for last. In either case, though, consider whether you should order groups by their relative importance. You might do this, for instance, with the ideas about Tiger Woods. Which of the qualities is most important in a role model? If you think that it is generosity, then you might want to present that quality first. If you think that hard work is a role model's most admirable trait, either present that quality first or save it for last, ranking and ordering the other two characteristics accordingly.

One common mistake that you should avoid as you work on organizing ideas is trying to use natural organization when you should use logical organization. It is not advisable, for example, to present your ideas to the reader in the order in which you thought of them. If you do that, you will have completely skipped steps 1 and 2 of the organization process. Nor do you want to try to use a story form to present information about a topic that is not really a story. For example, telling a story about the time that you actually met Tiger Woods and merely mentioning here and there the things about him that you admire is probably not the best way to address why he is a good role model.

EXERCISE 4.4   **Determining the Right Order for Ideas**

In what order would you place the groups that you created in Exercise 4.3? In the space provided, write each of your groups in order, numbered *1, 2, 3*, and so on.

EXERCISE 4.5   **Using Natural or Logical Organization**

Read each of the following main idea statements and then label each one **N** if it would lend itself to natural organization or **L** if it would require logical organization.

_____   **1.** You should register to vote and cast a ballot in every election.

_____   **2.** My performance in our school's talent show was not supposed to be funny, but it definitely turned out that way.

_____   **3.** Will Smith is a multitalented performer.

_____   **4.** Anyone can sew a lost button back on a shirt by following three simple steps.

_____   **5.** America needs to expand its railway transportation system.

_____ **6.** If you do not maintain a normal weight, you will put yourself at risk for several diseases and health problems.

_____ **7.** Americans could do more to conserve energy.

_____ **8.** There are three stages in a butterfly's life cycle.

_____ **9.** My wedding day was the happiest day of my life.

_____ **10.** Having brothers and sisters is better than being an only child.

The Modes of Development

As you think about the best way to organize your ideas, you will want to consider the common strategies for organizing ideas. Chapters 8 through 17 of this book provide in-depth explanations of these common patterns. The list that follows provides a brief description of each one:

- **Narration.** Tell a story from your own or someone else's experience. (See Chapter 8.)

- **Description.** Provide details about people, places, and things so that readers can picture them in their minds. (See Chapter 9.)

- **Process.** Explain the steps of a procedure. (See Chapter 10.)

- **Illustration.** Provide specific examples that illustrate the main idea. (See Chapter 11.)

- **Classification.** Group items into categories. (See Chapter 12.)

- **Division.** Examine the parts of something. (See Chapter 13.)

- **Comparison/Contrast.** Examine how two things are alike and/or different. (See Chapter 14.)

- **Cause and Effect.** Explain why something occurred or examine the results or outcomes. (See Chapter 15.)

- **Definition.** Explain the meaning of a term. (See Chapter 16.)

- **Argument.** Present a series of reasons to convince readers to change their minds or behaviors. (See Chapter 17.)

Often your thesis will either dictate or suggest organizing your essay according to one or more of these patterns. For example, the thesis "Driving over the speed limit can lead to many serious consequences" clearly indicates that the essay will discuss effects. Therefore, the essay's supporting points should be the different effects of speeding. The thesis "Although both are learning experiences, attending college is very different from attending high school" indicates comparison/contrast; thus, the supporting points should be in the form of points of comparison.

When you write a thesis, be aware of clue words that indicate an appropriate pattern for the supporting points. The following list provides some examples of phrases that often suggest a certain pattern:

Narration: *several events, a number of developments, over time*

Description: *features, characteristics*

Process: *three steps, several stages, process, procedure*

Illustration: *examples*

Classification: *types, categories, groups, classes, kinds*

Division: *parts, pieces, sections*

Comparison/contrast: *similarities, differences, likenesses, compares, contrasts*

Cause and effect: *causes, effects, consequences, reasons*

Definition: *defined, definition, is*

Argument: *reasons*

EXERCISE 4.6   **Matching a Thesis to a Mode of Development**

On the blank provided, write the mode of development suggested by each thesis statement.

1. Several events happen during the selection of a jury.

_____

2. Obesity has a number of negative consequences.

_____

3. Debit cards and credit cards may look alike, but they differ in important ways.

_____

4. To resolve a problem, try following George Polya's four-step procedure for problem solving.

_____

5. A hero can be defined as an individual who willingly endangers himself or herself to help others.

    ————————————————

6. You should not eat meat for three reasons.

    ————————————————

7. The two main parts of a baseball field are the infield and the outfield.

    ————————————————

8. The duck-billed platypus is one animal with some very odd characteristics.

    ————————————————

9. There are three types of parents.

    ————————————————

10. A few athletes may be good role models, but there are many more examples of those who are not.

    ————————————————

Outlining

During or after your completion of the three steps of the organization process, you should create an outline of your ideas. **Outlines** come in different forms, but they all list the ideas or information you will present in the order in which you will present them. The best outlines also indicate how ideas are related to one another. Regardless of their form, they all provide the writer with a guide to follow as he or she writes.

Myths About Outlining

When people object to creating an outline prior to writing, they usually argue that they can save time by skipping the outline and just working out their organization as they write. Or they may argue that it is pointless to create an outline when it never matches the finished product. Both of these arguments, however, rest on the following myths about outlining.

Myth #1: Skipping the outlining step saves time. On the contrary, failing to outline actually *adds* time to composition. When you do not spend time determining and writing down a plan of organization before you begin writing, you force your brain to juggle two challenging mental tasks (organizing and composing) at the same time. Because doing this is more complicated, the writing usually takes longer. Separating the outlining stage and working out the organization of your ideas before you begin to write can actually save you valuable time in the long run by making the writing step easier and therefore faster.

Myth #2: An outline is useless because the final paper rarely matches it. The outline is your best determination of your composition's overall structure. However, it is not cast in stone, and you may very well find better ways to organize your thoughts as you write. Just because you alter your original plan does not mean that it was not useful for getting you started.

Creating an outline of your ideas before you write will help you keep the overall big picture in mind as you concentrate on the smaller details. It will also prevent you from

- straying from your main point and including information or ideas that are irrelevant

- rambling or jumping from thought to thought in a manner that confuses the reader

- mixing different kinds of information together

- discussing an idea in the wrong place

Informal Outlines

If an outline is not a requirement of your assignment, and you are creating one just as a tool for yourself, then you are free to use any method that works for you. Informal types of outlines can take the form of brief lists of ideas in the order in which you want to discuss them. For example, the following sketch is an informal outline:

> Main idea: The Red Cross is a worthy organization that will make good use of your financial contribution.
>
> 1. Disaster relief services
>   - Provides shelter, food, water, health care to victims of floods, hurricanes, earthquakes, and other disasters
>   - Blood bank
>   - International in scope

   2. Training and education
      — teaches first aid and CPR, teaches swimming and lifeguarding, trains babysitters

   3. Uses its resources wisely and efficiently
      — more than 90 percent of every dollar it receives is used to pay for its programs and services

An informal outline can also take the form of branching. This form looks a lot like the clustering prewriting technique. You start with a topic and then draw "branches" of subtopics and details that radiate from the central topic. Here is an example of branching:

Main idea: People say that a swimming pool is too time-consuming and expensive to maintain, but it is worth the effort and cost.

⛤ **EXERCISE 4.7**   **Completing an Informal Outline**

Create an informal outline for the following main idea.

Main idea: Despite the crowds and traffic that are annoyances of city life, living in a large city is better than living in a small town.

Formal Outlines

When you think of an outline, you may picture one that includes Roman numerals. A **formal outline** is one that uses some combination of Roman numerals, letters, and/or Arabic numbers. One common type of formal outline, for example, uses all three:

> I. Main idea
>   A. Supporting detail
>   1. Statistic
>   2. Example
>   B. Supporting detail
>   1. Expert opinion
>   2. Data

In this type of outline, the Roman numerals correspond to the main ideas while the letters and Arabic numbers indicate supporting information. This is the type of outline that is usually a required part of longer assignments such as research papers because it serves as a kind of table of contents for a lengthy paper.

However, creating a formal outline is worthwhile even if it is not a required part of an assignment. This format not only is useful for showing the order of your ideas but also serves another valuable purpose: it clearly indicates your ideas' relationship to one another. Thus, as you write, one glance at this outline would help you keep in mind your overall structure of the entire paper, allowing you to stay organized *and* make important connections for your reader. Obviously, it takes some time to create a detailed outline like this, but the time and effort are worth it, for the composition process is then often faster and yields a more successful finished product.

WRITING FOR SUCCESS

The Many Uses of Outlines

The ability to create a good outline is a valuable skill to master because you will need this skill for many other personal and professional tasks. The following list briefly summarizes some of the many uses for outlines.

1. **A guide for an oral presentation.** Your delivery of a speech will often be much more effective if you use an outline and speak naturally rather than read a script.
2. **An agenda to use as a guide for a meeting.** Effective leaders know that an agenda in outline form can help make meetings more efficient and productive.

3. **A study guide for a textbook chapter.** Outlining a chapter is a very effective way to comprehend and recall its contents.
4. **Taking notes on a professor's lecture.** Use an outline form for your notes to help you better understand the information.
5. **A PowerPoint presentation.** One quick way to create an entire PowerPoint presentation is to simply outline it and let the PowerPoint program create the slides.
6. **A site map for a Web site.** A site map is an outline of all of the pages associated with a particular Web site, so you will need outlining skills to create one.

 **EXERCISE 4.8**   **Completing a Formal Outline**

Fill in the blanks in the following formal outline with the words and phrases in the list.

Main idea: Nursing is a great career.

Compensation	Improving public health through patient
Varied and interesting tasks	education
Vacations	Financial rewards
Intangible benefits	Exciting and fast-paced environment
High salary	Benefits of a nursing career
Overtime pay	Helping people who are suffering and in pain

I. _____

   A. _____

      1. _____

         a. _____

         b. _____

2. Fringe benefits
    a. Health insurance provided by employer

    b. _____

B. Working conditions

    1. _____

    2. _____

    3. Flexible schedule

C. _____

    1. _____

    2. _____

Organizing and Outlining: A Student Demonstration

In Chapter 3, you saw the prewriting generated by Juan, a student who was assigned to write about something everyone should learn how to do. Juan's thesis was

Being bilingual benefits you in different ways.

Next, Juan needs to complete the three-step organizing process. First, he circled relevant ideas in his freewriting:

I think that everybody should know how to speak at least two languages. America is a multicultural society many citizens speak languages other then english. My family and me speak spanish and english. One of my sisters is learning how to speak French too. She wants to visit France one day. Knowing two languages means I can communicate easily with more people This helps me at work especially. I can talk to Spanish-speaking customers which is an asset. I can travel more easily because I can speak to the people who live in many other countries. I want to learn how to speak other languages to increase my opportunities no matter where I go. And I can help others by translating One time I was in the emergency room with my son, he had the flu. I helped a family from Mexico communicate with the nurses to get there son treated for a cut finger.

Then he moved on to step 2 of the organizing process and discovered that he had already thought of several benefits. He next created groups of ideas:

<u>Helps me at work</u>
talk to Spanish-speaking customers

<u>Travel more easily</u>

<u>Help others by translating</u>
helped a family from Mexico communicate with the nurses

Although he discovered three good benefits to include in his essay, Juan noticed that he had not generated very many ideas yet, so he decided to do some more prewriting on his topic.

In step 3, he realized that natural organization would not apply to his topic, so he would have to logically order the groups. He decided that two of the benefits—helping others and traveling more easily—were benefits for his personal life. The third benefit related to his professional, or work-related, life. Because Juan felt that the professional benefit was probably the most important one in his life and in his readers' lives, he decided to discuss that benefit first. Helping others was the next most important benefit, so he decided to present that one second. He decided to save his discussion of traveling, his least important benefit, for last.

Finally, he created a brief, informal outline to guide him as he wrote his essay:

Main Idea: Being bilingual benefits you in different ways.
  1. Work
  2. Helping others
  3. Traveling

In Chapter 5, you will see how Juan completed the next step, composing his essay.

EXERCISE 4.9   **Preparing an Outline for Your Essay**

In Chapter 3, you generated some ideas about one of the following topics:

A significant decision that I made
Television
A time when I surprised myself
Men versus women

An unfair law
A solution to a problem

Then you wrote a main idea statement. Reread this main idea statement and examine the prewriting that you generated. Follow the three-step organization procedure. First, circle all of the words and phrases that seem relevant to your main idea. Next, group similar ideas and information together. Third, decide on the best order for those groups.

Finally, create either a formal or informal outline of your ideas. You will use this outline again in Chapter 5 when you actually write your essay.

CHAPTER 4 REVIEW

To review the main points in this chapter, write a brief response to each of the following questions.

1. How do you go about creating a framework for your ideas? What three steps are involved? Describe this process.

2. What types of topics arrange themselves with natural organization? Why?

3. For other topics, what must a writer do in order to determine a plan of logical organization?

4. What are two common types of logical order?

5. What is an outline? What should it do?

6. What are two myths about outlining? Why are they myths?

7. Why is it important to create an outline?

8. Describe the features of an informal outline and a formal outline.

CHAPTER 4 REVIEW

WebWork

For more practice with analysis and synthesis, the two skills underlying the organization process, complete the Paradigm Online Writing Assistant activities at **http://www.powa.org**. Click on "organizing" then "Analysis and Synthesis."

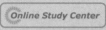 For more information and exercises, go to the Online Study Center that accompanies this book, at **http://www.college .hmco.com/pic/dolphinwriterthree**.

Writing the Essay

GOALS FOR CHAPTER 5

▶ Identify the parts of an essay and explain the purpose of each part.

▶ Identify the parts of a thesis statement.

▶ Revise ineffective thesis statements.

▶ Write effective thesis statements.

▶ Write introductions that use techniques for interesting readers and include necessary background information.

▶ Identify the parts of an essay's body.

▶ Identify the parts of a paragraph and explain the purpose of each part.

▶ Rewrite ineffective topic sentences.

▶ Use transitions to link sentences and paragraphs.

▶ Write conclusions using different methods for providing closure.

▶ Write an essay, connecting the body paragraphs with transitions.

In Chapter 3, you learned some prewriting techniques for generating ideas, including a main idea, and in Chapter 4, you practiced organizing and outlining ideas. This chapter focuses on the third step of the writing process, composing a draft of an essay.

   An **essay** is a multiparagraph composition that develops one idea or opinion, which is called the **thesis.** Like a paragraph, an essay focuses on one point and includes details that support that point. As a matter of fact, the parts of the paragraph often correlate to those of an essay, as the following diagram shows.

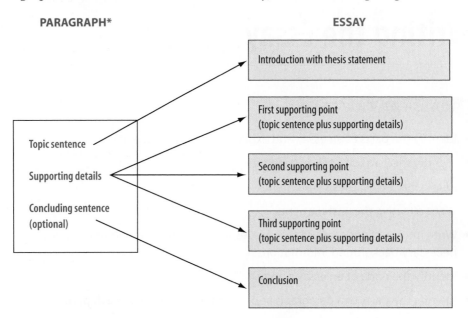

However, an essay is not just an expanded paragraph. For one thing, the thesis usually expresses an idea that requires more development than the idea expressed in a paragraph's topic sentence. Therefore, an essay is broader in scope and thus needs to be longer.

An essay has three main parts: an introduction, a body, and a conclusion. The **introduction** gives readers background information, gets them interested, and provides the thesis statement. The **body** is composed of several paragraphs that include all of the evidence to explain or prove the thesis. The **conclusion** provides a satisfying ending to the essay. Each of these parts is labeled in the essay that follows.

Three Steps to Better Writing

INTRODUCTION

When I was a senior in high school, my English teacher taught me some things about writing that finally began to make sense. Mrs. Murray made us write a paper a week, which was a lot more writing than I ever wanted to do. But I think I learned quite a bit by trying out some suggestions she gave us. I do not think I will ever say that writing is easy for me, but her techniques definitely help the process go more smoothly, and I still use them to this day. **The three most important things I learned are specific methods to use before, during, and after writing a paper.**

Thesis Statement

*For a review of paragraphs, see pages 111–112 in this chapter.

Mrs. Murray taught me, first of all, to explore ideas in different ways before I start writing. I used to just sit and stare at my blank paper, usually stressing out because my brain would not start working. But Mrs. Murray taught me how to freewrite and brainstorm to unlock my thoughts and get the ideas flowing. So now whenever I sit down to write a paper, I spend some time just jotting down random thoughts that pop into my head about my topic. I do not worry about grammar or spelling or organization. I just write, kind of like a warm-up exercise, and that helps me explore what I already know about my subject. This technique helps me decide what I want to say in my paper, so it helps me get started with a lot less anxiety.

Mrs. Murray's second helpful technique is one I use while writing the draft of a paper. She taught us to write a first draft with the "big picture" in mind. I used to stop all the time to worry about the little things, like the spelling of a word or the placement of a comma. But now I know that the first draft is when I am supposed to concentrate on the ideas themselves. So I usually write the first draft quickly, with my major thoughts and overall organization in mind. I try to get the "shell" of my paper figured out because I know I can go back later to fill in the blanks and fix my sentences. Sometimes, I just draw a blank line when I cannot think of the right word, or I might write a little note to myself in the margin of my paper. For example, I might scribble, "Add an example here" in the margin and then keep on writing. Doing this allows my brain to focus on the whole structure of the paper all at once, without getting distracted or sidetracked by the details. Once I get that overall structure nailed down, it is easier to go back and flesh it out.

The last thing Mrs. Murray taught me is something I do *after* I write a paper. As a matter of fact, it is also something I do after I get my graded paper back. I actually read and think about the teacher's suggestions. I confess that whether I had gotten a good grade or a bad one, I used to just stick my paper in a notebook, relieved to have another one done and out of my life. But Mrs. Murray taught us that one of the ways you can make writing easier on yourself is to learn from your mistakes. That means that you have to read the teacher's comments and suggestions carefully. It means that you have to try to understand your mistakes so you can avoid making them the next time you write. I used to hate seeing all of those corrections and notes all over my papers, but Mrs. Murray convinced me that teachers spend time writing those comments so that students can learn from them. And I believe the feedback I have gotten has helped me improve my writing skills, which has made the process less stressful.

BODY

It was in Mrs. Murray's class that I decided that writing is a fact of life, so I had better start learning some techniques that would make the process less agonizing for myself. I am glad I took her advice because now I dread writing a lot less, and my papers earn better grades.*

CONCLUSION

*Source: Doug Salisbury, "Three Steps to Better Writing," *Horizons,* Boston: Houghton Mifflin, 2004. Reprinted by permission of the Houghton Mifflin Company.

The remainder of this chapter will focus on writing and developing the different parts of the essay.

The Thesis Statement

In Chapter 3, you practiced generating a thesis as part of your prewriting practice. This thesis becomes the **thesis statement,** the sentence in the essay that states the main idea. Recall from Chapter 3 that a thesis has two parts: it states the topic of the paragraph, and it also states the writer's point about that topic. Notice how each of the following sentences contains both a topic and an idea about that topic.

Topic	*Point*
My hometown	is a great place to live.

Topic	*Point*
Americans	should do more to conserve energy.

Topic	*Point*
Studying in a group	is more effective than studying alone.

EXERCISE 5.1   **Identifying the Parts of Thesis Statements**

In each of the following thesis statements, circle the topic and underline the point the writer makes about that topic.

1. Teenagers should work only on weekends and not on school days.
2. Traveling with a group led by a tour guide makes trips easier and more enjoyable.
3. Violence on television, in movies, and in video games increases real-life violence.
4. The people who live next door to me are good neighbors.
5. For thousands of years, plants have been used for medicinal purposes.

Refining Your Thesis Statement

When you write thesis statements for essays of your own, remember that an effective thesis statement has three essential characteristics: it is a complete sentence that includes both a topic and a point, it is not too broad or too narrow, and it takes into account not just the topic but also the essay's audience and purpose.

First of all, a thesis statement must contain both of its required parts: a topic and some point about that topic. A topic in the form of a sentence fragment is not a topic sentence.

Incomplete:	Extreme sports
Complete thesis statement:	Extreme sports have been increasing in popularity for several reasons.
Incomplete:	Recent improvements in technology
Complete thesis statement:	Recent improvements in technology have given us the ability to get more accurate information more quickly.
Incomplete:	Sending astronauts to Mars
Complete thesis statement:	Sending astronauts to Mars should become one of America's priorities.

If you try to begin writing with only a topic in mind, then you will probably not produce a coherent and well-developed essay. When you are unsure about exactly what you mean to say, then your essay will probably ramble aimlessly. Make sure that before you begin to write, you have a complete thesis statement that includes both your topic and your point.

In addition to being complete, a thesis statement must also be appropriately specific. If an idea is too broad or too vague, it will not keep you properly focused as you write. For example, look at the following examples.

Too broad:	People can be very rude.
Too vague:	Something should be done about the quality of education in this country.

Neither of these statements expresses one clear idea, so each would probably lead to rambling when it came time to write. To improve these two statements, rewrite them to narrow the topic and/or the idea.

Many cell phone users are guilty of behaving rudely in public.

A merit pay system for teachers would help to improve the quality of public school education.

On the other hand, though, you do not want to make your thesis statement so specific or limited that you cannot develop it at all.

Too specific: Bill Clinton served two terms as U.S. president, from 1993 to 2001.

Because this sentence states a fact, there is not much more you can say about the topic. To improve it, broaden the topic and the idea.

During his two terms of office, Bill Clinton managed to achieve a number of needed improvements in this country.

Be aware that your thesis statement may not be perfect on your first try. You may have to work on it, experimenting with the wording and rewriting it, even after you have begun writing, until it says exactly what you want to express.

Look, for example, at one student's thesis. Lee was assigned to write about the topic "student success," so he generated ideas about studying. He came up with the following idea: *Studying with a group.* But then he realized that this phrase was not a complete sentence, so he revised it to read, *Studying with a group is more effective than studying alone.*

Another student, Jennifer, generated prewriting on the same topic and decided on this thesis: *Good study habits are important.* But then she realized that this statement was too broad and vague. She revised it to read: *Several study techniques will help you better understand and recall information for tests.*

As you can see, a thesis statement may not be perfect the first time you write it. If yours seems to be lacking something, do not proceed with writing the rest of the essay until you have figured out what is missing and have corrected the problem. If you are not sure of exactly what you are trying to communicate to your readers, then you will be in greater danger of rambling or failing to adequately develop what you want to say.

✦ **EXERCISE 5.2**   **Revising Ineffective Thesis Statements**

On the following blanks, rewrite each of the thesis statements that is either incomplete, too broad, too vague, or too specific. If the main idea seems complete and appropriately specific, write **OK** on the blank.

1. Boys and girls

_____

2. Modern medicine is amazing.

_____

_____

3. I have visited several foreign countries, such as England and France.

---

4. Something should be done about the problem of traffic in this country.

---

5. Every American student should be required to take a physical education course every year.

Considering Topic, Audience, and Purpose

So far, you have learned that effective thesis statements are complete and appropriately specific. As you evaluate the accuracy and effectiveness of your thesis statement, remember what you learned in Chapter 3 about the effects of audience and purpose on that statement. When you are composing your thesis statement, you will want to consider not only *what* you want to say but also *why* and *to whom* you want to say it. Therefore, in addition to the topic, there are two other factors—audience and purpose—that will affect how you express your thesis statement.

The first of these factors is your audience or readers. *Who* is going to read your writing? *What* do these people need to know or want to know about the topic? Your topic sentence should take into account this audience's needs and desires.

The second factor is your purpose. Do you want to inform your readers about your topic so they can learn something new? Or do you want to persuade them to believe what you believe about the topic? Your thesis statement should clearly reflect this purpose.

For example, consider the thesis statement "Running your own business and working for someone else both have their advantages and disadvantages." The writer intends to explain to someone who is interested in exploring different career options the pros and cons of self-employment and regular employment. But notice how the purpose of this next statement differs.

> You should start and operate your own business instead of working for someone else.

Although the audience is probably the same, the words *you should* indicate that the writer's purpose is persuasive.

> **EXERCISE 5.3**   **Identifying Topic, Audience, and Purpose in Thesis Statements**

A. Answer the question that follows each thesis statement by circling the letter of the correct response.

The fashions of a past era often become popular again about thirty years later.

1. The writer's purpose is to

   a. entertain readers with a story about fashion.
   b. inform readers about fashions that have been popular more than once.
   c. persuade readers to wear certain fashions.

Everyone should exercise at least three times a week.

2. The writer's purpose is to

   a. entertain readers by telling stories about people who exercise.
   b. inform readers about ways to exercise.
   c. persuade readers to exercise regularly.

My recent trip to Texas became an unexpectedly wild adventure.

3. The writer's purpose is to

   a. entertain readers with a story about a trip to Texas.
   b. inform readers about traveling in Texas.
   c. persuade readers to visit Texas.

People join groups and organizations for different reasons.

4. The writer's purpose is to

   a. entertain readers with an amusing story about someone who joined a group.
   b. inform readers about reasons why people join groups and organizations.
   c. persuade readers to join a group or organization.

Customer service in Japanese retail stores is superior to customer service in American retail stores.

5. The writer's purpose is to

   a. entertain readers with stories about Japanese and American customer service.
   b. inform readers about the differences between Japanese and American customer service.
   c. persuade readers that Japanese customer service is better than American customer service.

B. Use prewriting techniques to generate ideas and then write a topic sentence for each topic/audience/purpose set that follows.

Topic: A specific television show
Audience: People who watch television
Purpose: To inform

  6. Topic sentence: _____

Topic: A specific television show
Audience: People who have never seen the show
Purpose: To persuade

  7. Topic sentence: _____

Topic: A tradition or custom in your family
Audience: Your friends
Purpose: To entertain

  8. Topic sentence: _____

Topic: A tradition or custom in your family
Audience: People from a different culture
Purpose: To inform

  9. Topic sentence: _____

Topic: The death penalty
Audience: People who want to learn more about the subject
Purpose: To inform

  10. Topic sentence: _____

Topic: The death penalty
Audience: People who are in favor of using the death penalty as a form of punishment
Purpose: To persuade

  11. Topic sentence: _____

EXERCISE 5.4   **Writing Thesis Statements**

Prewrite on the topic "parents." Generate three thesis statements for different aspects of that topic and then write those three statements on the following blanks. Next, evaluate whether each statement is complete, appropriately specific, and suited to your audience and purpose. If you decide that the statement does not possess all three characteristics, rewrite it on the blank provided so that it does.

Thesis statement 1: _____

    Is it complete?   Yes _____   No _____

    Is it appropriately specific?   Yes _____   No _____

    Is it suited to audience and purpose?   Yes _____   No _____

    Revised thesis statement: _____

Thesis statement 2: _____

    Is it complete?   Yes _____   No _____

    Is it appropriately specific?   Yes _____   No _____

    Is it suited to audience and purpose?   Yes _____   No _____

    Revised thesis statement: _____

Thesis statement 3: _____

    Is it complete?   Yes _____   No _____

    Is it appropriately specific?   Yes _____   No _____

    Is it suited to audience and purpose?   Yes _____   No _____

    Revised thesis statement: _____

Reevaluating Your Outline

Once you have refined your thesis statement, you will need to reevaluate your outline to make sure that it still matches your main idea. Make sure this outline still includes the right kinds of supporting ideas, and decide if they are still listed in the right order. Make any necessary adjustments to your outline before you begin.

    Look, for example, at Lee's revised thesis statement and existing outline.

Studying with a group is more effective than studying alone.

    — Motivates you to study more regularly and for longer periods of time

— Groups can wander from the task at hand if members do not
stay focused
— Inconvenience of scheduling study sessions with others
— Talking aloud is a good learning strategy
— Others can clarify things you do not understand
— You can waste time covering info you already know

The outline includes some disadvantages of studying with a group, so the thesis statement and outline no longer match. Lee did not want to change his thesis statement, so he knew he would have to make a few changes to his outline. He dropped all of the disadvantages of study groups and just left the advantages.

Studying with a group is more effective than studying alone.

— Motivates you to study more regularly and for longer periods
of time
— Talking aloud is a good learning strategy
— Others can clarify things you do not understand

Now the outline matches the thesis statement.

 **EXERCISE 5.5**   **Evaluating Outlines**

In each of the following outlines, circle the point that does not match the thesis statement.

1. Thesis statement: People reduce stress in different ways.

A. Some people relax by working in their gardens.
B. For many people, financial worries are a major cause of stress.
C. Regular exercise helps many people release tension.

2. Thesis statement: Recent improvements in technology have given us the ability to get more accurate information more quickly.

1. The news and information on many Internet Web sites is updated daily or even hourly.
2. Satellites in orbit around our planet beam instantaneous communications to computers, TV stations, and even cell phones.
3. Medical equipment like the laparoscope allows doctors to heal their patients in hours or days rather than weeks.

3. Thesis statement: Laughter is good for your health.

1. Improves feelings of connection in family relationships and friendships
2. Improves immune system function
3. Lowers blood pressure
4. Reduces stress
5. Alleviates pain

The Introduction

The thesis statement generally appears in the **introduction,** or opening, of your essay. In addition to stating the thesis, the introductions of the essays you write should fulfill two additional purposes. Every introduction you write should get the readers' attention and provide necessary background information.

First of all, the introduction should grab readers' attention and get them interested in the essay's topic and the author's point about that topic. To make readers want to read on, you can use one of several methods.

Begin with an Anecdote. Everyone likes to hear stories, so you can tell a brief story that is related to your topic and leads to your main point. An anecdote is a tried-and-true technique for hooking readers' interest and making them want to continue reading.

> Fifth grade at recess: Time for softball. Two popular kids are picking teams, of course. First choice is Bobby McNeil, he of booming bat. Next is Johnny Pegg, the human glove. Then come the middle-of-the-packers. Then the picking of— aggh!—girls. Perfectly athletic and sound girls, but they're still girls. And they were all picked ahead of you, Sherman Green, who, last time we checked, is still technically a boy. The humiliation! We've all gone through the public, painful processes of selection: the high school dance, the college application process, the job interview, the singles bar—need I go on? This may explain our current obsession with the genre[1] that is consuming our TV dials: the reality show. (*Source:* Adapted from Rick Marin, "We're All Reality Stars," *USA Weekend,* Feb. 13–15, 2004, p. 14.)

----

1. genre: type

Begin with an Example. You can make the topic immediately interesting by showing how it relates to a specific individual. This technique may involve telling a story about that individual.

> Daniel Reardon's nightmare began at 5:30 a.m. with a call from the University of Maryland police. His 19-year-old son, Danny, had taken part in a fraternity drinking ritual and was unconscious. When Danny began college in fall 2001, his father, a dentist in Washington, D.C., had been confident that the teenager could take care of himself. After all, Danny had spent nine months after his high school graduation traveling across Europe. But Reardon hadn't counted on anything like this. When Danny passed out at about 11:30 p.m. on Feb. 7, 2002, fraternity members put him on a sofa, took his pulse and according to court records and police reports, took turns watching him. Early the next morning, Danny stopped breathing. Students at the fraternity house called for an ambulance about 3:30 a.m., but Danny's brain had ceased functioning when he reached the hospital. He died six days later. In one major respect, Danny was typical of many college undergraduates who die on or near campuses every year: He was a freshman who had been on campus only a few months. An analysis of 620 deaths of four-year college and university students since Jan. 1, 2000, finds that freshmen are uniquely vulnerable. They account for more than one-third of undergraduate deaths in the study, although they are only 24% of the undergraduates at those institutions. Some schools, however, are managing to combat this terrible problem using several effective tactics. (*Source:* Adapted from Robert Davis and Anthony DeBarros, "First Year in College is the Riskiest," *USA Today,* Jan. 25, 2006. Reprinted with permission.)

Provide an Interesting Fact or Statistic. You can also arouse readers' curiosity by providing some information that is surprising, startling, or even shocking.

> Every two seconds, a child dies of hunger here on planet Earth. That means 40,000 children die per day. Worldwide, 60 million people starve to death every year. Meanwhile, almost a third of Americans are overweight or obese. Clearly, U.S. citizens must do more to solve this problem. We can start by increasing our financial aid to struggling countries while also continuing to improve agricultural technologies for food production.

Provide a Direct Quotation. Beginning with a clever or humorous statement made by someone else can be a good way to get readers interested in the topic.

> John F. Kennedy once said, "Ask not what your country can do for you; ask what you can do for your country." These words resonate[1] more than ever today,

1. **resonate:** impact, affect

what with all of the obstacles and challenges our country faces in the wake of Hurricane Katrina, Hurricane Rita, and widespread poverty. People—the citizens of this great nation—need our help, and it is up to us to help them. We are all part of this country, and we need to support each other in times of need. Volunteering, either for a large-scale operation like Hurricane Katrina relief or for a small scale one like cooking at a local soup kitchen, can allow you to help your fellow citizens and make you an integral[1] part of other people's lives and welfare. Volunteering can make you feel better about yourself and about the world around you.

Ask Readers a Question. You can often draw readers into your essay by asking them questions to get them thinking about their own ideas or opinions about the topic.

> What is the most important of all the manners you can teach your child? Saying *yes, ma'am, yes, sir,* and so on? No. Saying *thank you?* No, but that's close. Opening doors for women and the elderly? No, and now you're getting cold again. "All right then! What?" Not interrupting adult conversations. "Who says?" Me, and I am a parenting expert, so that's the end of the discussion. Not interrupting adult conversations, including phone conversations, is the most important of all manners for several reasons. (*Source:* Excerpted from John Rosemond, "Teach Children the No. 1 Rule in Manners: Don't Interrupt," **http://www.rosemond.com/**)

Explain the Topic's Relevance or Significance to the Reader. Immediately connect the topic to your readers' interests, goals, or desires.

> If you are like millions of Americans, you have tried one of the thousand diets that purports[2] to help you lose weight faster. From the Atkins Diet to Jenny Craig to Weight Watchers, there is a diet for everyone. Obesity is a huge problem in America today, and many people feel—because of media pressure or just for personal reasons—that they have weight to lose. The problem is that it is harder to keep weight off than it is to lose it, which is why the diet industry is a multi-billion-dollar business. But there is no magic pill or secret to losing weight. All you must do is eat fewer calories, exercise more, and make an effort to maintain a healthy lifestyle for the rest of your life.

1. **integral:** necessary or essential   2. **purports:** claims

Begin with a Contradiction. Present to the reader some commonly held idea or opinion and then go on to contradict or refute it.

> Most people would say that successful businesspeople must have a lot of confidence. After all, they carry themselves with great poise[1] and can assert themselves in any situation. They can often command a room just by clearing their throats. However, studies have shown that the opposite is true—people in positions of power really think of themselves as imposters[2] who are just waiting to be found out by the people who work for them. Often, the most successful are the most insecure; they just work twice as hard as the rest of us to maintain the appearance of competence, coolness, and control.

EXERCISE 5.6 **Writing Interesting Introductions**

Choose two of the following thesis statements and complete the statements by filling in the blanks. For each thesis statement you choose, write on your own paper two different introductions, each of which uses a different technique for interesting the reader.

1. A relaxing day consists of _____.

2. _____ should be required reading for every parent.

3. I have the best time with _____.

4. _____ is a great singer.

5. In my spare time, I like to _____.

Another purpose of the introduction is to provide readers with necessary background information about the topic. After you have gotten readers interested, you may need to provide some facts or explanation about your topic so that they will understand the point you make in your thesis. Notice how in the following example the author interests readers by asking a question. But then she goes on to give some background information. She explains the cause of citizens' fear of terrorists, and she tells of one response to this fear: the creation of the "Minutemen." She then explains the purpose of this group. She needs to

---

1. **poise:** dignity, composure, and self-confidence

2. **imposters:** people pretending to be someone else

provide this brief orientation so that readers will know what she is referring to in her thesis statement.

> Are you afraid of terrorists? Since they hijacked several planes and attacked us on September 11, 2001, most Americans are at least a little concerned about dangerous immigrants repeating the carnage[1] of that terrible day. That is why so many people are advocating[2] the careful screening of legal visitors to this country and the recent measures taken to keep out illegal visitors, such as the millions of Mexican citizens who unlawfully cross the U.S. border every year. Some people have even gone so far as to form the "Minutemen," groups of armed citizens who volunteer to help patrol the U.S.–Mexico border. This organization says that its purpose is to prevent terrorists from entering this country. In reality, though, the Minutemen are wasting their time and energy by focusing their efforts in the wrong place.

Do not assume that readers will know all about your topic. Provide them with a brief orientation so that you are sure they have the information they need to understand your ideas. For example, look at the following thesis statement.

> The Head Start program has its critics, but the federal government should continue to fund that program.

What do you think readers will need to know before they can understand this point? The writer will need to answer the following questions: *What is the Head Start program? What is its purpose, and whom does it serve? Who are the program's critics, and what are their concerns? What has prompted the debate about the program's future?* If readers do not get the answers to these questions, they may not understand the thesis statement.

✴ **EXERCISE 5.7**   **Including Background Information in Introductions**

Choose two of the following thesis statements and fill in the blank if necessary. For each thesis statement, write on your own paper an introduction that provides necessary background information about the topic.

1. _____ is a very worthwhile charity.

2. Having three generations of family members living under the same roof has many advantages.

3. Driver's education classes should (or should not) be mandatory for everyone.

---

1. **carnage:** slaughter; killing   2. **advocating:** supporting; arguing for

4. _____ is one holiday that has completely lost its meaning.

5. Every young American should have to serve at least two years in the military.

To review, an introduction must fulfill three purposes: state the thesis, interest the reader, and provide necessary background information. However, an introduction may not necessarily fulfill these three purposes in the order in which they have been presented. In most cases, it will probably be best to get readers' attention and orient them _before_ stating the thesis, but there may be times when it seems most appropriate to begin the essay with the background information or even with your thesis statement. Just make sure each introduction you write accomplishes all three goals.

The Body of the Essay

The **body** of an essay supplies all of the ideas and information that explain or prove the point made in the thesis statement. The body consists of several body paragraphs, one for each separate idea or reason that supports the thesis. Each idea or reason is usually stated in a clear **topic sentence.** Then the rest of the paragraph develops this topic sentence with details such as facts, examples, observations, or other kinds of support.

The Paragraph

A **paragraph** can be defined as a group of sentences that all support or develop one particular idea about a topic. Paragraphs vary in length from just a few sentences to many sentences. A paragraph can stand alone, or it can be combined with other paragraphs to form a longer piece of writing, such as an essay.

The following diagram shows the form of a paragraph. The first sentence of a paragraph is indented five spaces from the left margin. The remaining sentences follow each other with only two spaces between them, and blank space follows the last word of the last sentence.

Indent
5 spaces

The purpose of a paragraph, particularly in a longer piece of writing, is to group related sentences together so that readers can clearly understand the writer's ideas. Imagine if the books or articles that you have read had contained no paragraphs and had presented thoughts and information in no particular order, leaving you to try to make sense of it all. Reading such a book or article would be a confusing and unpleasant task. Just as you expect writers to have grouped their sentences into related units of thought, the readers of your writing will expect you to have done the same with your own ideas.

A paragraph has two main parts: a topic sentence and a body. The topic sentence states the paragraph's main idea, and the remaining sentences—the body—develop that idea with more information and explanation.

The Topic Sentence

In Chapter 3, you practiced generating a thesis as part of your prewriting practice. In a paragraph, it is the **topic sentence** that states the main idea. But do not let the name fool you. This sentence does not just identify a topic. Just like a thesis, it has two parts: it states the topic of the paragraph, and it also states the writer's point about that topic. Notice how each of the following topic sentences contains both a topic and an idea about that topic.

Topic	*Point*
Any habit	can be broken.

Topic	*Point*
Environmental factors	are causing a sharp increase in asthma.

Topic	*Point*
All day-care employees	should be required to have a two-year college degree.

Remember that the term *topic sentence* might seem a little misleading, for the topic sentence does more than simply state the sentence's topic. It also states an *idea* about that topic.

EXERCISE 5.8   **Identifying the Parts of Topic Sentences**

In each of the following topic sentences, circle the topic and underline the point the writer makes about that topic.

1. Exercise is an important part of a healthy lifestyle.
2. *Wedding Crashers* was one of the funniest movies ever made.

3. Nursing is a rewarding career in many different ways.

4. All engaged couples should be required to take a course on marriage.

5. Although they live next door to each other, the two families have very different standards of living.

In a well-written paragraph, the topic sentence will be apparent. It will be the most general statement in the paragraph, and all of the other sentences will clearly develop the point that it makes. Topic sentences are often the first sentence of the paragraph, but they do not have to be. They can appear anywhere in the paragraph: at the beginning, in the middle, or at the end. Read the following paragraph and see if you can underline the sentence that expresses the main idea.

> Friends matter a lot during adolescence. Unlike most adults, who often try to improve many of a teenager's behaviors and skills, friends offer easier and more immediate acceptance and thus ease the uncertainty and insecurity of the adolescent years. They also offer reassurance, understanding, advice, and emotional and social support in stressful situations. The opportunity to share inner feelings of disappointment as well as happiness with close friends enables the adolescent to better deal with her emotional ups and downs. Furthermore, a capacity to form close, intimate friendships during adolescence is related to overall social and emotional adjustment and competence. (*Source:* Kevin L. Seifert and Robert J. Hoffnung, *Child and Adolescent Development,* 5th ed., Boston: Houghton Mifflin, 2000, p. 507.)

Did you underline the first sentence? That is the sentence in the paragraph that states the paragraph's main idea. Then the rest of the paragraph goes on to offer information that explains this statement.

EXERCISE 5.9   **Recognizing Topic Sentences in Paragraphs**

Underline the topic sentence in each of the following paragraphs.

1. The Toyota Camry has been the best-selling car in America for years, and overall, foreign car sales are increasing while American car sales are declining. Americans are choosing foreign brands like Toyotas, Hondas, and Hyundais over American brands like Fords and Chevrolets because they believe that foreign cars are better. Consumers have the perception, first of all, that the

quality of foreign cars is superior to that of American cars. People who have owned both kinds of cars say that foreign cars are put together better and are built to last longer. They also maintain that foreign cars are more reliable, needing less maintenance and fewer repairs than American cars. The price of foreign cars tends to be higher than that of American cars; however, consumers are willing to pay more because they think that foreign brands are a better long-term value.

2. Teaching is a satisfying career because it gives one the opportunity to have a positive influence upon young people every day. Teachers are in the position to inspire their students and to give them the knowledge and skills they need to be successful in life. Teaching is also a fairly secure, low-risk occupation with a good salary and many attractive benefits, such as health insurance and lots of vacation time. In addition, teaching brings status in society, for most people admire the work that teachers do. In fact, when a recent public survey asked which of eight professions (physician, lawyer, nurse, and journalist, among others) "provides the most important benefit to society," 62 percent of respondents put teaching first. Obviously, teaching is a great profession for many reasons. (*Source:* Adapted from Kevin Ryan and James M. Cooper, *Those Who Can, Teach,* 10th ed., Boston: Houghton Mifflin, 2004. Reprinted by permission of the Houghton Mifflin Company.)

3. Everybody uses "loaded language" to persuade people of something without actually making a clear argument for it. For example, a newspaper writer who likes a politician calls him "Senator Smith"; if he doesn't like the politician, he refers to him as "right wing [or left-wing] senators such as Smith." If a writer likes an idea proposed by a person, he calls that person "respected"; if he doesn't like the idea, he calls the person "controversial." If a writer favors abortion, she calls somebody who agrees with her "pro-choice" ("choice" is valued by most people); if she opposes abortion, she calls those who agree with her "pro-life" ("life," like "choice," is a good thing). (*Source:* Adapted from James Q. Wilson and John J. DiIulio, Jr., *American Government,* 8th ed., Boston: Houghton Mifflin, 2001, p. 257.)

When you write topic sentences for paragraphs of your own, remember that an effective topic sentence has some essential characteristics: it is a complete sentence that includes both a topic and a point, and it is not too broad or too narrow.

First of all, a topic sentence must contain both of its required parts: a topic and some point about that topic. A topic in the form of a sentence fragment is not a topic sentence.

Incomplete:	Men and women
Complete topic sentence:	Men's and women's friendships are very different.
Incomplete:	Jamie Foxx
Complete topic sentence:	Jamie Foxx is a multitalented performer.
Incomplete:	Computer literacy
Complete topic sentence:	Computer literacy is essential for today's college students.

If you try to begin writing with only a topic in mind, then you will probably not produce a coherent and well-developed paragraph. When you are unsure about exactly what you mean to say, then your paragraph will probably ramble aimlessly. Make sure that before you begin to write, you have a complete topic sentence that includes both your topic and your point.

In addition to being complete, a topic sentence must also be appropriately specific. If an idea is too broad or too vague, it will not keep you properly focused as you write. For example, look at the following examples.

Too broad:	Our local high school has a lot of problems.
Too vague:	Something should be done about the run-down playground equipment in the city park.

Neither of these statements expresses one clear idea, so each would probably lead to rambling when it came time to write. To improve these two statements, rewrite them to narrow the topic and/or the idea.

Overcrowding at our local high school is interfering with students' learning and undermining students' safety.

Taxpayer dollars should be used to renovate the playground in our city park.

On the other hand, though, you do not want to make your topic sentence so specific or limited that you cannot develop it at all.

Too specific: I have two children.

Because this sentence states a fact, there is not much more you can say about the idea. To improve the topic sentence, broaden the topic and the idea.

Both of my children are musically talented.

Be aware that your topic sentence may not be perfect on your first try. You may have to work on it, experimenting with the wording and rewriting it, even after you have begun writing, until it says exactly what you want to express.

EXERCISE 5.10 **Revising Ineffective Topic Sentences**

On the following blanks, rewrite each of the topic sentences that is either incomplete, too broad, too vague, or too specific. If the main idea seems complete and appropriately specific, write **OK** on the blank.

1. An easy but delicious dish to make

_____

2. Concerts are fun.

_____

_____

3. I scored an A on my science test.

_____

_____

4. Something should be done about our overcrowded schools.

_____

_____

5. Today's zoos are quite different from the zoos of a few decades ago.

_____

The Body of a Paragraph

The **body** of a paragraph includes all of the sentences that support, explain, or prove the idea expressed in the topic sentence. These sentences provide all of the evidence the reader will need in order to accept the main idea as true, and this evidence can take a variety of different forms, including

facts
statistics and other data
examples

stories
reasons
comparisons
descriptive details

In the following paragraph, the topic sentence is highlighted in bold. Read the paragraph and try to decide which of the different kinds of evidence in the preceding list is given to support the topic sentence.

Most people strongly dislike giving speeches. The mere thought of standing up in front of an audience to speak makes their hearts begin to beat faster and their stomachs begin to fill with butterflies. In fact, according to Gallup polls, fear of public speaking has for years been at or near the top of people's list of situations that provoke the most anxiety. Many have admitted that the thought of speaking in public terrifies them more than the fear of anything else, including heights, snakes, needles, flying, and even dying! I myself would become numb and almost paralyzed right before giving a speech. My hands would shake, my mouth would go dry, and my heart would race. I was sure that I would do or say something that would make everyone think that I was stupid, boring, or ridiculous.

This paragraph supports the topic sentence with descriptive details, facts gathered from polls, and an example (the writer's experience with public speaking).

You can think of the support in a body paragraph in terms of layers of development. A **layer of development** provides more specific information about a general idea stated in the sentence that came before it. Therefore, a layer of development anticipates and answers questions that pop into readers' heads as they read. For example, let us say that you write the sentence "Some people are fanatical about cleanliness." The words *fanatical* and *cleanliness* are relatively general terms that can mean different things to different people. As your readers read this sentence, they will probably wonder, *What do you mean by "fanatical about cleanliness"?* or *How are people fanatical about cleanliness?* Instead of going on to another new idea, you need to add some information—a layer of development—to answer these questions. In other words, you need to explain what you mean. So you might add this sentence:

My mother, for example, keeps her home absolutely spotless.

This sentence gives readers an example of a fanatically clean person. However, you should ask yourself, *Will my readers have any questions about this sentence?* They will probably wonder, for instance, *What do you mean by a spotless home?*

or *What does her home look like?* You might add yet another layer of development to answer these questions:

> She would not dream of letting any guest see any dust on her furniture or even
> one speck of dirt on her floors.

By adding these two sentences, it becomes much clearer to readers what you
mean by "fanatical about cleanliness."

Every time you write a sentence, ask yourself this question: *Is there some
idea here that I should explain more by giving another fact, detail, or example?*
There is no rule about how many layers of development should be included in a
paragraph. The number of layers you include will always depend upon the idea
or information in each different sentence you write. But if you get in the habit
of wondering if you just wrote something that might need further development,
then you will be less likely to leave readers guessing about what you really
mean, and your ideas will be clear.

EXERCISE 5.11   **Recognizing Sentences That Need Development**

For each of the following pairs of sentences, circle the letter beside the one that
needs to be explained with a more specific fact, detail, or example.

1. a. My sister is beautiful.
   b. My sister is tall, with blonde hair and gorgeous blue eyes.

2. a. The hurricane knocked out power lines and flooded some homes.
   b. The hurricane caused a lot of damage.

3. a. My five-year-old son can read, count to one hundred, and say hello in five
      languages.
   b. My son is very smart.

4. a. Running has many health benefits.
   b. Running has been shown to increase muscle tone, lower your heart rate
      and blood pressure, and improve lung capacity.

5. a. Sky diving is very exciting.
   b. Some people report feeling a sense of euphoria as they plummet to the
      earth during sky diving.

> **EXERCISE 5.12**   **Adding Layers of Development**

Each of the following paragraphs lacks adequate layers of development. On the blanks provided, add sentences that further explain or illustrate the idea in the preceding sentence.

1. Getting married has its advantages and disadvantages. Companionship is one long-term benefit of tying the knot. _____ Married couples are often better off financially, too. _____ _____. However, marriage also reduces one's freedom and autonomy[1]. _____ _____.

2. Almost everyone I know has at least one bad habit. _____, for example, _____. He/she _____. _____, too, has the bad habit of _____. For instance, _____. Then there's _____, who _____. He/she _____.

3. _____ is one of my favorite holidays. First of all, I enjoy _____. It _____. I also like _____. For example, _____ _____. But my favorite part of the celebration is _____. _____ _____.

When you are examining a paragraph to make sure it is adequately developed, consider using the following techniques.

Use different colors of highlighter markers to identify the layers in your paragraph. Use one color, such as yellow, to highlight the topic sentence, which is the most general sentence in the paragraph. Use another color, such as pink, to

1. **autonomy:** independence

highlight the second sentence, which should develop the first sentence. If the third sentence develops the second sentence, use yet another color to highlight it. If the third sentence develops the first sentence, highlight it with the same color that you used for the second sentence. Follow this same procedure for all of the other sentences in the paragraph. Then, after you have highlighted every sentence, see how colorful your paragraph is. In general, paragraphs that contain more colors are probably developing the main idea with sufficient details. A paragraph that is highlighted with only two colors, however, may need the addition of more specific information and examples.

Use the highlighting technique to determine the sentence in the following paragraph that needs more development.

> Lecturing is still a common method of delivering information to students in college classrooms. However, lectures are not always the best teaching method. For one thing, people do not remember most of what they hear. In fact, studies have shown that audiences retain only about 10 percent of the information presented to them in oral form. That percentage increases when students take notes, of course, but much information is still lost along the way. Lecturing also tends to be ineffective for today's students because they come to school steeped in visual experiences. They are used to being bombarded with images on television, in movies, in magazines and newspapers, and on billboards and signs. Therefore, many of them are simply not used to processing information presented only in an oral format, and they are not very good at it. Finally, lectures encourage passivity rather than participation in the creation of meaningful learning experiences.

Did you identify the last sentence as the one that needs more development? Following this sentence should be at least one layer of development that further explains what "passivity" and "meaningful learning experiences" are.

Count the sentences in your paragraphs. There is no magic minimum or maximum number of sentences for a paragraph. The number of sentences a paragraph contains will depend upon the main idea and the supporting information. However, if a paragraph contains only three or four sentences, it may be incomplete because it is not adequately developed. Get in the habit of scrutinizing short paragraphs, in particular, to make sure that they include enough layers of development.

Scan your drafts for the phrase *for example.* This phrase often begins sentences that really help readers grasp your ideas. If you never begin sentences this way, you may not be including the specific information your readers need in order to understand your thoughts on a topic.

EXERCISE 5.13   Identifying Sentences That Need Development

Underline the one sentence in each of the following paragraphs that is *not* adequately developed with more specific information or examples.

1. Houseplants offer homeowners a number of benefits. They act, first of all, as natural air fresheners. Not only do they help pull cooking odors from the air, but they also purify the air by removing toxic pollutants and by converting carbon dioxide into the oxygen that we breathe. They also make interior spaces seem more warm, inviting, and visually appealing. Houseplants also seem to benefit us mentally, too. Studies have shown that being near living, growing plants can help to improve our mood, lift depression, speed healing, and reduce feelings of stress.

2. Although you, like most applicants who enter the world of work, may not have a wealth of work experience, there are methods that you can use to "beef up" your résumé and to capitalize on the work experience that you do have. First, obtain summer jobs that will provide opportunities to learn about the field you wish to enter when you finish your formal education. For example, if you are interested in a sales position in a large corporation when you graduate, think about starting small: get a summer job in a local shop or in the mall to get retail sales experience. If you choose carefully, part-time jobs during the school year can also provide you with work experience that other job applicants may not have. (*Source:* Adapted from William M. Pride et al., *Business,* 7th ed., Boston: Houghton Mifflin, 2002, p. 202.)

3. According to researcher Theresa Amabile, there are three kinds of cognitive and personality characteristics necessary for creativity. The first one is expertise in the field of endeavor, which is directly tied to what a person has learned. The second essential element is a set of creative skills. These skills include persistence at problem solving, a capacity for divergent[1] thinking, the ability to break out of old problem-solving habits (mental sets), and a willingness to take risks. The final necessary characteristic is the motivation to pursue creative work for internal reasons, rather than for external reasons. For instance, creative people will produce artistic products for their own satisfaction and not just to receive rewards such as prize money. (*Source:* Adapted from Douglas A. Bernstein and Peggy W. Nash, *Essentials of Psychology,* 2nd ed., Boston: Houghton Mifflin, 2002, p. 228.)

1. **divergent:** different; departing from the conventional

Connecting Ideas with Transitions

Transitions are words and phrases whose function is to show the relationships between thoughts and ideas. The word *transition* comes from the Latin word *trans*, which means "across." Transitions bridge the gaps across sentences and paragraphs and reveal how they are related. The following box includes some common types of transitions with a few examples of each type.

Transitions that signal addition			
also	in addition	too	first, second, third
furthermore	finally	and	another

Transitions that show time order			
now	then	today	next
soon	later	finally	previously
eventually	meanwhile		

Transitions that indicate causes or consequences			
so	therefore	as a result	consequently
hence	because	thus	for this reason

Transitions that signal examples			
for example	for instance	in one case	as an illustration
to illustrate			

Transitions that signal comparisons			
also	too	likewise	similarly
however	but	yet	on the other hand
in contrast			

EXERCISE 5.14   **Adding Transition Words and Phrases**

Add appropriate transitions (as indicated by the words below the blank) in the blanks in the following paragraphs.

Preparing for a Job Interview

You have been asked to interview for a job you would like to have. Now what do you do to get ready? If you are like many people, you simply pick out an

contrast   outfit to wear, cross your fingers, and hope for the best. _____, if you really

want that job, you can do a lot more to make sure that your interview will be followed by a job offer. _____, you can prepare for a job interview in three   *example*
ways: research, rehearse, and use affirmations to build your confidence.

_____, you should do your homework by researching your potential   *addition*
employer. Find out what the company does or makes. Find out more about its procedures and goals. _____, find out more about the specific job for which   *addition*
you are applying. What would be your major responsibilities, and how would you fit into the whole organization? Use library sources such as magazine articles, company documents such as annual reports, and the company's Web site to find the information you need. If possible, talk to one or more of the company's current employees. _____, during your interview, you can more specif-   *time order*
ically explain how your skills and knowledge would help you do the job and fit into the organization. _____, if you were interviewing for a position as a   *example*
day-care worker and learned that the director of the day-care center promotes a certain style of discipline, you could mention this fact and explain how your own experiences have prepared you to use this disciplinary style. _____,   *cause or*
you will better communicate to the interviewer your enthusiasm for the job and   *consequence*
the company. _____, you will help him or her understand why you are the   *addition*
best person for the job.

_____, you must prepare by rehearsing. Most interviewers ask the same   *addition*
kinds of questions. _____, you should obtain a list of the most common in-   *cause or*
terview questions from an Internet source or a book about interviewing. They   *consequence*
will include questions such as *Why do you want to work for this company? What are your short-term and long-term goals?* and *What are some of your strengths and weaknesses?* Think carefully about your answers to these questions.

_____, practice answering them out loud, as though you were in the inter-   *time order*
view. Rehearsing ahead of time will allow you to give the interviewer more detailed, more coherent[1] responses. _____, you will show him or her that you   *cause or*
have good communication skills, an asset all employers want in their employees.   *consequence*

_____, build your self-confidence prior to an interview by using affirma-   *addition*
tions. An affirmation is a positive statement you say to yourself about your strengths or abilities. _____, you can think to yourself or say aloud, "I   *example*
have the experience and skills for this job," or "I am capable and intelligent,"
or "I am the best person for the job." _____, banish from your   *time order*
thoughts negative statements such as "I will probably say the wrong thing," or "I'm not good at interviewing." Employers want to hire competent people who

1. **coherent:** orderly and logical

believe in their own ability to get a job done. You cannot project these qualities if you yourself do not believe you possess them.

Today's job market is very competitive, and solid job-interviewing skills are a necessity. Everyone has to work harder to prove that he or she is the right person for the job. Using these three preparation techniques will increase your chances for professional success.

To review the parts of the essay's body, look at the following essay. The thesis statement, body, topic sentences, and supporting details have all been labeled.

Three Steps to Better Writing

INTRODUCTION When I was a senior in high school, my English teacher taught me some things about writing that finally began to make sense. Mrs. Murray made us write a paper a week, which was a lot more writing than I ever wanted to do. But I think I learned quite a bit by trying out some suggestions she gave us. I do not think I will ever say that writing is easy for me, but her techniques definitely help the process go more smoothly, and I still use them to this day. **The three most important things**

Thesis Statement **I learned are specific methods to use before, during, and after writing a paper.**

Topic Sentence Mrs. Murray taught me, first of all, to explore ideas in different ways before I start writing. I used to just sit and stare at my blank paper, usually stressing out because my brain would not start working. But Mrs. Murray taught me how to freewrite and brainstorm to unlock my thoughts and get the ideas flowing. So now, whenever I sit down to write a paper, I spend some time just jotting

Supporting Details down random thoughts that pop into my head about my topic. I do not worry about grammar or spelling or organization. I just write, kind of like a warm-up exercise, and that helps me explore what I already know about my subject. This technique helps me decide what I want to say in my paper, so it helps me get started with a lot less anxiety.

Topic Sentence Mrs. Murray's second helpful technique is one I use while writing the draft of a paper. She taught us to write a first draft with the "big picture" in mind. I used to stop all the time to worry about the little things, like the spelling of a word or the

Supporting Details placement of a comma. But now I know that the first draft is when I am supposed to concentrate on the ideas themselves. So I usually write the first draft quickly, with my major thoughts and overall organization in mind. I try to get the "shell"

BODY of my paper figured out because I know I can go back later to fill in the blanks and fix my sentences. Sometimes, I just draw a blank line when I cannot think of the right word, or I might write a little note to myself in the margin of my paper. For example, I might scribble, "Add an example here" in the margin and then keep on writing. Doing this allows my brain to focus on the whole structure of the paper all at once, without getting distracted or side-tracked by the details. Once I get that overall structure nailed down, it is easier to go back and flesh it out.

The last thing Mrs. Murray taught me is something I do *after* I write a paper. As a matter of fact, it is also something I do after I get my graded paper back. <u>I actually read and think about the teacher's suggestions.</u> I confess that whether I had gotten a good grade or a bad one, I used to just stick my paper in a notebook, relieved to have another one done and out of my life. But Mrs. Murray taught us that one of the ways you can make writing easier on yourself is to learn from your mistakes. That means that you have to read the teacher's comments and suggestions carefully. It means that you have to try to understand your mistakes so you can avoid making them the next time you write. I used to hate seeing all of those corrections and notes all over my papers, but Mrs. Murray convinced me that teachers spend time writing those comments so that students can learn from them. And I believe the feedback I have gotten has helped me improve my writing skills, which has made the process less stressful.

> Topic Sentence

> Supporting Details

It was in Mrs. Murray's class that I decided that writing is a fact of life, so I had better start learning some techniques that would make the process less agonizing for myself. I am glad I took her advice because now I dread writing a lot less, and my papers earn better grades.*

> CONCLUSION

EXERCISE 5.15   **Recognizing the Essay's Body and Its Parts**

In the following essay, draw a bracket (as in the preceding example) to label the body. Then underline and label the thesis statement and the topic sentence of each body paragraph.

Strategies for Problem Solving

If where you are is not where you want to be, and when the path to getting there is not obvious, you have a problem. The circle of thought suggests that the most efficient approach to problem solving would be <u>to first diagnose the problem, then formulate a plan for solving it, then execute the plan, and finally, evaluate the results to determine whether the problem remains.</u> But people's problem-solving skills are not always so systematic, which is one reason why medical tests are given unnecessarily, diseases are sometimes misdiagnosed, and auto parts are sometimes replaced when there is nothing wrong with them. Sometimes, the best strategy is not to take mental steps aimed straight at your goal. Psychologists have identified several strategies that work better for certain problems.

<u>When a problem is so complicated that all of its elements cannot be held in working memory at once, you can use a strategy called *decomposition* to divide it into smaller, more manageable subproblems.</u> Thus, instead of being overwhelmed by the big problem of writing a major term paper, you can begin by writing just an

*Source: Doug Salisbury, "Three Steps to Better Writing," *Horizons,* Boston: Houghton Mifflin, 2004, pp. 111–112. Reprinted by permission of Houghton Mifflin Company.

outline. Next, you can visit a library and search the Internet to find the information most relevant to each successive[1] section of the outline. Then, you can write summaries of those materials, then a rough draft of an introduction, and so on.

A second strategy is to *work backward*. Many problems are like a tree. The trunk is the information you are given; the solution is a twig on one of the limbs. If you work forward by taking the "givens" of the problem and trying to find the solution, it will be easy to branch off in the wrong direction. A more efficient approach may be to start at the twig end and work backward. Consider, for example, the problem of planning a climb to the summit of Mount Everest[2]. The best strategy is to figure out, first, what equipment and supplies are needed at the highest camp on the night before the summit attempt, then how many people are needed to stock that camp the day before, then how many people are needed to supply those who must stock the camp, and so on, until the logistics[3] of the entire expedition are established. Failure to apply this strategy was one reason that six climbers died on Mount Everest in 1996.

Third, try finding *analogies*[4]. Many problems are similar to others you have encountered before. A supervisor may find, for example, that a seemingly hopeless impasse[5] between coworkers may be resolved by the same compromise that worked during a recent family squabble[6]. To take advantage of analogies, the problem solver must first recognize the similarities between current and previous problems, and then recall the solution that worked before. Surprisingly, most people are not very good at drawing analogies from one problem to another. They tend to concentrate on the surface features that make problems appear different.

Finally, in the case of an especially difficult problem, a helpful strategy is to allow it to "incubate[7]" by laying it aside for a while. A solution that once seemed out of reach may suddenly appear after a person engages in unrelated mental activity for a period of time. Indeed, the benefits of incubation probably arise from forgetting incorrect ideas that may have been blocking the path to a correct solution.

As these strategies show, the best path to a goal may not necessarily be a straight line. In fact, obstacles may dictate going in the opposite direction. Try these techniques if you want to improve your problem-solving skills.

1. **successive:** following in uninterrupted order
2. **Mount Everest:** tallest mountain in the world
3. **logistics:** aspects of an operation or undertaking
4. **analogies:** comparisons
5. **impasse:** stalemate; situation in which no progress can be made
6. **squabble:** disagreement; argument
7. **incubate:** form or consider slowly over time

Source: Adapted from Douglas A. Bernstein et al., *Psychology,* 5th ed., Boston, Houghton Mifflin, 2000. Reprinted by permission of the Houghton Mifflin Company.

The Conclusion

In a brief essay, the **conclusion** is the very last paragraph. It is usually unnecessary to repeat or summarize all of the ideas you have just presented. Instead, think of the purpose of the conclusion as providing closure, or a satisfying ending, for the reader. View the conclusions you write as opportunities to wrap up your essay and to suggest how your readers might respond. Write your conclusion under the assumption that you have convinced your readers that the idea or opinion in your thesis is true. Now that they agree with you, what should happen next? To achieve closure, you might use one of the following methods.

Describe the Consequences of the Idea or Opinion in Your Thesis Statement. Briefly explain the effects of what you have just shown to be true.

> Looking back on my experience, I can honestly say that it made me a stronger person. While I was going through all of the pain and turmoil, I thought sometimes that I would die of a broken heart. But I did not. Somehow, I managed to keep going, and little by little, day by day, things slowly improved. Now I am stronger and more confident in my ability to handle life's ups and downs. I still miss Angelo, but losing him helped me mature and begin to take care of myself rather than expecting someone else to do it.

Make a Prediction That Arises from the Idea or Opinion in Your Thesis Statement. Tell what you think will happen in the future.

> No matter how cheap or convenient it becomes to get movies on DVD or to download them from pay-per-view services, people will still enjoy going to movie theaters. Movie theaters have long been a part of America's past, and they are sure to be a part of its future for many years to come.

End with a Suggestion That Readers Act in Some Way. Call readers to action, and ask them to do something such as join an organization, donate time or money, or make some kind of change.

> For all of these reasons, you should try to travel abroad whenever you get the opportunity. The next time you are considering vacation destinations, think seriously about visiting a foreign country. You will be glad you did, so get your passport and start broadening your horizons!

End with a Question That Keeps Readers Thinking. Just as you can begin an essay by asking questions that draw readers in, you can end with a question or two that encourages readers to continue reflecting upon the topic or issue.

> Clearly, there are ways to solve the problem of hunger and starvation on this planet. In a world of plenty, it is inexcusable to allow thousands of people to die every day because they do not even have a piece of bread to eat. Our generation can be the one that finally wipes out this problem once and for all, and we must. How can we continue to just stand by and let our fellow human beings starve to death?

EXERCISE 5.16   **Recognizing Methods of Concluding an Essay**

Write the answer to each question on the blank provided.

1. In the essay "Three Steps to Better Writing" on pages 124–125, which of the four techniques does the writer use to conclude the essay?

_____

2. In the essay "Strategies for Problem Solving" on pages 125–126, which of the four techniques does the writer use to conclude the essay?

_____

3. The technique used in the following conclusion is _____.

Obviously, a joint-custody arrangement following divorce is harmful to the children in several ways. It exposes them to ongoing parental conflict, undermines their sense of stability by forcing them to move back and forth between two households, and often confuses them by subjecting them to two different sets of values, rules, and expectations. Having the children live full-time in the home of one parent or the other might be difficult for one or both parents. But are not the children's needs and well-being more important than anything else?

Some Helpful Tips for Composition

1. As you write your essay, keep rereading your thesis statement to stay focused on the one point you want to develop. This will prevent you from including unnecessary or irrelevant information.

WRITING FOR SUCCESS

Tips for Successful Collaborative Writing

In your academic course work and in your career, you may have to collaborate, or work together, with others to write an essay, report, or other kind of document. When you do, you will want to follow all of the steps of the writing process that you have been learning about and practicing. However, you will have to include other people in each step of this process.

Your collaboration should begin with a meeting with everyone who will contribute to the project. At this meeting, you should all discuss your subject, your audience, and your purpose. Then, as a group, prewrite to generate ideas. Finally, organize those ideas into an outline.

At this point, you have two choices. One option is to divide the sections of the outline among the group members so that each person has one section to write. If the document is a long one, such as a research paper, this might be the best approach. Each member could work individually to write his or her assigned section, meeting periodically with the whole group to check that each piece of the draft still fits together with the others. Using this procedure, set deadlines for drafts and, if possible, have a group leader combine all of the

sections-in-progress into one document prior to each group work session. When a draft of the entire document is complete, the group can work together to revise it so that it has a consistent style. (For more information, see the Writing for Success box in Chapter 6.)

The other option is to have the whole group work together to compose the entire document. This method works best if the paper is relatively short. One person can serve as the "secretary" and take dictation as the other group members suggest sentences out loud. The benefit of this approach is being able to talk through ideas and wording for those ideas with others as you compose.

No matter what approach to composition you use, confine yourselves whenever your group meets to giving positive reinforcement and constructive criticism. Remember that each group member will bring different strengths to the task and that collaborative composition offers the chance to achieve the best possible end result by incorporating the ideas and talents of more than one mind. Therefore, you should focus on improving the finished product rather than on blaming people for their mistakes.

2. If you get stuck, go back and reread what you have written so far. Often, revisiting where you have been will act a springboard to propel you forward again.

3. As you write a first draft, stay focused on the overall big picture. Do not stop to worry about a particular word or to track down a piece of information you need. Instead, draw a blank or make a note in the margin about the missing detail and then keep writing. You can find the missing word or information later when you are concentrating on the details.

4. Be willing to go back to the prewriting and organizing stages if your ideas and information seem skimpy or if your ideas do not seem to be flowing logically from one to another.

◎ Writing an Essay: A Student Demonstration

In Chapter 4, you saw how Juan organized his ideas from his prewriting about something everyone should learn how to do. Here are his thesis and informal outline again:

> Main Idea: Being bilingual benefits you in different ways.
>   1. Work
>   2. Helping others
>   3. Traveling

Next, he began composing his essay. He started by examining his thesis statement and then decided that he could revise it to be a little more specific. His revised thesis statement became

> Being bilingual benefits you both professionally and personally.

Next, Juan evaluated his outline. He decided that it still included the ideas he wanted to discuss, in the order in which he wanted to discuss them. So he began composing his essay, devoting a paragraph to each of his points and including transitions to help readers follow his ideas from one paragraph to the next. Here is his first draft:

> I have been bilingual almost all of my life. My family is from Cuba, we spoke Spanish at home when I was a child. Then, we moved to the United States, and I learned to speak English. The older I get, the more I am realizing how knowing two languages helps you in life. Being bilingual benefits you both professionally and personally.
>
> First is work, the most important way. America is multicultural with many Spanish speaking residents. I work in a grocery store and interact with the public, so it benefits me to have the knowledge of another language. I can communicate with Spanish speaking customers, so I translate for other employees when nesessay, my manager considers me a valuble part of his team because I can do this.
>
> Being bilingual means that you can help people, too. One time I was in the emergency room with my son, he had the flu. I helped a family from Mexico communicate with the nurses to get there son treated for a cut finger. I like knowing that I have a skill I can use to help others.

Last, I can travel more easily because I know two languages. If I went to Spanish speaking countries I could talk to the residents. If I got lost, I would be able to get directions. I could get any information I need. This is a benefit to me because one day, when I finish my degree, I will hopefully be a manager, and I might have to travel overseas somewhere, I will be able to talk to coworkers in other countries to get my job done.

I would reccomend that all college students learn a second language. Your probably going to need it.

Notice that Juan did a good job of beginning with an introduction, discussing each point in a separate paragraph, and then ending with a conclusion. His essay is just a first draft, so it is not perfect. However, it is a good start. In Chapter 6, you will see how he revised and improved it.

 **EXERCISE 5.17**   **Writing Your Essay**

In Chapter 4, you created an outline for your main idea about one of the following topics:

A significant decision that I made
Television
A time when I surprised myself
Men versus women
An unfair law
A solution to a problem

Now write an essay that develops this main idea. First, compose your thesis statement. Then reevaluate your outline. Finally, follow your outline to write the essay, connecting the body paragraphs with transitions.

CHAPTER 5 REVIEW

To review the main points in this chapter, write a brief response to each of the following questions.

1. Define the terms *essay* and *thesis*; then discuss what you need to do in order to make your essay and thesis effective.

2. What are three essential characteristics of a good thesis statement?

3. What is the role of the introduction, and what three purposes must it fulfill?

4. What are some things a writer can do to get readers interested and make them want to read on?

5. What is the body of the essay, and what does it include? What is the role of the topic sentence?

6. What is a paragraph, and what is its purpose? What is the role of the topic sentence in a paragraph?

7. What are the two parts of a topic sentence? What makes a topic sentence effective?

8. What does the body of a paragraph include, and what does it provide? Why?

9. What is a layer of development?

10. What are modes of development, and what are their purpose?

11. What are transitions?

12. What is a conclusion, and what is its purpose? How can writers achieve closure in a conclusion?

WebWork

Go to the Essay Punch Web site at **www.essaypunch.com**. This Web site provides questions that you answer as you are guided step by step through the actual process of composing an essay. Follow the directions to create your own essay and then print out that essay.

Online Study Center   For more information and exercises, go to the Online Study Center that accompanies this book, at **http://www.college .hmco.com/pic/dolphinwriterthree**.

Revising

GOALS FOR CHAPTER 6

▶ Explain the difference between revising and editing.

▶ Name the three characteristics that should be evaluated as part of the revision process.

▶ Identify areas for revision in essays.

▶ Use a peer review sheet to identify needed revisions for an essay.

In Chapter 5, you practiced the third step in the writing process, composing a draft. However, even after an essay is written, you are still not quite finished. The fourth step of the process is revising.

Revising Versus Editing

Take a moment and think about the word *revision*. Notice that it includes the prefix *re-*, meaning "back or again," and the root word *vision*. So *revision* literally means "to look at again." Once you have written your essay, you need to look at it again to make sure that you have successfully explained your main idea for your readers.

Revising and editing, which makes up the fifth step of the writing process, are not the same things. When you revise an essay, you are looking for and then correcting larger-scale problems. In other words, you are evaluating and improving, if necessary, the way that your whole essay is organized or developed. Editing, which will be discussed in Chapter 7, involves examining the essay at the sentence and word levels and correcting errors in sentence construction, grammar, word choice, and spelling. It is best to accomplish revision and editing as two separate, distinct steps, for each process involves looking at different aspects of the essay.

133

To revise an essay, you will need to evaluate it for the three C's: completeness, cohesiveness, and coherence.

Revising for Completeness

When you examine an essay to make sure it is *complete,* or adequately developed, you evaluate two things. First of all, look at how many supporting points (reasons, examples, causes, effects, steps, types, features, parts, and so on) you included to support your thesis statement. Most of the time, you will need to include at least two points. But if you have included only two, are there additional points that would provide even more support for the opinion stated in your thesis?

Let us say, for example, that a student decided to support the thesis statement *Students drop out of high school for many different reasons.* Then she writes an essay that explains, first, how poor academic performance can lead to quitting and, second, how teenage pregnancy produces the same result. Do these two reasons sufficiently support the idea stated in the thesis? No, they do not. The thesis statement itself promises a discussion of *many* reasons; offering only two does not adequately develop the main idea. This student needs to go back to the prewriting stage to come up with more reasons to add.

The second thing to evaluate when checking for completeness is the amount of development provided in each individual body paragraph. Is the general idea presented in every topic sentence adequately developed with enough specific examples and other kinds of explanation? Has the writer anticipated and answered all of the readers' questions? Get in the habit of scrutinizing short paragraphs of only three or four sentences, in particular, to make sure that they are adequately developed.

For more discussion and practice with developing ideas in body paragraphs, refer back to Chapter 5.

EXERCISE 6.1   **Adequately Supporting the Thesis Statement**

For each of the following thesis statements, write additional supporting points (reasons, examples, and so on) on the blanks provided.

1. Thesis statement: Cell phones have benefited us in many ways.

A. They increase our safety.
B. They help us cope with emergencies.

C. _____

D. _____

E. _____

2. **Thesis statement:** Communicating via e-mail has both advantages and disadvantages.

   A. One advantage of e-mail is the ability to send someone information without having to track that individual down on the phone or in person.
   B. A disadvantage of e-mail is the possibility that messages sent will not be delivered or read.

   C. _____

   D. _____

   E. _____

3. **Thesis statement:** I would recommend _____ (my college, my dentist, a certain product, for example) for many reasons.

   A. He/she/it is a good value.

   B. _____

   C. _____

   D. _____

   E. _____

Revising for Cohesiveness

способность к сцеплению

If an essay is *cohesive,* all of its paragraphs and sentences "stick together" to support one main idea. In other words, a cohesive essay has unity because it focuses on and develops just one point.

After you determine that your essay includes enough supporting points that are adequately developed, the next step is to make sure that every paragraph and sentence in your essay relates to the idea presented in your thesis statement. When you are writing, it is easy to get side-tracked and to go off on tangents when new thoughts come to mind. Evaluating an essay for cohesiveness is the process of looking for any paragraph or sentence that does not directly relate to the main idea.

The following body paragraphs were written to support the thesis statement *Several new pieces of medical equipment are helping doctors diagnose illnesses in their early stages.* Which paragraph is not related to this thesis statement?

The magnetic resonance imaging (MRI) machine is one amazing medical advancement. Made up of a special scanner, a large magnet, and a powerful computer, the MRI takes detailed pictures of the inside of a patient's body. It is a safe, painless technique that allows doctors to "see" tissue inside your body without cutting the skin or taking x-rays. The computer images generated during an MRI exam help your doctor pinpoint and diagnose problems early.

The CT (computed tomography) scan, too, helps doctors detect problems and diagnose illnesses. This is a safe, painless x-ray technique that produces images that resemble "slices" of tissue. Using special scanning equipment, x-ray images are taken from many directions and then combined into computer-processed pictures. These pictures provide an excellent view of your body's bones, organs, and other tissue. They allow doctors to locate tumors, cancers, disorders in organs such as the liver or brain, and damage to the back or joints.

Once these problems are identified, they can be treated with an array of new drugs. Medicines that control high blood pressure, for example, are preventing heart attacks. Cholesterol medications, too, are helping people with heart disease. In addition, several amazing new drugs are helping cancer patients live longer or completely recover.

Did you identify the third paragraph as the one that is not related to the thesis statement? Because the thesis focuses on medical equipment that diagnoses problems, a paragraph about drugs that treat problems does not belong in the essay. The third paragraph prevents the essay from being cohesive.

To determine whether or not you have included any paragraph or sentence that prevents cohesiveness, try the following three techniques:

Make sure that each supporting point directly relates to the thesis statement. Does each point truly support the overall idea or opinion stated in the thesis? If it does not, it may need to be eliminated or revised so that it can be included.

Reexamine any especially long paragraphs in the essay. A relatively lengthy paragraph may have lost its focus on the idea stated in the topic sentence. Reread longer paragraphs to look for sentences that stray from the paragraph's main idea or the thesis statement.

Read the sentences of your essay backward, beginning with the last sentence. After you read each sentence, reread the thesis statement. Decide if each individual sentence truly relates to your essay's main idea.

EXERCISE 6.2   **Recognizing Sentences That Prevent Cohesiveness**

In the following essay, underline the sentences that do not directly relate to the essay's thesis statement.

Curb the Curfew

Currently, about 75 percent of larger U.S. cities, as well as many smaller towns, impose curfews upon young people. These curfews, which generally prohibit anyone under age eighteen from leaving home between 11 p.m. or midnight and 6 a.m., are intended to stop juvenile crime and mischief. In reality, though, they are doing more harm than good, and they should be eliminated.

First of all, curfews do not prevent crime. In fact, several surveys and studies of various American cities indicate that curfews have no effect on crime rates. Perhaps this is true because most juvenile crimes are not committed in the middle of the night; the majority of youth crimes happen right after school, between 3 and 6 p.m. Furthermore, teenagers who want to sell drugs or rob people in the middle of the night are not likely to let a curfew law deter them. Another tragic mistake that many young people make is dropping out of school.

Not only are curfew laws ineffective; they also create or exacerbate tension between teens and law enforcement agencies. These laws communicate to young people that adults believe they are immature and untrustworthy, so some teenagers rebel by engaging in mischief. In Detroit and New Orleans, for example, youth crime actually increased after curfews were instituted. In Los Angeles, gang violence continues to be a major problem despite efforts to persuade kids not to join gangs. In San Francisco, youth crime was reduced only after that city's curfew was eliminated.

Even worse, though, most curfew laws discriminate against minors. Juvenile crimes are committed by a tiny percentage of the teenage population, yet curfew laws restrict the movements of the innocent majority, preventing them from doing things like going for an early morning jog, being on time for a 6 a.m. sports practice, or participating in extracurricular activities that extend past 11 p.m. Parents should encourage their children to participate in extracurricular activities to develop their talents and skills. Consequently, judges from Washington, DC, to Florida have been striking down curfew laws for being unconstitutional.

Clearly, establishing curfews is not the way to go about preventing crime. Cities that impose a curfew should consider other, more effective anticrime strategies.

Revising for Coherence

In addition to being complete and cohesive, an essay needs to be coherent. If an essay is *coherent,* it makes sense because it offers a clear progression of thought. In other words, readers can easily follow the writer's ideas from paragraph to paragraph and, within paragraphs, from sentence to sentence.

Evaluating an essay's coherence involves examining its overall organization and its transitions. Specifically, you should answer these four questions about your draft:

Does Your Draft Match Your Outline? Your draft does not have to match the outline that you put together during stage 2 of the writing process. However, it was in stage 2 that you applied your powers of logical thinking to the organization process. You may very well have come up with a better organization plan during stage 3 as you were composing. If that is the case, then it does not matter at all that your final essay differs from your outline. Make sure, though, that the essay does not differ from the outline *by accident*. If you did not make conscious choices to change to a better organization plan as you wrote, and you strayed *unintentionally* from your initial outline, then your essay may have become disorganized.

Are Your Supporting Points Presented in an Effective Order? Now that you have written the draft, make sure that your supporting points still seem to be in the right order. Essays based on natural organization should include the major events or steps in chronological order. But for those essays based on logical organization, make sure that the supporting points make sense in the order in which they are presented. Be willing to move whole paragraphs around until the order seems logical.

Are Your Paragraphs Linked by Transitions or Other Information? Have you used transitions to indicate the relationship of a body paragraph to the one before it? See Chapter 4 for more information about transitions. In addition, you can strengthen the progression of thought by repeating, summarizing, or referring back to an idea or piece of information that was presented earlier.

Are the Details in Each Body Paragraph Where They Belong? Check each body paragraph to make sure that its examples and details belong with the particular supporting point of that paragraph. If you find a specific fact, example, anecdote, statistic, or other piece of information that belongs in a different paragraph, move it.

> **EXERCISE 6.3** **Evaluating the Coherence of an Essay's Body**

The following paragraphs make up the body of an essay. Read them and then answer the questions that follow.

Making a Good First Impression

1 Studies have shown that most interviewers decide whether or not to hire a candidate within the first four minutes of a job interview. Obviously, then, making a good first impression on the interviewer is extremely important. It could make the difference between getting a job offer and getting a "thanks but no thanks" letter a few days later in the mail. To ensure that an interviewer's first impression of you is a positive one, you should follow three steps.

2 The moment you first meet an interviewer, you must immediately communicate that you are a confident but friendly person. If you are sitting, stand up, look the interviewer directly in the eye, smile, and offer a firm handshake. Say, "It's nice to meet you, Mr. Smith" while you shake Mr. Smith's hand. Watch the interviewer's body language to gauge whether you are speaking too long; if the interviewer stops looking at you or begins to fidget, wrap up what you are saying and let him or her control where the dialogue goes next.

3 During what remains of your four minutes, make it clear to the interviewer that you have excellent communication skills. When you get to where you have been heading, continue to display good manners by not sitting until you are invited to do so. Listen carefully to the interviewer's questions, take a moment to collect your thoughts before you begin speaking, and give the answers that you rehearsed while preparing for the interview. As you speak, be aware of your own body language. Try to suppress nervous behaviors like jiggling a leg, but do use your gestures and facial expressions to communicate emotions like excitement, pride, and concern.

4 Exhibit politeness, poise, and interest. The interviewer will probably lead you to the place, such as an office or conference room, where the interview will occur. On the way, hold doors open for the interviewer and always follow him or her; do not lead. Stand up straight, walk briskly, and pay attention to what the interviewer is saying. If he or she is inclined to make small talk, join in the banter to help break the ice. Lean forward slightly to show that you are interested in what the interviewer is saying.

5 These techniques will help you make a good first impression in interview situations. They can also be adapted to enable you to be effective in other situations, such as a first date or a parent/teacher conference. No matter where you use these techniques, do not forget the old saying, "You don't get a second chance to make a first impression," and use these suggestions to get it right the first time.

1. Is there a better order for these paragraphs? How would you reorder them to improve coherence?

   _____

2. Which sentence in paragraph 2 belongs elsewhere in the body?

   _____

   In which paragraph should it be placed?

   _____

3. Which sentence in paragraph 3 belongs elsewhere in the body?

   _____

   In which paragraph should it be placed?

   _____

4. What transition could you add to the beginning of paragraph 4 to improve coherence?

   _____

Two Important Revision Tips

1. Allow time for your draft to sit for a few days between the writing and revising steps. If you give yourself a few days to provide some distance between you and the draft you wrote, you may be better able to see the aspects of it that could use improvement.

2. Often, it is difficult to evaluate your own writing. You may be so intimately connected with your creation that it might be challenging to see its flaws and to figure out how to fix them. Therefore, it is often beneficial to ask others—such as classmates, family members, coworkers, or friends—to read your draft and provide you with feedback about your essay's strengths and weaknesses. Get in the habit of allowing enough time to ask one or more people you know to read your essay and to offer their comments and suggestions. Even those who are not teachers can read your draft simply as readers and tell you what they like about it and what confuses them. Consider using some type of peer review sheet to guide your readers' feedback. These sheets ask reviewers to examine specific aspects of an essay and comment on each one. The following is an example of a peer review sheet that focuses on the specific qualities of an effective essay covered in this chapter.

Sample Peer Review Sheet #1

Writer: _____

Reviewer: _____

Topic of essay: _____

	Yes	No

1. Does the essay include a thesis statement that clearly states one main idea? _____ _____

Suggestions for improvement:

2. Does every paragraph in the essay support the main idea? _____ _____

Suggestions for improvement:

3. Does the essay seem complete, or adequately developed? _____ _____

Suggestions for improvement:

4. Is the essay organized effectively? _____ _____

Suggestions for improvement:

5. Has the author included transitions to help readers follow the progression of thought from one paragraph to the next? _____ _____

Suggestions for improvement:

6. Are the essay's introduction and conclusion effective?* _____ _____

Suggestions for improvement:

Additional suggestions for improvement:

*For more discussion of effective introductions and conclusions, see Chapter 5.

This sheet guides reviewers to evaluate the essay's thesis statement as well as its completeness, cohesiveness, and coherence.

Another version of a peer review sheet, which follows, is more general. It allows reviewers to comment on any strength or weakness they see.

Sample Peer Review Sheet #2

Writer: _____

Reviewer: _____

Topic of essay: _____

1. **State the essay's focus.** In your own words, write down what you believe the writer was trying to say.

2. **Offer a commendation.** What did you like best about this essay? Why? What did the writer do well?

3. **Ask a question.** What would you like to know more about? What was confusing or unclear?

4. **Make a recommendation.** Give the writer at least one specific suggestion for improving the essay.

If you use this type of review sheet, pay particular attention to your reviewer's response to the first item. The reader's understanding of the main idea should match your intention. If these two things do not match, you need to reevaluate the wording of your thesis statement as well as the supporting details you have included.

You may have noticed that these peer review sheets do not ask for information about the essay's errors in grammar and spelling. Those sentence- and word-level issues will be addressed in the next chapter.

WRITING FOR SUCCESS

Tips for Collaborative Revision

In Chapter 5, you learned some tips to help you with collaborative writing projects. When you work with others to write a document, you will also need to work together to examine the three C's: completeness, cohesiveness, and coherence. Have the group's leader distribute drafts of the paper to each group member. Everyone should then review the paper to make sure that nothing important has been left out, all ideas are fully developed, information is logically organized, and nothing irrelevant is included. While the group discusses areas for improvement, have a "secretary" take notes or actually make the needed changes. Be prepared to meet several times during the revision process, if necessary. Depending on how many changes are made during a work session, the group may need to look at several different drafts.

If different sections of the paper were written by different individuals, the group will also need to pay attention to the paper's style. The *style* of writing refers to the words that the writer has chosen and the way that sentences have been constructed, and it will vary from writer to writer. Make sure that the length of sentences, the type of sentences, and the level of vocabulary are all relatively consistent throughout the document. See Chapter 7 for more information about improving style.

Revising an Essay: A Student Demonstration

In Chapter 5, you saw the first draft of Juan's essay about something everyone should learn to do. Here is his draft again:

> I have been bilingual almost all of my life. My family is from Cuba, we spoke Spanish at home when I was a child. Then, we moved to the United States, and I learned to speak English. The older I get, the more I am realizing how knowing two languages helps you in life. Being bilingual benefits you both professionally and personally.
>
> First is work, the most important way. America is multicultural with many Spanish speaking residents. I work in a grocery store and interact with the public, it benefits me to have the knowledge of another language. I can communicate with Spanish speaking customers and translate for other employees when nesessay, my manager considers me a valuble part of his team because I can do this.
>
> Being bilingual means that you can help and assist people, too. One time I was in the emergency room with my son, he had the flu. I helped a family from Mexico communicate with the nurses to get there son treated for a cut finger. I like knowing that I have a skill I can use to help others.

Last, I can travel more easily because I know two languages. If I went to Spanish speaking countries I could talk to the residents. If I got lost I would be able to get directions. I could get any information I need. This is a benefit to me because one day when I finish my degree I will hopefully be a manager, and I might have to travel overseas some-where, I will be able to talk to coworkers in other countries to get my job done.

I would reccomend that all college students learn a second lan-guage. Your probably going to need it.

After Juan wrote this essay, he set it aside for two days. He was then ready to look at it again and evaluate it for the three C's. In addition, he asked one of his classmates to read his essay and complete a peer review sheet. Here is his classmate's feedback:

Peer Review Sheet

Writer: Juan _____

Reviewer: Tina _____

Topic of essay: The benefits of being bilingual _____

	Yes	**No**
1. Does the essay include a thesis statement that clearly states one main idea?	√	

Suggestions for improvement:

	Yes	**No**
2. Does every paragraph in the essay support the main idea?	√	

Suggestions for improvement:

You could reword the topic sentences to make each point clearer.

(continued)

Peer Review Sheet (*continued*)

	Yes	No
3. Does the essay seem complete, or adequately developed?		√

Suggestions for improvement:

Your supporting points need more development. See #4 below. After you move the details in the last paragraph, you may need to add more development to it.

4. Is the essay organized effectively? _____ √

Suggestions for improvement:

The overall order is good, but I think some of the details in the third body paragraph might belong in the first body paragraph.

5. Has the author included transitions to help readers follow the progression of thought from one paragraph to the next? √ _____

Suggestions for improvement:

6. Are the essay's introduction and conclusion effective? _____ √

Suggestions for improvement:

Maybe improve the conclusion?

Additional suggestions for improvement:

Your supporting points are very convincing!

Juan considered Tina's suggestions and revised his draft. His revision follows.

I have been bilingual almost all of my life. My family is from Cuba, we spoke Spanish at home when I was a child. Then, we moved to the United States, and I learned to speak English. The older I get, the more I am realizing how knowing two languages helps you in life. Being bilingual benefits you both professionally and personally.

First, speaking two languages helps you get more professional success at work. America is multicultural with many Spanish speaking residents. I work in a grocery store and interact with the public, it benefits me to have the knowledge of another language. I can communicate with Spanish speaking customers and translate for other employees when nesessay, my manager considers me a valuble part of his team because I can do this. One day when I finish my degree I will hopefully be a manager, and I might have to travel overseas somewhere, I will be able to talk to coworkers in other countries to get my job done.

When you are bilingual, you can often help and assist people, too. One time I was in the emergency room with my son, he had the flu. I helped a family from Mexico communicate with the nurses to get there son treated for a cut finger. Another time, I helped a lady in a store. She was trying to return something she bought but the clerk at the customer service counter did not speak Spanish. I translated for the lady, and helped her get her money back. I like knowing that I have a skill I can use to help others.

Last, knowing two languages makes traveling in some foreign countries easier. If I went to Spanish speaking countries I could talk to the residents. If I got lost I would be able to get directions. I could get any information I need. For example, I went to Puerto Rico. I had never been there before but I got around just fine because I knew how to speak the language.

I would reccomend that all college students learn a second language. It may take time and effort to do it, but it will be worth it. Your probably going to need it, and you will be glad you learned it.

In the next chapter, you will see how Juan got help with editing his essay and producing a final draft.

EXERCISE 6.4 **Revising Your Essay**

Ask one of your classmates to read the essay you wrote about one of the following topics:

A significant decision that I made
Television
A time when I surprised myself
Men versus women
An unfair law
A solution to a problem

Then ask that classmate to complete the following peer review sheet.

Sample Peer Review Sheet #1

Writer: _____

Reviewer: _____

Topic of essay: _____

	Yes	No

1. Does the essay include a thesis statement that clearly states one main idea?   _____ _____

Suggestions for improvement:

2. Does every paragraph in the essay support the main idea?   _____ _____

Suggestions for improvement:

3. Does the essay seem complete, or adequately developed?   _____ _____

Suggestions for improvement:

4. Is the essay organized effectively?   _____ _____

Suggestions for improvement:

5. Has the author included transitions to help readers follow the progression of thought from one paragraph to the next?   _____ _____

Suggestions for improvement:

6. Are the essay's introduction and conclusion effective?   _____ _____

Suggestions for improvement:

Additional suggestions for improvement:

Use the feedback on this sheet to decide what revisions to make to your essay. Also, evaluate the essay yourself for the three C's: completeness, cohesiveness, and coherence. Finally, rewrite your essay, making any necessary changes.

CHAPTER 6 REVIEW

To review the main points in this chapter, write a brief response to each of the following questions.

1. In its most literal sense, what does the word *revision* mean? What do you do when you revise an essay?

2. How should you evaluate your paragraphs? What should you look for?

3. When you are examining an essay to make sure it is complete or adequately developed, what should you do?

4. What is cohesiveness, and what makes an essay cohesive?

5. What makes an essay coherent?

6. What are the advantages of letting a draft sit for a few days between the writing and revising stages?

7. What are the advantages of letting others read your draft and provide feedback?

8. What are peer review sheets? How can they help you improve your writing?

WebWork

Most colleges and universities have writing labs or centers where students can go to get help with their writing. These writing centers, which are typically staffed by either teachers or students with excellent writing skills, usually offer one-on-one tutorials and/or assistance with the revision of a paper.

Many colleges have also created online versions of their writing centers. An online writing lab (OWL), which is also known as an online writing center, is a Web site on the Internet that often offers students online resources to help them with their writing. These resources usually include tutorials and exercises. Some of them even allow students to send their writing to staff members for feedback and advice.

Find out about the kind of help your own college offers. Go to your college's Web site on the Internet and locate information on that Web site about your college's writing lab or center. Then answer the following questions.

1. Does your school have a writing lab or center? If so, what resources and services does it offer?

2. If your school has an online writing lab or center, who staffs this lab? What is the procedure that a student follows to get help with a paper?

3. If your school does not have an online writing lab or center, search for a school that does. Use a search engine such as Google to locate schools with online writing facilities. Then answer questions 1 and 2.

Online Study Center   For more information and exercises, go to the Online Study Center that accompanies this book, at **http://www.college .hmco.com/pic/dolphinwriterthree**.

7

Proofreading, Editing, and Preparing a Final Draft

▶ Proofread and edit sentences for style, sentence errors, grammatical and mechanical errors, and spelling errors.

▶ Use a peer review sheet to identify errors that need editing.

▶ Prepare a final draft of an essay according to certain guidelines.

The fifth and final step of the writing process involves editing and preparing a final draft. When you reviewed your writing during the revision step, you were searching for large-scale errors such as problems with the overall organization or development of your idea. To edit your writing, you **proofread,** or search for errors at the sentence and word levels. In other words, you comb through the paper carefully, searching for grammatical and spelling errors and making adjustments to sentences to improve your overall style. **Editing** means making the necessary corrections. After locating and fixing errors, you prepare your final draft for submission.

This chapter briefly covers the kinds of errors you will need to find and correct as part of the editing stage of the writing process. For more information about how to recognize and eliminate errors of this type, see the Handbook at the end of this text.

Editing to Improve Style

The **style** of writing refers to the words the writer has chosen and the way in which sentences are constructed. There are many different kinds of writing styles, and you will surely develop your own style as you continue to improve your overall writing skills. Right now, however, you should concentrate on choosing words and constructing sentences so that your writing will be interesting, clear, and easy to read. You can do that by paying attention, especially during proofreading, to the length and type of your sentences as well as to the words you have selected.

Sentence Length

Writing that is composed mostly of very short sentences usually sounds dull and monotonous to readers. If readers are bored by your sentences, they will have a more difficult time concentrating on your meaning. Also, short sentences may not be making important connections, so readers may not fully understand your ideas. The following paragraph contains too many short sentences.

> I enjoy cooking. It is rewarding. The dishes I prepare nourish my family. These dishes also give them pleasure. Cooking gives me a chance to be creative, too. I like experimenting. I combine foods in unique ways. I try out new recipes. I modify them to suit my family's preferences. Plus, being in the kitchen relaxes me. The pleasant colors, textures, and aromas of cooking food delight my senses. I focus on mixing, stirring, chopping, frying, and baking. I usually forget about everything else. Sometimes I head to the kitchen on especially stressful days. Cooking can even be a form of meditation.

As this example shows, too many short sentences make the whole paragraph sound unsophisticated. But notice how the paragraph becomes clearer, easier to read, and less childish when the length of the sentences is varied.

> I enjoy cooking because it is rewarding. The dishes I prepare not only nourish my family but also give them pleasure. Cooking gives me a chance to be creative, too. I like experimenting by combining foods in unique ways and trying out new recipes that I modify to suit my family's preferences. Plus, being in the kitchen relaxes me, for the pleasant colors, textures, and aromas of cooking food delight my senses. When I focus on mixing, stirring, chopping, frying, and baking, I forget about everything else. Sometimes I head to the kitchen on especially stressful days because cooking can even be a form of meditation.

Now the paragraph includes a mix of shorter and longer sentences that not only are more pleasurable to read but also sound much more sophisticated.

If you have a tendency to write too many short sentences, try to combine some of them using the following techniques.

1. Join two sentences with a coordinating conjunction—*and, or, but, nor, for, yet,* or *so.*

Two short sentences:	Julie is an airline pilot.
	Her brother Jeff is a cruise ship captain.
Combined sentence:	Julie is an airline pilot, and her brother Jeff is a cruise ship captain.

2. Turn one sentence into a dependent clause and attach it to an independent clause.

Two short sentences:	She plays the piano.
	Her playing makes her dog howl.
Combined sentence:	When she plays the piano, her dog howls.

3. Embed the information of one sentence into another sentence.

Two short sentences:	Xavier is my neighbor.
	He grows a beautiful rose garden.
Combined sentence:	Xavier, my neighbor, grows a beautiful rose garden.

EXERCISE 7.1   Combining Sentences

On the blank provided, combine each group of sentences to write one new sentence. Try to use each of the three techniques for combining sentences at least once.

1. I want a career as a television news anchor.
I am majoring in journalism.

_____

2. Bob ate too many spicy chili dogs.
His stomach hurts.

_____

3. We are planning a trip to Washington, DC.
It is our nation's capitol.

_____

4. Mr. Hobbes slipped on the ice.
He is our mail carrier.
He broke his wrist.

_____

5. Temperatures increase.
The days get longer.
Spring flowers begin to bloom.

_____

Sentence Types

Another way to achieve a style of writing that is interesting is to vary not only the length but also the type of sentence you write. There are four types of sentences: simple, compound, complex, and compound-complex, which are illustrated next.

A **simple sentence** contains just one independent clause (one subject-verb relationship).*

    subject   *verb*

The **cashier counted** the money in the drawer.

A **compound sentence** contains two independent clauses. Each contains at least one subject and one verb* and could stand alone as a complete sentence.

   subject *verb*   *subject*   *verb*

My **aunt** **likes** cats, but my **uncle** **is** allergic to them.

A **complex sentence** contains a dependent clause and an independent clause.

     dependent clause   *independent clause*

If I am going to make an A on the exam, I will have to study.

*This relationship may include a compound subject and/or a compound verb. For more on compound subjects and verbs, see the Coordination section of the Handbook at the end of this text.

A **compound-complex sentence** includes a dependent clause and two independent clauses.

independent clause #1

dependent clause   *subject*   *verb*

As the final buzzer sounded,   Mike   shot   the ball, and

independent clause #2

subject   *verb*

it   went   into the basket.

When you check your sentences during the editing stage, determine the type of each sentence in your paragraph. Then, if you see that you are relying too heavily on simple sentences, combine some of them to add more variety.

EXERCISE 7.2   **Identifying Sentence Types**

On the blank next to each sentence, identify it as either simple (**S**), compound (**C**), complex (**CX**), or compound-complex (**CC**).

_____   **1.** Americans find celebrities fascinating.

_____   **2.** Many people view celebrity-watching TV shows like *Entertainment Tonight* regularly, and magazines like *People* and *InStyle* have many readers.

_____   **3.** They also search for information about popular stars on the Internet because they want to know about the clothing, activities, and lifestyle choices of the rich and famous.

_____   **4.** Some people copy the styles of stars if they can afford to do so.

_____   **5.** Although stars live in a very different world, we see them often on television or in movies or concerts, so they seem like friends or even distant relatives.

_____   **6.** News of their breakups, addictions, health problems, and bad decisions makes them seem like the rest of us.

_____   **7.** After hearing about celebrities' problems, people enjoy gossiping about them, and they use news of the stars' good and bad behaviors to confirm their own values and ethics.

_____   **8.** When celebrities manage to overcome their problems, some people feel inspired.

_____ **9.** Champion cyclist Lance Armstrong, for example, encouraged many cancer victims.

_____ **10.** Many Americans long to be celebrities themselves, so they pay attention to famous people.

Diction

Diction refers to the individual words you choose. These words affect your style, so you should make sure that they are appropriate in a number of respects. In particular, you should evaluate the appropriateness of your words' level of formality, specificity, emotion, and originality. To determine whether a word is appropriate or not, you must consider your readers and decide if the word is suitable for those readers.

First of all, evaluate your choices of words for their **level of formality.** Although each pair of words in the following chart are synonyms, notice that the words in the two columns vary in their level of formality.

Formal	_Informal_
apartment	pad
companion	buddy
brave	has guts
pilfer	rip off
gentleman	guy
suspicious	fishy
supervisor	head honcho
relax	take it easy
chicanery	monkey business
trepidation	cold feet

Many forms of writing, including academic papers and work-related documents, call for a relatively high level of formality. It is unlikely that the words labeled _informal_ in the previous chart would be appropriate in such documents, for readers expect a more elevated style. In contrast, more personal kinds of writing, such as e-mail messages and letters to family members and friends, can be much more informal. They are likely to include slang terms and conversational words like those in the chart labeled _informal_.

EXERCISE 7.3   **Identifying Inappropriately Informal Words**

The following passage was submitted to an English professor for an academic assignment that asked students to paraphrase a poem. Circle all of the words and phrases that are inappropriately informal.

Edgar Allan Poe's poem "The Raven" is about a dude who is chilling at home one winter night, reading books and trying to forget that he is bummed over the death of a chick named Lenore. He freaks out at the sound of a rustling noise, and when he opens the door to check it out, a big, black raven flies into the room and sits on a statue. He talks to the bird. He wants to know where it comes from, and he asks it if he will ever stop grieving for Lenore. But no matter what he says to the bird, he thinks it replies with the word *Nevermore*. By the end of the poem, this guy completely loses it.

You will also need to consider whether your words are **specific** enough. Specific words help readers form clear images in their minds so that they can grasp your meaning more easily. Using general or more vague terms makes it harder for readers to understand your ideas. Notice how the following revised sentences become clearer when the vague terms are replaced with more specific ones.

> *Too general:*   The play was amazing.
>
> *More specific:*   The running back leaped three feet in the air and caught the ball with his fingertips in one corner of the end zone.

Words like *play* and *amazing* do not provide the reader with very much information. In fact, the word *play* has different meanings, and it is impossible to know which one the writer intends in the first sentence. The revised sentence, however, contains more specific terms that provide readers with a lot more detail and help them form a clear mental image.

Which words in the following sentence are too vague and general? Circle them as you read the sentence.

Carl ate a lot of food quickly.

Did you circle the words *a lot, food,* and *quickly?* These are the words that provide relatively little information. If this sentence were rewritten to read "Carl gobbled two foot-long submarine sandwiches in fewer than four minutes," it would be much clearer for the reader.

⭐ **EXERCISE 7.4**   **Identifying Vague Words**

Rewrite each of the following sentences on the blanks provided to replace vague, general words and phrases with more specific words and phrases.

1. He is very talented in his sport.

My neighbor Don works for the electrical company; he is very talented in finding solutions for electrical problems

2. That child often behaves badly.

My son often behaves badly when he is tired and lack of sleep

3. She did well in school.

_____

4. The weather is terrible.

_____

5. The company is doing better now than it did last year.

_____

The next aspect of diction to examine is the **emotion** conveyed through the words you have chosen. Some words, like *cat,* are relatively neutral. That is, they carry no particular emotional suggestion. But compare *cat* with the word *kitty,* which indicates affection for that animal. Notice in the folllowing chart how some synonyms reveal information about the feelings of the person who chooses to use the word.

Neutral	*Emotional*
physician	healer
confident	cocky
thinking	daydreaming
change	reform
mixed breed	mutt
debate	argument
remind	nag
slim	svelte
finish first	triumph
spread out	sprawling
discipline	punish
leader	pioneer
persuade	pressure

When you are evaluating your word choices, think about what they reveal about your emotions. Although it is fine to feel strongly—either positively or negatively—about the subject you are writing about, you must also think about your reader, especially when your topic is a controversial one. You do not want to offend, insult, or annoy readers because if you do, they will reject your ideas. So make sure that your words are not inappropriately emotional.

For example, the following sentence contains emotional word choices.

> Bums and vagrants are hanging out in our city park, and our city must deal with this problem.

The words *bums* and *vagrants* have negative, judgmental connotations attached to them, so readers might be offended by the writer's lack of sympathy for those who lack a place to live. Revising the sentence to be less emotional by substituting a term like *homeless people* might be a good idea.

EXERCISE 7.5   **Identifying Inappropriately Emotional Words**

On the blanks provided, rewrite each of the following sentences so that it expresses the same idea through more neutral language.

1. Laws force business owners to include ramps for the handicapped.

_____

2. The two chicks were gossiping about their coworkers' feud.

_____

3. Advertisements dupe kids into believing lies.

_____

4. A gang of hoodlums loiters in the mall every weekend.

_____

5. The nerds in the engineering department pressured her to change her mind.

_____

_____

Finally, you will need to evaluate whether or not your word choices are **original.** In other words, locate and eliminate from your writing all **clichés,** overused expressions that everyone has heard before. The following are just a few examples of the thousands of clichés we hear often.

fresh as a daisy
black as night
chip off the old block
cute as a button
disappeared into thin air
music to my ears
quiet as a mouse
a piece of cake
nip it in the bud
let the cat out of the bag
like shooting fish in a barrel
mean as a snake
one foot in the grave
better than sliced bread
opened a can of worms
put my foot in my mouth
sleep like a log
tall, dark, and handsome
light at the end of the tunnel
up a creek without a paddle
the last straw
tough as nails
work like a dog

These expressions often creep into our writing because we have heard them over and over, and they naturally pop into our minds as we compose. But they make writing dull and unoriginal, so replace them with other words that mean the same thing.

Notice how the following revised sentences are more interesting than the versions containing clichés.

Sentence with cliché:	My new coworker has been a thorn in my side.
Revised:	My new coworker has been like an itch on my back that I cannot reach.
Sentence with cliché:	As the deadline approached, I was running around like a chicken with my head cut off.
Revised:	As the deadline approached, I was bouncing around like a ball in a pinball machine.

EXERCISE 7.6   **Eliminating Clichés**

Rewrite each of the following sentences to eliminate the clichés.

1. The senator had some skeletons in his closet.

_____

2. You are a sight for sore eyes.

_____

3. They were between a rock and a hard place.

_____

4. When she got the promotion, she was as happy as a clam.

_____

5. He went straight to bed and slept like a baby.

_____

Eliminating Wordiness

When you are examining the diction of your writing, one last problem to look for is **wordiness,** or unnecessary words. Clear writing always expresses an idea in as few words as possible. Wordy writing just makes it more difficult for readers to understand your thoughts, for the extra words slow them down and get in the way. Notice how the following wordy sentences express ideas that become clearer after the unnecessary words have been eliminated.

Wordy: Due to the fact that more than thirty-six inches of winter precipitation fell during the evening hours, our public school institutions have decided against having students and teachers report for classes on this day.

Revised: Because it snowed three feet last night, schools are closed today.

Wordy: At the appointed day and time, each and every citizen of America who is registered to vote should report to a polling place and participate in the election by casting a ballot for his or her candidates of choice.

Revised: On Election Day, all registered voters should go vote.

Always ask yourself, *Can I find a way to say this in fewer words?* Notice how in the second example, the shorter phrase *On Election Day* replaces *At the appointed day and time,* the phrase *all registered voters* substitutes for *each and every American citizen who is registered to vote,* and the phrase *go vote* takes the place of *report to a polling place and participate in the election by casting a ballot for his or her candidates of choice.*

It is quite natural to be wordy when you are writing your first draft and trying to find the right words for expressing your ideas. However, you should get in the habit of examining your drafts during the editing stage and eliminating the words that are not contributing anything. When you are examining your writing for wordiness, look for the following common expressions, which add unnecessary words.

Instead of . . .	*Use . . .*
due to the fact that	because
in order to	to
for the purpose of	to
in the near future	soon
in the event that	if
at this point in time	now
at the present time	now
at that point in time	then
in today's world	today
this day and age	today
has the ability	can
during the same time that	while
until such time as	until
in spite of the fact that	although
are of the opinion that	think
green in color	green
small in size	small
short in length	short
the reason is that	because
given the fact that	because
put forth an effort	try
a number of	some

Also, look for redundant expressions, which contain words that simply repeat each other. Here are a few common redundant expressions:

Instead of . . .	*Use . . .*
close proximity	proximity
each and every	each
he is a man who	he

(continued on next page)

my personal feeling	my feeling
first and foremost	first
is located in	is in
past history	past (or history)

Finally, develop the habit of examining the especially long sentences that you write. Ask yourself if you can pare these sentences down so that they say the same thing in fewer words.

EXERCISE 7.7   **Eliminating Wordiness**

On the blanks provided, rewrite each of the following sentences to eliminate unnecessary words.

1. In spite of the fact that she was displaying the signs and symptoms of bad health, she reported to her place of employment anyway.

   _____

2. During the same time that Carla was attending an institution of higher learning, she was also employed in a position in which she worked fewer than forty hours per week.

   _____

3. We are of the opinion that John is a person who has the ability to serve as an effective leader for our group of different individuals.

   _____

4. In the event that you do not review the information the instructor presented during class meetings, you will not achieve a grade that is high enough to be a passing score when you complete the test.

   _____

5. They have decided to enter into a marital relationship, and the reason is that they have deeply romantic feelings for one another.

   _____

Editing to Correct Major Sentence Errors

In addition to proofreading your drafts to ensure sentence variety and appropriate language and to eliminate wordiness, you will need to find and correct major errors in sentence structure. These errors include sentence fragments, run-on sentences, dangling or misplaced modifiers, and faulty parallelism.

Sentence Fragments

A **sentence** contains at least one independent clause with at least one subject-verb relationship that expresses a complete thought and ends with a period. A **sentence fragment** lacks either a subject, a verb, or both or is a dependent clause, which cannot stand on its own as a complete idea. The missing element(s) must be added for the sentence to be grammatically correct.

No subject:	Will sell her car
Corrected:	She will sell her car.
No verb:	A beautiful, sunny day
Corrected:	The day was beautiful and sunny.

or

A beautiful, sunny day lifts my spirits.

No subject or verb:	Looking for errors
Corrected:	Looking for errors, she carefully read over the paper.

or

She was looking for errors.

No subject or verb:	Beneath the surface of the water
Corrected:	The dolphin dove beneath the surface of the water.
Incomplete:	That we wanted to buy
Corrected:	The brand that we wanted to buy was sold out.
Incomplete:	Where I exercise
Corrected:	The gym where I exercise gets crowded at five o'clock.

Often, correcting a sentence fragment is a matter of attaching it to a sentence that comes before or after it.

Incorrect:	Because she is an excellent teacher. She won her school's Teacher of the Year award.
Correct:	Because she is an excellent teacher, she won her school's Teacher of the Year award.
Incorrect:	He brushes and flosses every day. To prevent cavities.
Correct:	He brushes and flosses every day to prevent cavities.

For more information about sentence fragments, including more practice in correcting them, see the Subordination section of the Handbook at the end of this text.

EXERCISE 7.8   **Correcting Sentence Fragments**

On the blanks provided, rewrite each of the following sentence fragments to correct them. You may need to add information to create complete sentences.

1. In the morning

_____

2. If you finish early

_____

3. Someone who loves animals

_____

4. To lose weight

_____

5. Driving to work every day

_____

Comma Splices and Run-on Sentences

A **comma splice** consists of two independent clauses that are separated with only a comma, which is inadequate punctuation.

> They laughed, the joke was very funny.
> The rain stopped, the skies cleared.

In both of these examples there are two complete thoughts expressed in two different independent clauses. However, they are separated with only a comma.

A **run-on sentence** consists of two independent clauses that are not separated by any punctuation.

> Ants had invaded the kitchen she called an exterminator.
> Sarah e-mailed Doug he did not get the message in time.

Comma splices and run-on sentences can be corrected in one of three ways. First of all, you could simply add a semicolon between the two independent clauses.

> They laughed; the joke was very funny.
> The rain stopped; the skies cleared.
> Ants had invaded the kitchen; she called an exterminator.
> Sarah e-mailed Doug; he did not get the message in time.

Or you could add a comma and an appropriate coordinating conjunction.

> They laughed, for the joke was very funny.
> The rain stopped, and the skies cleared.
> Ants had invaded the kitchen, so she called an exterminator.
> Sarah e-mailed Doug, but he did not get the message in time.

A third way to correct a run-on sentence is to add a semicolon and an appropriate conjunctive adverb or transitional expression followed by a comma.

> They laughed; in fact, the joke was very funny.
> The rain stopped; then, the skies cleared.
> Ants had invaded the kitchen; therefore, she called an exterminator.
> Sarah e-mailed Doug; however, he did not get the message in time.

For more information about comma splices and run-on sentences, including more practice in correcting them, see the Coordination section of the Handbook at the end of this text.

EXERCISE 7.9   **Correcting Comma Splices and Sentence Fragments**

On the blanks provided, rewrite each of the following comma splices and run-on sentences to correct them. Try to use each of the different methods for correcting these errors at least once.

1. The emergency room was busy, its waiting room was full.

_____

2. My car will not start, I need to take it to a repair shop.

_____

3. They expected only a handful of people to apply, hundreds filled out applications.

_____

Because of

4. She forgot to add baking powder the cake did not rise.

Although

5. Many people voted for her, she did not win.

_____

Misplaced or Dangling Modifiers

A modifier, especially an adjective, must be placed next to the word it describes. If a modifier is not next to the word or words it describes, it is called a **misplaced modifier.**

> **Flying overhead,** Professor Anderson pointed out the hawk.

In this sentence, the phrase *flying overhead* modifies *Professor Anderson* because those are the closest words to the phrase. Therefore, this sentence is saying that Professor Anderson was flying overhead. Actually, though, it is the hawk that is flying overhead. To correct this sentence, rewrite it so that the modifier is next to the word that it modifies.

> Professor Anderson pointed out the hawk **flying overhead.**

Misplaced modifiers can be phrases or single words. The word *only*, for example, is commonly misplaced.

> The baby *only* weighed four pounds.

In this sentence, the word *only* is modifying the verb, but it should be modifying the words *four pounds*. Therefore, it needs to be moved.

> The baby weighed *only* four pounds.

If the word the modifier is supposed to be describing is not in the sentence at all, the error is called a **dangling modifier.**

> Having lost the game, the fans were disappointed.

In this sentence, the modifier *having lost the game* is incorrectly describing *fans*. The fans did not lose the game; the players did. To correct the error, rewrite the sentence to add the missing information.

> Having lost the game, the players disappointed their fans.

For more information about dangling and misplaced modifiers, including more practice in correcting them, see the Basic Sentence section of the Handbook at the end of this text.

✺ **EXERCISE 7.10**   **Correcting Misplaced and Dangling Modifiers**

On the blanks provided, rewrite each of the following sentences to correct misplaced and dangling modifiers. You may need to add information to correct the dangling modifiers.

1. Hanging on a hook in the closet, I found my umbrella.

_____

2. I like to watch television cooking dinner.

_____

3. While hunting for the missing keys, a twenty dollar bill was found.

_____

4. Tossed into the air, the boy caught the popcorn in his mouth.

_____

5. When fishing for trout, patience is needed.

_____

Faulty Parallelism

When pairs or series of words, phrases, or clauses express parallel ideas, they must be parallel in structure.

> My grandmother spends her days sew**ing**, read**ing**, and visit**ing** friends.
>
> I am not sure **where** she went or **when** she will return.
>
> We agreed **that** Ashley is the most qualified candidate and **that** we should hire her.

Notice how changing the structure of one of the items in the pair or series makes the relationships in the sentence harder to understand.

> My grandmother spends her days sewing, reading, and visits to friends.
>
> I am not sure where she went or her return time.
>
> We agreed that Ashley is the most qualified candidate and hiring her is what we should do.

Not only are these sentences more difficult to understand, but their lack of balance also causes them to sound cumbersome and awkward.

Now read two more sentences that lack parallelism and try to determine how their structures change from the beginning to the end of the sentence.

> TV viewers love _American Idol,_ and _Survivor_ is enjoyed by them, too.
>
> The students are hoping that the professor's tests will be easy and to know all of the answers.

In the first sentence, the first independent clause is in the active voice, and the second is in the passive voice. To correct the error, change the second independent clause to the active voice: TV viewers love _American Idol,_ and they enjoy _Survivor,_ too.

The second sentence contains a dependent clause that begins with *that* and an infinitive phrase. To correct the sentence, change the infinitive phrase to a dependent clause: The students are hoping that the professor's tests will be easy and that they will know all of the answers.

For more information about faulty parallelism, including more practice in correcting it, see the Parallelism section of the Handbook at the end of this text.

EXERCISE 7.11   **Correcting Faulty Parallelism**

On the blanks provided, rewrite each of the following sentences to correct their faulty parallelism.

1. He enjoys bicycling, jogging, and tennis.

_____

2. Jeff has been not only to Spain, but Africa is a place to which he has traveled.

_____

3. She wrote postcards to tell her family where she had been and the things she had seen.

_____

4. Troy is an excellent guitarist and who also sings well.

_____

5. The doctor told her that she should drink a lot of fluids and to rest.

_____

Editing Errors in Grammar and Mechanics

In addition to locating and correcting major sentence errors—such as fragments, comma splices, dangling modifiers, and faulty parallelism—you will need to scan your writing for the many other kinds of grammatical and mechanical errors, including subject-verb agreement errors, errors in verb tense, and capitalization and punctuation errors. Of course, it can be difficult to identify these errors, especially if you did not realize that you had included them in the first place. Thus, one good technique for locating errors is to have others read your drafts and point them out. Consider adding questions about possible word- and sentence-level errors to the Peer Review Sheet you give your reviewers to fill out. Doing so will encourage your reviewers to look for very specific kinds of errors that may be reducing the effectiveness of your writing. You could add a page like the one that follows, for example, to your Peer Review Sheet.

	Yes	No
1. Does the writer include a mixture of sentence lengths and types?	____	____
Suggestions for improvement:		
2. Is the diction appropriately formal, specific, original, and emotional?	____	____
Suggestions for improvement:		
3. Is the writing free of wordiness?	____	____
Suggestions for improvement:		
4. Is the writing free of major sentence errors, such as sentence fragments, comma splices, run-on sentences, dangling or misplaced modifiers, and faulty parallelism?	____	____
Suggestions for improvement:		
5. Is the writing free of other grammatical and mechanical errors?	____	____
Suggestions for improvement:		

If you use a Peer Review Sheet, ask your reviewers to identify the specific locations of possible errors in your draft. Then make sure you correct all of those errors before or during your preparation of your final draft.

Another way to find errors is to learn to recognize them yourself. Increase your knowledge of grammar and mechanics so that you will stop making the same mistakes over and over again. Use the Handbook at the end of this text to review this material, and complete the exercises provided to make sure that you understand how to correct the various kinds of errors. Also, pay special attention to your instructors' comments. If an instructor identifies subject-verb agreement errors in a paper you have written, go to the Handbook and find out what subject-verb agreement errors are and how to correct them.

It is very important to correct errors in your writing because submitting a final draft that is marred with errors will undermine your credibility as a writer. When a paper contains errors, readers often question the writer's intelligence and overall writing ability, or they assume that the writer did not care enough about the document to ensure that it was error free.

Editing Spelling Errors

Your final draft should always be free of spelling errors. There are three ways to identify and correct errors in spelling.

1. **Use a computer spell-checker.** If you have an electronic version of your draft, use the spell-check feature of your word processing program to locate errors. Most of these spell-checkers will suggest possible alternative spellings for each error identified. Note, however, that these spell-checkers are not foolproof. They may actually ignore words that are incorrectly spelled. Therefore, use the next two methods in addition to this one.

2. **Ask someone to proofread your draft for spelling errors.** Ask someone you know who is a good speller to circle possible errors in spelling in your draft.

3. **Whenever you have the slightest doubt about the spelling of a word, look it up in a dictionary.** Always check the spellings of words you question in a book or online version of a dictionary. You can find several different online dictionaries at www.onelook.com.

> **EXERCISE 7.12**   **Proofreading a Passage for Grammatical and Spelling Errors**

Edit the following passage to correct grammatical and spelling errors. Cross out the errors and add corrections directly to the text of the passage.

Strategies for Problem Solving

If where you are is not where you want to be,

and when the path to getting there is not ob-

vious, you have a problem. The circle of thought

suggests that the most efficeint approach to

problem solving would be to first diagnose the problem, then formulate a plan for solving it, then execute the plan, and finally, evaluate the results. To determine whether the problem remains. But peoples' problem-solving skills are not always so systematic, which is one reason why medical tests are given unnecessarily, diseases are sometimes misdiagnosed, and the replacement of auto parts when there is nothing wrong with them. Sometimes, the best strategy is not to take mental steps aimed straight at your goal. Psychologists has identified several strategies that work better for certain problems.

When a problem is so complicated that all of it's elements cannot be held in working memory at once. You can use a strategy called *decomposition* to divide it into more smaller, more manageable subproblems. Thus, instead of being overwhelmed by the big problem of writing a major term paper, you can begin by writing just an outline. Next, you can visit a library and search the Internet to find the information most relevent to each successive[1]

1. **successive:** following in uninterrupted order

section of the outline. Then you can write summaries of those materials, then a rough draft of an introduction, and so on.

A second strategy is to work backward. Many problems are like a tree. The trunk is the information you are given, the solution is a twig on one of the limbs. If you work forward by taking the "givens" of the problem and trying to find the solution, it will be easy to branch off in the wrong direction. A more efficient approach may be to start at the twig end and work backward. Consider, for example, the problem of planning a climb to the summit of the world's tallest mountain. The best strategy is to figure out, first, what equipment and supplies are needed at the highest camp on the night before the summit attempt, then how many people are needed to stock that camp the day before, then how many people are needed to supply those who must stock the camp, and so on, until the logistics[1] of the entire expedition are established. Failure to apply this strategy was one reason that six climbers died on mount everest[2] in 1996.

1. **logistics:** aspects of an operation or undertaking

2. **Mount Everest:** tallest mountain in the world

Third, try finding analogies[1]. Many problems are similiar to others you have encountered before. A supervisor may find, for example, that a seemingly hopeless impasse[2] between coworkers may be resolved by the same compromise that worked during a recent family squabble[3]. To take advantage of analogies, the problem solver must first recognize the similarities between current and previous problems then he or she must recall the solution that worked before. Surprisingly, most people is not very good at drawing analogies from one problem to another. They tend to concentrate on the surface features that make problems appear different.

Finally, in the case of an especially difficult problem, a helpful strategy is to allow it to "incubate[4]" by laying it aside for a while. A solution that once seemed out of reach may suddenly appear after a person engages in unrelated mental activity for a period of time. Indeed, the benefits of incubation probly arise from forgetting incorrect ideas that may have been blocking the path to a correct solution.

1. **analogies:** comparisons
2. **impasse:** stalemate; situation in which no progress can be made
3. **squabble:** disagreement; argument
4. **incubate:** form or consider slowly over time

> As these strategies show, the best path
> to a goal may not necessarily be a straight
> line. In fact, obstacles may dictate going in the
> opposite direction. Try these techniques. If you
> want to improve your problem-solving skills.*

When you have finished correcting the errors in this essay, turn back to page 127 and compare your edits with the error-free version.

Preparing the Final Draft

After you have edited your paper for style and errors, you are ready to prepare your final draft for submission. You will, of course, need to follow your instructor's guidelines for final drafts. Regardless of your paper's final format, however, the paper should always be neat, clean, and professional looking. It should be typed or handwritten, as your instructor requires, and its appearance should reflect the fact that you have invested time and effort in your writing.

In general, both typed and handwritten final drafts usually have one-inch margins at the top, bottom, left, and right sides of the page. This means that the first sentence begins an inch from the top edge of the paper, and the last line on the page stops an inch away from the bottom edge of the paper. Each line begins one inch from the left edge of the paper and reaches all the way to one inch from the right edge of the paper. Every new paragraph is indented five spaces. Many instructors require assignments to be double-spaced, which means that a handwritten paragraph should skip every other line on the page. At the top of the first page, include your name and any other information the instructor wants you to list (such as course name or number and date).

Source: Adapted from Douglas A. Bernstein et al., *Psychology*, 5th ed., Boston: Houghton Mifflin, 2000, p. 262. Reprinted by permission of Houghton Mifflin Company.

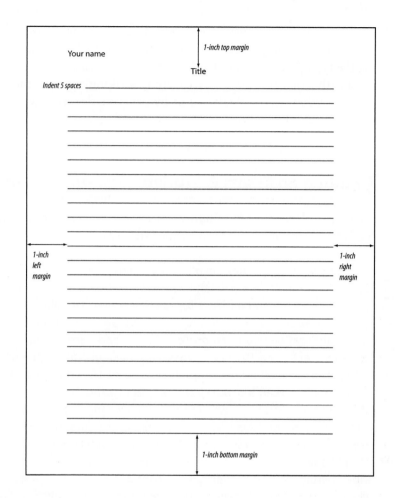

WRITING FOR SUCCESS

The Importance of Error-Free Professional and Personal Writing

Producing error-free essays for your academic courses will give you practice that you will need later to produce error-free professional and personal documents. It is important to eliminate errors from these documents because they can have serious consequences. Errors in legal documents such as contracts, for example, may very well cost you time and money. Errors in professional documents such as résumés can cost you jobs that you want, for employers may conclude that an individual who writes with errors has poor communication skills. Errors in business documents such as brochures or letters may lead potential customers to conclude that your product or service will be less than perfect, too. To avoid all of these negative effects of errors, work hard now to recognize and correct errors so that you will continue to do so even after you complete your college education.

After you have prepared your final draft, you should go over it one more time to look for **typographical errors,** which are accidental mistakes that occur during the typing or printing of a document. If you find such an error, you should always neatly correct it either by carefully striking through the error and writing the correction with a black pen or by covering the error with correction fluid and then writing the correction.

Editing an Essay: A Student Demonstration

In Chapter 6, you saw how Juan revised his essay about something everyone should learn to do. Here is his revised draft again.

I have been bilingual almost all of my life. My family is from Cuba, we spoke Spanish at home when I was a child. Then, we moved to the United States, and I learned to speak English. The older I get, the more I am realizing how knowing two languages helps you in life. Being bilingual benefits you both professionally and personally.

First, speaking two languages helps you get more professional success at work. America is multicultural with many Spanish speaking residents. I work in a grocery store and interact with the public, it benefits me to have the knowledge of another language. I can communicate with Spanish speaking customers and translate for other employees when nesessay, my manager considers me a valuble part of his team because I can do this. One day when I finish my degree I will hopefully be a manager, and I might have to travel overseas somewhere, I will be able to talk to coworkers in other countries to get my job done.

When you are bilingual, you can often help and assist people, too. One time I was in the emergency room with my son, he had the flu. I helped a family from Mexico communicate with the nurses to get there son treated for a cut finger. Another time, I helped a lady in a store. She was trying to return something she bought but the clerk at the customer service counter did not speak Spanish. I translated for the lady, and helped her get her money back. I like knowing that I have a skill I can use to help others.

Last, knowing two languages makes traveling in some foreign countries easier. If I went to Spanish speaking countries I could talk to the residents. If I got lost I would be able to get directions. I could get any information I need. For example, I went to Puerto Rico. I had never been there before but I got around just fine because I knew how to speak the language.

I would reccomend that all college students learn a second language. It may take time and effort to do it, but it will be worth it. Your probably going to need it, and you will be glad you learned it.

Next, he needed to look over his draft for word- and sentence-level errors. So he asked his peer reviewer, Tina, to help him find grammatical and mechanical errors and to help him polish his style. Tina completed the following addition to the first Peer Review Sheet.

Peer Review Sheet (page 2)

	Yes	No
1. Does the writer include a mixture of sentence lengths and types?	√	

Suggestions for improvement:

	Yes	No
2. Is the diction appropriately formal, specific, original, and emotional?	√	

Suggestions for improvement:

	Yes	No
3. Is the writing free of wordiness?		√

Suggestions for improvement:

	Yes	No
4. Is the writing free of major sentence errors, such as sentence fragments, comma splices, run-on sentences, dangling or misplaced modifiers, and faulty parallelism?		√

Suggestions for improvement:

I saw a few run-on sentences.

	Yes	No
5. Is the writing free of other grammatical and mechanical errors?		√

Suggestions for improvement:

I see several misspellings and comma errors.

After receiving Tina's feedback, Juan found the errors she mentioned and edited his paper to eliminate these mistakes. Then he typed his final draft according to his teacher's guidelines. Here, finally, is the draft he submitted.

The Benefits of Being Bilingual

by Juan Espinoza

I have been bilingual almost all of my life. My family is from Cuba, and we spoke Spanish at home when I was a child. Then we moved to the United States, and I learned to speak English. The older I get, the more I realize how knowing two languages helps you in life. Being bilingual benefits you both professionally and personally.

First, speaking two languages leads to more professional success. America is multicultural, with many Spanish-speaking residents. I work in a grocery store and interact with the public, so it benefits me to speak another language. I can communicate with Spanish-speaking customers and translate for other employees when necessary. Therefore, my manager considers me a valuable part of his team. One day, when I finish my degree, I will hopefully be a manager, and I might have to travel overseas somewhere. I will be able to talk to coworkers in other countries to get my job done.

When you are bilingual, you can often help people, too. One time I was in the emergency room with my son. He had the flu. I helped a family from Mexico communicate with the nurses to get their son treated for a cut finger. Another time, I helped a lady in a store. She was trying to return something she had bought, but the clerk at the customer service counter did not speak Spanish. I translated for the lady and helped her get her money back. I like knowing that I have a skill I can use to help others.

Last, knowing two languages makes traveling in some foreign countries easier. If I were to go to Spanish-speaking countries, I could talk to the residents. If I got lost, I would be able to get directions. I could get any information I need. For example, I went to Puerto Rico. I had never been there before, but I got around just fine because I knew how to speak the language.

I would recommend that all college students learn a second language. It may take time and effort to do it, but it will be worth it. You are probably going to need it, and you will be glad you learned it.

Because Juan completed all five steps in the writing process to create this essay, it is clearly developed, well organized, and easy to read and understand.

EXERCISE 7.13 **Editing Your Essay**

Ask one of your classmates to read the essay you wrote about one of the following topics:

A significant decision that I made
Television
A time when I surprised myself
Men versus women
An unfair law
A solution to a problem

Then ask that classmate to complete the following peer review sheet to help you identify errors that need correction.

Peer Review Sheet (page 2)

	Yes	No
1. Does the writer include a mixture of sentence lengths and types?	_____	_____
Suggestions for improvement:		
2. Is the diction appropriately formal, specific, original, and emotional?	_____	_____
Suggestions for improvement:		
3. Is the writing free of wordiness?	_____	_____
Suggestions for improvement:		
4. Is the writing free of major sentence errors, such as sentence fragments, comma splices, run-on sentences, dangling or misplaced modifiers, and faulty parallelism?	_____	_____
Suggestions for improvement:		
5. Is the writing free of other grammatical and mechanical errors?	_____	_____
Suggestions for improvement:		

Use the feedback on this sheet to edit your essay, and then prepare your final draft according to the following guidelines.

1. Type the essay with double-spacing or write it neatly by hand, skipping every other line on your paper.

2. All margins should be one inch.

3. Include a title for your essay and put your name somewhere at the top of the page.

CHAPTER 7 REVIEW

To review the main points in this chapter, write a brief response to each of the following questions.

1. What does editing mean? How do you edit your writing?

2. How would you define the term *style* in terms of writing?

3. What is the drawback to using very short sentences in your writing? What two things can you do to combine sentences?

4. What is a simple sentence?

5. What is a compound sentence?

6. What is a complex sentence?

7. What is a compound-complex sentence?

8. Define the term *diction*.

9. What is a cliché?

10. What is wordiness in writing?

11. In addition to proofreading your drafts for sentence variety, appropriate language, and wordiness, you should also find and eliminate major errors with regard to what?

12. What is a sentence fragment?

13. What is a comma splice?

14. What is a run-on sentence?

15. What is a misplaced modifier? a dangling modifier?

16. When pairs or series of independent clauses express parallel ideas, what must they be?

17. What are three ways to identify and correct spelling errors in your writing?

18. Regardless of a paper's final format, what should it always be?

19. What are typographical errors?

WebWork

After your instructors help you identify grammatical errors in your writing, you should find out how to correct these errors yourself so that you will not make the same mistakes over and over again. One useful tool for learning about grammar is the Guide to Grammar and Writing Web site at **http://grammar.ccc.commnet.edu/ grammar**. This Internet site not only explains grammatical concepts but also includes computer-graded quizzes that give you instant feedback so that you know immediately whether or not you have understood the information.

Find one of your graded papers and choose an error (like sentence fragments or faulty parallelism) that you made. Next, go to the Guide to Grammar and Writing Web site and find the tutorial about that particular error. Then complete at least one of the quizzes provided at the end of the lesson.

Online Study Center   For more information and exercises, go to the Online Study Center at **http://www.college.hmco.com/pic/ dolphinwriterthree**.

8 Narration

GOALS FOR CHAPTER 8

▶ Define the term *narration.*

▶ Describe the steps in writing a narrative essay.

▶ Write a narrative essay.

▶ Include vivid and figurative language in a narrative passage.

In Chapter 5 of this book, you practiced developing the main idea of an essay with various kinds of information and examples. In the next eleven chapters (Chapters 8–17), you will look more closely at different patterns, or modes, that will help you organize the development of your thesis statement or thesis. You will begin in this chapter with the narrative mode of development.

Writing a Narrative Essay

You probably use **narration,** or storytelling, fairly often. You tell stories about the things that happen to you, your friends, and your family members, and you also tell stories you have heard about other people's experiences. As a writer, you will need to be able to tell a good story in order to develop some point or idea. Sometimes, the story will be about something that happened to you. At other times, you will tell a story about something that happened to someone else. Read, for example, the following narrative passage.

It can take years to hit bottom with many drugs, decades with alcohol. But on steroids Chris Wash managed it in just 12 months, starting with a dream of playing for a top college basketball team and winding up on a highway over-pass, waiting for the moment to jump. In that time Wash, a 6-foot-2 guard on the Plano West High School team in Plano, Texas, went from a rangy[1] 180 pounds to a hulking[2] 230, with shoulders so big he could barely pull on his backpack in the morning. And he developed a whole new personality to match that intimi-dating physique[3]: depressed, aggressive, and volatile[4]. After a series of fights in his junior year, his coach threw him off the team, but by then building muscles had become an end in itself.

He switched from pills to injecting himself with steroids in the buttocks, often with a couple of friends, including a promising high-school baseball player named Taylor Hooton. That went on for several months, until one day Hooton was found dangling from his belt in his bedroom, an apparent suicide. Fright-ened, Wash gathered up his vials[5] and syringes and threw them down the sewer.

But an insidious[6] thing about steroids is that stopping them abruptly can lead to depression. A few weeks later, Wash drove to a bridge across a Dallas freeway and walked to the middle, looking down at the rushing traffic. Ulti-mately, he stepped back from the railing and called his mother to come get him.

After intensive therapy, he is now free of steroids, but he lost months of classes and had to transfer out of Plano West to finish up at an alternative high school for troubled kids that has no basketball team. "I could have had a scholarship to play ball in college," he muses. "Basketball was my life. It is who I was."*

This author wanted to develop the idea that steroids are dangerous drugs for young athletes. He tells a story about Chris Wash's experience to prove his point.

Whether you write about your own experiences or someone else's, you will need to incorporate some features that are common to all effective narratives. These essential features are discussed in the following sections of this chapter.

Determining a Main Idea and Writing a Thesis Statement

The first step in writing an effective narrative essay involves deciding on the point you want to make about the events you will relate. As you look at the de-tails you generated during the prewriting stage, ask yourself *why* you want to

1. **rangy:** having long, slender limbs
2. **hulking:** bulky or massive
3. **physique:** build or body type; physical type
4. **volatile:** hot-tempered
5. **vials:** small glass bottles, especially ones for medicines
6. **insidious:** sinister or dangerous

*Source: Adapted from Jerry Adler, "Toxic Strength," from Newsweek, Dec. 20, 2004. © 2004 Newsweek, Inc. All rights reserved. Reprinted by permission.

tell the story. Is there some moral or lesson that someone could gain from hearing the story? Does the story illustrate some truth about your life or the lives of others? Do you want to help readers learn something, or do you want to entertain them? These questions will help you decide on the one main idea you would like your readers to know or to accept. Then write a thesis statement to express this main idea.

For an example, look at a brainstorming sample generated by a student who was assigned to write about a time when she had learned something about herself. She decided to generate ideas about her battle to give up smoking.

- smoked cigarettes for 9 years, from age 16 to 25
- suddenly started to get chest pains
- could hardly breathe when climbing stairs, could not run or exercise
- worried that I would die, no one to raise my two-year-old daughter
- decided to quit
- went cold turkey, but addiction too strong
- read stop-smoking books
- tried hypnosis, did not work
- enrolled in a free stop-smoking course at hospital
- followed a program that gradually decreased amount of nicotine over several weeks
- smoked last cigarette on April 3, 2004
- still had to deal with cravings
- gained weight
- have not smoked since then

After completing this brainstorming, the student decided that she wanted to tell readers how quitting smoking taught her that she has the strength to overcome other problems. She wrote the following thesis statement.

Conquering my addiction to cigarettes taught me that I am strong and can achieve anything if I am determined enough.

As you complete this step in the process, remember what you learned in Chapter 4 about thesis statements. Specifically, a thesis statement includes both your topic (the incident or event) and the point you want to make about that topic.

EXERCISE 8.1 **Writing Thesis Statements for Narratives**

For each of the following topics, use some prewriting techniques to generate ideas on your own paper and then write a thesis statement you could use for a narrative essay.

1. A memorable occasion that I shared with a friend or loved one

Thesis statement: _____

2. A day that I now regret

Thesis statement: _____

3. An emergency or disaster that I witnessed or experienced

Thesis statement: _____

4. A painful moment

Thesis statement: _____

5. An interesting discovery

Thesis statement: _____

Selecting the Right Details for a Narrative

The next step toward writing an interesting narrative essay is selecting the right details to include. You cannot include everything that happened or every little detail because reading the finished product would be too tedious for your readers, and your point could get lost in irrelevant information. Therefore, you will have to examine your prewriting and decide which pieces of information are essential to your narrative. You will, of course, need to include all of the major, important events, so make sure you circle those events in your prewriting. Then you will need to think about the minor events in the story, evaluating each one in terms of its relationship to the main idea you want to express. If a minor event does not directly relate to your main idea, you will probably want to leave it out because providing unnecessary information slows down your story and makes it less interesting. Finally, you will need to consider the details of the events you will include and omit information that is not essential to the story.

   To decide what information is essential to your narrative, you will need to consider the story's parts, or structure. A story is based on a conflict, a struggle within a person or among two or more people who believe they have different goals. So you will need to include information that establishes the nature of that conflict. You will tell about the actions, statements, and behaviors that explain why the conflict is occurring. Then you will need to tell about the struggle that results from this conflict. What do the people involved do and say and think as they engage in the struggle? Finally, you will need to explain how the struggle turned out. How was the conflict finally resolved? Thinking of your story in terms of these parts will help you select the best details. If you question whether you should provide some piece of information, ask yourself if that information helps develop the conflict, the struggle, or the final outcome. If it does not, you may need to leave that information out.

For some practice in selecting details, look back at the student's brainstorming about quitting smoking (page 184). Put check marks next to details in the following list that seem important if the reader is to understand what happened.

_____ Her struggles on the two days she quit "cold turkey"

_____ The events at the hypnosis session

_____ The clothes the writer was wearing the day she quit smoking

_____ How she dealt with her cravings for cigarettes after quitting

_____ Health problems she has had since quitting smoking

_____ A fender-bender she was involved in on her way to buy the stop-smoking books

_____ A time when she had to take her daughter to the emergency room at the hospital at which the stop-smoking course had been held

You should have checked the first, second, and fourth items in this list. Knowing about the writer's clothing, her unrelated health problems, her car accident, and her daughter's trip to the emergency room is not essential to understanding the story. The other pieces of information, however, are important in helping readers see what happened and why.

EXERCISE 8.2   **Selecting Details for Narratives**

Choose one of the thesis statements you wrote for Exercise 8.1 and then list the major, important events that you would definitely need to include if you developed that statement in a narrative essay.

Organizing Details and Using Transitions

Of all the modes for writing, narratives tend to be among the easiest to organize. As a matter of fact, narratives naturally organize themselves because the events are almost always presented in chronological, or time, order. Of course, writers can move around in time as they tell their stories. In a flashback, for instance, a writer can take readers back to the past for a while before returning to the present to move the story forward again. However, the events in most narrative essays are simply told in the order in which they occurred. Preparing the outline, then, is usually just a matter of listing the important events in order, from beginning to end.

To help the reader understand the time frame of the events, writers include transitional words and phrases. The following list includes common time-related transitions.

first, second, third	next	as
before	soon	when
now	in the beginning	until
then	once	later
after	today	eventually
while	previously	last
finally	often	meanwhile
over time	during	
in the end	in, on, or by (followed by a date)	

In addition, writers include information about the passage of time, usually by using short phrases such as *in a few hours* or *after two weeks* or specific dates. When writing a narrative essay, you will usually begin a new paragraph every time there is a change of scene or a movement forward in time.

Notice how the writer of the following passage uses both time-related transitions and information about how much time has passed to help the reader follow the events in the story.

In the 1930s, my family and I were living under Hitler's[1] regime in Munich, Germany. As Jews, my parents realized that it was essential for us to leave, but no country would give us asylum[2]. **Then** a miracle happened—Italy opened its borders. **It was 1939** when we finally left, each of us taking only one suitcase and 10 marks[3].

1. **Hitler:** a German dictator during World War II who was responsible for the execution of millions of Jews
2. **asylum:** safe haven or sanctuary
3. **marks:** a European monetary unit

We went to Milan. My father, a tailor, and my mother, a seamstress, found jobs. I was 15—old enough to be employed as a maid. My brother, who was 12, was too young to work. Since none of us spoke Italian, we needed a lot of help, even to buy groceries.

We had been in Milan **for one year** when the Italian government (which had formed a full military and political alliance with Germany) began sending foreign Jews to the internment camp[1] Ferramonti in Calabria. The image we have of concentration camps cannot be applied here. We were treated well, had enough food, and could approach the guards freely.

One year later the government began assigning Jewish families to villages throughout Italy. My family was told we were going to Villanova d'Asti. My brother had befriended a boy who had no family in the camp. The boy asked my parents to take him with us, which they did. The townspeople, especially our landlady, made us all feel welcome. My parents found work in their trades; I did the housekeeping.

In the fall of 1943, our landlady, Signora Balbiano, came to inform us that Germans had begun arresting Jews in the south of Italy and suggested that it might be time for us to go into hiding in Zimone, a tiny mountain village in the north. She introduced us to the village priest, who found a barn for us to stay in. The townspeople knew we were living among them, so we were free to come and go and my father was able to continue working as a tailor.

One Sunday the priest told us not to leave the barn because a government search party looking for partisans[2] was on the way. The boy we had brought along did not heed the warning; he sneaked out to the village square to check the time on the church clock tower. **When he saw the soldiers,** he began to run. The men spotted him and followed him back to our barn. We were all arrested and sent to an Italian prison that was under German command. **After two months,** we were deported in cattle cars to Auschwitz[3]. **It took five days** to get there. My mother and I survived together, but that was the last time I saw my father and brother. I do not know what happened to the boy.*

---

1. **internment camp:** place where imprisoned Jews and others were confined during World War II; in general, a place of confinement for a specific group of people

2. **partisans:** followers or supporters
3. **Auschwitz:** one of Hitler's infamous death camps where Jews were executed

*Source: Excerpted from Thea Aschkenase, "It Was the Last Time We Were Together," *Newsweek,* Oct. 23, 2000, p. 11. © Newsweek, Inc. All rights reserved. Reprinted by permission.

EXERCISE 8.3   **Organizing Events in Narratives**

On your own paper, prewrite to generate ideas, and then complete each of the following thesis statements by filling in the blank. Then, on the other blanks provided, prepare an informal outline by listing the major events of the story in the order they occurred.

1. I had never been so proud as I was when _____.

_____

_____

_____

_____

_____

2. _____ was an experience that affected who I am today.

_____

_____

_____

_____

_____

3. I have some regrets about the way I handled _____.

_____

_____

_____

_____

_____

EXERCISE 8.4   **Recognizing Narrative Transitions**

Circle all of the transitions and time-related information in the following passage.

Boy's Love for a Dog a Bit More Than Priceless

I still remember the moment and the choice that had to be made. It was seven years ago, and our youngest son wanted a dog, so we had to decide whether to send one of the other kids to college or use practically the same amount of money to purchase a mutt for Tim.

We went with the dog. Huge mistake.

My instinct was to go to the city pound. Instead, Tim, his two older brothers and an older sister piled into the car, and we drove to a kennel that seemed to be located in an area where it would have been no surprise to see Hannibal Lecter[1] answer the door. The dogs had the same odor old socks and dirty towels do when they have been stuffed into a gym bag and left for days.

Tim headed toward the first puppy he made eye contact with: a 6-week-old chocolate Lab. It cost more than my first house, but the kid was in love.

Naturally, I insisted that they had to promise to take care of the dog—feed it, let it out, let it in—if they expected me to get it for them. Like kids everywhere, they looked me in the eye and lied.

At the time, Tim was a huge fan of Mo Vaughn[2]. So he named the chocolate Lab Mo. When Mo was 8 months old, a couple of things occurred to me: A. I was the one taking care of him, and B. Mo was a moron. He was like so many of these movie stars that appear on Letterman and Leno[3]: clearly stupid but very good-looking.

When Mo was 4, he began to let himself go. He would not stop eating, spent hours begging for people food and [found] people willing to feed him. He became the neighborhood garbage disposal.

He put on a lot of weight and became obese. He stopped running because he was just too heavy. He was only able to get off the floor or the driveway in stages. Are you picking up on a pattern of similarities here between the two Mo's?

Anyway, last week Tim called me at work. He said Mo was crying all the time and would not eat. Would not eat?

It took four of us—three strong young guys and me—to get Mo into the car for the drive to the vet. When we got to the animal hospital, they immediately treated Mo—and us—like human beings: they demanded money up front before they would look at him.

They took his blood pressure and gave him some prednisone, a CAT scan, an ultrasound, an MRI—I am not kidding—and a urine test. They took X-rays of his spine, neck, shoulders, and hips, and they could not agree on a diagnosis. They even suggested we take Mo to a neurologist.

"A neurologist?" I asked.

1. **Hannibal Lecter:** a sinister character from the novel and the film *Silence of the Lambs*
2. **Mo Vaughn:** a famous baseball player known for his large size and batting skills
3. **Letterman and Leno:** two late-night talk-show hosts

"It is just like treating a human," the vet told me.

The hospital even had visiting hours. The first night, Tim made me take him so he could see his dog. When we got home, he made me call the doctor to check his condition.

With the tab running, I figured I could have sent Mo to the Boca Raton Beach Club for the same amount I was spending to save an animal that did not have health insurance.

After 48 hours, the vet had answers: He told us that Mo basically had a doggie-version of attention deficit disorder[1] and that he was anemic[2] and a fat load that had to cut back on food. Or else.

"Or else what?" I wanted to know.

"He will die," I was told.

Mo is almost 8. That is 56 in doggie years. He is dumb, eats a ton, and does nothing other than sleep and drool. The kids are too lazy and self-absorbed to let him out when he barks at midnight. So, with this in mind, I began to wonder how many Big Macs and supersize fries would be required to get the job done, kind of the canine version of death by injection. A few hearty meals of grease-laden people food, and pretty soon I would have a lot of extra time on my hands.

Then something happened. Fate intervened. Like a last-minute call from the governor just as the condemned dog is being walked toward the death chamber, Tim wrote me a note on school composition paper. He put it in an envelope with five single dollar bills he had saved from some birthday.

Here is what he wrote: "Dear Dad. This is to help pay for Mo's hospital stay. Thank you for taking good care of Mo. Love, Tim."

So the dog came home. And he is here to stay because it turns out that Mo is Tim's best friend.*

EXERCISE 8.5   **Writing a Narrative Essay That Includes Transitions**

Choose one of the thesis statements and outlines you prepared in Exercise 8.3. Write the essay, including transitional words that indicate the time frame of the events.

1. **attention deficit disorder:** a disorder commonly affecting children in which they have trouble concentrating for long periods of time

2. **anemic:** suffering from anemia, a blood disorder in which red blood cells are diminished

*Source: Adapted from Mike Barnicle, "Boy's Love for a Dog a Bit More Than Priceless," *New York Daily News,* June 22, 2003, www.nydailynews.com. Reprinted courtesy of the author.

Using Vivid Language

Using vivid and interesting language is important in all types of writing. However, it is especially important in narrative writing, in which your goal is to enable readers to picture people and events in their minds. There are three kinds of vivid language that will help you re-create experiences in words.

Specific Words

You will create more vivid mental images for your reader if you choose specific words over more general ones. For example, the word *dance* is a relatively general term that includes many different kinds of dancing. So to help your reader picture the scene more clearly, substitute a more specific word, such as *waltz* or *moonwalk*. Instead of writing *magazine*, write *Reader's Digest*. Instead of writing *martial art*, write *karate*. And so on. The more precise your word choice, the sharper the picture becomes in the mind's eye of your readers.

Factual and Sensory Details

Like specific words, factual and sensory details will create more vivid mental images for your reader. **Factual details** offer information such as names, quantities, dates, and dimensions (height, length, width, weight). So in describing your own or someone else's actions, you might want to specify when and where these actions take place as well as how long they lasted. **Sensory details** provide information about what something looks, smells, tastes, sounds, or feels like. When you write narratives, include information about the sights, sounds, and other sensations of the scenes you are re-creating in words. Use adjectives, words that describe nouns (for example, *eighty, green, towering,* and *sensitive*), to provide these factual and sensory details.

One special type of factual detail in narratives is dialogue. **Dialogue** is the exact statements of the participants, enclosed in quotation marks. Consider including the exact words spoken by the people in your story because dialogue assists readers in picturing exactly what happened.

Action-Oriented Verbs

In narratives, especially, you will want to use action-packed verbs to describe the events and the participants' behaviors. So, instead of writing *Bob entered the room,* write *Bob strolled into the room,* which provides more of a mental picture of *how* he entered. Also, choose verbs that offer the most precise explanation of what happened. For example, instead of writing that Joe *spoke,* you might want to say that Joe *shouted* or *whispered.* The more specific the verb used, the easier it is for the reader to picture what happened.

Read the following passage and notice how the writer included all three kinds of vivid language to re-create the scene.

We were talking about books, drinking wine, and eating crusty pieces of baguette[1] when in a small, frightened voice Ann Brown suddenly said, "Dick?" And Dick said nothing. I looked across the table at him. His round, kind face was tinged[2] with blue. He was an extremely polite and modest man; probably he had been choking in silence for a minute already. Asthmatic, wheezing noises gurgled out of the back of his throat. His hands were white-knuckled, pressed flat against the table, and he was staring blindly into some deep middle space. His eyes bulged. For about five long seconds we stared at him, unbelieving, as the rattle from the back of his throat grew more savage and his face began to turn from blue to gray. "Dick?" Ann said again, almost shouting. Dick's hands scrabbled at the table edge, knocking over a glass. He stumbled backward, the chair toppling behind him. His gasps were growing deeper, inhuman. The color seeped from his face. And we sat gawking[3], a choir of stunned idiots, still rooted to our chairs.

Finally, a voice in my head spoke. It said that if I did not do something, anything, to help this man, I would never be able to live with myself. Before I knew it, I had slid out from behind the table and was standing behind him. Flashing through my brain were fractured images of all the HOW TO AID A CHOKING VICTIM posters I had seen countless times in restaurants and movie theaters but had never really looked at. I stood trying to put those shreds of knowledge together while Dick, unable to draw breath, began to shudder violently, his arms outstretched as if pinioned[4] to the air.

Desperate now, I shot a glance at Greg, the waiter who legally, like all waiters, was supposed to have HOW TO AID A CHOKING VICTIM memorized. He was standing off to the side, back against the wall, mouth agape[5], an expression of ignorant terror ruining the splendor of his handsome face. No help there.

1. **baguette:** a long French bread
2. **tinged:** slightly colored
3. **gawking:** gaping or staring
4. **pinioned:** bound
5. **agape:** hanging open

Only partially conscious of what I was doing, I put my arms around Dick's chest at the level of his sternum[1]. I made a fist with my right hand and capped it with my left and without pausing drove my fist at a slight upward angle into the soft area above his rib cage. He heaved and bent over, but otherwise his suffering did not abate[2]. The terrible, scorched sounds continued from the back of his throat, and the side of his face that I could see out of the corner of my eye was as gray as stone. Worse, I found myself looking over his shoulder at Ann Brown. The look of horror on her face was one of the most painful things I had ever witnessed. I was failing. Dick Brown was going to die, in my arms, in front of his wife.

It was after I had just jackhammered my fist into his chest for the fourth time (I was wired enough to lift a VW) that Dick was finally able to draw breath enough to cry out, half-distinctly, *"Please . . . stop . . . doing . . . that!"*

I released him at once. Apparently, I had been on the verge of breaking his ribs. Dick fell to his knees and was briefly sick. Once he had recovered, it was Ann who told me that my very first try had sent a large crust of bread shooting out of Dick's windpipe and onto the floor. The whole event had happened so quickly, she had been too shocked to say anything.

A little while later, we were gathered around the table again, as though nothing had happened. Except that when the food arrived, brought by a sheepish[3] and silent Greg, nobody touched it. We were like survivors in a lifeboat, afflicted with an overwhelming thirst. Ann Brown stared at her husband as if, any minute, he might disappear. Every so often she would turn to me, shake her head, and murmur, "You just saved my husband's life." Then she would fall to staring at him again.*

Were you able to picture this scene in your mind as you were reading? It is the author's use of vivid language that allows you to do that. He uses specific words, like *baguette* instead of just *bread*. He includes factual details, such as exactly how he performed the Heimlich maneuver. He includes sensory details, such as the colors of Dick's face and the descriptions of the sounds the choking man made. He includes dialogue, telling us what Ann and Dick said. And he includes action verbs like *stumbled, seeped, heaved,* and *jackhammered.*

---

1. sternum: breastbone

2. abate: decrease; end

3. sheepish: ashamed; shamefaced

Source: Adapted from John Burnham Schwartz, "On the Road," *Travel and Leisure,* April 2004, pp. 94–95. John Burnham Schwartz is the author of the novels *Bicycle Days, Reservation Road,* and *Claire Marvel. Reservation Road* is currently being made into a feature film, based on his screenplay.

EXERCISE 8.6 — Writing with Vivid Language

Rewrite each of the following sentences to substitute more specific words, add factual and sensory details, and use more action-oriented verbs.

1. An individual entered the building.

2. The job was very difficult.

3. The machine malfunctioned.

4. The woman's facial expression changed.

5. The people at the scene were suddenly overcome with emotion.

6. The animal was frightening.

7. Everyone at the event was having a good time.

8. The weather was not pleasant.

9. The young man looked as though he had been in a fight.

10. It was very hot outside.

EXERCISE 8.7 — Telling a Story with Vivid Language

Write a story about an experience in which a certain emotion (such as anger, jealousy, or sorrow) was dominant. Include all three kinds of vivid language to bring your story to life for the reader.

EXERCISE 8.8   **Describing a Photograph Using Vivid Language**

Use vivid language to describe what is happening in the following photograph.

Source: Baerbel/Schmidt/Getty Images

Using Figurative Language

Figurative language, or figures of speech, makes interesting, often clever comparisons between two unlike things in order to help the reader form a clear mental image of or better understand the thing being described. **Metaphors** are direct comparisons in which one thing is called another.

The moon was *a bright lamp* in the night sky.

Similes are indirect comparisons that use the word *like* or *as*.

A wealthy but unhappy woman, she was *like a bird imprisoned in a gilded cage.*

Personification describes an inanimate object or nonhuman by giving it human characteristics.

The wind *whistled* through the trees.
The tea kettle *shrieked* on the stove.

Try to come up with a few original comparisons to add to your own writing. They will add clarity and a spark of creativity to your descriptions. However, avoid clichés, overused and tired expressions such as "hungry as a bear," "sweet as sugar," and "happy as a clam."

Notice how in the previous story about saving a choking victim, the author calls the people at the table "a choir of stunned idiots" (a metaphor) and then later, after the crisis has passed, writes that they were "like survivors in a lifeboat, afflicted with overwhelming thirst" (a simile).

> ### EXERCISE 8.9   Recognizing Figurative Language

Underline the figurative language in the following passage. In the margin beside each underlined phrase, indicate the type of figurative language by writing the word METAPHOR, SIMILE, or PERSONIFICATION.

Mom Is Ready for Her Baby to Grow Up (Isn't She?)

From the kitchen window, in the slanted amber light of late afternoon, I see my baby working hard at what he loves best. First, he hurls a tennis ball against the backyard wall, then flings his body this way and that to catch the flying gold as it bounces back. On and on, one pirouette[1] after another, this ballet continues as I peel potatoes and quarter them for dinner.

Later he hauls out a tee and begins to swing his aluminum bat, aiming for deep left field and the adulation[2] of imaginary fans in the bleachers. While doing this, he talks to himself, a monologue of encouragement and instruction. At 7, my youngest loves baseball so much he is willing to eat clay, literally: to slide head first, to pounce on line drives, to run hard and backward for a high fly swallowed momentarily by the sun or the lights. When he does this, he reminds me of his father, the man who died when he was a baby, the man he cannot remember except for the photographs scattered about the house like markers to point him in the right direction. Then I cannot help but think: Nick would do him proud.

Nick doesn't worry about any of this, of course. He smiles at everybody as if the whole world loved him, and his jack-o-lantern grin brings to mind that Debbie Boone ballad of many moons ago, "You Light Up My Life." Indeed, that smile burns like a bonfire.

As I see him swinging off the tee, or skating and scootering around the block, I recognize a lump in my throat. Not only is he growing up, but I also am growing older. I know it will not be long before he asks me for the car keys. And after that, our life together will be a blur of events leading in one direction: away, away.

---

1. pirouette: a type of turn in ballet   **2. adulation:** excessive admiration

The water for the potatoes is leaping and licking the sides of the pot, but I pass through the sliding-glass door that divides my domain from his. Fearing I am calling him in, he makes a face until I wave him away.

"Play," I insist. "Play as much as you can before it gets dark."

And he does, as the wind picks up and I get a good, last, pungent[1] whiff[2] of little-boy sweat.*

EXERCISE 8.10   **Recognizing the Features of a Narrative Essay**

Read the following narrative essay and then answer the questions that follow by writing your responses on the blanks provided.

Aspirin for a Severed Head

I have been divorced two years this Thanksgiving.

I did not believe I would ever get over my divorce, which could not have been more painful, squalid[3], or banal[4]. We had just had a baby—not to save the marriage, I might add, but for the usual joyous, traditional, and misguided reasons.

I did not know the marriage needed saving. This shows my general naivete[5], something that divorce cures one of forever.

I became a single mother overnight, which is nothing like becoming famous overnight: I believe it is the emotional equivalent of having a stroke. While my estranged[6] spouse recuperated at the requisite[7] tropical island where frothy drinks are served with miniature parasols, I was left holding the diaper bag.

The timing could not have been worse, as I was left to raise our beautiful son at a time when eating or grooming seemed difficult and perhaps unnecessary. (Other activities, such as swan-diving off the roof, or driving my car into a cement piling, seemed easy and sensible.) I wanted to die. Unlike my spouse, I did not want Club Med[8]. I wanted Club Dead. Life as I knew it was over, my bills were doubled, and my fear and loneliness and sense of complete failure rose like bone dust into the night air.

During the first few weeks, my mother came to stay with me, positioned on the Pottery Barn Chair-and-a-Half[9], a kind of angelic sentinel[10] in sweat clothes.

1. **pungent:** sharp; biting
2. **whiff:** scent or hint of aroma
3. **squalid:** dirty or foul
4. **banal:** commonplace
5. **naivete:** innocence
6. **estranged:** separated from
7. **requisite:** required

8. **Club Med:** a chain of resorts in warm climates
9. **Pottery Barn Chair-and-a-Half:** a large chair sold by Pottery Barn, a housewares company
10. **sentinel:** lookout; guard

*Source: Adapted from Ana Veciana-Suarez, "Mom Is Ready for Her Baby to Grow Up (Isn't She?)," *Miami Herald,* April 8, 2001, www.miami.com. Copyright 2001 by *Miami Herald*. Reproduced with permission of *Miami Herald* in the format Textbook via Copyright Clearance Center.

She drank Diet Coke, and she listened, telling me stories from her own divorce. She had survived.

Of course, I did not die. Instead, I focused on my extraordinary son and drank chardonnay[1] every night. From the couch, which had become my battle station, I ordered a barrage[2] of mail-order items. I felt like crap every day.

I asked my mother, "How long?"

"Two years," she said. My brain did not accept this as viable information. Yes, my mother had been left at thirty-six with two kids, but that was in the '70s. I announced I could not last that long, that even next month was pushing it. She said, "Oh. Well. Everyone's different, honey."

I walked around my small town with a thought bubble over my head: Person Going Through a Divorce. When I looked at other people, I automatically formed thought bubbles over their heads. Happy Couple with Stroller. Innocent Teenage Girl with Her Whole Life Ahead of Her. Content Grandmother and Grandfather Visiting Town Where Their Grandchildren Live with Intact Parents. Secure Housewife with Big Diamond. Undamaged Group of Young Men on Skateboards. Good Man with Baby Who Loves His Wife. Dogs Who Never Have to Worry. Then every so often I would see one like me, one of the shambling, sad women without makeup, looking older than she is: Divorced Woman Wondering How This Happened.

I remember thinking, This just cannot last. Sooner or later my life is going to have to come back from the cleaners. I waited. I was not patient, but I waited. If there had been someone in a position of authority to upbraid[3] for this, I would have. I would have upbraided most severely.

I asked my divorced friends, "How long?"

"Two years," they said.

No no no no no, I thought. This is the new millennium, after all, and I felt certain things could be moved along if only the right therapists or books or audiotapes or workshops or aromatherapy could be found. I was open to seminars, Deepak Chopra, Marianne Williamson, Persian Sufis, and Doctor Phil[4]. I was as open as one can be without coming apart entirely. I was the village idiot of self-help.

I got all the books. *Spiritual Divorce, How to Rebuild When a Relationship Ends, Dumped, Crazy Time,* and even something called *The Good Divorce,* which at the time struck me as the Good Holocaust[5].

1. **chardonnay:** a type of white wine
2. **barrage:** bombardment
3. **upbraid:** scold; tell off
4. **Deepak Chopra, Marianne Williamson, Persian Sufis, and Doctor Phil:** self-help experts who give advice on how people can better their lives
5. **Holocaust:** the term used for the time during World War II when millions of Jews were confined and executed under Hitler's regime

Luckily, I had a good therapist. One with the ability to dispense Xanax[1].

My therapist said, "People tell you to get over it, but they do not tell you how." His insight that there is no magic bullet that will erase the pain and propel one into spanking-new shiny lives, free of lingering trauma, fear, and humiliation, was one I could certainly relate to. I felt relieved. I was not doing it wrong.

Time passed slowly, as when one is waiting for aspirin to work on one's severed head.

I got through the first Christmas. The first Valentine's Day. The first wedding anniversary. The first divorce anniversary. The pain slowly eased up; the psychic damage was beginning, if not to disappear, then to taper. I stopped wishing him dead, and started wishing him rich so he could send us more money. This did not happen.

And then, just as my mother said it would happen, one day I walked down the street with my son and realized I felt happy. Out of the woods.

When people say it takes two years, believe them. Statistically speaking, this is the point in time when one has gotten through it. There is some truth to this—also some rather flamboyant[2] falsehoods, especially when you have a child running around wearing his face and yours, entwined forever: You have done this; it cannot be undone. You will always have children together; they will almost certainly outlive the marriage in terms of years. It is beautiful and hard all at once. It is marriage and its Siamese twin[3], divorce. Divorce, which apparently has become the antidote to marriage, although the jury is decidedly out. In the end, it is just life.

Still, I easily relate to what Karen Karbo wrote in *Generation Ex*, "There is no statute of limitations[4] on wanting to strangle your ex." I would add that no such statute exists on feelings of affection, anger, and even love. You learn that you can love someone and be divorced from them at the same time, in the same way that you loved them before you were married—except now you know they are capable of ripping your heart out. This changes things considerably. It gives you what time gives you: perspective.

After a couple of years, you can appreciate your ex for who he is and realize that he is separate and distinct from you. You can feel a certain amount of warmth for him, as you do your alma mater[5], or your car. You can love a car, but you do not attach yourself to the car. You do not buy little gifts for the car, thinking you can win the car over. You do not lose sleep over whether the car thinks you are attractive or if the car is thinking of you too, right now. You do not especially care whether someone else drives the car.

---

1. **Xanax:** an antianxiety medication
2. **flamboyant:** showy; colorful
3. **Siamese twin:** a person born physically joined to his or her twin
4. **statute of limitations:** law limiting the time for legal action
5. **alma mater:** the institution from which someone graduated

Kierkegaard muses in *Love and Marriage,* "We read in fairy tales about human beings whom mermaids and mermen[1] enticed into their power by means of demonic music. In order to break the enchantment it was necessary in the fairy tale for the person who was under the spell to play the same piece of music backwards without making a single mistake. This is very profound, but very difficult to perform, and yet so it is: the errors one has taken into oneself one must eradicate[2] in this way, and every time one makes a mistake one must begin all over."

Right.

Or you can wait two years.*

1. Write, in your own words, the main idea of this essay.

_____

_____

2. What are the main events of this story?

_____

_____

_____

_____

_____

3. Describe the struggle and conflict of this story.

_____

_____

4. How was the conflict finally resolved?

_____

5. Which part of this story is especially easy for you to picture in your mind? Give examples of the vivid language (specific words, factual and sensory details, and action-oriented verbs) that the writer uses to narrate that part of the story.

_____

1. **mermen:** male versions of mermaids,   2. **eradicate:** wipe out
   underwater creatures of legend

*Source: Adapted from Suzanne Finnamore, "Aspirin for a Severed Head," in Jennifer Foote Sweeney, ed., *Life as We Know It: A Collection of Personal Essays from Salon.com,* New York: Washington Square Press, 2003, pp. 218–223. This article first appeared in *Salon.com,* at http://www.salon.com. An online version remains in the *Salon* archives. Reprinted with permission.

In Summary: Steps in Writing Narrative Essays

1. Prewrite to generate ideas and determine a main idea.
2. Select relevant details, including only events and information that are essential to understanding the main idea, and create an outline of the major events in chronological order.
3. As you write, include time-related transitional words and information. Also, use vivid language, including specific words, factual and sensory details, and action-oriented verbs. Try to include vivid language, too, to help the reader form a clear mental image of or better understand the thing being described.

CHAPTER 8 REVIEW

To review the main points in this chapter, write a brief response to each of the following questions.

1. What is a narrative?

2. What are the steps in writing an effective narrative?

3. What are three things that you should consider when thinking about what information is essential to your narrative?

4. Why do narratives naturally suggest a pattern of organization?

5. What is a flashback, and how can it be used in a story?

6. What should you do when preparing an outline for a narrative?

7. What are transitional phrases, and what purpose do they serve? List three examples of a transitional word or phrase.

8. What is the purpose of vivid language? What are three kinds of vivid language? Define each.

9. What is the purpose of figurative language?

10. Define the term *metaphor.*

11. Define the term *simile.*

12. What is *personification?*

Topic Ideas for Narrative Essays

Exercise 8.1 includes topic ideas you may want to develop into narrative essays. Here are some additional ideas.

- A historical event that fascinates you
- An important first day (of work, school, camp, and so on)
- An amazing or extraordinary event you witnessed or experienced
- An important learning experience
- A brush with death
- A childhood memory
- An amazing but true story
- An inspiring story
- The rituals or customs of a particular holiday
- A memorable celebration
- An accident, like the 1996 incident involving a three-year-old boy who fell eighteen feet into the primate exhibit at the Brookfield Zoo, near Chicago (see the following photograph)

Source: © Robert Allisson/Contact Press Images

For more on narrative essays, visit the Guide to Grammar and Writing Web site at **http://grammar.ccc.commnet.edu/grammar/composition/narrative.htm**. Read the information about narrative compositions and then answer the questions in the "Points to Ponder" box.

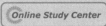 For more information and exercises, go to the Online Study Center at **http://www.college.hmco.com/pic/ dolphinwriterthree**.

Description

GOALS FOR CHAPTER 9

▶ Define the term *description*.

▶ Describe the steps in writing a descriptive essay.

▶ Write a descriptive essay.

▶ Recognize the dominant impression, details, organization pattern, and figurative language in a longer description.

▶ Recognize the features of a narrative/descriptive essay.

In Chapter 8, you examined the narrative as a method of developing an idea. In this chapter, you will focus on **description,** which provides details about what something or someone looks like, sounds like, smells like, and so on. Description is often used along with narration, for telling a story usually requires that you give some information about a scene or the people in it. However, description can also be a mode of development of its own. For example, read the following description of a beach in Puerto Rico.

> For generations, Puerto Rican families have made Sunday pilgrimages[1] from across the island to Luquillo Beach on a sweeping half-moon bay. The clans barbecue on the beach, frolic in the surf, and, when the day is done, stop by the kiosks[2] lining Road 3 to pick up a selection of traditional snacks for the ride home.

---

1. **pilgrimages:** journeys, often of a religious type

2. **kiosks:** booths or stalls

205

On weekends, it is like the Fourth of July. People park cars helter-skelter[1] along the highway, music blares from portable radios, and often there are concerts or festivals that seem to attract most of the island's 3.8 million residents.

But the beach remains beautiful, its white sands among the most photographed in the Caribbean. A coral reef outside the bay dissipates[2] the ocean waves, leaving only gentle waters—perfect for swimming—lapping at the shore.

And the numbered kiosks here—60 of them in all—still serve my favorite no-concessions[3]-to-cholesterol foods, as well as absolutely killer drinks. Try kiosk #42, also known as El Guayu Guaya del Zombie. Alberto Rivera, a.k.a. the Zombie, is usually there himself, serving coconut drinks in the shell. Or drop by #54 for the delicious *arepa de pulpo,* a crispy roll stuffed with vinegary octopus.*

This passage describes Luquillo Beach, providing information about what the place looks like, sounds like, and even tastes like, so that readers can form a mental image of it.

Writing a Descriptive Essay

Sometimes, you will need to develop a thesis statement by describing someone or something. When you describe, you provide factual and sensory details that help readers form a mental image of your subject. To write an effective description, you will need to include the essential features that are illustrated in the next sections.

Prewriting

Although you can use any of the prewriting methods described in Chapter 3 of this text to generate ideas for description, clustering is especially useful. Re-creating a person, place, or thing in words for your readers will require you to provide details related to all five senses, so you might want to add a group of

---

1. **helter-skelter:** in a chaotic disorganized manner
2. **dissipates:** dissolves
3. **concessions:** allowances; special considerations

Source: Adapted from Natalia de Cuba Romero, "Puerto Rico, Beach by Beach," *Caribbean Travel and Life,* December 2002, p. 97.

details for each sense to your cluster. For example, if you were going to describe an evening at the county fair, your cluster might look like this:

Determining a Main Idea and Writing a Thesis Statement

The first step in writing an effective descriptive essay involves deciding on the point you want to make about the subject you are describing. This point offers a **dominant impression,** an essential quality that you want to convey about your subject. Sometimes, you will know before you begin writing what your dominant impression will be. For example, if you are assigned to write about a place that is peaceful to you, then "peaceful" is your dominant impression, and you would select a subject that fits this impression. However, if you are assigned to write about your favorite room in your home, then you may not know what your dominant impression is until you generate some details.

For example, here is one student's list of details:

scent of baking cookies
dirty dishes piled high in the sink
round table ringed with chairs
books and magazines stacked on table
refrigerator covered with photographs
smell of brewed coffee
potted plants in the windowsill
warm from heat of oven
fruit in a basket
talk show on TV

When you consider this list of details, what one impression do most of them convey to you? Would you say this room seems to be comfortable? Cozy? Cluttered? Inviting? Certain details in the list match each of these characterizations. If the student were to write a thesis statement for an essay about this room, she might write something like this:

My kitchen, my favorite room in my house, is a cozy and inviting place.

Almost all of the details in this particular example would convey that impression. However, be aware that other lists of details might suggest more than just one dominant impression. Think for a moment about what you would see, hear, smell, taste, and feel as you were sitting in a mall. Your list of details would be long, and it would probably include everything from the sound of music playing to the smell of coffee, pizza, and burgers in the food court to the cool feeling of the air conditioning on your skin. Different writers might choose to convey different dominant impressions about this scene. One writer might find the subject to be a vibrant and exciting place, another writer might describe it as warm and cozy, and a third could consider it noisy and annoying. In your essay, the thesis statement should clearly indicate the dominant impression that you will convey.

As you complete this step in the process, remember what you learned in Chapter 4 about thesis statements. Specifically, a thesis statement includes both your topic (the person or thing being described) and the point you want to make about that topic.

EXERCISE 9.1   **Writing Thesis Statements for Descriptive Essays**

For each of the following topics, use some prewriting techniques to generate ideas for your own paper, and then write a thesis statement that you could use for a descriptive essay.

1. My favorite celebrity

Thesis statement: _____

2. My favorite place to relax

Thesis statement: _____

3. A site with historical significance

Thesis statement: _____

4. A delicious meal

Thesis statement: _____

5. A special or meaningful object

Thesis statement: _____

Selecting the Right Details for a Description

The next step in writing an interesting descriptive essay is selecting the right details to include. You cannot include every detail about your subject because your essay would be too long and too tedious to read, and your point would get lost in irrelevant information. Therefore, you will have to examine your prewriting and decide which pieces of information will convey your dominant impression. Circle every detail that supports the idea in your thesis statement, and ignore the other details.

For some practice in selecting details, think back to the previous example about describing a mall. On the blank next to each of the following details, write an **L** if you think that detail suggests "lively and exciting," a **W** if the detail suggests "warm and cozy," and an **N** if the detail suggests "noisy and annoying." Some details might warrant more than one label.

_____ scent of coffee brewing

_____ smell of pizzas and hamburgers

_____ large group of teenagers talking and laughing loudly

_____ kiosk vendors hawking their wares

_____ sound of water in a courtyard fountain

_____ sounds of thumping pop music inside clothing stores

_____ sound of baby crying

_____ store display windows with trendy new fashions

_____ people walking and talking on cell phones

_____ couples strolling hand in hand

Did you label the details in this list *W, W, L/N, L/N, W, L/N, N, L, L/N,* and *W*? This is how you would go about deciding which details match your dominant impression.

EXERCISE 9.2   **Selecting Details for Descriptive Essays**

Choose one of the thesis statements you wrote for Exercise 9.1; then, on your own paper, list the details that you would definitely need to include if you developed that statement in a descriptive essay.

Organizing Details and Using Transitions

Once you have circled all of the appropriate details in your prewriting, you next need to decide how to organize these details. Descriptions require some type of spatial organization. In other words, this organizational pattern orients the specific details for the reader by explaining how those details relate to one another in space. Some common spatial patterns for arranging details are

front to back (or vice versa)
left to right (or vice versa)
top to bottom (or vice versa)
inside to outside (or vice versa)
near to far (or vice versa)

Descriptive details can also be arranged using a narrative pattern. For example, if you are describing a parade that passed before you, you could describe each element of the parade in chronological order.

The best pattern is often dictated by the subject itself. For example, if you are describing a house, you might use an outside-to-inside pattern. If you are describing a landscape, however, it would be more appropriate to use a near-to-far or left-to-right pattern. Once you have selected a pattern, list your details in that order in your outline. Follow your outline as you write to avoid jumping around. Particularly in descriptions, readers must understand the details' arrangement in order to create a mental picture.

As you write descriptions, use transitional words that help your reader understand how the details are related. The following list includes common spatial transitional words.

above	to the left, to the right	overhead
below	nearby	underneath
under	in the distance	between
inside	on top	among
outside	at the bottom	across
toward	in the center	next to
away	close by	far away
in front	in back	up
down		

Usually, you will begin a new paragraph each time you switch to another major part or area of your description.

Notice in the following passage how the spatial transitional words and information, which are boldfaced, help you organize the details in your mind and form a mental picture of the subject.

The new National World War II memorial **on the Mall in Washington** is set **between the Lincoln Memorial and the Washington Monument.** It has two semicircles of pillars, each representing a state or a territory, arrayed[1] **on either side of two forty-three-foot-tall arched entry pavilions** symbolizing the European and Pacific theatres of the war. There is a formal entrance **on the Seventeenth Street side, directly in line with the Lincoln Memorial,** but most people enter through one of the pavilions, walking **under a ten-foot-wide bronze laurel wreath suspended from a bronze ribbon held in the beaks of bronze eagles set atop columns.**

From there, one descends a gentle, curving ramp to the level of the Rainbow Pool and the granite plaza. The pool is the focal point not only because it is huge and occupies **the center of the plaza** but also because its newly restored fountains give the memorial much of its visual energy.

1. **arrayed:** arranged; collected

Freedom Wall, **on the west side of the plaza,** contains more than four thousand gold stars, each representing a hundred war dead. The words *HERE WE MARK THE PRICE OF FREEDOM* are engraved in a **low stone panel** in **front of the wall,** but the dead are not identified by name. (*Source:* Adapted from Paul Goldberger, "Down at the Mall," *The New Yorker,* May 31, 2004, pp. 82–84)

EXERCISE 9.3   **Organizing Details in Descriptive Essays**

On your own paper, prewrite to generate ideas and then complete each of the following thesis statements by filling in the blank. Then, on the other blanks provided, prepare an informal outline by listing the major details in an appropriate type of spatial order.

1. An object that is special and meaningful to me is my _____.

_____

_____

_____

_____

_____

2. _____ is a unique person whom I know.

_____

_____

_____

_____

_____

3. _____ is my favorite place to relax.

_____

_____

_____

_____

_____

EXERCISE 9.4   **Recognizing Spatial Transitions**

Circle all of the transitional words and space-related information in the following passage.

German artist Emanuel Leutze's famous oil-on-canvas painting *Washington Crossing the Delaware* (1851) is a symbolic and romanticized commemoration[1] of George Washington's crossing of the Delaware River in 1776 during the American Revolutionary War.

In the center, Washington himself, striking a dramatic pose, is the painting's focal point. He stands near the front of the small boat, his head emphasized by the unnaturally bright sky above him, his face turned toward the rising sun. Right behind Washington are two figures supporting the American flag, the design of which actually did not exist at the time of this event.

Washington and the flag seem to radiate light, but the scene beneath them is in darker tones, with red highlights repeated throughout the painting. The thirteen people around Washington represent a cross section of the American colonies, including a man in a Scottish bonnet and a man of African descent facing backward [and standing] next to each other in the front, western riflemen at the bow and stern, two farmers in broad-brimmed hats near the back (one with bandaged head), and an androgynous[2] rower in a red shirt, possibly meant to be a woman in man's clothing. Surrounding the boat is a wide river filled with chunks of ice to emphasize the difficulty of the crossing. (*Source:* Adapted from "Washington Crossing the Delaware," Wikipedia, http://en.wikipedia.org/wiki/Washington_Crossing_the_Delaware)

© Bettmann/CORBIS

1. **commemoration:** celebration; memorial   2. **androgynous:** neither male nor female

EXERCISE 9.5   **Writing a Descriptive Essay That Includes Transitions**

Choose one of the thesis statements and outlines you prepared in Exercise 9.3. Write the essay, including transitional words that indicate how the details are arranged in space.

Using Vivid and Figurative Language

On pages 192–201 of Chapter 8, you learned how to include vivid language (specific words, factual and sensory details, and action-oriented verbs) and figurative language (metaphors, similes, and personification) in your writing. Just as these types of language help readers of narratives form clear mental images, they also bring descriptive essays to life. Notice how the following descriptive passage uses all of these kinds of vivid and figurative language.

Revenge Has Deep Roots

When I went out to get my newspaper from my lawn the other morning, I felt the skin pebble along my spine. Hairs rose on my arms like ghostly filaments[1]. I knew something was wrong with the picture.

With a cold pinch in the gray October dawn, I noticed that all the trees on my Queens street were ablaze in the riotous red, orange, and brown colors of fall. Up and down the street, fulvous[2] leaves crinkled on the other yellowing lawns and clattered at the curbs in a swirling celebration of the season of the witch.

A gust of wind blew. Leaves showered like gold doubloons[3] from every tree on my quiet block.

Except mine.

As Halloween crept upon us like an ebony cat at midnight, The Tree that I have been at war with since I first moved into my house six years ago was still a lush and verdant[4] green. I hefted my newspaper, sagging with dark news of war, mass executions, beheadings, and a divisive election too close to call, and stared up into The Tree. It shook its full mop of green leaves like a rock star in a heavy-metal conniption[5].

The wind blew again, like a gale of hideous laughter.

I glared at The Tree's roots, which were bursting through the sidewalk like a fat man splitting a pair of cheap sneakers. I gazed up at its tough coarse bark

1. **filaments:** fine threads or wires
2. **fulvous:** dull yellow
3. **doubloons:** gold coins formerly used in Spain and Spanish America
4. **verdant:** lush, green
5. **conniption:** hysterical fit caused by extreme excitement or anger

and into its thriving mass, sparkling with photosynthesis. It outthrust its thick, proud trunk, flexed its twisty limbs, branches clawing and flaunting its veiny green leaves.

I got the message. I knew the score. I had seen this bullying arrogance before. What The Tree was really doing was telling me that although I had plotted last year to have it uprooted or cut down, all The City would do was prune it, and so now it was payback time. Now with a nurturing spring and rainy summer swelling its rootball, it was back!

Back from the half-dead.

The Tree was ready for a Halloween dress rehearsal of what it had planned for me this long, cold, and blood-curdling winter.

Over the years, The Tree had awakened me with its icy fingers tapping on my midnight windows. It sent clouds of pollen to whip me into allergic seizures, served as a gangplank[1] for clan reunions of squirrels that held Thanksgiving banquets in my attic walls. In summer, The Tree hung with swollen hives of killer wasps that forced me out of my yard and into the house.

The Tree served as bombardier[2] school for every local bird that used my car for target practice. Once, it sent a 20-foot, 200-pound section of limb crashing to my lawn, like an omen marking the spot where I should plant my FOR SALE sign.

I am convinced that The Tree has been planning revenge on me for my life as a writer, for adding to the felling of endless cousin trees that hold the ink of my 30-year stream of words on paper. I believe that when I called the bureaucracy[3] to ask to have The Tree cut down, The Tree intercepted my calls that traveled through the telephone wires that stretched through its branches.

The Tree knows when I am home, when I sleep, when I rise. Sees when I leave. It listens and watches and conspires. The Tree knows when I am watching a once-in-a-lifetime sporting event and gets even by disrupting my cable service.

Once when my fax line ceased working, Verizon sent a repairman who discovered that a squirrel had chewed through the cable. A squirrel on a mission from The Tree.

When a local politician helped get the Parks Department to prune The Tree last year, I felt a slight pang of victor's sorrow. After a long battle, you sometimes acquire a begrudging[4] respect for your adversary[5]. As the tree pruner's saw buzzed, biting deep into The Tree's tough limbs, I watched the nestling birds explode to flight, wasps scatter to the winds, and squirrels scamper to other trees.

I was left with a defeated enemy standing like a war memorial at my curb.

Still, I thought little of The Tree over the last year. But then last week the squirrels returned to my attic. The birds again turned mine into the only polka-dot car in the neighborhood.

---

1. **gangplank:** walkway, usually from a boat
2. **bombardier:** someone who releases bombs
3. **bureaucracy:** system of government
4. **begrudging:** without generosity; unwilling
5. **adversary:** opponent or challenger

And then as I stood on the lawn last week, I realized it was so healthy, so far back from the dead that it was the only tree on the block that had not yet begun to shed its leaves in the dying season.

The Tree is now a member of the undead, a tree of the living dead, and I tremble at what ghoulish tricks and hellish treats it has in store for me this year, starting with Halloween. . . .*

Notice how the author includes all three kinds of figurative language. For example, he uses metaphors such as "the tree is now a member of the undead." He includes similes such as "Halloween crept upon us like an ebony cat at midnight" and "It shook its full mop of green leaves like a rock star in a heavy-metal conniption." And he personifies The Tree in many ways, giving it the ability to bully, plan revenge, listen to phone calls, get even, and plan to play tricks.

 **EXERCISE 9.6**   **Writing with Vivid Language**

Write an essay about a person, place, or thing you know well. As you describe this person, place, or thing, try to incorporate the three different types of vivid language and at least one example of each kind of figurative language.

EXERCISE 9.7   **Describing a Photograph Using Vivid Language**

Use vivid language to describe the scene in the following photograph.

Source: Digital Vision/Getty Images

Source: Denis Hamill, "Revenge Has Deep Roots," *New York Daily News,* October 21, 2004, p. 7. *New York Daily News,* L.P. Reprinted with permission.

EXERCISE 9.8   **Recognizing the Features of a Descriptive Essay**

Read the following essay. Then answer the questions that follow by writing your responses on the blanks provided.

A Ride Aboard the Ferrocarril Mexicano Railway

The locomotive's diesel engine growls as we climb higher into the Sierra Madre Mountains, deep in Central Mexico. Clinging precariously[1] to steep canyon rims, it leads a line of railcars on a fantastic journey through tight mountain passes and narrow tunnels, chugging ever forward toward Los Mochis on the country's West Coast.

Not wishing to miss a bit of the majestic beauty outside the train windows, I stand in the gangway between the cars and lean out the open portal. Letting the wind sweep through my hair, I drink in the sights and sounds of the Ferrocarril Mexicano Railway train ride.

Warm afternoon light flows across the mountain tops, painting the distant mountains shades of pink, purple, and misty blue. Waterfalls cascade from steep mountain sides. People wave from colorful settlements nestled in isolated valleys. A river rages through the ravine.

"This is like being at an IMAX movie[2], only it is real," declares Syma Waxman, a lung transplant nurse from St. Louis.

The trip from Chihuahua City southwest to Los Mochis has been labeled one of the most spectacular train rides in all the world. Originally conceived by American investor Albert Kinsey Owen, and named Chihuahua al Pacifico, the railway took more than 90 years to complete. It now stands as one of the world's finest engineering marvels with 39 major bridges and 86 tunnels. Crossing the Mexican states of Chihuahua and Sinaloa, it travels through terrain otherwise accessible only on foot or by burro[3].

Traveling nonstop, the 420-mile trip takes only 13 hours. That's *mas o menos,* of course (which means "more or less" and sums up the Mexican attitude toward time). But we, looking for adventure, elect to stop along the way, staying with families, hiking into the countryside, and exploring the local culture. By doing so, we get an up-close view of a land richly blessed with natural beauty, much of it, as yet, unspoiled by man.

Undoubtedly, one of the highlights of the trip is the Barrancas del Cobre—the Copper Canyon. When the train skids to a halt in Divisadero, we disembark to find a view of the canyon that spans the entire horizon. A labyrinth[4] of more than 200 gorges, the Copper Canyon covers 25,000 square miles and is four times the size of the Grand Canyon.

---

1. **precariously:** shakily; unstable
2. **IMAX movie:** movie shown in a large, surround-sound theatre
3. **burro:** donkey
4. **labyrinth:** maze

It is here that we encounter the indigenous[1] Tarahumara Indians, a shy people with mahogany skin and deep black eyes, who are fabled for their running ability. While staying at nearby Areponapuchi, our host Armando Diaz walks with us around the canyon rim. We meet the Indians in their homes and watch them make adobe[2] bricks and handicrafts.

Another favorite stop is Cerocahui, a picturesque[3] mountain town near Urique Canyon. When the sun sets, the night grows black as tar. I walk to a nearby field and watch stars bloom in the night sky.

While I enjoy the scenery, my most indelible[4] memories are of the people. I melt when a young hustler who carries my bags admits he'd like to be *el presidente* someday. And there is Armando Diaz, who in his younger days descended into the canyon and emerged leading burros carrying silver—every day. I will never forget Miguel, a handsome sailor in the Mexican Navy who stated with a knowing smile, "The money is better in the U.S., but life is better in Mexico."

Near the end of our trip, I again stand by the gangway breathing the mountain air. Approaching the town of Creel, we round a curve, and I spy two boys no older than 7 sitting on a rock. Instead of waving, the snaggle-toothed[5] youngster on the left whistles to me. Without hesitation, I blow the boys a kiss. They collapse in giggles, their laughter a mere reflection of the joy I feel at having passed this way.*

1. What is the dominant impression conveyed by this description?

_____

_____

2. How does the author organize the details of her description?

_____

_____

_____

3. What part of the author's description was particularly vivid for you? How did the author use factual and sensory details to paint the scene?

_____

1. **indigenous:** native or original to an area
2. **adobe:** earthen brick; building made of adobe
3. **picturesque:** scenic; pretty
4. **indelible:** impossible to remove
5. **snaggle-toothed:** without all of one's teeth; missing teeth

*Source: Cassandra M. Vanhooser, "Adventure," *Southern Living,* September 2001, pp. 46, 48. © *Southern Living.* Reprinted by permission.

4. Find an example of figurative language used in the essay and write it on the blank.

_____

_____

_____

The Narrative/Descriptive Essay

Narrative essays, which you learned about in Chapter 8, often include descriptive details about the people, places, and things involved in a story. Likewise, the details in descriptive essays may be organized chronologically, as they are in the essay "Revenge Has Deep Roots" on pages 214–216. A descriptive essay may also incorporate one or more stories. As you can see, narration and description are a natural and common combination. For an example, read the narrative/descriptive essay in Exercise 9.9.

EXERCISE 9.9   **Recognizing the Features of a Narrative/Descriptive Essay**

Read the following essay. Then answer the questions that follow by writing your responses on the blanks provided.

The Intruder

A dank January day, rain mixed with sleet. I looked out the bedroom window, wishing for something better. In front of the brownstone across the street, workmen tossed trash into a large Dumpster. I wondered who was doing so much renovation. There on the sidewalk was a kitchen cupboard, cream-colored enamel with a pale green inside. In the Dumpster, a table with the same colors rested next to a twin-size mattress. Barrels of clothing were thrown in, mingling with everything else.   1

A workman standing in the Dumpster stepped on something that rebounded, so he sat down unexpectedly. I smiled. At first I could not figure out where the endless stream of refuse was coming from. Then I noticed two open windows on the top floor of the brownstone.   2

I have always envied the person in that apartment because of its balcony, where each year someone put plants out without fear that they might be blown down in a high wind. The ledges in my building are too narrow. Flowerpots across the street still contained dried remnants of summer's bounty.   3

4   In early December every year, someone placed a red plastic wreath in each window. In the abundance of my Christmas decorations, I would glance across the street and unkindly consider that somewhat tacky acknowledgement of the season.

5   The man in the Dumpster began breaking things apart with a sledgehammer. The pale green and cream paint showered the mattress and the pink underwear, the color of World War II rayon[1].

6   Then I remembered an incident two years ago. While I wandered the endless aisles of crackers at the local market, a very small gray-haired woman spoke to me.

7   "I do not mean to intrude, but I suppose you know me."

8   I tried to figure out where and when we might have met.

9   "I live across the street from you on the fourth floor of the brownstone. I feel I have known you for 38 years. I just want you to know I am not snooping. I just look."

10   I smiled, and asked, "I hope you like my paperwhites and amaryllis[2] in the windows during the winter."

11   "Oh, yes, they are so beautiful. I remember your boy when he was little. He used to stand at the window every morning, Monday through Friday, to wave goodbye to his father, who crossed the street to wave back. Then I watched your son with his blue book bag head off to school. Each year, he was bigger and the books were heavier it seemed."

12   I felt very uncomfortable. "My son moved out of the city."

13   "Oh, I see. I live alone."

14   "So do I now. My husband died."

15   "I am sorry. I have always wondered what the roofs of the buildings on my side of the street look like from your apartment."

16   "Not Paris, but I have spent lots of time staring at them."

17   "I do like to see your Christmas lights." Silence. "My name is Camille."

18   "My name is Jane." I paused, and then, "We should have tea sometime so you can see your roof from my perspective." I scribbled my phone number on a scrap of paper.

19   "Thank you. I just want you to know I do not snoop."

20   I smiled, "Thank you."

21   Instantly I regretted giving her my number. Her voyeurism[3] angered and also frightened me. On the way down the block, I realized that indeed I had been living in my apartment for 38 years. She had reminded me. I had moved in as a

---

1. **rayon:** a flimsy type of synthetic material from which clothing can be made
2. **paperwhites and amaryllis:** types of flowers or plants
3. **voyeurism:** watching others for pleasure; persistent observance

bride, and she had been watching all those years. Surreal[1]. Haunting. I cherished the anonymity[2] the city provided, but now I realized my privacy had been invaded. I went upstairs, lifted the curtain, and looked across the street. I thought I saw shelves or books or maybe music scores, but perhaps it was only reflected light on the windows.

But she had remembered things I had forgotten.   22

Ants in their tunnels touch feelers while passing as they follow their routine   23
paths. But we run our labyrinths[3] of market aisles, subways, and hallway tunnels alone, touching so seldom that each encounter evokes reactions, stretching far beyond a day, not to be forgotten. She never phoned. Never saw her rooftops.

The sound of the sledgehammer reverberated[4] in my being as resoundingly   24
as the ax cutting the trees in "The Cherry Orchard[5]." The Dumpster was filling. No one was there to pack a life into cardboard boxes to send to Good Will[6]. The red wreaths must have been someplace among all those other treasured things.*

1. The author begins and ends this essay with the description of a scene outside her window. What is the dominant impression of her description?

_____

_____

2. In paragraphs 1 through 5, what spatial pattern is used to organize the descriptive details? Give some examples of transitional words that helped you figure out what pattern is being used.

_____

_____

_____

3. The narrative is in the form of a flashback in the middle of the essay. What is the point of this flashback?

_____

_____

1. **surreal:** strange; dreamlike
2. **anonymity:** state of being unknown
3. **labyrinths:** mazes
4. **reverberated:** echoed; bounced back
5. **"The Cherry Orchard":** a play by Russian playwright Anton Chekhov

6. **Good Will:** a place where you can bring discarded or unwanted items that will be given or sold to the poor

*Source: Jane Bendetson, "The Intruder," *New York Times Magazine,* Feb. 28, 1999, p. 92. © 1999 by Jane Bendetson. Reprinted by permission.

4. What is the point of the metaphor in paragraph 23?

_____

_____

5. The author says that her neighbor's voyeurism angered and frightened her. Do her feelings change when she sees the woman's apartment being cleaned out?

_____

_____

_____

6. What part of the author's description was particularly vivid for you? How did the author use factual and sensory details to paint the scene?

_____

In Summary: Steps in Writing Descriptive Essays

1. Prewrite to generate ideas and determine a main idea.
2. Select relevant details, including only information that is essential to understanding the main idea, and create an outline using an appropriate type of spatial order.
3. As you write, include space-related transitional words and information. Also, use vivid language, including specific words, factual and sensory details, and figurative language.

_____

_____

_____

_____

_____

_____

_____

_____

_____

To review the main points in this chapter, write a brief response to each of the following questions.

1. What is the purpose of description?

2. How can the clustering method of prewriting be helpful?

3. What is the *dominant impression* in writing?

4. How do details relate to your dominant impression in an essay?

5. How do spatial organizational patterns help in writing?

6. What is the purpose of including vivid and figurative language in your writing?

7. Why are narration and description a natural and common combination in writing?

Topic Ideas for Descriptive Essays

Exercise 9.1 includes topic ideas you may want to develop into descriptive essays. The following are some additional ideas.

- A public gathering place on your campus
- An accident scene
- The contents of a desk, drawer, closet, or other storage place
- A fruit or vegetable
- A family heirloom
- Your favorite hangout
- A person with a distinctive style
- A _____ place (messy, busy, chaotic, serene, vibrant, and so on)
- Utopia
- Your favorite season
- Your best friend

■ The scene in the following photo

Source: RubberballRF/Jupiter Images

WebWork

For more information about descriptive essays, visit the Purdue University Online
Writing Lab at **http://owl.english.purdue.edu/handouts/general/gl_describe.html**.
Then use a search engine such as Google or Yahoo! to find photographs of a person,
place, or thing that is special or meaningful to you for some reason. For example, find
photographs of a place where you have vacationed or of a famous person who has
inspired you, or of a work of art you have always admired. Study the photographs to
help you remember some of the details and then write a description.

 For more information and exercises, go to the Online Study
Center at **http://www.college.hmco.com/pic/**
dolphinwriterthree.

10

Process

GOALS FOR CHAPTER 10

▶ Define the terms *directive process* and *informative process*.

▶ Describe the steps in writing a process essay.

▶ Write a process essay.

▶ Recognize the purpose, steps, organizational pattern, and transitional words used in a process essay.

Process is an explanation of how something is done or should be done. There are two types of process: directive process and informative process. A **directive process** provides directions for accomplishing some task. The goal of this type of process is to give readers the information they need in order to re-create the process themselves. Recipes, instructions for assembling a toy, and "how-to" articles are all examples of directive process analysis. The following passage illustrates directive process.

How to Make a Lasting Change

Many of us struggle to better ourselves in various ways, always seeming to fall short, somehow, and to stay mired[1] in destructive routines. However, when someone makes a serious commitment to transform his or her life, it is possible. Once people understand that change is a process—a developmental progression with distinct steps to move through—then our capacity to alter behavior is quite impressive. While the key to success varies from person to person, experts agree that certain attitudes and behaviors both prior to and during the change process help predict who will make it.

1. **mired:** caught up in; stuck or entangled

225

Suppose you want to lose 20 pounds. First and foremost, you really have to be ready to do it and understand that the pros outweigh the cons, that being heavy has harmful consequences, for one thing, and that losing weight has tangible[1] benefits, like improved health. People who are committed to working hard at dieting and who view it as a major undertaking rather than a minor episode are more likely to stick with a program, and the more confidence you have in your ability to lose weight, the more likely it is that you will.

Once you decide that you are indeed prepared to break a bad habit, it is essential to set realistic goals—like losing one or two pounds a week versus a full suit size—and to come up with an equally sensible plan of attack. Research on lasting change shows that it tends to be incremental[2], so that the body, the relationship, or the organization has a chance to adapt. For example, instead of trying to halve your daily caloric[3] intake or to cut all carbohydrates overnight, dieters can throw away the first bite of every meal, eventually building to two bites in the second week, three in the third, and so on.

It is also important to cleave to your strengths and interests while pursuing change. Those who want to get into better shape and love the outdoors should try cycling, not a stuffy gym. If you enjoy interacting with people, work out with a friend. Keep track of your development in a visible way, such as charting weight loss or graphing your heart rate and stamina[4]. Find a healthy alternative to your problem behavior, like chewing sugarless gum instead of smoking, and be sure to reward your efforts—promise yourself a massage for every five pounds lost, perhaps, or a shopping spree once you reach your goal weight.

Lastly and most important, do not give up if you tumble off the wagon now and then. When people who slip once equate the slipping with a fall, a lapse becomes a relapse. They are back to drinking again, smoking again, overeating, or not exercising at all, and they feel like a failure. They view it as evidence of their inability to change, and they give up entirely. To be a triumphant changer, however, you should see a setback as a reason to recommit to your goal, and then get back on the horse immediately.*

This passage teaches readers how to make lasting change in their lives by explaining the process as a series of steps. Note that this passage directly addresses the reader with the words *you* and *your*. In a directive process, it is appropriate to do so because you are teaching the reader how to do something.

1. **tangible:** physical; real or solid
2. **incremental:** accumulating or increasing over time
3. **caloric:** having calories
4. **stamina:** staying power; strength or endurance

*Source: Adapted from Carolyn Kleiner Butler, "50 Ways to Fix Your Life," *U.S. News and World Report,* Dec. 27, 2004/Jan. 3, 2005, p. 32. Copyright © 2004 *U.S. News and World Report,* L.P. Reprinted with permission.

Informative process provides information about how some process works. The goal of this type of process is to explain a procedure so that readers can understand it, not so that they can re-create it. Thus, an essay or article that explains how bees make honey or how e-mail works is designed to inform the reader about the process. The next passage illustrates informative process.

──────────────────── **How Air Bags Work** ────────────────────

When a car crashes, the force required to stop the forward motion of the people inside of it is very great because the car's momentum[1] has changed instantly while that of the people has not. The air bag is designed to slow the passengers' speed to zero with little or no damage, so it has only a fraction of a second and a small space—the distance between a passenger and the steering wheel or dashboard—to work with. Even that tiny amount of space and time is valuable, however, if the system can slow the passenger evenly rather than forcing an abrupt halt to his or her motion.

Before a crash occurs, the air bag, which is made of a thin nylon fabric, is folded into the steering wheel, dashboard, seat, or door. Attached to it is a sensor. When a collision force equal to running into a brick wall at 10 to 15 miles per hour occurs, there is a mass shift that flips a mechanical switch. This switch closes an electrical contact, telling the sensors that a crash has occurred. The sensors receive information from an accelerometer[2] built into a microchip.

Instantly, the air bag's inflation system mixes sodium azide with potassium nitrate to create a large volume of nitrogen gas. This gas then rapidly inflates the bag, which literally bursts from its storage site at up to 200 miles per hour— faster than the blink of an eye! A second later, the gas begins to quickly dissipate[3] through tiny holes in the bag, deflating the bag so that the person can move. Even though the whole process happens in only one-twenty-fifth of a second, the additional time is enough to help prevent serious injury.*

This passage explains what happens when an air bag inflates after a car crash so that readers can *understand* the process rather than *perform* the process. Note that the writer does not directly address the reader as *you,* as he or she would when writing a directive process.

1. **momentum:** motion
2. **accelerometer:** instrument for measuring acceleration

3. **dissipate:** disperse or dissolve

*Source: Adapted from "How Air Bags Work," courtesy of HowStuffWorks.com, http://auto .howstuffworks.com/airbag1.htm.

To write effective process essays of either type, follow the principles presented in the next section.

Writing a Process Essay

Some thesis statements need to be developed with an explanation of how something is done or should be done. When you develop an idea with process, you explain the steps in a procedure using chronological order.

Determining a Main Idea and Writing a Thesis Statement

The thesis statement of a process essay will identify the process you are explaining and will state the goal or end result of this process.

Anyone can learn how to give up a bad habit.

The thesis statement may also identify the number of steps in the process. Thus, for example, an essay for an explanation of the life cycle of a butterfly might begin with this thesis statement:

Caterpillars are transformed into butterflies in three stages.

EXERCISE 10.1   **Writing Thesis Statements for Process Essays**

For each of the following topics, use some prewriting techniques to generate ideas on your own paper and then write a thesis statement you could use for a process essay.

1. Registering for a college course

Thesis statement: _____

2. A household chore

Thesis statement: _____

3. A process involved in one of your hobbies

Thesis statement: _____

4. How a device, tool, or piece of equipment works

Thesis statement: _____

5. How you reduce stress

Thesis statement: _____

Organizing Details and Using Transitions

Most process essays, like narrative essays, are naturally organizing. The writer breaks the process down into a series of clear steps and then presents those steps chronologically, in the order in which they occur. Other process essays may take the form of a series of tips or advice. In that case, the writer must determine the best order for presenting those tips if they are not chronologically related. Order of importance is a common pattern to use for those types of tips. Your outline for your essay should list the steps or tips in the order in which you will discuss them.

As you write, show how the steps in the process are separated from and related to one another by including either transitional words or organizational markers. In a process that presents the steps chronologically, transitional words will help the reader follow the order of the steps in time. The following list includes common process transitions.

first, second, third	next	as
before	soon	when
now	in the beginning	until
then	once	later
after	often	meanwhile
while	finally	last
in the end	afterward	

Notice how the writer of the following passage uses process transitions (in bold print) to help the reader follow the steps in the procedure.

———————— **Hanging Pictures 101** ————————

According to my mother, all you need to hang multiple picture frames properly is a good eye, a few nails, and a pair of hard-heel shoes for hammering. But for those who do not have Mom's innate[1] sense of balance and proportion—or her shoe collection—we have gathered tips for hanging an arrangement of frames with precision.

First of all, attach one D-ring hanger to each side of the frame with a small screw, marking measurements one-third of the way from the top of the frame.

Second, use wire cutters to cut a length of picture wire in a gauge (or weight) appropriate for the weight of each frame. The wire's length should be about one and a half times the width of the frame. Fold the wire in half with the center point landing about halfway between the top of the frame and the D-ring hangers. Pull the wire ends through the D-ring hangers, and wrap the wire around two or three times.

1. **innate:** inborn; instinctive

Next, determine where to hang the pictures on the wall. Consider making a template[1] of each picture with paper. Hang these with tape to make sure you like the positioning. As a good rule of thumb, place pictures at eye level (about 5 feet 8 inches). If you are hanging them over furniture, put them six to eight inches above the piece.

Once you have determined the placement of all of the pictures, use a level to draw a pencil line across the wall. This line ensures that the pictures will hang along the wall at the same height. A laser level with push pins can be attached to the wall to keep your hands free for drawing. The laser projects a visible level line. Use a metal straightedge to keep the pencil steady. Mark along the line where each picture hook will go on the wall.

Then, install picture hooks with screws along the pencil line on the wall. Lightweight pictures also can be hung on one-inch finishing nails. If a frame weighs more than ten pounds, insert screws into wall studs, or use wall anchors.

Finally, position the wire hanger on the picture hook. After all frames are hung, use the level to straighten the arrangement. To keep each frame from slipping, add a bit of sticky putty, available at hardware stores, to the bottom corners to hold them in place.

Now, step back, and enjoy your gallery-worthy display.*

Organizational markers—such as numbers, bullet points, or headings—are also useful in helping the reader follow your ideas. You may want to identify the steps in the process as Step 1, Step 2, and so on. In the following essay, for example, the author chooses to present the steps in a numbered list.

Fire Building 101

Step 1: This may seem obvious, but it will still make a big difference. Make sure the damper is open. (The damper is inside and up beyond the fireplace opening at the beginning, or throat, of the chimney. Feel around or use a flashlight to find the handle that pivots it open.)

Step 2: Place your kindling (preferably strips of softwoods such as pine—not pressure-treated or painted [wood] because [that produces] toxic fumes) or your fire starter under the andirons toward the back of the firebox. Andirons or metal grates are important because they elevate the firewood, providing air circulation underneath.

---

1. **template:** pattern; model or guide

*Source: Adapted from Amy Bickers Mercer, "Hanging Pictures 101," *Southern Living*, July 2004, pp. 122–123. Copyright © 2004 *Southern Living*. Reprinted by permission.

Step 3: Start off with two or three pieces of firewood, and place them on the back of the andirons. Next, crumple a piece of newspaper, and place it on top of the logs.

Step 4: Light the newspaper first, and then the kindling. The burning newspaper will help create a draft to draw smoke up the chimney. With the blaze set, replace the fire screen, and sit back and enjoy the glow.*

If you are presenting a series of tips that are not chronologically related, however, you could separate them into sections labeled with headings or marked with bullet points.

EXERCISE 10.2 **Organizing Details in Process Essays**

On your own paper, prewrite to generate ideas and then complete each of the following thesis statements by filling in the blank. Then, on the other blanks provided, prepare an informal outline by listing the major steps in chronological order or the major tips in order of importance.

1. If you want to _____, follow these steps.

_____

_____

_____

_____

_____

2. _____ is a process that occurs in three distinct stages.

_____

_____

_____

_____

_____

*Source: Robert Martin, "Fire Building 101," *Southern Living,* Dec. 2003, p. 99.

3. To be a better _____, here are some tips.

_____

_____

_____

_____

EXERCISE 10.3 **Recognizing Process Transitions**

Circle all of the transitional words and time order information in the following essay.

Giving Lessons

We are a nation of givers. In 2002, as the stock market lost nearly a quarter of its value, as millions of people lost jobs, and as many others lost sleep worrying about terrorism and imminent[1] war, Americans nonetheless gave a record $241 billion to charitable causes. While foundations and corporations contributed a good chunk of the philanthropic[2] pie, the overwhelming majority of those billions—more than 80 percent—was given by ordinary Americans. Tapping a vast national reservoir of goodwill, two thirds of households, rich and poor, reached deep into their pockets in 2002 and pulled out an average gift of $2,499, according to estimates from Giving USA, a publication of the American Association of Fundraising Counsel Trust for Philanthropy.

Charitable giving, whether of $1 or $1 million, gives each of us a chance to affect the greater good. *U.S. News* talked to philanthropic experts for advice on ensuring that your charitable investments are sound:

The first step is to identify a cause. It is the most basic decision a donor can make. What do you care about? It may be an issue that reflects passionately held beliefs or personal experience. "I know what it is to be hungry," says Vanessa Lazar, 30, whose year-long brush with homelessness prompted her and her friends to start raising money for starving Ethiopians. "To think of someone going without food just does something to me." Similarly, losing a family member to lymphoma[3] may spur one to support cancer research, while a nature buff may want to help conserve wildlife.

After narrowing down a cause, investigate organizations working in that area. The process may seem daunting. Thousands of groups may be working on your particular cause. A keyword search for "literacy," for instance, results in

1. **imminent:** about to happen
2. **philanthropic:** charitable; promoting human welfare

3. **lymphoma:** a type of cancer that affects the lymph nodes

over 2,700 organizations, from Books for a Better World, a Phoenix group that builds libraries in developing countries, to First Book, a Washington, DC, outfit that gives books to low-income children in the United States. Pare that universe down with a series of questions: Do you want to give locally, nationally, or internationally? Will your gift support research or provide direct service? Are you more comfortable with a big organization or a small group on a shoestring[1] budget? Bear in mind, there is no right answer.

Then choose the charity. First, verify that the organization is certified a non-profit by the Internal Revenue Service, crucial to obtaining a tax deduction for your donation. Experts also suggest giving to groups you know. "There really is a logical reason why people give to their alma maters[2]," says Christine Letts, associate director of Harvard's Hauser Center for Nonprofit Organizations.

Second, consider volunteering, which is another prime way to learn about the inner workings of an organization. Andrew Schechtman, a 36-year-old family practitioner in San Jose, CA, volunteered in Liberia for a year with the international health group Doctors Without Borders, treating malnutrition, malaria[3], and war wounds. Now, safely back in the States, Schechtman donates money to the group. "I know from experience that they are stingy," he says, "so I know my money is going to be well spent."

Failing firsthand experience, donors can consult community foundations, which make grants to local nonprofits in more than 650 areas nationwide. "We can connect you with staff who have expertise in the area you are exploring," says Stuart Appelbaum, vice president of development for the Minneapolis Foundation. The Council on Foundations' Web site (www.cof.org) lists community foundations that you can tap for assistance.

When you have narrowed down the beneficiary[4] of your largess[5], you will need to decide the form of your gift. The majority of Americans—the nearly two thirds of givers who do not claim tax deductions—simply make modest donations, a practice most nonprofits appreciate. But money is not everything. Many cash-strapped groups seek used computers. A list of them can be found at www.sharetechnology.org. For your privacy, be sure to erase the hard drive, and get a receipt from the group for tax purposes. Cell phones can also be recycled. Send your old mobile to CollectiveGood in Tucker, GA, and designate a charity from the list at www.collectivegood.com. CollectiveGood will send half the phone's resale price ($3 to $4) to the charity.

Finally, consider donating time. Many charities, especially struggling or smaller groups, could not survive without volunteers. State budget cuts have forced the

---

1. **shoestring:** consisting of little money
2. **alma maters:** the institutions from which people have graduated
3. **malaria:** an infectious disease transmitted by mosquitoes
4. **beneficiary:** recipient
5. **largess:** the generous giving of gifts, money, or favors

Vision homeless shelter in Luzerne County, PA, to lay off several staffers. Without a roster of 3,000 volunteers to undertake tasks like supervising overnight shifts, the shelter—now housing 35 men—would close its doors.*

> ### EXERCISE 10.4   Writing a Process Essay That Includes Transitions
>
> Choose one of the thesis statements and outlines you prepared in Exercise 10.2. Write the essay, including transitional words that indicate the order of the details.

Developing a Process Essay

While the thesis statement and pattern of organization for a process essay tend to be relatively easy to generate, writers must take care to include all of the essential information about the procedure. Have you ever tried to put something together by following unclear or incomplete instructions? The process was probably time-consuming and frustrating. So to help readers easily re-create or comprehend the procedure you are explaining, do not make any assumptions about the readers' knowledge and do not leave out even the smallest critical detail. You must anticipate all of your readers' questions and make sure that you provide answers.

Avoid Making Assumptions. Considering your intended audience is very important if you are going to explain the process clearly enough for readers to understand it or follow it. How much basic knowledge will your readers have about your subject? How much will readers know about the materials involved in the process? If you refer to an *Allen wrench* or a *zipper footer,* will your readers know what that is? Will you need to provide definitions of terms, or can you be reasonably sure that readers will know what the terms mean? Will readers know how to accomplish minor steps—such as "thread the needle," "whisk together the ingredients," or "contract your abdominal muscles"—or should you explain those, too?

Include Relevant Details and Information. As you write your process, make sure that you do not overlook any essential steps or materials, especially for minor actions or events. For example, if you tell readers to breathe in, do not forget to tell them to breathe out. Also, be very specific. If you tell readers to sit, specify whether they should sit in a chair or on the floor. If you tell readers to attach two things, specify whether that attachment should be made with glue, nails, screws, or something else.

*Source: Adapted from Joellen Perry, "Giving Lessons," *U.S. News and World Report,* Dec. 8, 2003, pp. 46–56. Copyright © 2003 *U.S. News and World Report,* L.P. Reprinted with permission.

EXERCISE 10.5 **Recognizing Assumptions and Missing Details**

The following passage attempts to teach readers how to pick a lock. Read the passage and then answer the questions that follow.

How to Pick a Lock

The first step in picking a lock is to insert the tension wrench into the keyhole and turn it in the same direction that you would turn the key. This turns the plug so that it is slightly offset from the housing around it. This creates a slight ledge in the pin shafts.

While applying pressure on the plug, you insert a pick into the keyhole and begin lifting the pins. The object is to lift each pin pair up to the level at which the top pin moves completely into the housing, as if pushed by the correct key. When you do this while applying pressure with the tension wrench, you feel or hear a slight click when the pin falls into position. This is the sound of the upper pin falling into place on the ledge in the shaft. The ledge keeps the upper pin wedged in the housing so that it won't fall back down into the plug.

In this way, you move each pin pair into the correct position until all of the upper pins are pushed completely into the housing and all of the lower pins rest inside the plug. At this point, the plug rotates freely, and you can open the lock.

Conceptually, the lock-picking process is quite simple, but it is a very difficult skill to master. Locksmiths have to learn exactly the right pressure to apply and what sounds to listen for. They also must hone their sense of touch to the point where they can feel the slight forces of the moving pins and plug. Additionally, they must learn to visualize all the pieces inside the lock. Successful lock picking depends on complete familiarity with the lock's design.*

1. What terms would you need to have defined in order to re-create this process?

_____

2. Which of the tools that the author mentions are unfamiliar to you?

_____

3. As you read this passage, what other questions did you have that were not answered?

_____

_____

_____

*Source: Adapted from Tom Harris and Marshall Brain, "How Lock Picking Works," courtesy of HowStuffWorks.com, http://home.howstuffworks.com/lock-picking6.htm.

EXERCISE 10.6   Recognizing the Features of a Process Essay

Read the following essay. Then answer the questions that follow by writing your responses on the blanks provided.

How Tattoos Work

It is virtually impossible to walk through a mall without spotting people of all ages with tattoos. Tattoos come in all shapes and sizes, and they can appear almost anywhere on someone's body. Permanent cosmetic studios also tattoo on eyebrows, eyeliner, and lip liner for those who want their makeup to be permanent. In these cases, you may not even know that you are looking at a tattoo!

Tattoos have steadily gained popularity in the last decade—a trend that shows little sign of slowing down. In this essay, we will look at how the tattooing process works.

Early Tattooing Methods

An amazing variety of tattooing methods developed in different cultures. In North and South America, many Indian tribes routinely tattooed the body or the face by simple pricking, and some tribes in California introduced color into scratches.

Many tribes of the Arctic and Subarctic, mostly Inuit, and some people in eastern Siberia made needle punctures through which a thread coated with pigment (usually soot) was drawn underneath the skin. In Polynesia and Micronesia, pigment was pricked into the skin by tapping on a tool shaped like a small rake.

The Maori people of New Zealand, who are world famous for their tattooing, applied their wood-carving technique to tattooing. In the moko style of Maori tattooing, shallow, colored grooves in distinctive, complex designs were produced on the face and buttocks by striking a small bone-cutting tool (used for shaping wood) into the skin. After the Europeans arrived in the 1700s, the Maori began using the metal that settlers brought for a more conventional style of puncture tattooing.

The Maori had a custom of preserving the heads of their tattooed leaders after death as precious family possessions. Over time, they began to trade some of the heads to collectors for firearms and iron tools. This practice, which explains why there are some of these heads in European museums, was short-lived because of the fighting and political turmoil it caused.

Modern Tattooing

Today, tattoos are created by injecting ink into the skin. Injection is done by a needle attached to a hand-held tool. The tool moves the needle up and down at a rate of several hundred vibrations per minute and penetrates the skin by about one millimeter.

What you see when you look at a tattoo is the ink that's left in the skin after the tattooing. The ink is not in the epidermis, which is the layer of skin that we see and the skin that gets replaced constantly, but instead intermingles with cells in the dermis and shows through the epidermis.

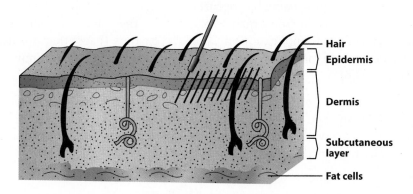

The cells of the dermis are remarkably stable, so the tattoo's ink will last, with minor fading and dispersion[1], for your entire life!

The Tattoo Machine

The basic idea of the electrically powered tattoo machine is that a needle moves up and down like one in a sewing machine, carrying ink into your skin in the process. Today, a tattoo machine is an electrically powered, vertically vibrating steel instrument that resembles a dentist's drill (and sounds a little like it, too). It is fitted with solid needles that puncture the skin at the rate of 50 to 3,000 times a minute. The sterilized needles are installed in the machine and dipped in ink, which is sucked up through the machine's tube system. Then, powered by a foot switch much like that on a sewing machine, the tattoo machine uses an up-and-down motion to puncture the top layer of the skin and drive insoluble, micrometer-sized particles of ink into the second (dermal) layer of skin, about one-eighth inch deep.

Sterilization

Much of the tattoo application process focuses on safety, since any puncture wound—and that is what a tattoo machine is doing to your skin—holds the potential for infection and disease transfer.

The only acceptable method of sterilization for killing every living microorganism is an autoclave, a heat/steam/pressure unit (used in hospitals) that achieves and maintains 250 degrees Fahrenheit (121°C) under 10 pounds of pressure for 30 minutes or up to 270°F (132°C) under 15 pounds of pressure for 15 minutes. (Most units run a 55-minute cycle from a cold start.)

1. **dispersion:** dispersal or scattering

Most tattoo materials—inks, ink cups, gloves, and needles—are used only once to eliminate the possibility of contamination of materials. All reusable materials, such as the needle bar and the tube, must be completely cleaned, put into special pouches, and sterilized in the autoclave. Indicator strips on the packages change color when processing has occurred.

Other equipment includes razors (for shaving the skin, since hair clogs up the tubes and hinders application) and plastic barriers (bags) that are used on spray bottles, tattoo machines, and clip cords to prevent cross-contamination.

Prep Work

The tattoo artist, who has washed and inspected hands for cuts or abrasions and disinfected the work area with an EPA-approved viricidal[1], dons fresh gloves and generally follows this procedure:

- Places plastic bags on spray bottles
- Explains the sterilization process to the client
- Opens up single-service, autoclave-sterilized equipment in front of the client
- Shaves and disinfects (with a mixture of water and antiseptic green soap) the area to be tattooed

With the outline (stencil) of the tattoo in place—or the outline of a custom tattoo drawn by hand onto the skin—the actual tattooing begins.

Making the Outline

Using one single-tipped needle, the artist starts at the bottom of the right-hand side and works up (lefties generally start on the left side) so that the stencil will not be lost when the artist cleans a permanent line. For single-needle work, a thinner black ink than that used for shading is used because thinner ink can be easily wiped away from the skin without smearing.

As this happens, the tattoo machine is buzzing and smooth, clear lines should be emerging as the needle pierces the skin, applies the ink, and gradually lifts out of the skin in a steady motion. (Experts say this point is where the professionals show their mettle[2]: In order to create clear lines and proper depth, the tattoo artist must understand how deep the needles actually need to go to produce a permanent line. Not going deep enough will create scratchy lines after healing, and going too deep will cause excessive pain and bleeding.)

Shading

Once the outline is complete, the area is thoroughly cleaned with antiseptic soap and water. Then, the outline is thickened and shading is added. The tattoo

---

1. **viricidal:** able to kill viruses   2. **mettle:** courage; grit

artist will use a combination of needles. If this step is not done correctly, shadowed lines, excessive pain, and delayed healing will result. Again, everything must be autoclaved before use.

Using a thicker, blacker ink, the artist goes over the outline, creating an even, solid line. Shading creates special effects. Each tattoo artist works differently, depending upon his or her training and preference.

Color

After the shading is done, the tattoo is cleaned again and is now ready for color. When applying color, the artist overlaps each line of color to ensure solid, even hues with no "holidays"—uneven areas where color has either been lifted out during healing or where the tattoo artist simply missed a section of skin.

The tattoo is again sprayed and cleaned, and the tattoo artist applies pressure, using a disposable towel to remove any blood and plasma excreted during the tattooing process. According to medical experts, some bleeding always occurs in tattooing, but under normal conditions (no alcohol or illegal drugs in the system, no fatigue, no tattooing over scar tissue), most stops within a few minutes after the tattoo is completed. (Reputable tattoo artists will not tattoo those who are sick, drunk, high, or pregnant, and they will not apply pornographic, racist, or gang tattoos.)

Caring for a New Tattoo

Taking care with a new tattoo can prevent health problems and also ensure that the quality of the image is protected. Here is what you need to do:

- Remove the bandage from the tattoo one to two hours after completion.
- Wash it gently with cool or lukewarm water, using a mild antibacterial soap.
- Pat it dry. (Do not rub!)
- Apply very thin coats of Bacitracin or A&D Ointment (not regular petroleum jelly) and work them well into the skin. (If you can see the ointment on your skin, you are using too much, and it could pull color out of your skin, tattoo artists warn.)
- Do not soak the tattoo in water or let the shower pound directly on it.
- Avoid sun, sea, and swimming pool until it has healed.
- Refrain from picking at any scab that may form—it will fall off as it heals, usually in one to three weeks.
- Use ice packs if swelling or redness occurs.
- Call your doctor if you have even the slightest signs of infection!*

*Source: Adapted from Tracy V. Wilson, "How Tattoos Work," http://people.howstuffworks.com/tattoo.htm. Courtesy of HowStuffWorks.com.

1. What is the thesis of this essay? Where is it stated?

   _____

   _____

2. What kind of order is used to arrange the major steps explained in this essay?

   _____

3. What is a process transitional word or phrase that the author uses? Do you think the author should have used more process transitional words throughout the rest of the essay?

   _____

   _____

4. Does the writer make any assumptions about the reader's knowledge, or does she leave out any crucial details? Explain your answer.

   _____

5. If you have a tattoo, does your own experience match the author's explanation of the procedure? If not, how did your experience differ? If you do not have a tattoo, do you think you now understand the process involved in getting one? What are your unanswered questions?

   _____

In Summary: Steps in Writing Process Essays

1. **Write a thesis statement that mentions the process and the end result.**
2. **Organize the steps in the process.** Create an outline that lists these steps in chronological order or in another kind of order, as appropriate.
3. **Develop each step with all of the essential information.** Make sure that you define terms, explain the use of materials, and describe each step as is appropriate for your intended readers. Use transitional words to help readers understand how the steps are related.

To review the main points in this chapter, write a brief response to each of the following questions.

1. Define the term *process*.

2. What are the two types of process?

3. What is a directive process, and what is its goal?

4. What is an informative process, and what is its goal?

5. What is a thesis statement, and what purpose does it serve in a process essay?

6. What are the different ways in which you can organize a process essay?

7. What purpose do transitional words and organizational markers serve in a process essay? What are some common transitional words? What are some examples of organizational markers?

8. What are some ways in which you can help readers easily re-create or comprehend the procedure you are explaining?

Topic Ideas for Process Essays

Exercise 10.1 includes topic ideas that you may want to develop into process essays. The following are some additional ideas.

- How to _____ (serve a tennis ball, catch a fish, set up a fish aquarium, use an Internet search engine, choose the right pet, and so on)

- How to make _____ (enchiladas, a new friend, a piñata, a basket, and so on)

- How to prepare for a _____ (job interview, date, exam, party, speech, and so on)

- How to conquer _____ (an addiction to cigarettes, clutter, disorganization, procrastination, obesity, and so on)

- How _____ works (e-mail, adoption, a courtroom trial, recycling, and so on)

- How _____ is done (air traffic control, a manufacturing process, a medical procedure, and so on)

- A skill that everyone should learn (e.g., listening, changing a tire, flossing teeth, changing a diaper, and so on)

- How a process in nature occurs

- How a machine works

- How to fold a paper crane (see the following series of pictures):

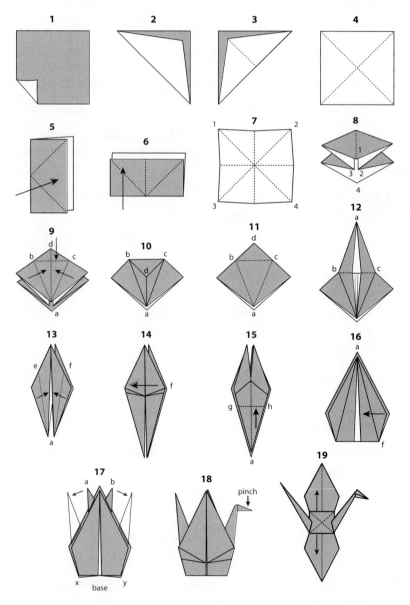

Source: http://www.sadako.com/howtofold.html

WebWork

Go to St. Cloud State University's Literacy Education Online (LEO) Web site at **http://leo.stcloudstate.edu/acadwrite/process.html**. Review the list of questions to consider when writing a process essay. Then read the sample process essay. Evaluate the effectiveness of this essay by answering the following questions.

1. Is the thesis statement clearly stated? Is the goal or end result clear?

2. Are the details clearly organized? Does the writer use adequate transitional words and/or organizational markers?

3. Does the writer make any assumptions about the reader's knowledge?

4. Did the writer overlook any steps or not include mention of essential materials?

5. What suggestions for improvement would you offer this writer?

Online Study Center For more information and exercises, go to the Online Study Center at **http://www.college.hmco.com/pic/ dolphinwriterthree**.

11

Illustration

▶ Define the term *illustration*.

▶ Describe the steps in writing an illustration essay.

▶ Write an illustration essay.

▶ Recognize the features of an illustration essay.

Illustrating ideas by providing specific examples is a valuable way to help readers understand ideas. We often make general or vague statements or use abstract terms that readers will not be able to understand or correctly interpret if we do not provide one or more examples. Look, for instance, at the following statement.

Life has to end; love does not.

Do you immediately understand what the writer means by this statement? You probably need additional clarification and explanation. If the writer provides an example, this idea will become much clearer.

We have been lectured in America, perhaps too often, that we need to "live in the present," to "get on with our lives." But I have spoken with a great many people who say they have known the one true love of their lives, and the lesson is always the same: Life has to end; love does not.

Take Marge Jackson, of Canton, Ohio, who will turn 90 this year. Her first "date" with Harvey was on Valentine's Day, 1932, when he drove her around in a borrowed car. They would visit on the front porch. They would roller-skate in the street. He knew she loved to dance, so he secretly took dance lessons to woo her. And once they were married, the dancing never stopped. He would come in from the garage and say, "OK, ballerina, once around the floor," and they would twirl around the kitchen to the music on the radio.

Illustration   **245**

Their marriage lasted 53 years. The night before he died, she shampooed his hair in a hospital bathroom. When visiting hours were over, she snuck back for one more kiss.

"I knew you would come back," he said.

Harvey has been gone nearly 14 years now, but Marge keeps his picture on her dresser and his suit in the closet, and some nights she pats a little of his talcum powder on her cheek so that, when she lies on the pillow, it smells like he is there. "I am not losing my mind," she says. "I am just missing him." Marge may be by herself, but she is not alone. When she "has a chat" with her husband at night, looking at an old Valentine he made for her, wearing a pat of his talcum powder, she wants no pity. "My life began when I met Harvey," she says. It just did not end when she lost him.

Her favorite song—the one they played at her wedding—begins with the lyrics "I'll get by, as long as I have you. . . ." For her and many others, they get by because, in their own way, they still do have sweethearts who make them smile—not because they were once in love but because they still are.*

To illustrate the main idea, this passage provides one long, extended example of a woman who is still in love with her husband years after his death. After you have read this example, the idea stated in the thesis statement probably makes a lot more sense.

Other passages, like the one that follows, might offer several examples instead of just one long example.

Giving Kids Candy Is Anything but Sweet

My wife and I try to lead by example. We routinely exercise and demonstrate, not preach, the merits of a well-rounded diet. We have firm rules on dessert and candy intake—only after balanced meals and once per day. But I am now coming to the realization that I am naive to believe that our effort to exert control over such matters will have an impact.

After my five-year-old son finished his 45-minute gymnastics class a few days ago, the coach rewarded him with a Hershey's Kiss. At my seven-year-old daughter's school carnival last month, children were encouraged to purchase "candy grams" for each other—a bargain at only 50 cents for a full-size Snickers, Baby Ruth, or Three Musketeers bar. Social norms being what they are, if you did not receive at least five or six candy bars, you simply were not popular. Last weekend both children returned home from birthday parties with their own gift bags, which, of course, contained an assortment of treats.

*Source: Adapted from Mitch Albom, "They Never Stopped Loving," *Parade*, Feb. 8, 2004, pp. 6–7. © 2004 Mitch Albom. All rights reserved. Mitch Albom is the author of the best-selling books *Tuesdays with Morrie* and *The Five People You Meet in Heaven*.

When I made a routine deposit at our local bank recently, the teller offered both of my children a lollipop. The most popular store in downtown Wheaton, IL, is a narrow alley of a shop that you literally have to enter single file. It sells only candy. For $1, you can purchase a large bag of it. Every night there is a line out the door. It is viewed as a nostalgic part of Wheaton's charm. The thing that disturbs me most of all is that there is now a basket of candy on display at our family physician's office so that children can grab a piece at the end of their exam. Why would my kids listen to my ranting about eating healthy when they get candy at the doctor's office?

Our calendar now dictates more candy-based giving, too. Let us be honest— many kids equate Easter with getting candy from an imaginary bunny. Giving a box of chocolates to your loved ones on Valentine's Day is a sign of affection. Not giving chocolates to your spouse on Valentine's Day is akin to[1] forgetting an anniversary.

Last year our Halloween-candy intake was so significant that I taught my daughter how to use PowerPoint[2] to graph the quantity of different kinds of candy she had received—it was a unique "bar" chart, to say the least. (She had scored 14 Snickers, 12 Three Musketeers, and 10 Hershey's.) By early December, I have usually thrown away all the remaining Halloween candy in a fit of frustration sparked by the most recent pediatric dental visit. That is about the time our neighbors start showing up with plates of Christmas cookies.*

In the previous passage, the author provides multiple examples to illustrate his point that he's fighting a losing battle when it comes to keeping his kids away from candy.

Writing an Illustration Essay

Some thesis statements will need to be illustrated with specific examples. When you develop an essay using illustration, you give specific instances that back up the claim you make in your main idea.

1. **akin to:** similar to; of the same kind

2. **PowerPoint:** a type of computer program that allows one to prepare slide presentations

Source: Excerpted from Dave Beasley, "Giving Kids Candy Is Anything but Sweet," *Newsweek,* April 18, 2005, p. 20. © *Newsweek,* Inc. All rights reserved. Reprinted by permission.

Determining a Main Idea and Writing a Thesis Statement

A thesis statement that will need to be developed with one or more examples usually states a general observation or opinion:

> In today's society, cheating is widespread.

> Many drugs and medical advancements have helped humans live longer, healthier lives.

> My mother has always been good at turning setbacks into opportunities.

To prove that the observation in each of these thesis statements is valid, each essay would need to be developed with one longer example or several shorter examples.

EXERCISE 11.1   **Writing Thesis Statements for Illustration Essays**

For each of the following topics, use some prewriting techniques to generate ideas on your own paper and then write a thesis statement you could use for an illustration essay.

1. A quality of most of today's college students
   Thesis statement: _College students ~~spend~~ a lot of time on video or computer games._ [handwritten: Most of the ... good or bad ... shouldn't spend]

2. A person with a lot of _____ (patience, stubbornness, talent, common sense, and so on)
   Thesis statement: _A person with a lot of talent can ~~usisly help~~ less make a good career in every day life_ [handwritten]

3. A necessary ingredient of a good marriage
   Thesis statement: _Good marriage has to base on love and respect._ [handwritten]

4. An important skill for our modern world
   Thesis statement: _Knowledge is an important skill for our morden world_ [handwritten]

5. An individual (or group) who is doing good things for the world
   Thesis statement: _Dalai LAMA speaks about peace in whole world_ [handwritten]

Selecting Relevant Examples

In Chapter 9, you learned to convey a dominant impression in a description by carefully choosing the right details. Similarly, illustration must incorporate only those examples that develop the main idea. Whether you choose to include one example or several, all examples must directly relate to the point you are trying to make. So if you are trying to illustrate the point that many cell phone users are rude, you would choose several examples of your encounters with people who were inconsiderate of others while talking on their cell phones. You would not bring up people who do not demonstrate this rude behavior.

To discover the best examples, begin by prewriting. Then weed out any example that does not exactly match your main point.

EXERCISE 11.2   **Selecting Relevant Examples**

For each of the following thesis statements, circle the letter of the example in the list that would not develop the thesis statement.

1. Thesis statement: My friend Judy is a kind and thoughtful person.

   a. She always gives her seat on the subway to passengers who are older than she is.
   b. She volunteers at an elementary school where she helps struggling students learn to read.
   c. She is working on completing a master's degree in computer science.

2. Thesis statement: Sports heroes are not always good role models for children.

   a. Several professional baseball players have pumped up their muscles with steroids, leading teenagers to begin imitating them.
   b. Many professional players, after overcoming significant obstacles, have gone on to set new records.
   c. Quite a few sports stars have recently been arrested for crimes ranging from assault to drunk driving.

3. Thesis statement: My grandmother has a lot of energy.

   a. She enjoys reading best-selling novels and biographies in her spare time.
   b. She walks three miles three mornings per week and takes water aerobics classes at the YMCA two days per week.
   c. She volunteers twenty hours per week in a busy hospital emergency room and still manages to get to all of her six grandchildren's games and performances.

4. Thesis statement: First impressions are often inaccurate and misleading.

   a. When James and I first met, I disliked him, but we have since become best friends.
   b. My boss told me that during my job interview, I convinced him that I had the personality characteristics and skills to do the job.

c. My friends Juan and Becky were sure that the initial attraction between them was love at first sight, but after just two weeks of dating, they both lost interest in each other.

5. Thesis statement: High school football games are as much about socializing as they are about following the competition on the field.

a. Adults chatter to each other about their children who are playing in the band, twirling a color flag, or coming out of a huddle.

b. Parents and children stop by to greet their favorite teachers and catch up on news while an endless parade of teenagers walks back and forth in front of the bleachers like television show extras.

c. Many members of the community who do not even have children at the high school will come to a game because it is an exciting sports event.*

Including Adequate Examples

After prewriting to generate the examples you want to include, consider whether or not you are providing an adequate number of examples. Readers will not be able to understand or agree with your point if they do not feel as though they have been given enough information. If you are presenting a controversial idea or one that is difficult to believe, you will have to provide sufficient examples to get the reader to accept that idea. For example, if you are trying to convince readers that cheating is rampant among college students, you will need to provide several examples to persuade a skeptical reader that this opinion is valid. If you give only one example, you will not have offered enough evidence to support your point.

If you decide that one extended example will provide adequate support, then make sure that you fully develop that example with plenty of detail. (See "Developing an Illustration Essay" later in this chapter.)

EXERCISE 11.3   Adding Examples

Read the following passage. Then, on the blanks provided, list two or three additional examples that the writer could add to better support the essay's main idea.

Over the last ten years, our lives have been enriched by many amazing technological advancements. In particular, it is difficult to imagine living without the

Source: Adapted from Nick Patterson, "Southern Journal," *Southern Living,* Oct. 2001, p. 200.

many great products that we rely on now for entertainment and for communication with friends and family members.

For example, I would not want to ever have to give up my digital music player. This light, compact electronic device allows me to listen to music wherever I go, and the quality of the sound is excellent. Plus, I do not have to bother with CDs or cassette tapes; I simply buy and download from the Internet the songs that I want.

Additional examples: *2 παραγραφα*

_____

_____

_____

_____

_____

_____

_____

_____

_____

Organizing Details and Using Transitions

If you include several examples in support of your main idea, you will need to decide on the best order in which to present them. Sometimes, the order will not matter. If all of your examples are equal in importance, you can arrange them in any order. At other times, though, some examples will be more significant than others. In that case, you should decide whether to present the most important examples first or save them for last. In the essay about cheating college students, for instance, you might want to present your strongest example first so that readers will not dismiss your point out of hand and stop reading. Then save the weaker evidence for later in the essay, after you have convinced your readers that your thesis is valid.

After you have decided on the best order for your examples, list them in that order in an outline. Then, as you write, make sure that you include transitional words to help readers follow your organization and progression of thought. Some common illustration transitional phrases are

for example   an illustration of this is
for instance   one example
to illustrate   another example (or instance)
in one case   a case in point is

Notice as you read the following passage how the illustration transitional words, which are highlighted in bold, help you move from one example to the next.

In a city defined by small spaces—cabs, elevators, cramped apartments, and crowded sidewalks—it is often cause for bewilderment that New Yorkers would willingly choose to live with giant-breed dogs. But many big-dog owners are religiously attached to their choice of pet.

Jaime Stankevicius, **for example,** is an opera singer who shares a Chelsea[1] studio with his Great Dane, Avalon. Avalon stands 6 feet 3 inches tall on his hind legs and weighs 140 pounds. His nails are trimmed with a Dremel rotary power tool. He consumes $30 to $50 worth of food a week. When Avalon makes his daily trek through Chelsea, people stare in disbelief. "Does this guy live in a New York apartment?" asks one man.

Another example is Brutus, an English mastiff who now weighs 160 pounds. At first, Brutus lived with his owner, Barry Kellman, in the 740-square-foot apartment Kellman shared with his wife. But when Mrs. Kellman got pregnant, she said Brutus was too much to bear. Mr. Kellman paid $55 a night for overnight boarding at Biscuits & Bath Doggy Gym, but when those bills began adding up, he did the next logical thing (in his mind): he rented an $1,800-a-month, one-bedroom apartment for Brutus and found him a human roommate. Eventually, Mr. Kellman's marriage ended, and he is now sleeping on the couch in Brutus's apartment while they look for a bigger place.*

---

1. **Chelsea:** a neighborhood in New York City

*Source: Adapted from Andrea Elliott, "Rooming with the Big Dogs," *New York Times,* May 25, 2004, pp. B1, B7.

⊛ **EXERCISE 11.4** **Organizing Details in Illustration Essays**

On your own paper, prewrite to generate ideas and then complete each of the following thesis statements by filling in the blank. Then, on the other blanks provided, prepare an informal outline by listing the examples you would include in an appropriate order.

1. You can tell a lot about people by observing _____.

_____

_____

_____

_____

_____

2. People who _____ are usually _____.

_____

_____

_____

_____

3. _____ is a specific habit of successful people.

_____

_____

_____

_____

_____

⊛ **EXERCISE 11.5** **Recognizing Illustration Transitions**

Circle all of the illustration transitional words in the following passage.

Verbal Shorthand

I do not know why it is, but people who have been married for a long time tend to cut corners when it comes to spoken language. In fact, if it were not for pronouns, I do not think many of us could communicate at all. A single word may convey several meanings, thoughts, or requests, but somehow each partner knows exactly what the other is saying at any given time. My wife and I are guilty of using such verbal shorthand.

One example is our use of the word *it*. If my wife asks me to turn it down, I know she means the TV, if it is on. Otherwise, she is talking about the thermostat. See what I mean. *It* covers many bases. My wife may say, "Please put it back together when you are through." I understand that she is referring to the newspaper. "It is about time for it to come," I might proclaim. This could mean the mail, the paper, the bus, or the cab we called, depending upon the time and context. When I exclaim, "I have had it for now!" my wife knows that I am frustrated with whatever project I have been working on and ready for a nap. If I head toward the garage, she may say, "Do not forget to fill it up." She means the car. But if I am in the backyard and she says the same thing, I know she means the birdbath. If she calls from the laundry room and inquires, "Is it on yet?" she means, *Are the commercials over and is the program starting?*

A second good example is our use of the word *that*. When my wife says, "You had better do something for that," I know that she has heard me sneeze. When she is in another room and admonishes[1], "That will spoil your appetite," she has heard the rustle of my candy-bar wrapper. When she says, "I think you can do better than that," I have either just finished mowing the lawn, trimming the hedge, or (in winter) shoveling the sidewalk and driveway.

Yet another word that we use as a shortcut is *he*. She may say: "You would think he would be cold out there without a coat." If she is looking out our north window, I know she means Harry next door. If the south window, it is neighbor Bob. But when she asks, "Has he been out yet?" she means Earl, our dog.

As a final illustration, there is the word *one*. While in the laundry room, she might remark, "We have got to get a new one before long." She means the washing machine. When my wife proffered[2] a box of assorted chocolates the other evening and asked which I preferred, I said, "The one in the corner." I got the one I wanted. I did not have to say, "the chocolate, nougat, and caramel-covered macadamia nut cluster." She knew.*

⭐ **EXERCISE 11.6**   **Writing an Illustration Essay That Includes Transitions**

Choose one of the thesis statements and outlines you prepared in Exercise 11.4. Write the essay, including transitional words that indicate how the details are related.

1. **admonishes:** scolds; gives a warning   2. **proffered:** offered; held out

*Source: Adapted from George Beiswinger, "Verbal Shorthand," *Smithsonian*, Aug. 2001, p. 108. Adapted by permission of George Beiswinger. Originally appeared in *Smithsonian* magazine, August 2001.

Developing an Illustration Essay

If you have decided to develop your illustration essay with several shorter examples, you will probably only briefly mention each one. Thus, you will probably write just one to three sentences to explain each example.

If you have decided to include just one extended example, however, you will need to develop this example with even more specific detail. These specific details will often take the form of narratives or descriptions, which were discussed in Chapters 9 and 10. As you are developing each example with one or both of these modes, remember what you have learned about structuring a narrative, creating a dominant impression in a description, using descriptive language such as specific words and factual and sensory details, and all of the other principles of effective narration and description.

Look back at the passage about love that lasts (pages 244–245); it is developed in part with a narrative. The story includes details about what happened, what both people said, and how they behaved.

EXERCISE 11.7   **Recognizing the Features of an Illustration Essay**

Read the following essay. Then answer the questions that follow by writing your responses on the blanks provided.

A World Without "F's"

1   School is out. What did your children learn this year? Across the country, one poisonous lesson was pumped into the systems of self-esteem-inflated students: There is no such thing as failure.

2   Christine Pelton, a now-famous former biology teacher at Piper High School in Piper, Kansas, resigned last month when her school board—pressured by angry parents—refused to support her flunking of nearly 30 students who plagiarized[1]. Two lesser-known teachers also refused to play along with the education establishment's dumbing-down games. They tried to give out Fs, too. Their reward for showing children that slacking off has consequences? Humiliation, intimidation, and litigation[2].

3   Erich Martel, a history teacher at Wilson Senior High School in Washington, DC, issued an F last year to a girl who took his Advanced Placement American history course. It was enough to prevent her from graduating. But when the school held its commencement[3] ceremony, there was the student—strolling across the stage in her cap and gown.

---

1. **plagiarized:** copied someone else's work and presented it as one's own

2. **litigation:** legal action

3. **commencement:** graduation ceremony

4   Martel checked the school's computer system. The student's grade had been boosted to a D. "It was a feeling of being sabotaged[1], a feeling of being undermined, that for reasons that have nothing to do with the student's performance, there are shortcuts around a teacher's legitimate grade," Martel told the *Washington Post* last week. And he wasn't alone. Martel discovered at least eleven cases in which students' grades were raised without the knowledge of his fellow teachers.

5   One student earned a D, which her father protested because his daughter "needed a high grade-point average" to go to college. The teacher relented and gave the student a chance to retake a final exam. Her score was even lower. The teacher kept the original grade. But Martel later discovered that it had been changed to a "P" (for "Pass"). "I could not believe it," the overruled teacher, Anexora Skvirsky, said. "I am absolutely alarmed. It is uncalled for. It is intolerable. It is like cheating. It is like lying. It is like fraud." Like?

6   As for those responsible for altering the grades, the DC schools are sending a consistent message: Screw up, move up. The assistant high school principal who changed the grade of Martel's student is now a principal at an elementary school in the district. And Wilson High's former principal, who also altered grades, is now an assistant superintendent overseeing the city's high schools. She justifies the grade changes because they were "unfair."

7   "Unfair" is the same gripe that came from the parents of a high school senior at Sunrise Mountain High School in Glendale, Arizona. When their daughter flunked a required English class, which she needed to pass in order to graduate, Mom and Dad did the natural thing in a no-consequences world: They hired a lawyer.

8   In a missive[2] that would make the parody[3] writers at the satirical[4] magazine, *The Onion*, blush, attorney Stan F. Massad demanded that teacher Elizabeth Joice "take whatever action is necessary to correct this situation so that it can be settled amicably[5]. Failing that, you will force us to institute litigation." Massad claimed that his client "has been very sick, unable to sleep or eat and she has been forced to seek medical attention. To say that she has experienced Severe Emotional and Physical Distress over this matter is an understatement."

9   Turning up the sob-story volume, Massad bemoaned: "The student was all ready to graduate and, now, at the eleventh hour, she is told that she will not. As you know, the student is on the Student Council, and she was looking forward to speaking at the Graduation Ceremonies. It is certainly a shame that this

1. **sabotaged:** deliberately defeated or hindered something
2. **missive:** letter or memo
3. **parody:** related to humor that mocks or ridicules
4. **satirical:** related to sarcastic or mockingly witty attacks meant to expose vice or folly
5. **amicably:** good-naturedly; agreeably

young lady's life has now been ruined forever." (The full text of the bullying letter is available at http://www.azcentral.com/news/articles/0611lawyerletter.On .html.)

10   The *Arizona Republic* reported that just hours before her graduation last month, the student was allowed to take a retest—over Joice's objections. The student passed the retest and got her diploma. Life, she has learned from her litigious[1] parents and obsequious[2] school officials, is one big do-over.

11   Whiny parents wonder why public schools have abandoned standards, forsaken accountability[3], and adopted appeasement[4] as their primary educational mission. Oh, who could be to blame for such an abysmal[5] abdication[6] of responsibility? Who?*

1. What is the thesis of this essay?

_____

_____

2. Does the author offer several examples or just one extended example in support of her thesis statement?

_____

3. What mode organizes the details of the example that is developed in paragraphs 3 and 4?

_____

4. Does the author use any illustration transitions? Do you think that she should add more? If so, where should these transitions be added?

_____

_____

5. After reading this essay, do you agree with the author's thesis statement? Why or why not?

_____

1. **litigious:** relating to legal action
2. **obsequious:** fawning; submissive
3. **accountability:** responsibility
4. **appeasement:** attempts to bring peace, quiet, or calm, often at the expense of principles

5. **abysmal:** terrible; awful
6. **abdication:** giving up responsibility or power

Source: Michelle Malkin, "A World Without "F's," *Santa Barbara News-Press,* June 20, 2002, p. A15. Reprinted by permission.

In Summary: Steps in Writing Illustration Essays

уместные, относящиеся к делу

1. **Select relevant examples.** Make sure that each example matches your main idea or thesis.
2. **Plan to include a sufficient number of examples.** You might be able to provide just one extended example, but ask yourself if you could illustrate your point better if you provided several examples.
3. **Organize your examples.** Determine if some of your examples are more important than others and arrange them accordingly.
4. As you write, **develop each example (as appropriate) with narration or description.** Refer to Chapters 9 and 10 to review the principles of writing effective stories and descriptions.

To review the main points in this chapter, write a brief response to each of the following questions.

1. Define the term *illustration* as it relates to essay writing.

2. How can you use examples in an illustration essay?

3. Discuss the role of the thesis statement in an illustration essay.

4. Discuss the role of examples in an illustration essay and the importance of using an adequate number of examples. Discuss how you can arrange examples in your essay, depending on whether they are equal in importance or not.

5. List three common illustration transitional phrases.

6. What are the two modes often used to develop longer, extended examples?

Topic Ideas for Illustration Essays

Exercise 11.1 includes topic ideas that you may want to develop into illustration essays. The following are some additional ideas.

■ Current American obsessions

■ Food fads

- Dangerous habits of today's drivers
- A person I know who is _____ (open-minded, addicted, compassionate, lacking in self-awareness, creative, and so on)
- Taking risks *(positive or negative)*
- A quality that all successful people possess
- A good _____ (parent, friend, employee, boss, teacher, doctor, and so on)
- A specific quality of today's _____ (teenagers, senior citizens, and so on)
- Agree or disagree: Technology has made the world a better place to live.
- A specific quality of today's music, video games, or movies
- Agree or disagree: The book is always better than the movie.
- A specific advantage or disadvantage of being a celebrity
- Role models

 **Web**Work

For some good examples of writing that uses illustration, visit **http://grammar.ccc .commnet.edu/grammar/composition/examples.htm**.

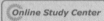 For more information and exercises, go to the Online Study Center at **http://www.college.hmco.com/pic/ dolphinwriterthree**.

Classification *(process to put things in the groups*

GOALS FOR CHAPTER 12

▶ Define the term *classification*.

▶ Describe the steps in writing a classification.

▶ Write a classification essay.

▶ Recognize the features of a classification essay.

Sometimes you will need to show how the elements of a subject that contains different types or parts can be distinguished from one another. Grouping like things together—which is called *classifying*—often helps readers better understand both the larger thing and the relationships among its elements. The passage that follows, for example, classifies people into two types: "go-backs" and "close-outs."

------ **The Real Digital Divide** ------

I conducted an informal poll among friends and discovered that the world does indeed consist of two kinds of people: go-backs and close-outs. It was information I could not readily accept. For me, hitting the back button when navigating a Web site is such a natural, no-brainer way to traverse[1] the Internet that I could not believe there might be other, equally effective ways to move around in cyberspace[2].

As I thought about it, I realized that Web navigation is something most of us teach ourselves according to some intuitive[3] sense of order and direction. Given that, I began to wonder what a person's navigational preference might say about his or her personality.

1. **traverse:** move over; travel over
2. **cyberspace:** the electronic medium of computer networks

3. **intuitive:** instinctive; untaught

259

Go-backs, it seemed to me, would be people who like having links to the past and probably have many long-term friendships. Go-backs are probably impulsive Web users, the kind of people who start out looking for research on the consumer-confidence index and end up on a site about the Whirling Dervishes of southern Turkey. Because go-backs are also insecure about technology, they need a digital handrail to guide them back to where they started. In the world of the Internet, go-backs are the impetuous[1] kindergartners who climb over the schoolyard fence, get into trouble, and then beg the teacher to give them a second chance. Go-backs are my people.

Now, let us talk about close-outs. People who shut down Web pages when done with them are clearly more decisive and confident than go-backs. They are forward thinkers who gather data, make decisions, and emphatically[2] stand by them. They do not dawdle, which makes them reliable, but they may have a tendency to be a bit brash[3]. Close-outs scare me.

In conducting my poll, I was pleased to discover that the writers and editors I work best with are just like me. They like to go back. Like Dorothy[4], we believe there is no place like home. I was, however, astonished to learn that I live with a close-out, which actually helps to explain some of our arguments. "Honey, let us go back to when you first got upset," I might say to my beloved close-out, whose initial response typically is: "No. It is over. I am not talking about this anymore."*

The previous passage groups people into two different categories based upon how they like to navigate the Internet and then offers descriptive details about each group.

The topic you have chosen for your essay will dictate a need for classification. For instance, if you need to explain a large topic, like architectural style, the reader may comprehend it more readily if you classify the major types of architectural styles. Notice how the following passage, for example, classifies people who do not vote into five different types.

We have identified five types of nonvoters. Nearly three out of ten (29 percent) of nonvoters can be described as "Doers." They are relatively avid news consumers who follow politics and public affairs regularly. They are extremely upbeat about the state of the Union and tend to be more positive than other nonvoters about a wide variety of governmental and social institutions. Doers tend to be more involved than members of the other nonvoter clusters in their

1. **impetuous:** impulsive and thoughtless
2. **emphatically:** forcefully; determinedly
3. **brash:** boldly defiant

4. **Dorothy:** a character in the film *The Wizard of Oz*

Source: Adapted from Shari Caudron, "The Real Digital Divide," in *Horizons* (Boston: Houghton Mifflin, 2004), pp. 173–174. Reprinted by permission of Houghton Mifflin Company.

communities. Five percent of the Doers say they volunteered on a political campaign last year and still failed to vote.

One-quarter of all nonvoters can be described as the "Unplugged." Compared with the other four clusters of nonvoters, the Unplugged are disproportionately[1] young—59 percent are under the age of 30, including 41 percent who are between the ages of 18 and 24. These are among the most information-deprived of all nonvoters. While 40 percent of the Doers say they read a newspaper six or seven days a week, only 7 percent of the Unplugged say they read a newspaper that often. The unplugged also watch television news less than any other group of nonvoters. Not surprisingly, the Unplugged tend not to follow politics, rarely discuss public policy with family or friends, and say they pay little attention to a campaign.

Fourteen percent are what we call the "Irritables." Compared with other groups of nonvoters, Irritables are disproportionately older. They tend to follow politics and public affairs fairly closely, with 42 percent saying that they follow developments in this area most of the time. One-quarter of this group say they read a newspaper six or seven days a week—a significantly higher level of daily readership than either the Don't Knows or the Unplugged. Sixty-four percent of the Irritables say they watch a television news broadcast at least six days a week. Half of the members of this cluster say they followed campaign stories at least fairly closely. Irritables see little difference between the political parties, and they are much more likely than Doers to feel that it makes no difference who is elected.

Twelve percent of the likely nonvoters can be classified as "Don't Knows." They have little or no interest in politics, have little interest in the news, and profess[2] little knowledge about the candidates or the institutions that govern their lives. Don't Knows are generally pessimistic about their elected officials and a wide variety of social institutions. In general, they are also more likely than members of other nonvoter blocks to express no opinion about the various institutions.

Twenty percent of nonvoters can be described as "Alienated[3]." As the cluster name would imply, 63 percent of the Alienated feel that the country has gotten off on the wrong track—29 percentage points higher than among the Doers. Alienated voters also take a dim view of politicians, political institutions, and a number of social institutions, as well. For instance, 39 percent of the Alienated have an unfavorable opinion about the Supreme Court, while the comparable figure among Doers is 11 percent. Among all nonvoters, the Alienated are the most

1. **disproportionately:** unevenly; unequally
2. **profess:** declare; claim
3. **alienated:** withdrawn; separated

likely to express unfavorable opinions about their local school boards, their local city councils, and even religious institutions.*

To write effective classification essays, follow the principles presented in the next sections of this chapter.

Writing a Classification Essay

Classification focuses on the distinguishing features of various people or things and groups like things together. To successfully classify a subject, you will need to apply an organizing principle, find the best order for the resulting groups, and develop your ideas with descriptive details and/or examples.

Applying an Organizing Principle, Determining a Main Idea, and Writing a Thesis Statement

Things can be classified a number of different ways. For example, think of how many ways there are to classify people. We can group people according to personality type by using categories such as the ones from the Myers-Briggs personality inventory or by grouping people according to whether they possess "Type A" characteristics or "Type B" characteristics. We can classify them according to socioeconomic class into groups that we could label *lower class, middle class,* or *upper class.* We can group them by the type of work they perform: blue collar or white collar. We can group them according to social groups: popular people, jocks, nerds, loners, and so forth. These different ways of classifying are based on an *organizing principle,* a basis for the groupings. In the previous examples, personality, socioeconomic class, line of work, and social group are the different organizing principles. When classifying things, make sure you apply only *one* organizing principle to avoid overlap among different groups. You should avoid concluding, for instance, that your groups are blue-collar workers, the middle class, and the upper class because some of the blue-collar workers might also belong in the middle-class or upper-class categories.

When you write your thesis statement, consider naming your categories if you have just a few. For example, you could write: "The three types of parenting styles are authoritarian, permissive, and authoritative." However, if there are numerous categories, you might write a more general thesis statement: "There are many different kinds of love."

*Source: Adapted from The Pew Charitable Trusts, September 2001, www.pewtrusts.com/pdf/pp_medill _highlights.pdf. Reprinted by permission of The Pew Charitable Trusts.

EXERCISE 12.1 **Applying Organizing Principles for Classification**

For each topic given, think of two different organizing principles and then generate
three groups that would result from the application of each principle.

[handwritten: Age (1) ocets of (high school) 2) 20s 3) older adults]

1. **Topic: Students**

   [handwritten: GPA (high, average, low)]

   Organizing Principle #1: *knowlege*   Organizing Principle #2: *hobbies activi-ties*

   Groups: Groups:

   Smart   *a lot of different hobbies*

   average   *1 or 2 hobbies or activity*

   stupid   *no at all*

2. **Topic: Women (or men)**

   [handwritten: sports fan (huge fan, average, not at all)]

   Organizing Principle #1: *weight*   Organizing Principle #2: *cooking*

   Groups: Groups:

   obess, above average   *high (gurmet)*

   normal, average   *average*

   anorexic, below average   *low (fast food)*

3. **Topic: Shoppers**

   Organizing Principle #1: *frequency*   Organizing Principle #2: *spending money*

   Groups: Groups:

   every 1-3 days   *saver*

   once a week   *average*

   once a month   *spenders*

   method of purchase (Internet, phone, store)

EXERCISE 12.2 **Writing Thesis Statements for Classification Essays**

For each of the following topics, use some prewriting techniques to generate ideas
on your own paper, and then write a thesis statement that you could use for a classification essay. *[handwritten: сначала опред-то принцип и 3 группы, затем опред-то замечан-]*

1. **Relatives**

   Thesis statement: *Holidays - perfect time for commu-nication with your relatives*

2. **Fears**

   Thesis statement: *There are some simple fears, which people have in the childhood.*

3. College professors

Thesis statement: _____

4. Stress

Thesis statement: _____

5. Jobs

Thesis statement: _____

Organizing Details and Using Transitions

Once you have determined your groups, organizing a classification essay tends to be relatively easy. You simply devote at least one paragraph of the essay to each group. However, you will need to determine if these groups should be discussed in a particular order. They may be equal, making their order irrelevant. However, if one group is significantly larger than others, you might consider arranging them from largest to smallest, or vice versa. If the classification is based upon other quantities, such as dollar amounts, you might consider arranging them in ascending or descending order. Also, consider whether you should organize them by order of importance.

As you write, make sure that you include transitions to help readers follow your pattern of organization and train of thought. Classification essays present a series of groups or categories, so they typically include transitional phrases such as these:

first	second	third
one category	a second kind	another type
the first group	the next group	the last group

As you read the following excerpt from an essay, notice how the bold transitional words help to point out the two categories.

Differing Learning Styles

A *learning styles* approach to teaching and learning is based on the idea that all students have strengths and abilities, but each student may have a preferred way of using these abilities. Some researchers have identified four basic learning styles. **The first type,** the *mastery style* learner, absorbs information concretely; processes information sequentially, in a step-by-step manner; and judges the value of learning in terms of its clarity and practicality. For example, a middle-school student with a mastery learning style might enjoy learning geometry because it helps him or her figure out problems with a building or craft hobby.

The second type of learner is the *understanding style* learner, who focuses more on ideas and abstractions; learns through a process of questioning, reasoning, and testing; and evaluates learning by standards of logic and the use of evidence. A geometry student with this style might benefit from testing several triangles to deduce[1] the principle that the angles all add up to 180 degrees.

The *self-expressive style* learner, **the third type**, looks for images implied in learning; uses feelings and emotions to construct new ideas and products; and judges the learning process according to its originality, aesthetics[2], and capacity to surprise or delight. A geometry class that included making three-dimensional mobile sculptures by combining classic geometric forms might appeal to a student with the self-expressive learning style.

The fourth type is the *interpersonal style* learner. Like the mastery learner, the interpersonal learner focuses on concrete, palpable[3] information; prefers to learn socially; and judges learning in terms of its potential use in helping others. Students with interpersonal styles might enjoy learning geometry in groups, especially if they were able to use what they learned in a project, such as building part of a house for a low-income family.*

EXERCISE 12.3   Organizing Details in Classification Essays

On your own paper, prewrite to generate ideas and then complete each of the following thesis statements by filling in the blank. Then, on the other blanks provided, prepare an informal outline by listing the examples you would include in an appropriate order.

gon-mo npeg-ue u cgeeamo 3 намеро-pue

1. In my experience, there are _____ types of friends.

Organizing principle—time (location, where, (y)ou usually meet friends)

1) long-time friends, whom I know since I was a child

2) less-time friends, whom I know since I was a student

3) short-time friends, whom I know since I started to work

1. **deduce:** use reason to discover
2. **aesthetics:** beauty; good taste
3. **palpable:** easily felt or evident

*Source: Adapted from Kevin Ryan and James M. Cooper, *Those Who Can, Teach*, 10th edition, Boston: Houghton Mifflin, © 2004, p. 44. Used by permission of Houghton Mifflin Company.

2. Goals fall into one of _the three_ categories.

long term time
career, personal, education
most important _short term,_ _achieved_
somewhat important _long term_ _unachieved_
less important _life long terms_ _in process of achieving_

3. There are _____ types of drivers.

reckless _age_ _skills_
careful _teenagers_ _exellent_
very careful _adults_ _average_
seniors _poor_

⭐ **EXERCISE 12.4** **Recognizing Classification Transitions**

Circle all of the classification transitional words in the following essay.

The Seven Deadly Nyms

Virtuous Internet searching takes more than hard work and clean thinking—you must keep constant vigilance against the seven deadly nyms that can play the devil with your search results.

When was the last time you thought—really thought—about how you choose the words you enter into search engine query[1] boxes? Did you know there are literally hundreds of words that are virtually guaranteed to produce the worst possible results, no matter how good the search engine?

Most experienced searchers are familiar with "stop words," or words that many search engines completely ignore. The engines ignore stop words because they are common words that typically modify other words and carry no meaning themselves, such as "the," "who," "it," and so on. Though using stop words in your queries can cause problems, there are far more insidious[2] culprits[3] that

1. **query:** question
2. **insidious:** deceitful; tricky
3. **culprits:** offenders

you should avoid like the plague. These words are the class of search terms I call the *seven deadly nyms*.

The first deadly nym is a set of words called *contronyms*, or Janus[1] words. A contronym is a single word that has multiple meanings that contradict the others. Some common contronyms include

Fast—moving quickly versus firmly stuck in place
Hysterical—overwhelmed with fear versus outrageously funny
Root—establish something new versus dig out completely

The second deadly nym is a group of words known as *heteronyms*. Heteronyms are similar to antagonyms[2], with a subtle difference. Heteronyms are words that are spelled identically but have different meanings when pronounced differently (*bow, desert, object, refuse*).

Heteronyms can sometimes be the result of melioration[3], or the acquisition of a positive meaning by a word that has traditionally had a negative meaning. *Bad* is an example. In its original sense, *bad* means nasty, spoiled, broken, etc. But pronounced "baad," it takes on the slang meaning that's just the opposite: good, cool, or fashionable. A particularly insidious example of a melioration is the word *factoid*, which means "a piece of unverified or inaccurate information that is presented in the press as factual, often as part of a publicity effort, and that is then accepted as true because of frequent repetition," according to dictionary.com.

Watch out for the opposite of heteronyms: *polyonyms*. These are different words that have the same meaning (*Jupiter, Zeus, Oden*). Depending on what you are looking for, you might miss some important information if you use only one variant of a polyonym. For best results, find and use them all.

For the spelling-challenged, *homonyms* are the most pernicious[4] deadly nym. Homonyms are words that have the same sound but a completely different meaning (*to, too, two*). Some homonyms are also contronyms—words that are spelled and pronounced like another word but have a different origin and meaning.

The fifth deadly nym is the *capitonym*, a word that changes pronunciation and meaning when it is capitalized. Capitonyms are commonly words that become proper nouns when capitalized: amber is a yellow, orange, or brownish-yellow fossil resin[5]; Amber is the eighth-grade softball team captain. You polish

1. **Janus:** two-faced god of Roman mythology
2. **antagonyms:** another word for *contronyms*
3. **melioration:** improvement; becoming more positive

4. **pernicious:** harmful; destructive
5. **resin:** solid or semisolid substance of plant origin

silver with ammonia and silicon, though you would never dream of applying the same to a Polish sausage.

Next up are *caconyms*. A caconym is an erroneous name, especially in taxonomic classification[1]. While caconyms might be useful for tracking down archaic[2] or outdated usage, you are likely to end up with inaccurate information if you use them in search queries.

The seventh deadly nym is the obscure but lethal *exonym*, especially if you are searching for nonlocal information. An exonym is a place name that foreigners use instead of the name that natives use (Cologne: Koln; Florence: Firenze; Morocco: Maroc). Beyond provoking a chuckle from locals, using exonyms as search terms will likely net results biased toward foreign information, which may not be as accurate as home-grown content.

The next time you are tempted to nym, think before you type. Abstain[3] from nyms and you will likely end up choosing far better query terms and be blessed with the fruits of virtuous search.*

EXERCISE 12.5   **Writing a Classification Essay That Includes Transitions**

Choose one of the thesis statements and outlines you prepared in Exercise 12.3. Write the essay, including transitional words that indicate how the details are related.

Developing a Classification Essay

You will usually develop each group of your classification essay with descriptive details and examples. For example, let us say that you are writing about the monarchy form of government, and you are classifying three different types of monarchy: absolute, constitutional, and limited. As you describe each type, you will present details about the characteristics of each kind of monarchy, and you will also want to illustrate each type by giving examples of specific countries that base their governments upon one of these types.

1. **taxonomic classification:** an ordered system of grouping things together

2. **archaic:** no longer current

3. **abstain:** refrain; hold oneself back

*Source: Adapted from Chris Sherman, "The Seven Deadly Nyms," SearchEngineWatch.com, Aug. 7, 2002, http://searchenginewatch.com/searchday/article.php/2160501.

EXERCISE 12.6   **Recognizing the Features of a Classification Essay**

Read the following essay. Then answer the questions that follow by writing your responses on the blanks provided.

I'm Terribly Sorry. Really.

In a deeply therapeutic[1] culture, apologies function like secular[2] sacraments[3]. But more and more people demand them, while fewer and fewer are willing to give them. So instead of "I did it and I am sorry," we get fake apologies and conditional ones. Some examples:

The basic conditional apology. Secretary of Education Rod Paige said to the National Education Association, "If you took offense at anything I said, please accept my apology." If? He had said the NEA is a terrorist organization.

The misdirection conditional. Sen. Christopher Dodd claimed that Sen. Robert Byrd, a former member of the Ku Klux Klan[4], would have been a great senator at any time in history, including the Civil War. Dodd's "if" statement said: "If in any way, in my referencing the Civil War, I offended anyone, I apologize." This made it sound as though someone was hounding Dodd for mentioning the Civil War.

The I-gotta-be-me conditional. After turning a press conference into a brawl, boxer Mike Tyson explained: "I responded as I saw fit. In the process, things that I said may have offended members of the audience. To these people I offer my apologies."

The subject-changing, head-scratching conditional. In 1985, after saying that South African bishop Desmond Tutu was "a phony," Jerry Falwell[5] said he meant that Tutu could not speak for all South Africans. Falwell offered an apology if the bishop thought he was being impugned[6] as a person or a minister. Oh. So that is it.

The subject-changing, head-scratching nonapology. When Jane Swift served as lieutenant governor of Massachusetts, she used state employees to baby-sit her infant daughter. Asked to explain, she said: "I will not apologize for trying to be a good mother."

1. **therapeutic:** having or exhibiting healing powers
2. **secular:** worldly rather than spiritual
3. **sacraments:** religious acts
4. **Ku Klux Klan:** racist organization in America
5. **Jerry Falwell:** an American Baptist minister and conservative activist
6. **impugned:** attacked as false or questionable

The I-was-misunderstood nonapology. Sen. Trent Lott blamed "a poor choice of words" for his suggestion that the segregationist[1] Strom Thurmond of 1948 should have been elected president.

The incomprehensible conditional. Rep. Corrine Brown recently called U.S. policy on Haiti a racist policy concocted by a "bunch of white men." When a Mexican-American assistant secretary of state objected, Brown issued a conditional apology to Hispanics, saying that she meant to indict[2] whites only, adding, "You all [nonblack people] look the same to me." Luckily for her, Brown is a Democrat, so her remarks went nowhere in the media.

The "regret" nonapology. In finally acknowledging his perjury[3] and the Monica Lewinsky affair[4], President Clinton said: "I know that my public comments and my silence about this matter gave a false impression. I misled people, including even my wife. I deeply regret that."

The accusatory conditional. "If, in hindsight, we also discover that mistakes may have been made, . . . I am deeply sorry," said Cardinal Edward Egan of New York, while apologizing (sort of) for bishops who failed to deal with sex scandals in the Roman Catholic clergy. "Hindsight" means that the critics are just second-guessers who were not there.

The accusatory nonconditional. "Your government failed you. . . . And I failed you," said Richard Clarke at the 9/11[5] hearings. But his book makes clear that he does not believe he failed anyone. What he means is that President Bush failed the nation. No one has ever buried a severe accusation in a pitch-perfect Oprah-fied[6] apology like Clarke.

The historical apology for what other people did. President Clinton apologized for U.S. support of dictators during the Cold War and for the deposing[7] of Hawaii's Queen Liliuokalani by the Cleveland administration in 1893. Most of these apologies are low cost or cost free. For instance, I would like to apologize here for the U.S. invasion of Canada in the War of 1812. There. I feel better already.

The "it happened" nonapology. After 14 years of denials, Pete Rose[8] finally admitted he had bet on baseball games. He wrote: "I am sure I am supposed to act

1. **segregationist:** someone who supports separating people of different races, classes, or ethnic groups
2. **indict:** accuse of wrongdoing
3. **perjury:** deliberately giving false or misleading testimony while under oath
4. **Monica Lewinsky affair:** President Clinton had an extramarital affair with Lewinsky, who was working as an intern at the White House
5. **9/11:** on September 11, 2001, terrorists attacked several targets in the United States
6. **Oprahfied:** in the style of Oprah Winfrey, a popular television talk-show host
7. **deposing:** removing from power
8. **Pete Rose:** a former Major League baseball player

all sorry or sad or guilty. . . . Let's leave it at this: I'm sorry it happened, and I'm sorry for all the people, fans, and family it hurt. Let's move on."

The sincere but responsibility-shrinking apology. In 2003, Arnold Schwarzenegger met the barrage[1] of sexual accusations against him by saying, "I was on rowdy movie sets, and I have done things that were not right, which I thought then [were] playful. . . . I am deeply sorry about that, and I apologize because this is not what I'm trying to do." This is the most effective political apology any of us will probably live to see. The problem is that Schwarzenegger was accused of much more serious offenses against women than the words *rowdy* and *playful* can reasonably cover. He minimizes while apologizing. Quite brilliant, really.*

1. What is the thesis of this essay?

_____

_____

2. What organizing principle(s) does the author apply to his topic? How many categories result from the application of this organizing principle?

_____

3. The author's types of apologies might be placed in one of four larger groups: conditional apologies, nonapologies, nonconditional apologies, and sincere apologies. Do you think the essay would be more effective or easier to understand if the different kinds of apologies were grouped together in these larger categories? Regroup the author's thirteen kinds of apologies into these four groups.

_____

_____

_____

_____

_____

_____

_____

_____

_____

1. **barrage:** overwhelming outpouring

Source: John Leo, "I'm Terribly Sorry. Really." *U.S. News and World Report,* May 10, 2004, p. 13. Copyright © 2004 *U.S. News and World Report,* L.P. Reprinted with permission.

4. The author substitutes bold subheadings for classification transitions. Do you think that this technique is an effective substitute? Why or why not?

_____

5. What is the author's attitude toward his subject? How do you know?

_____

_____

_____

6. Do you agree with the author that "more and more people demand them [apologies], while fewer and fewer are willing to give them"?

_____

In Summary: Steps in Writing Classification Essays

1. **Select an organizing principle.** Apply just *one* principle to sort items into appropriate groups.
2. **Decide on the best order for presenting the categories.** If appropriate, arrange the groups in ascending or descending order. As you write, use transitional words to help readers understand the relationships among the types.
3. **Develop each type or category with descriptive details and examples.**

To review the main points in this chapter, write a brief response to each of the following questions.

1. What is classification?

2. What is an organizing principle?

3. Why should you be careful to use just one organizing principle for classification?

4. When should you state your specific categories in a thesis statement for a classification essay?

5. In what order should you arrange the categories of a classification?

6. What are some common classification transitional words and phrases?

7. What kinds of details are commonly used to develop classification essays?

Topic Ideas for Classification Essays

Exercise 12.1 includes topic ideas you may want to develop into classification essays. Here are some additional ideas:

- Neighbors   *friends / nuetral / enemies*   *relationship with neibors*
- Crimes
- Computer users
- Communication
- Bosses or coworkers
- Teenagers
- Social classes

- Intelligence
- Sports fans
- Movies
- Tests
- Attitudes
- Personalities

WebWork

Go to **http://www.buowl.boun.edu.tr/students/types%20of%20essays/
Classification%20Essay.htm**. Read the sample classification essay. Then evaluate the
effectiveness of this essay by answering the following questions.

1. On what organizing principle is the classification based? Is the thesis clearly stated?
   Are the topic and/or categories clear?

2. Are the categories clearly organized? Are they presented in an appropriate order?
   Does the writer use adequate transitional words?

3. Is each type or category adequately developed with details and/or examples?

4. What suggestions for improvement would you offer this writer?

Online Study Center For more information and exercises, go to the Online Study
Center at **http://www.college.hmco.com/pic/
dolphinwriterthree**.

Division

GOALS FOR CHAPTER 13

▶ Define the term *division*.

▶ Describe the steps in writing a division essay.

▶ Write a division essay.

▶ Recognize the features of a division essay.

Sometimes you will need to show how the elements of a subject that contains different components or parts can be separated from one another. Breaking a large or complex thing down into its parts—which is called *dividing*—often helps readers better understand both the larger thing and the relationships among its elements. The passage that follows, for example, divides college sports programs into three main parts.

The National Collegiate Athletic Association splits its membership of U.S. colleges and universities into three divisions: Division I, Division II, and Division III. Division I member institutions have to sponsor at least seven sports for men and seven for women (or six for men and eight for women) with two team sports for each gender. Each playing season has to be represented by each gender as well. There are contest and participant minimums for each sport, as well as scheduling criteria. For sports other than football and basketball, Division I schools must play 100 percent of the minimum number of contests against Division I opponents—anything over the minimum number of games has to be 50 percent Division I. Men's and women's basketball teams have to play all but two games against Division I teams; for men, they must play one-third of all their contests in the home arena. Schools that have football are classified as Division I-A or I-AA. I-A football schools are usually fairly elaborate programs. Division I-A teams have to meet minimum attendance requirements (average 15,000 people in actual or paid attendance per home game), which must be met once in a rolling two-year period. Division I-AA teams do not need to meet minimum attendance requirements. Division I schools must meet minimum financial aid awards for their athletics program, and there are maximum financial aid awards for each sport that a Division I school cannot exceed.

Division II institutions have to sponsor at least four sports for men and four for women, with two team sports for each gender, and each playing season represented by each gender. There are contest and participant minimums for each sport, as well as scheduling criteria—football and men's and women's basketball teams must play at least 50 percent of their games against Division II or I-A or I-AA opponents. For sports other than football and basketball there are no scheduling requirements. There are no attendance requirements for football, or arena game requirements for basketball. There are maximum financial aid awards for each sport that a Division II school must not exceed. Division II teams usually feature a number of local or in-state student-athletes. Many Division II student-athletes pay for school through a combination of scholarship money, grants, student loans, and employment earnings. Division II athletics programs are financed in the institution's budget like other academic departments on campus. Traditional rivalries with regional institutions dominate schedules of many Division II athletics programs.

Division III institutions have to sponsor at least five sports for men and five for women, with two team sports for each gender, and each playing season represented by each gender. There are minimum contest and participant minimums for each sport. Division III athletics features student-athletes who receive no financial aid related to their athletic ability, and athletic departments are staffed and funded like any other department in the university. Division III athletics departments place special importance on the impact of athletics on the participants rather than on the spectators. The student-athlete's experience is of paramount[1] concern. Division III athletics encourages participation by maximizing the number and variety of athletic opportunities available to students, placing primary emphasis on regional in-season and conference competition.*

Your topic will dictate a need for division. For instance, if you need to explain a complex topic, such as the description of a machine or a large entity, to

1. **paramount:** highest; most important

Source: Adapted from "What's the Difference Between Divisions I, II, and III?" from "Earth Observatory Experiments: Rainforest Biome," http://www.ncaa.org/about/div_criteria.html.

your reader, dividing it into its parts will help you present your details in an orderly way. Notice how the following passage, for example, divides the four-billion-year-old history of Earth into eras and periods.

To better understand Earth's history, scientists have come up with a number of divisions that they use to measure time. Specifically, they divide the four billion years that the planet has existed into four main eras. Monumental[1] changes mark the end of one time period and the beginning of another.

The Precambrian Era, dating from 4.5 to 544 million years ago, marks the period of Earth's history from its initial formation to the beginning of life. During this time range, our Earth went through vast changes. The Earth had solidified from the solar disk left over from the Sun's own formation. The Moon formed, setting the stage for later tidal fluctuations[2]. As the Earth cooled, it developed its initial atmosphere that contained no oxygen, [nevertheless] setting the stage for the development of the first life forms, prokaryotes. From their interaction with the then prevalently[3] carbon dioxide and sulfur-rich atmosphere, they slowly altered, developing into the first eukaryotes and creating yet another profound change in Earth, the production of oxygen.

As the atmosphere slowly became enriched in oxygen, complex multicellular organisms evolved, and the curtain had fallen upon one era of Earth's history to arise in a new era, the Paleozoic. With one of the greatest events in life's theater on Earth, the Precambrian Explosion marked a moment when an abundance of fossils showed a vast increase in the numbers and diversity of life. Later shown to be a more gradual increase in Earth's diversity, this was still the most significant increase in life forms on our new, young planet. The era ended with a mass extinction caused by the impact of a comet or asteroid about 250 million years ago.

The third era is the Mesozoic Era. Dating from 245 to 65 million years ago, the Mesozoic (Middle Animals) Era, the age of the dinosaurs, marks the beginning of land animals and plants. During this era, gymnosperms[4] first evolved, invading deep into new territory away from shores where water was plentiful. As these new plants moved inland, animals soon followed. The dinosaurs evolved, flourished in every habitat on land, then reinvaded the oceans. The Mesozoic ended as the dominant dinosaurs died after a meteor struck the Earth, changing the environment.

The fourth and final era is the Cenozoic Era. Dating from 65 million years ago to the present, the Cenozoic Era began with a truly big bang, a meteor

---

1. **monumental:** massive; enormous
2. **fluctuations:** changes
3. **prevalently:** mostly; predominantly
4. **gymnosperms:** type of plant

crashing into the Earth, causing a mass extinction of the large, dominant life forms of the Mesozoic Era, the dinosaurs. This event also marked the beginning of the Age of Mammals as mammals slowly invaded those niches[1] left open by the extinct dinosaurs. During this era, birds, angiosperms (flowers), insects, and bony fish have proliferated[2] through nearly every habitat on Earth.*

To write effective division essays, follow the principles presented in the rest of this chapter.

Writing a Division Essay

Division is a way of understanding a larger thing in terms of its smaller parts. To write an effective division essay, you need to determine the major and minor parts, decide on the best order for presenting those parts, and develop each part with descriptive details, examples, and possibly even an explanation of how the parts work together.

Determining the Parts and the Main Idea and Writing a Thesis Statement

The first step in division is deciding what the *major* parts are. For example, if you were going to divide a baseball field into its major parts, how would you do it? You could say that a baseball field has two major parts: the infield and the outfield. Each of the field's other, smaller parts—such as the bases—can be discussed in terms of one of these major parts. Center field, for example, is part of the outfield while home plate is part of the infield. If you were examining an organization, you could break it down into its major divisions or departments and then examine its other parts in terms of those major divisions. Doing this creates an orderly hierarchy that helps the reader more easily see how all of the parts relate to one another.

When you write your thesis statement, consider either naming the major parts or at least identifying how many there are.

1. **niches:** functions or positions

2. **proliferated:** grew or multiplied at a rapid rate

Source: Adapted from Kevin C. Hartzog, "Geological Time Scales," Oct. 15, 2002, http://www.starsandseas.com/SAS%20Evolution/SAS%20geoltime/geotime_precamb.htm. Reprinted by permission.

EXERCISE 13.1   Determining the Parts

Think of two different ways to divide each of the following subjects. Write the major parts of each division on the blanks provided.

1. Geographical areas of the United States
   Main parts of Division 1: _south, middle, north_
   Main parts of Division 2: _pacific, mountian, central, eastern_

2. Periods in your lifetime
   Main parts of Division 1: _childhood, teenager, adulthood_
   Main parts of Division 2: _school, college, work, retirement, eldery_

3. A certain group of people or a team
   Main parts of Division 1: _freshmen, junior, sophmore, senior_
   Main parts of Division 2: _starters, juniors, varsity_

EXERCISE 13.2   Writing Thesis Statements for Division Essays

For each of the following topics, use some prewriting techniques to generate ideas on your own paper, and then write a thesis statement that you could use for a division essay.

family time.

1. Parts of a typical weekday _different parts: rising time, work time, evening, family time_
   Thesis statement: _My usual day is divided in three_

2. A specific body part _thigh, shin, foot_
   Thesis statement: _The human being's leg is divided in three sections_

3. A specific area _Chicago—city is divided by ethnic groups of people: Chinatown, Little Italy, Greektown, Ukraine village_
   Thesis statement:

4. A ceremony (a wedding, graduation, bar mitzvah, and so on) _preparation, official part, celebration_
   Thesis statement: _A wedding ceremony is divided in three parts_

5. A movie, TV program, or video game _beginning, the heart, end of the story_
   Thesis statement: _The movie's divided on 3 parts_

Organizing the Parts and Using Transitions

To prepare to compose, create an outline that clearly groups the minor parts in terms of the major parts and reveals the relationships among all of these parts. Although you do not necessarily have to use a formal Roman numeral outline, this format will allow you to show the relationships among all of the parts. An outline for the division of the body's cardiopulmonary system, for example, might look like this:

> I. Cardiopulmonary system
>   A. Cardiovascular system
>   1. Heart
>   2. Blood vessels
>   a. Arteries
>   b. Veins
>   B. Respiratory system
>   1. Mouth
>   2. Nose
>   3. Trachea
>   4. Diaphragm
>   5. Lungs

This outline first divides the whole system by its major parts: the cardiovascular system and the respiratory system. Then it breaks those two systems into smaller parts by naming the components of each one.

After you group the minor parts with the major parts, you will need to decide the order in which to present them. Sometimes the order does not matter. For example, in the essay about the cardiopulmonary system, you might be able to discuss either the cardiovascular system or the respiratory system first. However, in other division essays, the parts are best arranged by either time order, spatial order, or order of importance. If you are dividing the parts of a ceremony, you might want to present them in the order in which they occur, arranging them in time order. If you are dividing the parts of a machine or an organ in the body, you might want to present them in a spatial order, such as left to right or top to bottom. The two main parts of a baseball field, for example, might be arranged from closest to farthest. If you are dividing a group of some kind, you might want to use the order of importance for presenting its various parts. Make sure your outline reflects the order you have chosen.

As you write, include appropriate transitional words to help the reader understand the relationships. If you use time order, include narrative transitions (see Chapter 8 for a list of these transitional words). If you use spatial order, include spatial transitions (see Chapter 9). If you use order of importance, you will include transitional words such as those in the following list.

first, second, third
next
last
finally
the most important part
most important
above all
least important

As you read the following passage, notice how the bold transitional words and information help to point out the parts.

The Stringed Instruments of an Orchestra

In most orchestras, four instruments make up the string section. These are the violin, the viola, the cello, and the double bass. All are generally played with a bow, although they may also be plucked with one's finger to create a different type of sound. The bow is a long, narrow piece of wood and is strung with a type of hair. Each of the four stringed instruments is a different size and is composed of different strings, as described next.

The violins make up **one part** of the string section. They are the smallest of the stringed instruments in the orchestra. The violin is also the highest sounding instrument of the string family. It has four strings (G, D, A, and E) and is played by placing the instrument under one's chin and drawing the bow across the strings. There are generally two sections of violins in an orchestra, which are referred to as the first and the second violin sections. The first section plays one written part to the music and the second section plays another. A person who plays the violin is referred to as a violinist.

Another part of the string section includes the viola. This instrument looks very similar to the violin; however, it is larger. It is played in a similar fashion to that of the violin, but it is a deeper-sounding instrument. It also has four strings: the C, G, D, and A strings. Most orchestras have one viola section. A person who plays the viola is referred to as a violist.

The third component of a string section is the cello, a larger instrument than both the violin and the viola. It also has a deeper sound. It is played by standing the instrument on the floor and placing the cello between one's legs. Similar to the violin and viola, the cello is played by drawing a bow across the strings. The strings on a cello are C, D, G, and A. Most orchestras have one section of cellos. A person who plays the cello is referred to as a cellist.

Finally, the double bass is the largest stringed instrument in an orchestra. It has the lowest pitch of all four of the stringed instruments described here. It is played by standing the instrument on the floor and drawing a bow across the strings. Unlike a cello, the double bass is played by standing behind it or sitting on a tall stool because of the large size of the instrument. The strings on a double bass are E, A, D, and G. Most orchestras have one double bass section. A person who plays the double bass is referred to as a bassist.*

EXERCISE 13.3 **Organizing Details in Division Essays**

On your own paper, prewrite to generate ideas and then complete each of the following thesis statements by filling in the blank. Then, on the other blanks provided, prepare an informal outline by listing the parts that you would include in an appropriate order.

1. The _____ I use regularly is made up of _____.

   _____

   _____

   _____

   _____

2. _____ is one business with an efficient division of labor.

   _____

   _____

   _____

   _____

3. _____ can be divided into _____ main parts.

   _____

   _____

   _____

   _____

*Source: Adapted from "The Four Types of Stringed Instruments of the Orchestra," 2002, http:// il.essortment.com/instrumentofth_rgju.htm. © 2001 by PageWise, Inc. Used with permission.

> **EXERCISE 13.4**   **Recognizing Division Transitions**

Circle all of the division transitional words in the following essay.

The Earth's atmosphere is most commonly divided into five layers or "spheres": the troposphere, stratosphere, mesosphere, thermosphere, and exosphere.

Closest to Earth is the *troposphere*. The word *troposphere* stems from the Greek word *tropos*, meaning "turning" or "mixing," because it is the most turbulent[1] part of the atmosphere. Most weather occurs in this layer. The temperature of this layer, which starts at Earth's surface and ends between seven kilometers at the poles and 17 kilometers at the equator, decreases with height.

The next layer, the *stratosphere,* ranges from 7 to 17 kilometers to about 50 kilometers from Earth's surface. In this layer, the temperature increases with height because [the layer] absorbs heat from the ultraviolet rays of the Sun. Commercial airline jets typically cruise in the lower stratosphere because it is a stable layer where there is little turbulence.

Above the stratosphere is the *mesosphere,* which comes from the Greek word *mesos,* meaning "middle." It is located 50 to 85 kilometers above Earth's surface, below the minimum altitude for spacecraft and above the maximum altitude for aircraft. Its temperature decreases with height. It is in the mesosphere where millions of meteors burn up on a daily basis.

Beyond the mesosphere is the *thermosphere,* which begins at about 85 kilometers above Earth's surface and ends at about 640 kilometers. It is named for the Greek word for "heat," *thermos.* Depending on solar activity, temperatures in this area can rise to 2,000 degrees Fahrenheit.

The uppermost layer of the atmosphere is the *exosphere,* from the Greek word *exo,* meaning "out or outside." It is here in this thin layer that some of Earth's atmospheric gases escape into outer space. The exact altitude at which the exosphere ends and space begins is not well defined.*

> **EXERCISE 13.5**   **Writing a Division Essay That Includes Transitions**

Choose one of the thesis statements and outlines you prepared in Exercise 13.3. Then write an essay, including transitional words that indicate how the parts are related.

1. **turbulent:** restless or disturbed

Source: National Weather Service, "Layers of the Atmosphere," July 12, 2006, www.srh.weather.gov/srh/jetstream/atmos/layers.htm.

Developing the Parts in a Division Essay

Usually, the parts within a division essay are developed with descriptive details and examples. However, you might also need to explain how the parts work together. For example, if you were to write that essay about the cardiopulmonary system, you would probably combine these methods of development. In your explanation of the heart, for example, you would use descriptive details to help the reader picture its size, shape, and other physical characteristics. Then you would probably need to use process to explain what the heart does and how it works with the other parts of the system.

EXERCISE 13.6 **Recognizing the Features of a Division Essay**

Read the following essay. Then answer the questions that follow by writing your responses on the blanks provided.

Federal Discretionary and Mandatory Spending

1   The federal budget can be divided into two types of spending according to how Congress appropriates[1] the money: *discretionary* and *mandatory.*

2   Discretionary[2] spending refers to the portion of the budget which goes through the annual *appropriations process* each year. In other words, Congress directly sets the level of spending on programs which are discretionary. Congress can choose to increase or decrease spending on any of those programs in a given year. The discretionary budget is about one-third of total federal spending. The pie graph on the next page indicates how discretionary spending was divided up in fiscal year 2005.

3   About half of the discretionary budget is "national defense," a government-defined function area that roughly corresponds in common parlance[3] as "military." However, this category does not include foreign military financing, security assistance, and other programs commonly thought of as military. Other types of

Total Budget:	$2.47 trillion
Mandatory:	$1.5 trillion
Discretionary:	$960 billion

Mid-Session Review, Budget of the U.S. Government, FY2006.

1. **appropriates:** sets apart for a specific use
2. **discretionary:** available for use as needed
3. **parlance:** speech or conversation

discretionary spending include the budget for education, many health programs, and housing assistance.

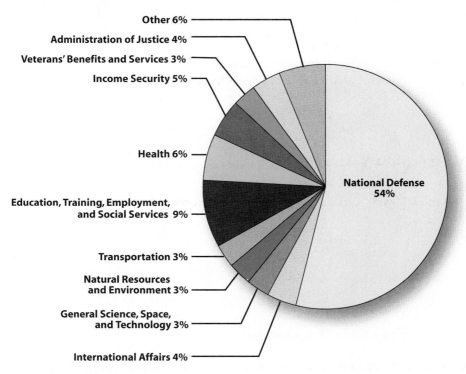

Other 6%
Administration of Justice 4%
Veterans' Benefits and Services 3%
Income Security 5%
Health 6%
Education, Training, Employment, and Social Services 9%
Transportation 3%
Natural Resources and Environment 3%
General Science, Space, and Technology 3%
International Affairs 4%
National Defense 54%

© 2005 National Priorities Project, Inc.
Other: energy, agriculture, commerce and housing credit, community and regional development, general government and the administration of Medicare and Social Security.

4   Mandatory spending includes programs, mostly *entitlement*[1] programs, which are funded by eligibility rules or payment rules. Congress decides to create a program, for example, Food Stamps. It then determines who is eligible for the program and any other criteria it may want to lay out. How much is appropriated for the program each year is then determined by estimations of how many people will be eligible and apply for Food Stamps.

5   Unlike discretionary spending, Congress does not decide each year to increase or decrease the Food Stamp budget; instead, it periodically reviews the eligibility rules and may change them in order to exclude or include more people.

1. **entitlement:** a government program that guarantees and provides benefits to a particular group

6   Mandatory spending makes up about two-thirds of the total federal budget. By far the largest mandatory program is Social Security, which makes up one-third of mandatory spending and continues to grow as the age demographic of the country shifts toward an older population. The following pie graph shows the breakdown of different types of mandatory spending in fiscal year 2005.*

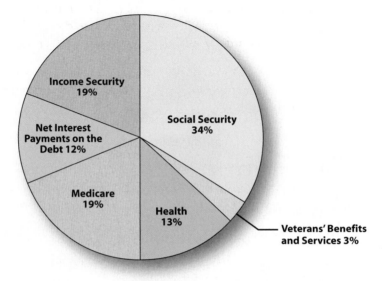

© 2005 National Priorities Project, Inc.

1. Into how many parts does the author divide the federal budget?

_____

2. Upon what does the author base this division?

_____

3. Into how many different parts does the author divide the discretionary budget? Into how many different parts does the author divide the mandatory budget?

_____

_____

_____

_____

_____

_____

_____

*Source: Office of Management and Budget, Budget of the United States Government, FY2006. Reprinted by permission of The National Priorities Project.

4. What are some of the other modes of development used to help readers understand the parts of the budget?

_____

_____

5. This writer includes a table and two pie graphs to help illustrate the parts of the subject. Did these visual aids help you better understand the federal budget? What other kinds of visual aids would be appropriate and effective in division essays?

_____

_____

In Summary: Steps in Writing Division Essays

1. **Divide the subject into its major parts.** Group minor parts with their major parts.
2. **Create an outline that shows the relationships of major and minor parts.** If appropriate, arrange the parts using time order, spatial order, or order of importance. As you write, include transitional words that reveal how the parts are related.
3. **Develop each part with descriptive details, examples, and/or explanation of how the parts work together.**

CHAPTER 13 REVIEW

To review the main points in this chapter, write a brief response to each of the following questions.

1. What is division?

2. What is the first step in writing a division essay?

3. What should be included in a thesis statement for a division essay?

4. What should an outline for a division essay include?

5. What are some of the best ways to arrange the information in a division essay?

6. What are some common transitional words and phrases for division essays?

7. How are division essays often developed?

Topic Ideas for Division Essays

Exercises 13.1 and 13.2 include topic ideas that you may want to develop into division essays. Here are some additional ideas:

- An animal breed, such as dogs or horses

- Classes in society

- An analysis of the ingredients of a particular product

- The components of _____ (a landfill, blood, a school board, and so on)

- A historical period

- A specific body part or system

- A major exam (e.g., the SAT, ACT, or the final exam of a course)

- A geographic region, such as a country, state, city, or town

- A certain population

- A place (e.g., an emergency room or an assembly line)

- An analysis of an artistic work

- Parts of a particular document, such as an essay or business letter

- Earth or the solar system

- A theatre, such as the one in the following diagram, or another building or structure

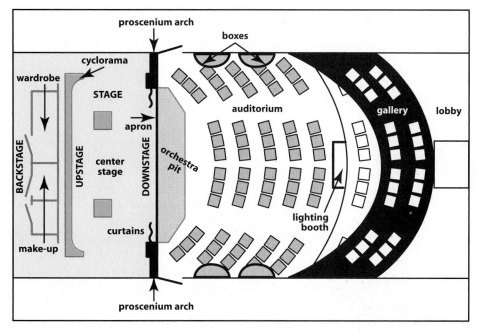

Source: http://www.knowitall.org/kidswork/theater/workzone/diagram/thdiagram.swf

backstage: the area where the performers prepare for the performance and wait when they are not onstage

wardrobe: the room where the costumes for the show are kept

makeup: the room where makeup and wigs are applied to performers

cyclorama: a curved cloth at the back of the stage that creates the illusion of unlimited space

stage: the floor area where the performance takes place

upstage: the back area of the stage

center stage: the middle area of the stage

downstage: the area of the stage closest to the audience

curtains: the large piece of fabric that separates the audience from the stage

apron: the part of the stage that is in front of the curtain near the audience

proscenium arch: an arch that frames the stage for the audience

orchestra pit: the area where the orchestra sits

auditorium: the area in the theatre where the audience sits

boxes: the small groups of seats in the private balconies

lighting booth: the control room for the stage-lighting instruments

gallery: the upper-level seating area in the auditorium

lobby: the area outside the auditorium where the audience gathers

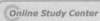

WebWork

Go to the How Stuff Works Web site at **www.howstuffworks.com**. Browse the site and then select a specific object that interests you. Study the description of it and any diagrams provided, and then write an analysis of the object's main parts.

Online Study Center For more information and exercises, go to the Online Study Center at **http://www.college.hmco.com/pic/ dolphinwriterthree**.

Comparison/Contrast

GOALS FOR CHAPTER 14

▶ Define the terms *comparison* and *contrast*.

▶ Describe the steps in writing a comparison/contrast essay.

▶ Write a comparison/contrast essay.

▶ Recognize the features of a comparison/contrast essay.

When you *compare* two things, you examine the similarities between them. When you *contrast* two things, you examine the differences between them. Comparison, contrast, or a combination of both is useful for developing ideas in compositions. Presenting a study of how two people, places, things, or ideas are alike or different is a good way to help your readers understand something about the two subjects. For example, read the following passage.

If you think it is just foreign policy that separates America from Europe, reflect for a moment on your summer. More than likely, you were at work for most of the past three months while most of Europe seems to have hung up a "Gone Fishing!" sign. The numbers support the perception. If you include vacations and public holidays, Europeans take off about six to seven weeks a year. Americans average about 10.2 days of vacation each year plus public holidays.

Do the Europeans have it right? Not exactly. In Europe, leisure is a matter for law. The European Union has just mandated[1] a minimum of four weeks' vacation for all member countries. In the United States, there is no law like that. Would you like Washington to lay down the law on vacations? It is hardly thinkable. It seems to me that our freely expressed choices have defined a pattern very different from that of Europe, one not amenable[2] to generalized rules.

1. **mandated:** required

2. **amenable:** agreeable

Europeans tend to take longer vacations, but over 60 percent of Americans prefer shorter trips. The average American spends only 4.3 nights of vacation away from home, down from six nights about 25 years ago. Micro-vacations are all the rage, ranging from a few hours at a spa to a weekend jaunt. Weekend trips compose more than half our leisure travel. Of course, there are practical reasons for the difference. More continental Europeans than Americans live in cramped flats[1], so they want to get out, while more Americans tend to own their own homes with backyards and are less inclined to leave. Second, [Americans] have a much higher proportion of families where both spouses work, so it is not easy to organize private time for a long family vacation beyond much more than a week or two, especially when you factor in schools, summer camps, and the like. And third, Americans tend to work longer hours because, by and large, they enjoy it while many Europeans do not. Roughly 85 percent of Americans are "broadly satisfied" with their jobs, a much higher proportion than in Europe.

So it is no wonder Europeans want all the time off they can get and that European labor unions push for more time off while American unions push for more money. We value money and more stuff; they value more leisure time.*

This passage contrasts Americans' and Europeans' amount of vacation time. After reading this passage, we understand the differences between attitudes about work and play on both sides of the Atlantic Ocean.

You can also help your reader understand an idea by offering a brief comparison called an *analogy*. An analogy explains one subject in terms of another subject that the reader already understands. The following is an example of an analogy.

> Society is like a pot of soup. It needs different and contrasting ingredients to give it body and flavor and lasting nourishment. It is compound, not simple; not like wine that drugs us, or caffeine that agitates us, but a blend to satisfy the most divergent[2] palates[3].
>
> Of course, this is an ideal, an impossible vision never to be fully realized in any given society. But it is what we should aim at, rather than promoting some brew that is to one taste alone. It may take another thousand years to get the recipe just right.†

1. **flats:** apartments   3. **palates:** tastes
2. **divergent:** different

Source: Adapted from Mortimer B. Zuckerman, "All Work and No Play," *U.S. News and World Report,* Sept. 8, 2003, www.usnews.com.
†*Source:* Excerpted from Sydney J. Harris, *Clearing the Ground* (Boston: Houghton Mifflin, 1986), p. 13.

In this analogy, the author compares societies to soup and to beverages. These comparisons help readers see his point about the need for diversity in society. When you can relate a new subject to something your readers already know about, you can increase their understanding of the new subject.

Comparison and contrast are also useful methods for persuading readers to favor or choose one thing over another.

Neat People Versus Sloppy People

I've finally figured out the difference between neat people and sloppy people. The distinction is, as always, moral. Neat people are lazier and meaner than sloppy people.

Sloppy people, you see, are not really sloppy. Their sloppiness is merely the unfortunate consequence of their extreme moral rectitude[1]. Sloppy people carry in their mind's eye a heavenly vision, a precise plan that is so stupendous, so perfect, it cannot be achieved in this world or the next.

Sloppy people live in Never-Never Land. Someday is their métier[2]. Someday they are planning to alphabetize all their books and set up home catalogs. Someday they will go through their wardrobes and mark certain items for tentative mending and certain items for passing on to relatives of similar shape and size. Someday sloppy people will make family scrapbooks into which they will put newspaper clippings, postcards, locks of hair, and the dried corsage from their senior prom. Someday they will file everything on the surface of their desk, including the cash receipts from coffee purchases at the snack shop. Someday they will sit down and read all the back issues of *The New Yorker*.

For all these noble reasons and more, sloppy people never get neat. They aim too high and wide. They save everything, planning someday to file, order, and straighten out the world. But while these ambitious plans take clearer and clearer shape in their heads, the books spill from the shelves onto the floor, the clothes pile up in the hamper and closet, the family mementos accumulate in every drawer, the surface of the desk is buried under mounds of paper, and the unread magazines threaten to reach the ceiling.

Sloppy people cannot bear to part with anything. They give loving attention to every detail. When sloppy people say they are going to tackle the surface of the desk, they really mean it. Not a paper will go unturned; not a rubber band will go unboxed. Four hours or two weeks into the excavation[3], the desk looks exactly the same, primarily because the sloppy person is meticulously[4] creating new piles of papers with new headings and scrupulously[5] stopping to read all the old book catalogs before he throws them away. A neat person would just bulldoze the desk.

1. **rectitude:** virtue or integrity
2. **métier:** calling or specialty
3. **excavation:** digging
4. **meticulously:** precisely
5. **scrupulously:** carefully

Neat people are bums and clods[1] at heart. They have cavalier[2] attitudes toward possessions, including family heirlooms. Everything is just another dust-catcher to them. If anything collects dust, it has got to go and that is that. Neat people will toy with the idea of throwing the children out of the house just to cut down on the clutter.

Neat people do not care about process. They like results. What they want to do is get the whole thing over with so they can sit down and watch the rasslin'[3] on TV. Neat people operate on two unvarying principles: Never handle any item twice, and throw everything away.

The only thing messy in a neat person's house is the trash can. The minute something comes to a neat person's hand, he will look at it, try to decide if it has immediate use, and, finding none, throw it in the trash.

Neat people are especially vicious with mail. They never go through their mail unless they are standing directly over a trash can. If the trash can is beside the mailbox, even better. All ads, catalogs, pleas for charitable contributions, church bulletins, and money-saving coupons go straight into the trash can without being opened. All letters from home, postcards from Europe, and paychecks are opened, immediately responded to, then dropped in the trash can. Neat people keep their receipts only for tax purposes. That is it. No sentimental salvaging of birthday cards or the last letter a dying relative ever wrote. Into the trash it goes.

Neat people place neatness above everything, even economics. They are incredibly wasteful. Neat people throw away several toys every time they walk through the den. I knew a neat person once who threw away a perfectly good dish drainer because it had mold on it. The drainer was too much trouble to wash. And neat people sell their furniture when they move. They will sell a La-Z-Boy recliner while you are reclining on it.

Neat people are no good to borrow from. Neat people buy everything in expensive little single portions. They get their flour and sugar in two-pound bags. They wouldn't consider clipping a coupon, saving a leftover, reusing plastic nondairy whipped cream containers or rinsing off tin foil and draping it over the unmoldy dish drainer. You can never borrow a neat person's newspaper to see what is playing at the movies. Neat people have the paper all wadded up and in the trash by 7:05 a.m.

Neat people cut a clean swath[4] through the organic[5] as well as the inorganic world. People, animals, and things are all one to them. They are so insensitive. After they have finished with the pantry, the medicine cabinet, and the attic,

---

1. **clods:** stupid people
2. **cavalier:** careless
3. **rasslin':** wrestling
4. **swath:** path or strip
5. **organic:** living

they will throw out the red geranium (too many leaves), sell the dog (too many fleas), and send the children off to boarding school (too many scuff marks on the hardwood floors).*

This humorous passage compares sloppy people and neat people, focusing on the virtues of sloppy people and the negative qualities of neat people. It is designed to persuade readers that sloppy people are better than neat people.

To write effective comparison/contrast essays, follow the principles presented in the next sections.

Writing a Comparison/Contrast Essay

Comparison and contrast are ways of understanding something in relation to its similarities to or differences from something else. To write an effective comparison/contrast essay, you need to determine your points of comparison, decide on the best order for presenting those parts, and develop each point with descriptive details and examples.

Determining the Main Idea and Points of Comparison and Writing a Thesis Statement

To write an effective comparison/contrast essay, it is important, first of all, to decide *why* you are comparing and/or contrasting your two subjects. Do you want readers to understand one of the subjects by seeing how it resembles something with which they are already familiar? Do you want to show that the two subjects are more different than readers think they are? Do you want to prove that one of the subjects is better than or preferable to the other subject? Your answers to these questions will lead you to determine your purpose, which will affect how you formulate your thesis statement. For example, the following thesis statement focuses on how two subjects are very different.

The married lifestyle is much different from the single lifestyle.

This thesis statement suggests that an informative and relatively objective comparison will follow. If you want to persuade your reader that one lifestyle is better than the other, though, you would need to change the thesis statement.

The married lifestyle *is better than* the single lifestyle.

*Source: Suzanne Britt, "Neat People versus Sloppy People," in Mary Lou Conlin, *Patterns Plus,* 7th ed. (Boston: Houghton Mifflin, 2002), pp. 169–171. Reprinted by permission of the author.

After you write a working thesis statement, decide which features of the two subjects would be most appropriate to discuss to prove your main point. In proving the previous thesis statement, you would probably need to examine the different aspects of the two lifestyles, such as amount of companionship, degree of independence, and level of financial security.

In the passage about neat people and sloppy people, the writer wants to persuade the reader that sloppy people are better. In order to accomplish that, she compares their attitudes, goals, emotions, and methods.

After deciding on the right points of comparison, you will need to make sure that you examine both subjects in terms of those points. Therefore, in an essay about the single lifestyle and married lifestyle, you would need to discuss the typical income and budget of a single person, and then you would need to devote equal attention to the typical income and budget of a married person. You would not compare the budget of a single person to the higher degree of companionship in a marital relationship. Doing so would be "comparing apples and oranges," as the saying goes, and you would not truly be contrasting the two subjects. To avoid this type of faulty comparison, it is important to outline your ideas, the topic of the next section.

EXERCISE 14.1   **Determining Points of Comparison**

For each of the following topics, determine three points of comparison and write those points on the blanks provided. Then write down the main idea that would arise from your comparison of these points.

1. Topic: Studying alone versus studying with a group

   Points of comparison: _____ *Ideas* _____

   problem solving _____ *motivation* _____

   work load _____ *discussing things effectively* _____

   Main idea: _____ *Studing with a group is more _____ than*
   alone, because it's more helpfull
2. Topic: Two of my good friends *in getting different*

   Points of comparison: *ideas, work load and problem solving.* _____

   age   common interests _____

   distanation _____

   Main idea: _____
   The differences between two of my good
   friends are age, distanation, character

3. Topic: Two brands of the same product

Points of comparison: _____ *quality* _____

_____ *price* _____

_____ *attractive package* _____

Main idea: _____ *More preferable brand of the*

same product would that one, what has

is better quality, less price and more

attractive

package

 EXERCISE 14.2   **Writing Thesis Statements for Comparison/Contrast Essays**

For each of the following topics, use some prewriting techniques to generate ideas on your own paper, and then write a thesis statement you could use for a comparison/ contrast essay.

1. Two different areas of the same town or city

Thesis statement: _____

2. Men and women

Thesis statement: _____

3. Two different ways of doing something

Thesis statement: _____

4. Two places where I have lived

Thesis statement: _____

5. Renting versus buying

Thesis statement: _____

Organizing Points of Comparison and Using Transitions

Organization is especially important in comparison/contrast essays because when you are juggling two different subjects and examining several features of each of those subjects, your reader can easily become lost if your composition is not clearly organized. Thus, after you have chosen your points of comparison, you must give careful thought to how you will arrange your discussion of these points to help your reader follow your ideas. There are two major patterns to choose from when organizing the points of a comparison/contrast essay.

The Whole-by-Whole Pattern of Organization. The first pattern, whole-by-whole, first looks at all of the points of comparison for one whole subject and then turns to a discussion of those same points of comparison for the other subject. An outline of this pattern looks like this:

I. Comparison of Subject A and Subject B
   A. Subject A
      1. Point of comparison #1
      2. Point of comparison #2
      3. Point of comparison #3
   B. Subject B
      1. Point of comparison #1
      2. Point of comparison #2
      3. Point of comparison #3

The advantages of using this pattern are mostly for the writer because he or she only has to concentrate on one subject at a time. However, it often asks more of readers, who are burdened with the task of remembering what was said about the first subject as they read about the second subject. Often this pattern also requires readers to make necessary connections or distinctions between the two subjects on their own. The second pattern of organization, however, eliminates these problems.

The Point-by-Point Pattern of Organization. In a point-by-point organization pattern, the writer alternates back and forth between his two subjects, arranging his or her composition according to the points of comparison. An outline of this pattern looks like this:

I. Comparison of Subject A and Subject B
   A. Point of comparison #1
      1. Subject A
      2. Subject B
   B. Point of comparison #2
      1. Subject A
      2. Subject B
   C. Point of comparison #3
      1. Subject A
      2. Subject B

This pattern usually makes it easier for the reader to see the similarities and/or differences between two subjects. Also, it allows the writer to make clearer, more explicit connections for the reader about the two subjects. However, it does require the writer, who is switching back and forth from one subject to the other, to be more attentive to thought progression. In addition to dividing the information into distinct paragraphs, the writer can also prevent the reader from getting lost by using clear transitions to signal similarities, differences, or the movement from one subject to another. The following lists include many of the common comparison and contrast transitional words.

Comparison transitions

also	similarly	similar to
too	in like manner	in the same way
likewise	just like, just as	along the same line

Contrast transitions

however	nevertheless	in contrast
but	on the one hand/on the other hand	conversely
yet	unlike	even though
although	rather	still
instead	on the contrary	nonetheless
in opposition	actually	whereas
in spite of	despite	in reality
just the opposite	while	as opposed to
though	unfortunately	

As you read the following excerpt from an essay, notice how the bold transitional words help to point out similarities and differences.

——— The Difference Between Male and Female Friendships ———

If there is one prototypical[1] image of women sharing friendship, it is that of two friends sitting across a table from each other, clutching their coffee cups, talking feelings. If there is a similar image of men, it is of buddies sitting together watching television, talking football.

We know these images are simplistic, and women and men are both guilty of stretching them to make assumptions about each other's friendships that range from the stereotypical[2] to the bizarre. Men never talk about anything but sports, women say in frustration. Women talk only about clothes, men retort[3]. Both sexes

1. **prototypical:** standard or typical
2. **stereotypical:** oversimplified; unfairly generalized
3. **retort:** reply

get trapped in vast generalizations, but the differences between the same-sex friendships of men and women are real. Decades of research cannot be ignored. A long list of studies tell men and women what they already know: men and women talk about different things in different ways.

Men are less likely to talk about personal subjects with other men than women are with other women. As Letty Pogrebin, author of *Among Friends,* summed it up, "The average man's idea of an intimate exchange is the average woman's idea of a casual conversation."

What else do the researchers show? Men's friendships are based on shared activities. Men who do things together, paint that house, change that tire, feel close. Women's friendships, **on the other hand,** are based on shared feelings. Women who share secrets, troubles, relationships, feel close.

If you had a camera you could videotape the gender gap. Women literally touch each other more; they sit closer together, focus on one-to-one sharing. **But** when men talk about what they do with their friends, you get a different portrait: men doing things together in groups.

The research list goes on. Men do not criticize their friends as much as women. **However,** neither do they communicate the kind of acceptance women count on from their friends. Men put shared interests highest among the reasons they bond with a friend. Women, **though,** first want friends who share their values. And even men tend to view their friendships with women as closer and more intimate than those with other men.*

EXERCISE 14.3   **Organizing Details in Comparison/Contrast Essays**

On your own paper, prewrite to generate ideas and then complete each of the following thesis statements by filling in the blanks. Then, on the other blanks provided, prepare an informal outline by listing the points you would include in an appropriate order.

1. I expected _____ to be _____, but my actual experience was much different.

_____

_____

_____

_____

Source: Adapted with permission of Simon and Schuster Adult Publishing Group, from "I Know What You Mean: The Power of Friendship in Women's Lives" by Ellen Goodman and Patricia O'Brien. Copyright © 2000 by Ellen Goodman and Patricia O'Brien. All rights reserved.

2. A comparison of _____ and _____ reveals that

_____ is better.

_____

_____

_____

_____

3. _____ and _____ are more similar than they
are different.

_____

_____

_____

_____

EXERCISE 14.4   **Recognizing Comparison/Contrast Transitions**

Circle all of the comparison/contrast transitional words in the following essay.

Obits Are the Ultimate Democracy

On the day after my fifty-seventh birthday, while morbidly[1] glancing at the Sunday *New York Times'* obituary[2] page, I ran into this pair of headlines: "Danny Dark, 65, Whose Voice Spurned StarKist's Charlie Tuna." And right next to it, "Stuart Hampshire, 89, Moral Philosopher, Dies."

I had never heard of either of these men. Had their obits run on different days, or different pages, I would have skipped them. But juxtaposed[3], they became an irresistible Odd Couple[4]. In journalism, as in real estate, nothing is more important than placement.

Stuart Newton Hampshire was born in Lincolnshire, England. As a young man, he studied at Oxford, "where he befriended Isaiah Berlin[5]."

Danny Dark (original name: Daniel Melville Croskery), on the other hand, was born in Oklahoma City, educated at Tulsa (Oklahoma) Central High School

1. **morbidly:** somberly; grimly
2. **obituary:** published notice of a death
3. **juxtaposed:** placed side by side
4. **Odd Couple:** two roommates—one neat and one messy—from a play, film, and TV series titled *The Odd Couple*

5. **Isaiah Berlin:** a twentieth-century political philosopher and historian

"under the guidance of an English teacher named Isabelle E. Roman and at Drury College, in Springfield, Missouri."

Hampshire's career was launched with the publication of his first book, *Spinoza,* which "examined the seventeenth-century philosopher Benedict Spinoza, whose thinking left an imprint on the author's own world view." After *Spinoza,* Hampshire taught at Oxford and University College, London. In 1963, he was appointed chairman of the Department of Philosophy at Princeton University.

For Danny Dark, too, 1963 was a breakout year. Having honed[1] his broadcasting skills at radio stations in Tulsa, Cleveland, Miami, New Orleans, and St. Louis, he was hired as a deejay[2] by KLAC-AM in Los Angeles.

At Princeton, Hampshire became an influential voice in the campus debate over the morality of the war in Vietnam. In contrast, a continent away, Dark became an influential voice-over[3]. Over the years, he appeared in dozens of TV and radio commercials and as the voice of Superman in a cartoon series. He was the guy who said, "Sorry, Charlie," to Charlie the Tuna in the StarKist ad. And "This Bud's for you."

Although they traveled different roads, Stuart Hampshire and Danny Dark each reached the pinnacle[4] of his profession. In 1979, Professor Hampshire was knighted by Queen Elizabeth. Similarly, Dark was posthumously[5] dubbed "the voice-over king" by the *Times.*

I doubt that Danny Dark and Stuart Hampshire ever met. It is unlikely they even knew of one another. Maybe Hampshire heard Dark's voice on TV or radio; if so, he had no way of knowing to whom it belonged. Moral philosophers and commercial voice-over artists have one thing in common: They are not likely to become household names.

I cannot help wondering how Hampshire and Dark would feel about being paired on the obit page. Perhaps the professor, a man for whom "esthetics[6], ethics and political philosophy were all part of the same intellectual quest," would be disconcerted[7] to find himself ushered into eternity next to a chap who made his living proclaiming, "Raid kills bugs dead!" in the pay of Raid Ant and Roach Killer.

Danny Dark, however, probably would not mind sharing a billing with Professor Hampshire. Nobody who does anonymous work in Hollywood can have much of an ego. Besides, Dark's the one whose picture ran in the *Times.*

The obits are the most democratic section of the newspaper. A guy can be an Oxford don[8] or a Drury College dropout, chronicle Spinoza for a living or hawk tuna fish—it does not matter. Work hard, do well, and you have got a

1. **honed:** sharpened
2. **deejay:** disc jockey (a radio announcer)
3. **voice-over:** voice of an unseen narrator
4. **pinnacle:** top; highest point
5. **posthumously:** occurring after one's death

6. **esthetics:** branch of philosophy that focuses on beauty
7. **disconcerted:** upset
8. **don:** professor

shot at a three-column sendoff. Just do not imagine you have any control over where you are going—or who is going next to you.*

EXERCISE 14.5 **Writing a Comparison/Contrast Essay That Includes Transitions**

Choose one of the thesis statements and outlines that you prepared in Exercise 14.3. Write the essay, including transitional words that indicate how the points are related.

Developing the Points in a Comparison/Contrast Essay

Because comparison/contrast essays examine the features of two subjects to show how they are alike and/or different, you will often use descriptive details and examples to develop each point of comparison. For example, if you were to write an essay about riding a motorcycle versus driving a car, you would want to add specific descriptive details when you compare sensory stimulation. You would want to mention the wind in your hair, the smells, and the sounds. If you were to compare the relative sense of freedom to be had on or in each vehicle, you might want to illustrate that by providing examples of specific rides from your experience. These kinds of details help the reader understand each point better.

EXERCISE 14.6 **Recognizing the Features of a Comparison/Contrast Essay**

Read the following essay. Then answer the questions that follow by writing your responses on the blanks provided.

———— Coalition of the Differing ————

1 The Americans and the British have not always seen eye to eye—neither in war nor wardrobe. In fact, during World War II the U.S. and British commands had such a terrible time communicating with one another that in 1943 they commissioned anthropologist[1] Margaret Mead to determine why. The Americans complained that the British were secretive and unfriendly; the British insisted that the Americans were simpleminded and boastful. The allies argued about everything.

1. **anthropologist:** person who studies the origins, behavior, and culture of humans

*Source: Adapted from Zev Chafets, "Obits Are the Ultimate Democracy," *New York Daily News*, June 30, 2004, www.nydailynews.com. Reprinted by permission of the author.

2   Mead discovered that the two cultures possessed fundamentally different world views. One simple way to demonstrate this was to ask an Englishman and an American a single question: What is your favorite color? American servicemen quickly came up with a color, but the British asked, "Favorite color for what? A flower? A necktie?"

3   Mead concluded that Americans, raised in a melting pot, learned to seek a simple common denominator[1]. To the British, this came across as unsophisticated. Conversely, the class-conscious British insisted on complex categories, each with its own set of values. Americans interpreted this tendency to subdivide as furtiveness[2]. (After all, a person who cannot name a favorite color must be hiding *something*.) "The British show an unwillingness to make comparisons," Mead wrote. "Each object is thought of as having a most complex set of qualities, and color is merely a quality of an object."

4   The allies eventually overcame their differences and rallied to defeat Hitler[3], but for decades afterward you could see Mead's revelations reflected in the men's fashions of Britain and America. For Yanks[4], what mattered was an overall "look." An American boy learned from his father, his schoolmates, and ads for Hickey Freeman suits that the goal was to combine elements that complemented one another: *the tie goes with the jacket, the shoes go with the belt.* To the British, on the other hand, what mattered more than the whole was its parts. Where a postwar American male might have been neatly described as "the man in the gray flannel suit," an Englishman of the same era was "the man in the gray flannel suit—also wearing plaid socks, a striped shirt, paisley tie, and checked jacket with a floral handkerchief in the pocket."

The Duke of Windsor in 1967. © *Condé Nast Archive/CORBIS*

5   Note the famous 1967 Patrick Lichfield photograph of the Duke of Windsor in which the abdicated[5] king appears in almost precisely this out-

1. **common denominator:** commonly shared trait
2. **furtiveness:** secretiveness; sneakiness
3. **Hitler:** German dictator who led the Nazi Party during World War II

4. **Yanks:** Americans
5. **abdicated:** gave up power

fit. To the duke, each piece of clothing no doubt had, as Mead observed, its own "complex set of qualities" having nothing to do with the others. And yet, was there another gentleman of this era who more exemplified[1] British sartorial[2] style? (He even gave his name to the Windsor knot.)

6　　It is impossible to say just when these national dress codes began eroding, but by the turn of the millennium they were gone. One night in London not long ago, I was walking back to my hotel (near Savile Row) when I saw framed through a pub window a group of lads standing together at the bar. They might as well have been college kids in Atlanta, or Barcelona, or Moscow; there was not a single sartorial clue that identified them as English. They projected what might be called an "urban" look, the blank, shapeless offering from brands such as Banana Republic and J. Crew. To wit, an untucked shirt, a one-size-fits-all sport coat and baggy trousers rolled up above black, square-toed shoes as big as the boxes they came in. What would dear Margaret Mead have made of this snapshot? Probably, that much of the men's world has a new style, one that reflects not tribal differences but global similarities.

7　　But let us not despair. After all, men's fashion history does have a way of turning out surprises. Take, for example, the January 2003 menswear shows in Milan. One of the most startling moments came when designer Miuccia Prada launched a male model down the runway wearing a loud print shirt, striped pants, and a wild patterned tie, all topped off with a checkerboard 1970s Bear Bryant[3] hat. It was a rig that would have made the Duke of Windsor proud.*

1. What is the thesis of this essay?

_____

_____

2. What are the author's two main points of comparison?

_____

3. Does the author organize his information using a whole-by-whole or point-by-point pattern?

_____

4. List two comparison/contrast transitional words or phrases that the author uses in this essay.

_____

1. **exemplified:** illustrated or represented
2. **sartorial:** related to tailored clothing
3. **Bear Bryant:** an American college football coach

Source: Patrick Cooke, "Coalition of the Differing," *Smithsonian*, June 2003, p. 112. Reprinted by permission of the author.

5. The author points out how popular fashion can reflect a society's worldview and attitudes. Would you agree that today's "bland" urban look is an attempt to reflect "global similarities"? Would you say that modern Americans express through their clothing choices their desire—either conscious or unconscious—to fit in and be like everyone else? Or would you argue that modern Americans are more interested in projecting individualism? Explain your answer.

In Summary: Steps in Writing Comparison/Contrast Essays

1. **Determine a main idea and points of comparison.** Decide on the purpose of your comparison, and then select relevant points of comparison. Make sure that you apply these points to both subjects.
2. **Choose an organizing pattern for the points of comparison.** Use either a whole-by-whole or point-by-point pattern for arranging ideas, and include transitions to help your reader follow these ideas.
3. **Develop each point of comparison.** Use descriptions, examples, or any other kind of details to explain each point.

CHAPTER 14 REVIEW

To review the main points in this chapter, write a brief response to each of the following questions.

1. What are you doing when you compare two things? What are you doing when you contrast two things?

2. What is an analogy?

3. What is the first step in writing a comparison/contrast paper?

4. What are points of comparison, and why should they be carefully selected?

5. What are the two major comparison/contrast patterns of organization? How do they differ from one another?

6. What are some common comparison/contrast transitional words and phrases?

7. What kinds of details are often used to develop comparison/contrast essays?

Topic Ideas for Comparison/Contrast Essays

Exercises 14.1 and 14.2 include topic ideas that you may want to develop into comparison/contrast essays. Here are some additional ideas:

- Two politicians, entertainers, athletes, actors, and so on
- Your generation versus your grandparents' generation
- Small town versus city life
- Past versus present
- Two jobs that you have held
- Private school versus public school
- Being self-employed versus working for someone else
- Democrats versus Republicans
- Bottled water versus tap water
- Flying versus driving
- Two instructors
- Shopping at the mall versus shopping online
- Two forms of exercise

- Moving around versus staying in one place
- The two buildings in the following photograph

Mitchell Funk/Getty Images

Work

For more discussion and examples of comparison/contrast outlines, go to The Write Place at **http://leo.stcloudstate.edu/acadwrite/comparcontrast.html**.

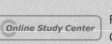   For more information and exercises, go to the Online Study Center at **http://www.college.hmco.com/pic/dolphinwriterthree**.

Cause/Effect

GOALS FOR CHAPTER 15

▶ Define the terms *cause* and *effect*.

▶ Describe the steps in writing a cause/effect essay.

▶ Write a cause/effect essay.

▶ Recognize the features of a cause/effect essay.

People like to understand why something happened. We ask questions such as *Why do people become terrorists?* and *Why has soccer become so popular among American youth?* When we ask questions such as these, we are trying to determine the *causes* of, or reasons for, an occurrence. We also like to understand the consequences of the things that happen. So we ask questions like *How has the influx of Hispanic immigrants affected America?* and *What will happen if public school education is not improved?* These types of questions lead to an analysis of the *effects,* or results, of an occurrence.

Essays often develop an idea by explaining causes, discussing effects, or doing both. The following passage, for example, focuses on causes.

--------- ## The Unfair Portrayal of Latinas on Television ---------

I have watched a lot of television since I was a little child. Now that I am in my late twenties, I can still say with great certainty that there has never been a positive role model for me, as a Puerto Rican-American female, on television. Most of the roles that I have seen Latina women play have been that of the maid, the fast woman that all of the men want to date, or the non-English-speaking next-door neighbor.

Why is that? Why aren't there any great role models for young Latina girls on American television? I think one reason is that it has taken a long time for Hispanic women to assert themselves in society. For many years, the female in the Hispanic household, while the head of the household in many respects, has taken a back seat in the dominant male culture of the Hispanic world. So I do not think many people in American society think of Latina women as bold, beautiful, talented, and ambitious.

Another reason for the lack of Latina women in prominent roles on television is because of American culture overall. You do not see too many women of any color, never mind Hispanic women, on television. Black women suffer the same fate as the women in my culture—they play the maid, the sassy best friend (if they are lucky), or the shop worker. You rarely see any women of color play a lawyer, a doctor, or a professional in any capacity.

I think because of the bias that exists on television, many Latina girls do not think of becoming actresses or professional women. So the trend will continue.

Latina women need to assert themselves and show the world that they have the talent and brains to be whatever they want so that another generation of young girls does not have to live in a void where people who look and act like them do not exist.*

The previous essay presents two reasons for the lack of positive Latina role models on television.

This next example focuses only on effects.

What Pets Bring to the Party

Like deities[1] and tax law, your beloved pet works in mysterious ways. Science cannot explain the power of the pooch or the Karma[2] of the kitty, but numerous studies have shown that furry companions—just by their presence—can help lower blood pressure and cholesterol levels, raise chances of survival after a heart attack, reduce loneliness and depression, and spread all-round good cheer.

Any owner will tell you how much joy a pet brings. For some, a critter provides more comfort than a spouse. A 2002 study by Karen Allen of the State University of New York at Buffalo measured stress levels and blood pressure in people—half of them pet owners—while they contended with performing five minutes of mental math or holding a hand in ice water. Subjects completed the tasks alone, with a spouse, a close friend or with a pet. People with pets fared best. Those tested with their animal pals had smaller spikes in blood pres-

---

1. **deities:** gods

2. **Karma:** Buddhist and Hindu belief that people are rewarded and punished for their actions and conduct

Source: Adapted from Maria Gonzalez, "The Unfair Portrayal of Latinas on Television," in *Horizons* (Boston: Houghton Mifflin, 2004), p. 263. Reprinted by permission of Houghton Mifflin Company.

sure and returned most quickly to baseline heart rates. With pets in the room, people also made fewer math errors than when figuring in front of spouses or friends. In another study, Allen put a group of hypertensive[1] stockbrokers on blood-pressure-lowering drugs and told half of them to adopt a pet. Six months later, the new pet owners showed less than half the blood-pressure surge of their peers while performing stressful tasks—and, again, made fewer math errors. It seems people feel less nervous around pets, says Allen, who thinks it may be because pets do not judge.

In part, it is that capacity for unconditional support that makes pets such good company. A study reported last fall suggests that having a pet dog not only buoys[2] your spirits but may also help you trim your gut. Researchers at Northwestern Memorial Hospital spent a year studying thirty-six portly people and their equally pudgy dogs on joint diet-and-exercise programs; a separate control group of fifty-six people without pets was put on a solo program. On average, people lost about eleven pounds, or 5 percent of their body weight. Their canine sidekicks did even better, losing an average of twelve pounds, more than 15 percent of their body weight. Pup owners did not lose any more weight than the pup-less but, say researchers, got more exercise overall—mostly with their dogs—and found it rewarding instead of a chore.

No scientific study has deconstructed exactly why pets boost our well-being, but for most pet lovers that probably does not matter. It is enough to know that like many of the other basic joys in life, a pet's affection is simple, easy, and mercifully unconditional.*

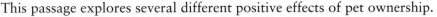

This passage explores several different positive effects of pet ownership.

To write effective cause/effect essays, follow the principles presented in the rest of this chapter.

Writing a Cause/Effect Essay

Explaining causes is a way to help readers understand *why* something happened, and explaining effects is a way to help readers understand the *consequences* of something. To write an effective cause/effect essay, you need to generate ideas

1. **hypertensive:** having high blood pressure

2. **buoys:** raises

Source: Sora Song, "What Pets Bring to the Party," *Time,* Jan. 17, 2005, p. A38. © 2005 Time, Inc. Reprinted by permission.

about the relationships among your cause(s) and/or effect(s), determine your thesis statement, organize your causes and/or effects based on their relationships, and develop each cause or effect with descriptive details and examples.

Generating Ideas, Determining the Main Idea, and Writing a Thesis Statement

After you have selected an occurrence or phenomenon to examine, you will need to generate some ideas about its causes, effects, or both. As you begin to explore your topic, you might find it useful to create a diagram, a visual representation of the relationships among the causes and effects. A student who chose to write about obesity, for example, created the following diagram.

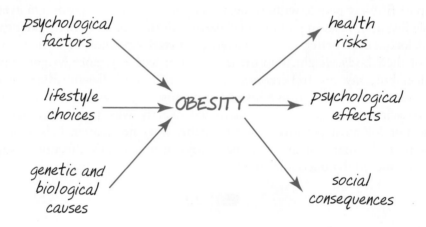

The causes are listed on the left, and the arrows indicate that each one contributes to obesity. Arrows drawn outward from the subject indicate its various effects. This diagram focuses only on *immediate* causes and effects, those that are the direct reasons for and the direct consequences of the occurrence. Depending on the topic, it may also be appropriate to present some of the *remote* causes, or ultimate roots of a situation, and/or the remote effects, or long-term consequences. Adding some of these remote causes and effects might change parts of the diagram as follows:

poverty $\longrightarrow$ lifestyle choices $\longrightarrow$ OBESITY $\longrightarrow$ loss of self-esteem $\longrightarrow$ decline in achievement

Thus, to truly do justice to your subject, you may need to discuss a *chain reaction* of causes or effects rather than just the immediate causes alone.

As you continue prewriting to generate ideas, spend some time thinking about the relationships in your diagram, adding to them or altering them as appropriate. For example, the student who created the first diagram about obesity may want to consider whether "psychological effects" and "social consequences" are two separate effects, or if one causes the other in a chain reaction. Also, beware of oversimplifying complex factors or consequences. For example, you would be going out on a limb if you asserted that consumption of fast food is the number one cause of obesity in the United States. Other contributing factors may be just as important. So spend some time thoroughly evaluating each cause or effect to make sure that the relationships are complete, reasonable, and logical. Then, when you think your diagram accurately reflects these relationships, you can determine your main idea.

The main idea of a cause/effect essay usually states some point about the relationships you discover in your diagram. Are there multiple causes for one occurrence, or is there a chain reaction of events that ultimately leads to the occurrence? Is one cause more to blame than others? Are there several effects of a particular occurrence, or does this occurrence set off one chain reaction of immediate and remote effects? What conclusion can you draw from the relationships among all of the causes and/or effects? Studying your diagram will help you draw this conclusion and then write a thesis statement that incorporates this conclusion. From the revised sample diagram, for instance, you might draw the conclusion that the psychological causes of obesity lead to a weight problem that breeds even more psychological and social problems. Thus, a thesis statement might read:

> Although psychological factors can lead a person to overeat, the resulting obesity simply breeds a new set of psychological problems, creating a vicious cycle that is difficult to break.

This thesis statement focuses on one specific cause and one specific effect. If you wanted to present a broader, more comprehensive look at the subject, you might write one of the following thesis statements.

Obesity has three main causes. *(causes only)*

Obesity results in a number of serious consequences. *(effects only)*

Many different factors contribute to obesity, leading to damage of one's body, mind, and relationships with others. *(causes and effects)*

EXERCISE 15.1   **Generating Cause/Effect Diagrams**

For each of the following topics, draw a diagram of the cause-and-effect relation-ships in the space provided.

1. A choice that you made

2. A fear that you have

3. One of your personality traits

EXERCISE 15.2   **Writing Thesis Statements for Cause/Effect Essays**

For each of the following topics, use some prewriting techniques to generate ideas on your own paper, and then write a thesis statement that you could use for a cause/effect essay.

1. E-mail

Thesis statement: _____

2. An important decision

Thesis statement: _____

3. Divorce

Thesis statement: _____

4. Stress

Thesis statement: _____

5. A particular invention or discovery

Thesis statement: _____

Organizing Causes and/or Effects and Using Transitions

Creating a diagram of cause-and-effect relationships like the one in the previous section not only will help you discover ideas but will also organize them. The relationships you discover among the causes and effects will assist you in determining the best arrangement of your details. If you were going to develop the thesis statement *Obesity has three main causes*, your informal outline for the essay might look like this:

1. Psychological factors
2. Lifestyle choices
3. Genetic and biological causes

When you are determining the best order for the information, it is important to evaluate the order of each cause or effect in case it is somehow related to another one. Look for time order or causal order among reasons or consequences that initially look like they are separate. If you are exploring the effects of obesity, for example, you might decide that the loss of self-esteem leads to unsatisfying interpersonal relationships. In that case you would need to discuss the loss of self-esteem (an immediate psychological effect) *before* you discuss damaged relationships (a more remote social effect). In the case of separate, unrelated factors or effects, consider whether some are more important than others. If so, arrange them using order of importance. For instance, if you decide that lifestyle choices are the most significant cause of obesity, you would need to discuss that reason *first* instead of second.

As you write, be sure to add transitional words that help the reader understand the cause-and-effect relationships. Some of the most common cause/effect transitional words are

so	consequently
therefore	as a consequence
as a result	due to
thus	hence
because of	for this reason
in response	one cause, a second cause
	one reason, another reason

Notice how the writer of the following essay uses cause/effect transitional words (in bold) to help the reader follow the relationships.

Colleges may be becoming the major breeding ground of Internet addiction. For example, when the dropout rate at Alfred University in Alfred, New York, more than doubled recently, Provost W. Richard Ott wanted to find out why. He could not see any logical explanation for why so many students who had arrived in college with SAT scores of 1,200 or higher would fail so quickly. An in-house survey revealed that 43 percent of these dropouts had been staying up late logged on to the Internet. "It is ironic," Ott said. "We have put all this money in for an educational tool, and some students are using it for self-destruction." A number of factors contribute to such rampant[1] Internet overuse.

One cause is free and unlimited Internet access. When freshmen register today, they get a student ID card, a meal card, and most important, a free personal e-mail account. They've got no online service fees to pay, no limits to their time logged on, and computer labs open for their convenience round the clock. It is an Internet user's dream.

---

1. **rampant:** widespread and growing without restraint

A **second cause** is huge blocks of unstructured time. Most college students attend classes for twelve to sixteen hours per week. The rest of the time is their own to read, study, go to movies or parties, join clubs, or explore the new environment outside their campus walls. Many forget all those other activities and concentrate on one thing: the Internet.

The third contributing factor is freedom from parental control. Away from home and their parents' watchful eyes, college students have long exercised their new freedom by engaging in pranks, talking to friends at all hours of the night, sleeping with their boyfriends and girlfriends, and eating and drinking things Mom and Dad would not approve of. Today, they utilize that freedom by hanging out in the MUDs[1] and chat rooms[2] of cyberspace[3], and no parent can complain about online service fees or their refusal to eat dinner with the family or help out with chores.

Then there is the fourth contributing factor, the full encouragement of faculty and administrators. Students understand that their school's administration and faculty want them to make full use of the Internet's vast resources. Abstaining[4] from all Net use is seldom an option; in some large classes, professors place required course materials solely on the Net and engage in their only one-on-one contact with students through e-mail! Administrators, of course, want to see their major investments in computers and Internet access justified.

Yet another cause of Internet overuse is the desire to escape college stressors. Students feel the pressures of making top grades, fulfilling parental expectations, and, upon graduation, facing fierce competition for good jobs. The Internet, ideally, would help make it easier for them to do their necessary course work as quickly and efficiently as possible. Instead, many students turn to their Net friends to hide from their difficult feelings of fear, anxiety, and depression.

And a final cause is social intimidation and alienation. With as many as 30,000 students on some campuses, students can easily get lost in the crowd. But when they join the faceless community of the Internet, they find that with little effort they can become popular with new "friends" throughout the United States and even the world. Why bother trying to socialize on campus?*

1. **MUDs:** types of multiplayer computer games
2. **chat rooms:** an online forum in which people communicate with one another
3. **cyberspace:** electronic medium of computer networks, where online communication takes place
4. **abstaining:** refusing to participate

Source: Excerpt adapted from "Fraternities of Netheads" by Kimberly Young, from *Caught in the Net,* 1998, pp. 174–179. Copyright © 1998 Kimberly Young. Reprinted with permission of John Wiley and Sons, Inc.

⟡ **EXERCISE 15.3** **Organizing Details in Cause/Effect Essays**

On your own paper, prewrite to generate ideas and then complete each of the following thesis statements by filling in the blank. Then, on the other blanks provided, prepare an informal outline by listing the points that you would include in an appropriate order.

1. _____ was one decision that affected me in a number of ways.

_____

_____

_____

_____

2. For _____ reasons, I decided to _____.

_____

_____

_____

_____

3. I decided to _____ because _____, but _____ was the end result instead.

_____

_____

_____

_____

⟡ **EXERCISE 15.4** **Recognizing Cause/Effect Transitions**

Circle all of the cause/effect transitional words in the following essay.

One in seven Americans has no health insurance. Therefore, they have little or no access to medical care. Most are between the ages of 18 and 44. These are not only the poor. A third of them earn at least $50,000 but still cannot afford the rising health insurance premiums and at the same time support their families and educate their children. Millions more lost their coverage when they were laid off from their jobs. Many retirees too young to qualify for Medicare[1] have also been forced into the ranks of the uninsured.

1. Medicare: a publicly funded health insurance program for the elderly and disabled in America

How did all this come about?

Because of the great advances in medicine, health-care costs have skyrocketed. Due to all of the new sophisticated tests and procedures—such as MRIs, CT and PET scans, and the costly breakthroughs in treating cancer, heart disease, and infection—progress has been expensive.

Because we are living so much longer (life expectancy increased in the last century from about 50 years to almost 80 for women and 74 for men), we also are prone to such chronic conditions as heart failure, arthritis, Parkinson's, paralysis after stroke, and Alzheimer's. As a result, we need more medications, more doctors' visits and other professional support, and more rehabilitation programs. Many of the elderly, alone and unable to fend for themselves, need long-term custodial care.

Thus, in order to pay for this explosion of medical success, insurers have had to raise their premiums, which millions can no longer afford. If you are still working, chances are good that your mandatory contributions to your health insurance have risen by 50 percent. Companies struggling to compete in the global market have had to cut back on the extent of coverage they provide their employees.

All of these problems have, consequently, given birth to the HMO[1]. While they try to make medical care affordable, most HMOs are businesses, too, and must turn a profit. You do not have to be a mathematician or an accountant to realize that, in order to do so, the HMO must spend less on your health than the premiums you pay. That means you are allowed fewer consultations, tests, and days in the hospital. As for providing the medications you need, the HMO—not your doctor—has the final say. Its focus is on the cost of the drug rather than its effectiveness.

Hence, the quality of health care in this country has declined overall. It is still the best in the world—for those who can afford whatever it costs.*

EXERCISE 15.5 **Writing a Cause/Effect Essay That Includes Transitions**

Choose one of the thesis statements and outlines that you prepared in Exercise 15.3. Write the essay, including transitional words that indicate how the causes and/or effects are related.

1. **HMO:** health maintenance organization, a type of health insurer in the United States

*Source: Adapted from Dr. Isadore Rosenfeld, "We Must Fix Health Care," *Parade*, Aug. 15, 2004, p. 5. © 2004 Parade Publications. All rights reserved.

Developing the Points in a Cause/Effect Essay

Whether the explanation of a cause-and-effect relationship has been scientifically proven (such as the effects of laser eye surgery) or is based upon educated opinion (such as the causes of cheating in college), readers will expect writers to provide them with plenty of evidence to support that explanation. This evidence can be in the form of examples, observations, facts, statistics, expert testimony, or even personal experiences. Therefore, you will often use the other modes, particularly narration, description, illustration, and process, to develop your ideas.

EXERCISE 15.6   **Recognizing the Features of a Cause/Effect Essay**

Read the following essay. Then answer the questions that follow by writing your responses on the blanks provided.

—————————————— **Jingle Bell Schlock** ——————————————

If I hear "Frosty the Snowman[1]" one more time, I wll rip his frozen face off.

It is a scientific fact, or should be, that Christmas music can turn you into a fruitcake. It either sends you into a Pavlovian[2] shopping trance, buying stupid things like the Robosapien[3], or, if you hear repeated Clockwork-Orange[4] choruses of "Ring, Christmas Bells" drilling into your brain with that slasher-movie staccato, makes you feel as possessed with Christmas spirit as Norman Bates[5].

I have never said this out loud before, but I cannot stand Christmas. Everyone in my family loves it except me, and they cannot fathom why I get the mullygrubs, as a Southern friend of mine used to call a low-level depression, from Thanksgiving straight through New Year. "You are weird," my mom says. This from a woman who once left up our Christmas tree until April 3, and who listens to a radio station that plays carols 24/7 all month.

My equally demonic sister has a whole collection of rodents dressed in holiday clothes that she puts up around her house. There is a mouse Santa Claus and mouse Mrs. Claus and mice elves and a miniature Christmas village with mice, and some rat Cinderella coachmen in pink waistcoats and rats in red velvet vests and more rats, wearing frilly red-and-white nightshirts and nightcaps and

1. **"Frosty the Snowman":** a popular Christmas carol
2. **Pavlovian:** related to reflex responses that were investigated by Ivan Pavlov, a psychologist who conditioned dogs to salivate at the sound of a bell
3. **Robosapien:** a toy-like robot
4. **Clockwork-Orange:** related to the 1962 science fiction novel *A Clockwork Orange* by Anthony Burgess and film made from it
5. **Norman Bates:** a serial killer in the film *Psycho*

holding little candles, leading you up the steps to bed. It is beyond creepy. I keep fretting that it is going to be like "Willard[1]" meets "The Nutcracker[2]," where they come alive and eat her like a Christmas pudding.

My mom and sister both blissfully sat through *It's a Wonderful Life*[3] again on Thanksgiving weekend, while even hearing a mere snatch of that movie makes me want to scarf down a fistful of antidepressants—and join all the other women in America who are on a holiday high—except our family doctor is a Scrooge[4] about designer drugs[5], leaving me to self-medicate as Clarence[6] gets his wings with extra brandy in the eggnog.

I have given a lot of thought to why others' season of joy is my season of doom—besides the obvious fact that yuppies[7] have drenched the holidays in ever more absurd levels of consumerism. I think it has to do with how stressed out my mom and sister would get on Christmas Day when I was little. I remember them snapping at me; they seemed tense because of all the aprons to be sashed and potatoes to be mashed. (In our traditional Irish household, women slaved and men were waited on.)

It might be exacerbated[8] by the stress I feel when I think of all the money I have spent on lavishing boyfriends with presents over the years, guys who are now living with other women who are enjoying my lovingly picked out presents which I'm no doubt still paying for in credit card interest charges.

I was embracing my Christmas black dog the other day when I read a *Times* article so scary it made my hair—and my genes—curl. It was about how severe stress can make a woman age very rapidly and prematurely, looking years older than her chronological age, because the stress causes the DNA in our cells to shrink, and sort of curl down on itself, until the cells can no longer replicate[9]. "When people are under stress they look haggard[10], it is like they age before your eyes, and here is something going on at a molecular level" that reflects that impression, said one of the researchers, Dr. Elizabeth Blackburn of the University of California at San Francisco.

1. **"Willard":** a horror movie about rats
2. **"The Nutcracker":** a famous ballet that includes mice as characters
3. *It's a Wonderful Life:* a popular Christmas film
4. **Scrooge:** miserly character in Charles Dickens's novella *A Christmas Carol*
5. **designer drugs:** mood-altering drugs that have been modified to attempt to get around existing drug laws
6. **Clarence:** in the film *It's a Wonderful Life,* Clarence is an angel who is trying to earn his wings by helping the main character
7. **yuppies:** nickname for professional people of upper-middle-class America (young urban professionals)
8. **exacerbated:** worsened
9. **replicate:** reproduce, repeat, or copy
10. **haggard:** appearing worn and exhausted

So now, on top of all the stress related to having a president and vice president who scared us to death about terrorists to get re-elected, I have to be stressed about the fact that my holiday stress might cause me to turn into an old bat—instantly, just like it happened in Grimm's fairy tales, when a girl would be cursed and suddenly become a crone[1]. Or just like this Christmas doll my sister brought home once that had an apple for a head; her face looked all juicy and white at the start of the week and then by the end of the week, it was all discolored and puckered.

I flipped through the hot new self-help book by Gordon Livingston, a psychiatrist from Columbia, MD, *Too Soon Old, Too Late Smart: Thirty True Things You Need to Know Now.* One of them is the cardinal[2] rule of anxiety: Avoidance makes it worse; confrontation gradually improves it.

Yep. I definitely need to rip Frosty's face off.*

1. In your own words, state the main point of this essay.

_____

_____

2. In the following space provided, create a diagram of the cause-and-effect relationships in this essay.

1. crone: ugly, withered old woman   **2. cardinal:** most important

*Source: Maureen Dowd, "Jingle Bell Schlock," *New York Times,* Dec. 5, 2004, p. WK13. Reprinted by permission of The New York Times Company, Inc.

3. What one cause/effect transition is used in this essay? Do you think the author could improve the essay by adding more transitions?

_____

_____

4. Do you think the author is justified in her dislike of the Christmas holiday? Why or why not?

_____

In Summary: Steps in Writing Cause/Effect Essays

1. **Create a diagram of cause-and-effect relationships.** Then use this diagram to generate ideas and to explore the topic so that you can draw a conclusion that will become your thesis.
2. **Organize the cause-and-effect relationships into an outline.** Evaluate what seem to be separate causes and effects for time order or causal relationships, and order them accordingly. If different causes and effects are unrelated, decide whether they should be arranged by order of importance.
3. **As you write, develop each cause or effect with sufficient evidence.** Use narration, description, illustration, or the other modes to offer readers plenty of evidence in support of your explanations.

CHAPTER 15 REVIEW

To review the main points in this chapter, write a brief response to each of the following questions.

1. What are you trying to determine when you examine causes? What are you trying to understand when you analyze effects?
2. Why is a diagram useful for generating ideas about causes and effects?
3. What are immediate causes and effects?
4. What are remote causes and effects?
5. What determined the best arrangement for your details in a cause/effect essay?

CHAPTER 15 REVIEW

6. What are some common cause/effect words and transitional phrases?

7. What modes of development are often used to develop cause/effect essays?

Topic Ideas for Cause/Effect Essays

Exercises 15.1 and 15.2 include topic ideas you may want to develop into cause/effect essays. Here are some additional ideas:

- An addiction or obsession
- A social problem
- A specific law or proposed law
- Increased longevity
- Credit card debt
- Reality TV shows
- "Extreme" sports like skydiving and rock climbing
- Why people attend college
- A current trend or fad
- A historical event
- Stereotypes
- Prejudice
- Stress
- Poverty
- A natural or scientific phenomenon

- Learning disabilities
- Explain how the situation in the following photograph came about

Karl Weatherly/Getty Images

WebWork

A graphic organizer, or diagram, can help you generate and organize ideas for cause/effect papers. Choose one of the topics in the list of "Topic Ideas for Cause/Effect Essays" on pages 324–325 then print one of the graphic organizers at **http://www.enchantedlearning.com/graphicorganizers/causeandeffect/**. Complete the diagram to generate and organize ideas for your topic.

Online Study Center For more information and exercises, go to the Online Study Center at **http://www.college.hmco.com/pic/ dolphinwriterthree**.

16 Definition

GOALS FOR CHAPTER 16

▶ Define the term *definition*.

▶ Describe the steps in writing a definition essay.

▶ Write a definition essay.

▶ Recognize the features of a definition essay.

The definition mode involves explaining what a term means. Writers include shorter definitions, those that require only a sentence or two, to make sure readers will understand the meaning of a term that may be unfamiliar. For example, if you were writing about computers for a general audience, you would want to briefly define the technical terms you intend to discuss.

Definitions can also be extended, requiring a longer passage or a whole essay to develop. Abstract or general terms, new terms, and terms that have changed meaning, for example, often require longer definitions and explanations. Look at the following example, which defines the abstract quality *American spirit*.

Souls of Steel: Reflection on the Amazing Resilience of the American Spirit

By Steve and Cokie Roberts

Following the tragic events of September 11, 2001, the spirit of America was scarred and scorched, but the signs of resistance and recovery are everywhere. Some are flashed across our television screens: the stock market reopening only days after the disaster of September 11; President Bush holding up the badge of a New York policeman who died saving others at the World Trade Center. And some signs are small and personal: an Arabic Baptist church in Washington, DC, flying an American flag; a firefighter dodging traffic not far from the Pentagon to collect donations in a boot overflowing with cash.

What is the true meaning of this familiar phrase "American spirit" that comes so easily to the lips of commentators like us? How has it imprinted our national identity for more than 200 years, and how will it shape our future?

Think of how steel is made. Like steel, our spirit is stronger than iron because the steelmaking process adds alloys[1] to the basic element found in nature and then tempers[2] them under fire to create a new, harder substance. In the process of making the American spirit, alloys of virtue and memory, heroism and hardship, are continually added to the raw materials of America's past and fused in the forge[3] of history.

Here are those elements we believe are essential to the American spirit that will continue to define who we are and what we will become.

Diversity.   Americans do not look alike or worship alike. They do not play the same games or eat the same foods. The victims of the World Trade Center attack came from eighty different countries. And with the shameful exception of African slaves and Native Americans, what distinguishes this country's history is that our citizens, or their ancestors, chose to come here.

Years ago, when we lived in Greece, we interviewed a young man who was leaving for America the next day. We asked him why he was going. Because, he answered, if I stay here, no matter how hard I work, I can go only so far. In America, there is no limit. That man added one small drop—of energy, of effort, of hope—to the spirit-making process.

Tolerance.   Precisely because we are so diverse, tolerance is an essential American trait, but it has been abused in times of fear and insecurity. More than 100,000 loyal Japanese Americans were interned[4] during World War II. McCarthyism[5] ruined countless lives and reputations. In the days after the terror of September 11, Arabic grocery stores were stoned, mosques[6] were defaced[7], [and] dark-skinned citizens were insulted and even assaulted. One Indian woman said a car pulled up beside her and the driver yelled, "Go back where you came from!"

If Americans went back where they came from, there would not be many of us left. President Bush touched the right chord when he visited a mosque near the White House and then told a joint session of Congress, "We are in a fight for our principles, and our first responsibility is to live by them." Tolerance is not a luxury of peace.

1. **alloys:** mixtures of two or more metals
2. **tempers:** hardens and strengthens by heating
3. **forge:** furnace in which metals are heated
4. **interned:** confined
5. **McCarthyism:** a movement in the 1950s to identify and penalize Americans who were suspected of supporting Communism
6. **mosques:** Muslim houses of worship
7. **defaced:** spoiled or ruined on the surface

Resilience. The immigration process acted as a natural experiment in hybridization[1]. Courage, tenacity[2], and ambition came over on those boats loaded with newcomers. The timid and tentative[3] stayed behind.

No wonder the stock market was up and running so fast after September 11. Many of the traders and brokers who accomplished that feat[4] probably could not tell you much about Betsy Ross, but they shared her spirit. Ross was twenty-four in 1776 when her husband, a militiaman, was killed in a gunpowder explosion; she took over the family upholstery business. A year later she was making flags for naval vessels, including the first version of the Stars and Stripes[5].

Ingenuity. The World Trade Center was built because our economy draws the best minds and hearts from other countries to our shores. Once here, they have had room to discover and create. The very size of America has always imbued[6] people with a sense of infinite possibility. For the pioneers, the enormous task of clearing and civilizing such a vast area meant they had to be practical. We are not much for ideology[7] or theory. "American know-how" is a cliché[8], but it is one born out of experience. Americans from Henry Ford[9] to Bill Gates[10] have always believed in what works, not what should work.

Patriotism. The stock market plunged after September 11, but any company that made flags was in great shape. Volunteers flooded relief efforts and blood banks. Young people who never had known adversity felt the stirring of an unfamiliar emotion: love of country.

Patriotism and courage take many forms. The cops and firefighters who died saving others are heroes. But it also takes courage to criticize national policy that you think is wrong. U.S. Representative Barbara Lee, D-Calif., the lone dissenting[11] voice when Congress broadened President Bush's warmaking power, was no less a patriot than the lawmakers who backed the president.

Faith. We have no official faith, no national church. But the United States is by far the most churchgoing country in the developed world. Perhaps it is the lack of an enforced orthodoxy[12] that gives different forms of spirituality room to breathe and bloom.

1. **hybridization:** crossbreeding; mixing together
2. **tenacity:** holding firmly
3. **tentative:** uncertain; hesitant
4. **feat:** achievement
5. **Stars and Stripes:** American flag
6. **imbued:** inspired or influenced
7. **ideology:** body of ideas or beliefs
8. **cliché:** an overused expression or idea
9. **Henry Ford:** founder of the Ford Motor Company
10. **Bill Gates:** cofounder of Microsoft, the world's largest computer software company
11. **dissenting:** disagreeing
12. **orthodoxy:** traditional, established faith

Every generation of Americans adds its own alloys, addresses its own adversaries. September 11 was our trial by fire. Today, the steel in our spirit is stronger for it.*

The previous passage defines the term *American spirit* by describing its six elements and illustrating each one.

The next example defines the new term *twixters*.

Michele, Ellen, Nathan, Corinne, Marcus, and Jennie are friends. All of them live in Chicago. They go out three nights a week, sometimes more. Each of them has had several jobs since college; Ellen is on her seventeenth, counting internships, since 1996. They do not own homes. They change apartments frequently. None of them are married, none have children. All of them are from 24 to 28 years old.

Thirty years ago, people like Michele, Ellen, Nathan, Corinne, Marcus, and Jennie did not exist, statistically speaking. Back then, the median[1] age for an American woman to get married was 21. She had her first child at 22. Now it all takes longer. It is 25 for the wedding and 25 for baby. It appears to take young people longer to graduate from college, settle into careers, and buy their first homes. What are they waiting for? Who are these permanent adolescents, these twentysomething Peter Pans[2]? And why can't they grow up?

Everybody knows a few of them—full-grown men and women who still live with their parents, who dress and talk and party as they did in their teens, hopping from job to job and date to date, having fun but seemingly going nowhere. Ten years ago, we might have called them Generation X, or slackers, but those labels do not quite fit anymore. This is not just a trend, a temporary fad, or a generational hiccup. This is a much larger phenomenon, of a different kind and a different order.

Social scientists are starting to realize that a permanent shift has taken place in the way we live our lives. In the past, people moved from childhood to adolescence and from adolescence to adulthood, but today there is a new, intermediate phase along the way. The years from 18 until 25 and even beyond have become a distinct and separate life stage, a strange, transitional never-never land between adolescence and adulthood in which people stall for a few extra years, putting off the iron cage of adult responsibility that constantly threatens to crash down on them. They are betwixt and between. You could call them *twixters*.†

1. **median:** average

2. **Peter Pan:** a fictional little boy who refuses to grow up

---

*Source: Adapted from Steve and Cokie Roberts, "Souls of Steel," *USA Weekend*, October 14, 2001, http://www.usaweekend.com/01_issues/011014/011014spirit.html. Originally appeared in the October 14, 2001, issue of *USA Weekend*. Reprinted with permission.
†Source: Excerpted from Lev Grossman, "Grow Up? Not So Fast," *Time*, Jan. 24, 2005, pp. 42–44. © 2004 Time Inc. Reprinted by permission.

Writing a Definition Essay

Defining a term involves explaining it so that readers can understand it. To write an effective definition essay, you need to determine how you will define the term in your thesis statement and then select other modes—such as narration, illustration, or process—that you can use to generate, organize, and develop your ideas.

Determining a Thesis Statement

If you decide that you will need to write an extended definition to explain your subject to your reader, your first step will be to determine your main point about your subject before you begin to write. Your thesis statement will probably provide a general definition of the term you have chosen. For example, a thesis statement for an essay defining the word *addiction* might read:

> An addiction is a physiological or psychological dependence upon a habit-forming substance or activity.

The main idea of a definition essay can also be implied. That is, you can present all of your details as you develop the essay and then allow the reader to draw a conclusion about the meaning of the term.

EXERCISE 16.1 **Writing Thesis Statements for Definition Essays**

For each of the following topics, use some prewriting techniques to generate ideas on your own paper and then write a thesis statement that you could use for a definition essay.

1. True love *is a deep feeling, when one person*
   Thesis statement: *wants to be with another all the time and be part of his life.*

2. A gentleman or lady
   Thesis statement: *Gentleman is a well-behaved high-principled and noble man.*

3. Courage
   Thesis statement: *Courage is ability to face life challenges, difficulties and problems.*

4. Good parent
   Thesis statement: _____

Good parent is a parent, who loves and cares about his children.

5. Success *is all goals, which everybody makes and reaches during the life*

Thesis statement: _____

Generating Ideas

After you have written a general definition for your thesis statement, the next step is to determine the most effective methods of development. Definitions are usually developed with one or more of the other modes, so your first step is asking the question *What would be the best way to explain this term to the reader?* One or more of the following modes can be useful in developing a definition essay.

- **Tell a story.** For instance, you could define what being *cool* is by narrating a story about a person who behaved in a "cool" way.

- **Provide descriptive details.** You could define what a *good day-care center* is by describing the essential physical characteristics that all good day-care centers should have.

- **Give examples.** Illustration is commonly used as a method of development for definition. The previous passage about *twixters,* for instance, provides numerous examples that illustrate the term's meaning.

- **Classify or divide.** You could also classify the parts of the subject into categories or divide it into its parts to help define what the subject is. For example, you could define what *love* is by classifying its different types.

- **Explain how something is done.** Process analysis can help to define a term by explaining how the subject works. You could define the term *stress,* for example, by describing each step in the body's stress response.

- **Explain causes and effects.** You could explain the reasons for the topic's existence or discuss the consequences of its existence. An essay that defines *depression,* for example, could explain what can lead to feelings of depression; it might also explore the effects of depression.

- **Compare or contrast.** You could offer an analogy, comparing the term or idea you are defining or explaining to something with which the reader is already familiar. Or you could use contrast, explaining what the term *does not* mean. For example, if you are defining a *workaholic,* you might want to distinguish one from a person who is not a workaholic. Contrast can also involve explaining how the thing or idea being defined is different from something else. In an essay defining the word *addiction,* for instance, the writer could contrast addictive use of a substance with nonaddictive use of the substance.

Which modes seem appropriate for developing each of the following thesis statements?

Intelligence is not just one thing; it comes in many different types.

The *bystander effect* is the name for a situation in which the *more* people who are present, the *less* likely it is that someone in need will be helped.

As William Butler Yeats said, "Education is not the filling of a pail, but the lighting of a fire."

Any one of these three thesis statements could be developed with a narrative that includes descriptive details. For example, you could relate a personal story or tell a tale about someone else to help readers understand the meaning of the term.

In addition, you could develop the first thesis statement with classification and description by categorizing the different types of intelligence and giving details about each type. Comparison/contrast would be another suitable mode of development because you could explain the similarities and differences among the various types of intelligence.

You might illustrate the second thesis statement with an explanation of the cause-and-effect relationships involved in the phenomenon. Using one or more examples would also help you develop the idea.

You could illustrate the third thesis statement with either one long example or a series of examples. You could contrast the two educational methods ("filling of a pail" versus "lighting of a fire"), and you could also explain the outcomes of each method.

After selecting the appropriate modes for your topic, spend some time prewriting to generate ideas for each of these modes. For example, if you are going to write about obsessions by using illustration, brainstorm to identify the names of people whom you would label obsessive. If you are going to define the term *fast food* by using process, list all of the steps that fast-food restaurants use to manufacture, cook, and sell their products.

EXERCISE 16.2 **Determining Modes of Development for Definition Thesis Statements**

For each of the following thesis statements, briefly explain on the blanks provided which two modes would best develop the main idea.

1. My definition of the word *patriotism* has changed over time.

_____

_____

_____

2. Most of us have been fortunate to have had at least one really great teacher.

_____

_____

_____

3. A team player is someone who can work cooperatively with others for the greater good and success of the team.

_____

_____

_____

4. Being spiritual differs greatly from being religious.

_____

_____

_____

5. A *blog*, which is short for *Web log,* is a kind of online journal, a collection of Web links and commentaries that is maintained and updated by just one person.

_____

_____

_____

Organizing a Definition Essay and Using Transitions

You may choose to use just one of the other modes for developing your ideas, or you might combine several different modes. If you will be using multiple modes to define or explain your subject, you will need to decide on the best order in which to present them and then create an outline that reflects this order. Often, one of the modes will provide the organizing structure for the entire essay while another mode or modes are used to provide layers of development. For example, for the thesis statement

A true friend is someone who knows all about you and likes you anyway

you might organize the entire essay by using a series of examples of different friends. Then you could develop each point of comparison with narratives or descriptive details.

As you write, be sure to add transitional words that can help the reader discern the relationships among the details. The transitional words that you include will depend upon the specific modes you have chosen to develop your ideas. However, because illustration is a common mode for defining ideas, you are likely to use illustration transitional words such as *for example* and *for instance*.

EXERCISE 16.3   **Organizing Details in Definition Essays**

On your own paper, prewrite to generate ideas and then complete each of the following thesis statements by filling in the blanks. Then, on the other blanks provided, prepare an informal outline by listing the details that you would include in an appropriate order.

1. Evil is _____.

_____

_____

_____

_____

2. To understand _____, one must understand the meaning of the term _____.

_____

_____

_____

_____

3. _____ and _____ are often used to mean the same thing, but they are actually very different.

_____

_____

_____

_____

EXERCISE 16.4 **Recognizing Transitions in a Definition Essay**

Circle all of the transitional words in the following essay.

Traditional neighborhood developments (TNDs) are urban undertakings that hark back[1] to the days when walking—not driving—got people where they needed to go. Other hallmarks such as tree-lined streets and detailed dwellings remain the desired results. Homes in these communities are designed with porches that are close to the street. This relationship of house to property edge maximizes yards and allows residents to keep an eye on their surroundings.

One old example of a TND is Charleston, South Carolina. Just the mention of this legendary Southern city conjures up images of shady porches and tranquil gardens mingling with well-worn cobblestone streets and bustling markets. Apart from its picturesque

1. **hark back:** return

appeal, the town's longevity and success rest in the fact that it works.

Another example is the much newer community of I'On, located in Mount Pleasant, South Carolina. Named in honor of Jacob Bond I'On, War of 1812 hero, this community seeks to create a pleasing mix of indoor and outdoor spaces connected by pedestrian-friendly streets. Begun in 1998, I'On does not just blindly copy Charleston; its goals are to achieve the best of both worlds—good design principles and systems that are timeless, coupled with modern materials and building techniques that are durable and low-maintenance.

First of all, the residences in Charleston are different from one another. Likewise, I'On's residences are not only different in size and shape but also vary architecturally. The unifying key is that each house is the same distance from the street, but owners are free to create residences that have their own style.

Secondly, color is used to distinguish one house from another. Charleston's famed Rainbow Row merits its name because each individual house is denoted by a different, and often bold, color. Similarly, the townhouse district in l'On adopts the same device. Whether attached or divided by a narrow alley, the dwellings are almost identically designed, yet their individual colors visually separate them.

Porches are a third element of the TND. Aside from their aesthetic[1] appeal, porches provide the best eyes to the street. Residents who can closely monitor their streets and sidewalks are more likely to interact with each other.

A final feature of the TND is the fence. In both Charleston and l'On, elements such as an ivy-covered garden wall, a whitewashed picket enclosure, or even a solid hedgerow define outdoor space. They let you know who owns what and where you can and cannot go. They also provide privacy and protection. That's why these secluded gardens and yards are able to exist side by side with well-traveled sidewalks and busy streets.*

1. aesthetic: related to beauty or good taste

Source: Adapted from Robert Martin, "Lessons for Today," *Southern Living, Favorites* (Special Issue), Spring 2004, pp. 92–95. © 2004 *Southern Living.* Reprinted by permission.

EXERCISE 16.5 **Writing a Definition Essay That Includes Transitions**

Choose one of the thesis statements and outlines that you prepared in Exercise 16.3. Write the essay, and use transitional words that indicate how the details are related.

Developing the Details in a Definition Essay

Once you have selected the appropriate mode (or modes) for developing your definition, you will follow the specific guidelines for that mode to provide the necessary details. For example, if you use illustration to develop your definition, remember the principles of writing effective illustration. If you use cause/effect, remember that set of principles, and so on.

EXERCISE 16.6 **Recognizing the Features of a Definition Essay**

Read the following essay. Then answer the questions that follow by writing your responses on the blanks provided.

Fellow Nerds: Let's Celebrate Nerdiness!

By Tom Rogers

I am a nerd. While the Internet boom has lent some respectability to the term, narrow-minded and thoughtless stereotypes[1] still linger. Nerds are supposedly friendless, book-smart sissies who suck up to[2] authority figures. Some of our image problems stem from our obsession with mastering every inane detail of our interests. But to call us suck-ups is nonsense. We often horrify those in authority with our inability to understand, let alone follow, societal norms.

Like most nerds, I did not know I was one until I started school. There I quickly found out that my enthusiasm for answering the teacher's questions made others feel I was deliberately trying to make them look bad. My classmates were not shy about expressing their feelings on the playground. Fortunately, I was tall and stood my ground, a bluff that helped repel bullies. But mostly I survived by learning to keep quiet in the classroom.

I became a high-school teacher because I realized there were lots of young nerds growing up who needed to know that being a nerd was not just OK but

1. **stereotypes:** oversimplified generalizations

2. **suck up to:** seek favor or attention from

something wonderful. Unfortunately, they were not likely to hear this even from teachers, although virtually every modern blessing from democracy to electric motors originated with a nerd. Some, like Thomas Paine[1], were idealistic; others, like Tesla[2], eccentric. Newton[3] was arrogant and Einstein[4] absent-minded. All of them are now considered geniuses. But make no mistake: seventeen-year-old versions of these men, placed in modern American high schools, would instantly be labeled as nerds.

I raised two nerd sons and a daughter, who describes herself as a nerd sympathizer, partly because I did not have the cleverness to raise "cool" kids, but also because, selfishly, I wanted nerds to talk to. Every year I invite my Advanced Placement[5] physics students to my house for study sessions before the AP test. Last year one student nerd's mother told me that her son had returned home and talked for hours about how awesome it was to have found a nerd family. Unfortunately, the world's response to our family has not always been so enthusiastic.

When my sons were still in school, they were often picked on by classmates. My older boy, a pale and unathletic kid, was an easy target. When his middle-school science teacher asked if anyone could name some elements, my son recited the periodic table[6] from memory. Thanks to events like that, he endured nerd hell at the hands of bullies when waiting for the school bus every afternoon. We tried karate classes and pep talks to bolster his defenses, but he was never able to win his tormentors' respect. He was just too small.

My boys were often misunderstood by their teachers, too. My younger son's middle-school social-studies teacher rigidly insisted that he take notes. When he refused, she publicly told him he would never graduate from high school. My son was perfectly capable of taking notes, but in typical nerd fashion, he could not bring himself to comply because it was illogical. He could easily remember what the teacher had said. Writing it down cut into his thinking time.

Clearly, my son would have to give his teacher what she wanted, but it had to be done with style. We discussed options. These included taking notes in one of the foreign languages he studied as a hobby. I discouraged it because he had learned some colorful foreign terms and was capable of describing his teacher in

1. **Thomas Paine:** intellectual and scholar who helped generate support for the American Revolution with his powerful writings
2. **Tesla:** accomplished scientist and inventor of the late nineteenth and early twentieth centuries
3. **Newton:** influential scientist of the late seventeenth and early eighteenth centuries
4. **Einstein:** physicist who is widely regarded as the most important scientist of the twentieth century
5. **Advanced Placement:** program that offers high school students the opportunity to earn college credit
6. **periodic table:** a table of 116 chemical elements

ways that could make a sailor blush. Finally, we agreed he would write his notes backward.

For six months he transcribed his teacher's lectures backward. When I held my son's notes up to a mirror, they were perfectly readable. I should not have been surprised. As a small child he had entertained us by turning books upside down and reading them backward. I waited for a complaint from his teacher, but she never noticed.

Despite childhood trials, both of my sons remain devoted nerds. My older son became conversational in four foreign languages and has hitchhiked around Europe three times. And these days no one would mistake him for a sissy. On one occasion a group of Russian policemen threw him a party after he accepted their invitation to take a mid-December dip in a spring filled with near-freezing water.

My younger son proved his teacher wrong and graduated from high school. He scored 1600 on the SAT and was asked to give a speech before five hundred educators and politicians who had gathered to honor education. It was his one moment of visibility. As I waited for him to talk, my stomach flip-flopped. I had no idea what he was going to say. He rose from his seat and delivered ten minutes of stand-up comedy on being a nerd. The audience laughed until they cried. I cried. Afterward a young nerd paid him his highest compliment: "Thank you for what you have done for our people." No, our kind does not fit the stereotypes, but yes, there is something wonderful about being a nerd.*

1. What is the thesis of this essay, and where in the essay is it stated?

_____

_____

2. What are the two primary modes of development used throughout the essay?

_____

3. The author focuses on nerd stereotypes that are, in his opinion, inaccurate. In your own words, write a one-sentence definition of the term *nerd* that the author of this essay would be likely to accept as valid.

_____

4. Write a one-sentence definition of a label that has been used to describe you or a group with whom you associate (examples: liberal, conservative, jock,

*_Source:_ Tom Rogers, "Fellow Nerds: Let's Celebrate Nerdiness!" *Newsweek,* Dec. 11, 2000, p. 14.
© 2000 *Newsweek,* Inc. All rights reserved. Reprinted by permission.

slacker, teacher's pet, and so on). If you used this definition as the thesis statement of an essay, what modes of development would you use to develop it?

_____

In Summary: Steps in Writing Definition Essays

1. **Determine your main idea.** Write a general definition of your term to serve as your thesis statement.

2. **Decide on your modes of development and generate ideas.** Choose one or more modes for developing your definition and then prewrite to generate ideas.

3. **Organize and develop ideas.** Follow the guidelines for the specific mode(s) you have chosen to organize and explain your ideas.

CHAPTER 16 REVIEW

To review the main points in this chapter, write a brief response to each of the following questions.

1. What are you doing when you use the definition mode of development?

2. What are two kinds of definitions?

3. What kinds of words are often good candidates for longer definitions?

4. What does the thesis statement of a definition essay usually provide?

5. How are definition essays usually developed?

6. Why are illustration transitions common in definition essays? What are some of these transitional words?

CHAPTER 16 REVIEW

Topic Ideas for Definition Essays

Exercise 16.1 includes topic ideas that you may want to develop into definition essays. Here are some additional ideas:

- A word related to one of your hobbies or interests
- A term used by a particular group (such as a social group, ethnic group, or family) to which you belong
- A word that is overused or abused
- An emotion (fear, anger, sorrow, and so on)
- A value (responsibility, loyalty, neatness, and so on)
- A certain type of person (a wise person, a genius, an ambitious person, and so on)
- Marriage
- Good and/or evil
- Noise pollution
- Heaven or hell

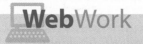

WebWork

Go to the Wisdom Quotes Web site at **http://www.wisdomquotes.com/** and select a category that interests you. Then click on the link for that category and read what others have had to say on that subject. Use their ideas to help you write a thesis statement that defines the topic. If you were to write an essay to develop this thesis statement, which modes would you use?

Online Study Center   For more information and exercises, go to the Online Study Center at **http://www.college.hmco.com/pic/ dolphinwriterthree**.

Argument

GOALS FOR CHAPTER 17

▶ Define the term *argument*.

▶ Describe the steps in writing an argumentative essay.

▶ Write an argumentative essay.

▶ Recognize the features of an argumentative essay.

There will be many occasions when you will need to convince a reader to do something or to change his or her belief about something. You may need to write an academic research paper arguing that online learning is as effective as traditional classroom-based learning. You may have to write a memo or report to convince your boss to implement a certain change at work. Or you may want to write a letter for your newspaper's editorial page to convince citizens to vote for a particular candidate for public office or to oppose a proposed change for your community. This type of writing is termed argumentative because you are *arguing* a certain position. Argumentative writing attempts to persuade the reader to accept a certain viewpoint.

The following passage, for example, argues against using the abbreviated language of instant messaging.

Instant Nonsense

By Lynne Truss

The good news about young people and their obsession with instant messaging? It may not entirely destroy the English language. The bad news? I worry that it's setting teenagers and children back when it comes to their command of language and the written word. How long will it be before Shakespeare[1] editors are

---

1. **Shakespeare:** seventeenth-century English playwright and poet

forced to translate Hamlet's[1] most famous speech for the benefit of younger readers: "2B or N2B: that is the FAQ"?

Frankly, I'm a bit alarmed by the impact of instant messaging. Already, more than 13 million U.S. teens use it, according to research from Pew Internet and American Life Project. E-mail, of course, paved the path for instant messaging and text messaging, and both are notorious[2] for taking maximum shortcuts. Teachers now find themselves grading essays by students who insist on the validity of "U" and "4" as substitutes for words that were, when you think about it, quite short in the first place. Oh, and let's not forget about "emoticons[3]," like :) to say "I'm happy" or :(for "I'm sad."

You may object that this code-speak is the innocent work of young people who will grow out of it. But look at your own correspondence. Isn't "BTW" now accepted for "by the way," and "COB" for "close of business"? With onslaught comes acceptance. English embraces change; its academic exponents[4] pride themselves on never saying a word against it. Instant messaging, therefore, has been greeted by the guardians of language as a brilliant marriage of speech, symbol, and written word.

What worries me, however, is this: If young people cling to their own version of written English, will they ultimately not recognize real words? Already, a large shift in attitude toward the written word has taken place. Whereas older people regard writing as the higher use of language, many young people see writing only as a rather poor substitute for speaking.

"So it's the future of literature at stake now, is it?" I hear you ask in exasperation. "Aren't you like those uncool fuddy-duddies[5] in the 1960s who said that Bob Dylan[6] was going to destroy poetry?" Time will tell, I suppose. But at least Dylan worked within the same language as Wallace Stevens and Walt Whitman[7]—or even the seventeenth-century poet John Donne. A fan of Dylan could still read Donne. What we face now is something far more radical and disrespectful of language. What we do about it is up to us. As always, I'm personally torn: stand and fight to the death, or go to bed and pull the covers over my head? As Hamlet might sigh, "To sleep, perchance to dream"—only, of course, instead of "sleep," he'd write |-I.*

1. **Hamlet:** character in one of Shakespeare's plays who begins a famous speech with the line "To be or not to be: that is the question."
2. **notorious:** known widely and unfavorably
3. **emoticons:** collections of numbers, letters, and/or punctuation marks that represent certain facial expressions
4. **exponents:** supporters or defenders
5. **fuddy-duddies:** old-fashioned people
6. **Bob Dylan:** an American singer-songwriter
7. **Wallace Stevens and Walt Whitman:** two American poets

Source: Lynne Truss, "Instant Nonsense," *USA Weekend,* October 22–24, 2004, p. 18. Originally appeared in *USA Weekend,* October 22–24, 2004. Reprinted by permission.

In the previous passage, the author provides two reasons why the shortcuts of instant messaging are a bad idea. First, the writer argues that instant messaging will destroy young people's ability to use standard English. Second, she argues that instant-messaging language will affect literature in general.

Writing an Argumentative Essay

Arguing for or against something involves offering convincing reasons in support of your position. To write an effective argumentative essay, you need to consider your audience's needs and goals, write a persuasive thesis statement, select relevant reasons and acknowledge opposing arguments, and develop your reasons with sufficient logical or emotional evidence.

Thinking About Your Audience

Many of the other modes of development usually focus either on the writer and his or her thoughts and experiences (narration, description) or on the subject itself (comparison/contrast, cause/effect, definition). Argumentative writing, in contrast, focuses on the *reader*. Because the whole purpose of persuasive writing is to persuade, or convince, the reader, the whole essay revolves around the kinds of reasons and evidence that the reader will need in order to accept the idea presented in the writer's thesis statement.

Thus, the first step in planning an argumentative essay is to carefully consider the targeted reader. Whether this is one person or many, remember that arguments are not directed at people who agree with the writer. Writing an essay for those who already concur with the thesis would be a waste of time. Instead, argumentative essays are directed at readers who either disagree with the writer's viewpoint or have not yet made up their minds.

Once you have determined exactly who needs to be persuaded to accept your thesis, spend some time thinking about that reader's (or those readers') needs, goals, and potential objections. At this point, at least informally analyze your readers. What do they probably believe right now? What do you think their goals and priorities are? To what parts of your argument will they object? Can you think of ways to overcome those objections? As you plan and write your essay, you will often return to this analysis to guide you in making decisions about *what* to include and *how* to include it.

EXERCISE 17.1   Considering Your Audience

For each of the following argumentative thesis statements, consider who the best audience would be. On the blanks provided, identify the most likely audience and briefly describe the members' needs, goals, and potential objections.

1. I should not be penalized for turning in my assignment two days late.

student — teacher

2. I deserve a promotion.

worker — boss

3. The legal drinking age should be lowered to eighteen.

voters (congress)

4. Children under the age of three should not be allowed to watch television.

parents

5. Junk food should not be sold in vending machines on public school campuses.

school officials, parents

Determining Your Thesis Statement, Relevant Reasons, and Opposing Arguments

Your analysis of your readers will affect, first of all, your choice of a thesis statement and supporting reasons. It will also help you to determine how to refute those readers' objections to your ideas.

The Persuasive Thesis Statement. Persuasive thesis statements usually have several important characteristics.

1. Persuasive thesis statements clearly state the behavior or belief that they want the reader to adopt after reading the essay. And to reflect their persuasive purpose, these types of thesis statements often include words and phrases like *should, must, ought to,* and *have to.* For example, read the following thesis statements.

   > Every healthy American should become an organ donor.

   > This university's administration must figure out a way to provide more parking for students.

   > The residents of this community ought to oppose the construction of a new Wal-Mart.

   Each of the previous statements clearly states the change in belief or behavior that the writer is advocating.

2. Persuasive thesis statements are also assertive. They do not include tentative or hedging words and expressions like "I believe that" or "*maybe* you should." They take a stand, and they confidently ask the reader to accept that stand as true and valid.

3. Persuasive thesis statements often include the agent of the action; in other words, they state exactly who should make or bring about this change. In the previous statements, healthy Americans, the university's administration, and the residents of a certain community are the ones being asked to alter either a belief or a behavior.

4. Persuasive thesis statements ask the reader to make changes that are logical and reasonable. Again, a consideration of your audience will guide your composition of your thesis statement. Although you might want them to make a very big change, you must consider whether you should initially argue for that big change or for some intermediate, shorter-term change that will, you hope, ultimately lead to the bigger change. For instance, will readers who believe the American tax system is currently just fine think it is reasonable for you to ask them to support eliminating the current system altogether and creating a completely new one from scratch? Probably not. No matter how eloquent and well-reasoned your argument is, you likely will not be able to convince them, so you might have to adjust your thesis statement to argue an idea that is more within the realm of possibility for them. You could argue instead that the current tax system needs to be reformed in certain ways.

EXERCISE 17.2   **Writing Thesis Statements for Argumentative Essays**

For each of the following topics, use some prewriting techniques to generate ideas on your own paper and then write a thesis statement you could use for an argumentative essay.

1. Dress codes

Topic sentence: _____

2. Raising the minimum wage

Topic sentence: _____

3. A needed change in America's educational system

Topic sentence: _____

4. A subject that everyone should study in school

Topic sentence: _____

5. Something illegal that should be legal

Topic sentence: _____

relevent — существие
относится. к делу

Supporting Reasons. Just as a consideration of your reader determined your thesis statement, your analysis of your audience should also guide your choice of supporting points. Often, there are many different reasons in support of a particular opinion. However, not all of these reasons may be *relevant* to your target audience. Therefore, in the planning stages of writing your essay, you will need to decide which reasons most closely match your readers' priorities and goals.

For example, if you intend to argue to drivers that they should give up driving their cars to and from work and instead use mass transportation (such as the bus, subway, or train), you would need to consider these readers' priorities. Typical employed people are concerned about time, money, safety, convenience, and stress reduction. Thus, they will respond to reasons that relate to time saved, financial benefits, accident statistics, ease of use, and the elimination of hassles. These readers may be less likely to be convinced by reasons—such as environmental issues—that are unrelated to their *main* concerns, so you could leave those points out.

EXERCISE 17.3 **Selecting Relevant Supporting Reasons**

For each of the argumentative thesis statements you wrote for Exercise 17.2, identify the target audience on the following corresponding blank and then list two or three supporting reasons that would be relevant to that audience.

1. Audience: _____

Supporting reasons:

_____

_____

_____

2. Audience: _____

Supporting reasons:

_____

_____

_____

3. Audience: _____

Supporting reasons:

_____

_____

_____

4. Audience: _____

Supporting reasons:

_____

_____

_____

5. Audience: _____

Supporting reasons:

_____

_____

_____

Opposing Arguments. One special feature of argumentative essays is the acknowledgment of opposing arguments, which is also known as making *concessions*. When you make a concession, you mention one or more of your opponent's arguments, and then you go on to refute that argument by explaining how your position is stronger, more logical, or more valid. Making concessions to the opposing arguments indicates to your reader that you understand the entire issue, not just your side of it. It also allows you to expose the weaknesses in opposing arguments by explaining how they are flawed.

Argumentative essay writers do not explain an opposing argument in detail. They merely mention it and then go on to refute it. Concessions can be dealt with in one section of the essay, but they are often most effective when you match each concession to one of your supporting points and use the supporting point as a refutation of the opposing argument. For example, if you assert that using mass transportation results in time being saved, someone who disagreed with you could point out that driving a car to a destination often takes less time than taking a bus there. To refute this argument, you could point to statistics indicating how much time a driver can actually end up wasting in traffic jams on busy workdays. You could also point out that unlike driving, time spent commuting via mass transportation allows a person to do other things while riding. The following example, which includes a concession in italic type, demonstrates one way of doing this.

> *You might think that riding the bus would take more time than simply driving yourself to and from work.* However, using mass transportation actually gives you time to get things done that would otherwise take up additional hours of your day. When you drive, all you can do is drive. But when you ride a bus, you can pay bills, read, or even work on a laptop computer. Thus, you are utilizing the time more wisely.

If you decided to include the argument that using mass transportation reduces stress, someone who disagreed with you might point out that having to be at a bus or train stop at a certain time creates time pressures. Or he or she might say that riding in crowded buses or cars is stressful. In turn, you could counter with information about the stress caused by driving in heavy traffic every day. The following example includes both the concession (in italic type) and the response.

> *Drivers may argue that driving is less stressful than riding the bus.* They probably do not realize, however, how much stress they put themselves through by driving back and forth to work in traffic.

Notice that both of these concessions to the opposing argument are mentioned very briefly in just one sentence. Notice also that the transitional word *however* signals the end of the concession and the beginning of the writer's argument.

Other contrast transitional words, such as *but, on the other hand, though,* and *nevertheless,* are also appropriate in signaling such a shift. Concessions themselves often begin with words and expressions such as *admittedly, of course, it is true that,* and *I concede that.*

As you develop the habit of incorporating concessions into your argumentative essays, choose your words carefully to avoid insulting or offending readers. Remember that they either disagree with you or are undecided and that they are likely to believe many of the opposing arguments you are going to refute. Therefore, when you make concessions, use language that is sensitive to your readers. Do not suggest that the opposing argument (and, thus, the people who believe it) is uninformed or ignorant. It is probably best to avoid using aggressively judgmental words such as *ridiculous* or *silly* when you mention an opposing argument. Instead, gently refute each one with logical, well-reasoned explanations of your own viewpoints.

As you read the following essay, notice how the author incorporates concessions (in bold print) to the opposing argument.

Don't Dumb Down the Military

By Nathaniel Fick

I went to war as a believer in the citizen-soldier. My college study of the classics idealized Greeks who put down their plows for swords, returning to their fields at the end of the war. As a Marine officer in Afghanistan and Iraq, however, I learned that the victors on today's battlefields are long-term, professional soldiers. Thus the increasing calls for reinstating the draft[1]—and the bills now before Congress that would do so—are well intentioned but misguided. Imposing a draft on the military I served in would harm it grievously[2] for years.

I led platoons of volunteers. In Afghanistan, my marines slept each night in holes they hacked from the rocky ground. They carried hundred-pound packs in addition to their fears of minefields and ambushes, their homesickness, loneliness, and exhaustion. The most junior did it for $964.80 per month. They didn't complain, and I never wrestled with discipline problems. Each and every marine wanted to be there. If anyone hadn't, he would have been a drain on the platoon and a liability[3] in combat.

In Iraq, I commanded a reconnaissance[4] platoon, the Marines' special operations force. Many of my enlisted marines were college-educated; some had been to graduate school. All had volunteered once for the Marines, again for the

1. **draft:** required enrollment in the armed forces
2. **grievously:** seriously
3. **liability:** something that holds one back
4. **reconnaissance:** related to exploration or inspection of an area to gather information

infantry[1], and a third time for recon. They were proud to serve as part of an elite unit. Like most demanding professionals, they were their own harshest critics, intolerant of their peers whose performance fell short.

The dumb grunt[2] is an anachronism[3]. He has been replaced by the strategic corporal. Immense firepower and improved technology have pushed decision-making with national consequences down to individual enlisted men. Modern warfare requires that even the most junior infantryman master a wide array of technical and tactical skills.

Honing[4] these skills to reflex, a prerequisite for survival in combat, takes time—a year of formal training and another year of on-the-job experience were generally needed to transform my young marines into competent warriors. The Marine Corps demands four-year active enlistments because it takes that long to train troops and ensure those training dollars are put to use in the field. One- or two-year terms, the longest that would be likely under conscription, would simply not allow for this comprehensive training.

Some supporters of the draft argue that America's wars are being fought primarily by minorities from poor families who enlisted in the economic equivalent of a Hail Mary pass[5]. They insist that the sacrifices of citizenship be shared by all Americans. The sentiment is correct, but the outrage is misplaced. There is no cannon-fodder[6] underclass in the military. In fact, front-line combat troops are a near-perfect reflection of American male society.

Yes, some minority men and women enlist for lack of other options, but they tend to concentrate in support jobs where they can learn marketable skills like driving trucks or fixing jets, not throwing grenades and setting up interlocking fields of machine gun fire. African-Americans, who comprise nearly 13 percent of the general population, are overrepresented in the military at more than 19 percent—but they account for only 10.6 percent of infantry soldiers, the group that suffers most in combat. Hispanics, who make up 13.3 percent of the American population, are underrepresented at only 11 percent of those in uniform.

The men in my infantry platoons came from virtually every part of the socioeconomic spectrum. There were prep-school graduates and first-generation immigrants, blacks and whites, Muslims and Jews, Democrats and Republicans. They were more diverse than my class at Dartmouth[7], and far more willing to act on their principles.

1. **infantry:** soldiers trained to fight on foot
2. **grunt:** an infantryman in the U.S. military
3. **anachronism:** something that is out of its proper time or order
4. **honing:** sharpening
5. **Hail Mary pass:** in football, a long pass thrown in desperation at the end of a game
6. **cannon-fodder:** soldiers regarded as likely to be killed or wounded in combat
7. **Dartmouth:** a college in New Hampshire

The second argument most often advanced for a renewed draft is that the military is too small to meet its commitments. Absolutely true. But the armed forces are stretched thin not from a lack of volunteers but because Congress and the Pentagon are not willing to spend the money to expand the force. Each of the services met or exceeded its recruiting goals in 2003, and the numbers have increased across the board so far [in 2004]. Even the Army National Guard, often cited as the abused beast of burden in Iraq, has seen re-enlistments soar past its goal, 65 percent, to 141 percent (the figure is greater than 100 because many guardsmen are re-enlisting early).

Expanding the military to meet additional responsibilities is a matter of structural change: if we build it, they will come. And build it we must. Many of my marines are already on their third combat deployment[1] in the global war on terrorism; they will need replacing. Increasing the size of the active-duty military would lighten the burden on every soldier, sailor, airman, and marine. Paradoxically[2], a larger military becomes more sustainable than a smaller one: fewer combat deployments improves service members' quality of life and contributes to higher rates of enlistment and retention. For now, expanding the volunteer force would give us a larger military without the inherent liabilities of conscription[3].

And while draft supporters insist we have learned the lessons of Vietnam and can create a fair system this time around, even an equitable draft would lower the standards for enlistees. Defense Secretary Donald Rumsfeld was chastised[4] for saying Vietnam-era draftees added no value to the armed forces. But his error was semantic[5]; the statement was true of the system, if not of the patriotic and capable individuals who served.

The current volunteer force rejects applicants who score poorly on its entrance aptitude exam, disclose a history of significant drug use, or suffer from any of a number of orthopedic[6] or chronic injuries. Face it: any unwilling draftee could easily find a way to fail any of these tests. The military, then, would be left either to abandon its standards and accept all comers, or to remain true to them and allow the draft to become volunteerism by another name. Stripped of its volunteer ideology[7], but still unable to compel service from dissenters[8], the military would end up weaker and less representative than the volunteer force—the very opposite of the draft's intended goals.

Renewing the draft would be a blow against the men and women in uniform, a dumbing down of the institution they serve. The United States military

1. **deployment:** positioning troops to ready for combat
2. **paradoxically:** with apparent contradiction
3. **conscription:** required enrollment in the armed forces
4. **chastised:** criticized

5. **semantic:** related to meaning in language
6. **orthopedic:** related to the skeletal system of the body
7. **ideology:** set of ideas or beliefs
8. **dissenters:** people who disagree

exists to win battles, not to test social policy. Enlarging the volunteer force would show our soldiers that Americans recognize their hardship and are willing to pay the bill to help them better protect the nation. My view of the citizen-soldier was altered, but not destroyed, in combat. We cannot all pick up the sword, nor should we be forced to—but we owe our support to those who do.*

EXERCISE 17.4 **Determining Concessions**

For each of the supporting reasons you listed in Exercise 17.3, write a concession on the following blanks.

1. _____
_____
_____

2. _____
_____
_____

3. _____
_____
_____

4. _____
_____
_____

5. _____
_____
_____

Organizing an Argumentative Essay and Using Transitions

After you decide on the reasons you will offer in support of your argument, your next major consideration will be the order in which to present these reasons. Order of importance is the most common pattern for arranging reasons. There-

*Source: Nathaniel Fick, "Don't Dumb Down the Military," *New York Times*, July 20, 2004, www.nytimes.com. © 2004, *The New York Times*. Reprinted with permission.

fore, rank each of your reasons in importance, and then let your analysis of your readers guide you in your decision about whether to discuss them in order from most important to least important or vice versa, from least important to most important. If your readers are very busy decision-makers, consider beginning with your strongest, most important reason, the one that will be most likely to persuade them. If you are reasonably sure that your readers will be willing to read the entire essay, giving your entire argument careful consideration, consider saving your strongest reason for last so that it will be the one they remember best after they have finished reading.

As you write, do not forget to include transitional words that help readers follow you from one point to the next. Some of the most common argumentative transitional words and phrases are

first, second, third
one reason, another reason, and so on
most importantly
for one thing
next
lastly
finally
another
in addition
furthermore
also

Notice how the writer of the following passage uses argumentative transitional words (in bold type) to help the readers follow the supporting reasons.

People who like to hunt for sport would have us believe that they provide a valuable service to nature and to society by curbing animal overpopulation. In reality, though, nature does not need any help from humans to maintain its delicate balance, and communities are harmed far more than they are helped by the practice of sport hunting.

First of all, sport hunters often destroy property. Many of them, for example, think nothing of trespassing; littering; damaging gates, fences, or other structures; or disposing of dead animals improperly. Land owners do not want to have to clean up the messes some hunters leave behind; therefore, they are becoming more and more reluctant to allow hunters on their property.

More importantly, though, sport hunting is dangerous to humans, livestock, and pets. According to the International Hunter Education Association, in 2004, hunters were responsible for accidents that killed 42 people and injured 403 others. Although most hunters try to behave responsibly, many more are inexperienced, careless, or even intoxicated. As a result, anyone or anything in their line of fire—including other hunters, hikers, innocent bystanders, cows, horses, dogs, and cats—could be in danger of being shot.

Finally, sport hunting is harmful because it promotes violence, cruelty, and unethical behavior. Hunting is a blood sport, one that glorifies killing other sentient[1] beings, often for no reason other than seeing them die. It is true that many hunters eat the meat of the animals they kill; however, many hunters shoot creatures purely for fun. In fact, they kill many animals—such as raccoons, rodents, squirrels, and birds—that they have no intention of using for food.

The primary interest of people who hunt is not to help nature or their fellow human beings. They do it because they take pleasure in killing things, and it is time for everyone to admit that their hobby is damaging rather than beneficial.

 EXERCISE 17.5   **Organizing Reasons in Argumentative Essays**

On your own paper, prewrite to generate ideas and then complete each of the following thesis statements by filling in the blank. Then, on the other blanks provided, prepare an informal outline by listing the supporting reasons that you would include in an appropriate order.

1. _____ should be mandatory.

_____

_____

_____

_____

2. _____ should be outlawed once and for all.

_____

_____

_____

3. _____ is a worthy cause (or charity).

_____

_____

_____

_____

1. **sentient:** conscious; capable of perception or feeling

EXERCISE 17.6 **Recognizing Argumentative Transitions**

Circle all of the argumentative transitional words in the following passage.

Buy a Used Car: Three Reasons to Say In with the Old

By Deanna Mascle

You know it is time to buy a replacement for your vehicle. Repair bills are looming on the horizon or eating into your checking account. Every time you turn around something seems to be going wrong—both large and small annoyances make driving an ongoing hassle. Once you have made the decision to go car shopping, the first question you must face is whether to go new or used. Here are three reasons you should buy a used car.

The top reason to buy a used car is that new cars are a losing proposition. New cars depreciate fast. Did you know that as soon as you drive a new car off a dealer lot it will instantly depreciate between $1,000 and $2,000. After the first three years most cars are worth only about 60–70 percent of their original value. However, if you buy a used car then you will have to pay a lot less for a nice car and you will not have to worry about that depreciation.

Once upon a time buying a used car was a risky proposition. There was a good chance you could buy a lemon or a car that had been used and abused or even been in an accident. Today the savvy consumer does not have to face these risks, which leads to the second reason for buying a used car. It is safer (and less risky) than it has ever been before. Many reputable dealers offer one-owner vehicles that are still on warranty so that takes some risk out of the equation, but in addition today there are many research tools available on the Internet to help you learn about the reputation and performance history for the particular vehicle model you are considering, plus you can even run the vehicle identification numbers to determine if a specific vehicle has been in an accident. It is probably a lot less risky to buy a used car than a new unproven vehicle that might turn out to be a lemon. You can also get a pretty accurate value for a vehicle so you know how much you should pay.

Finally, buying a used car takes a lot of the stress out of new car ownership while still letting you enjoy the benefits of a new vehicle. Dealers will give a vehicle a turnout so it will have that new car smell, but because you do not have to worry about the price you paid, you can sit back and enjoy your new-to-you vehicle without worrying about tempting fate. Plus, many dealers have more room to deal on a used car than they often do with a new car so you have more bargaining power.

So if you are looking to buy a car, then you should consider buying a used car because it will save you money, it is safer than ever before, and it is less stressful.*

EXERCISE 17.7 **Writing an Argumentative Essay That Includes Transitions**

Choose one of the thesis statements and outlines that you prepared in Exercise 17.5. Write the essay, including transitional words that indicate how supporting the reasons are related.

Developing Your Supporting Reasons with Evidence

As you develop each reason that supports your thesis, be aware of the two kinds of evidence you can offer and plan to include the kind that is more likely to convince your reader. The first type is *logical* evidence, which includes facts, statistics, expert opinion, and examples. This type of evidence consists of the hard data and observable facts that will appeal to your readers' reason and intellect. If you want to argue for using mass transportation instead of driving to work, for instance, you can provide specific details about the cost of taking the bus versus the cost of driving. You could also provide statistics that compare the safety of bus riders to the safety of drivers.

The second type of evidence is emotional. This evidence appeals to readers' needs and feelings, such as the need for fun or friendship and the desire to be a good parent. Think of television commercials, which attempt to sell us many products—from perfume to beer to peanut butter—by appealing to our desires to be attractive, well liked, loving to our children, and so on. These types of arguments can also be effective in argumentative essays, too. For example, you could argue that by using mass transportation, you are increasing your own safety and thus also doing something important for your children. This particular argument appeals to readers' love and concern for their families. However, beware of basing entire academic arguments on emotional evidence. Readers of academic and professional arguments will expect the majority of your evidence to be factual and logical.

As you incorporate both logical and emotional kinds of evidence in support of your argument, make sure that you avoid *logical fallacies*, arguments that are flawed in various ways because they are based on careless thinking or on delib-

*Source: Adapted from Deanna Mascle, "Buy a Used Car: 3 Reasons to Say In with the Old," *EzineArticles,* November 27, 2006, http://ezinearticles.com/?Buy-A-Used-Car:-3-Reasons-To-Say-In-With-The-Old&id=370558.

erate attempts to distract the reader. Some of these fallacies are based on a lack of sufficient evidence. For example, a writer may simply repeat a point over and over without ever offering any real proof in support of it. Or the writer may jump to conclusions on the basis of very little evidence. Other fallacies arise from flawed relationships. For example, a writer might claim that one thing led to another without considering the other factors that could have been at work, or he or she might carelessly compare two things that are really more different than they are alike. Still other fallacies take the form of personal attacks against those who believe the opposing arguments or try to persuade the reader based on what other people—such as celebrities—believe. Alert readers will detect such fallacies, which weaken your arguments.

EXERCISE 17.8   Recognizing the Features of an Argumentative Essay

Read the following essay. Then answer the questions that follow by writing your responses on the blanks provided.

Society Is Dead, We Have Retreated into the iWorld

I was visiting New York last week and noticed something I would never thought I would say about the city. Yes, nightlife is pretty much dead (and I am in no way the first to notice that). But daylife—that insane mishmash[1] of yells, chatter, clatter, hustle, and chutzpah[2] that makes New York the urban equivalent of methamphetamine[3]—was also a little different. It was quieter.

Manhattan's downtown is now a Disney-like string of malls, riverside parks, and pretty upper-middle-class villages. But there was something else. And as I looked across the throngs on the pavements, I began to see why.

There were little white wires hanging down from their ears, or tucked into pockets, purses, or jackets. The eyes were a little vacant. Each was in his or her own musical world, walking to their soundtrack, stars in their own music video, almost oblivious to the world around them. These are the iPod[4] people.

Even without the white wires you can tell who they are. They walk down the street in their own MP3[5] cocoon, bumping into others, deaf to small social cues, shutting out anyone not in their bubble.

Every now and again some start unconsciously emitting strange tuneless squawks, like a badly tuned radio, and their fingers snap or their arms twitch to some strange soundless rhythm. When others say "Excuse me" there's no

1. **mishmash:** collection or mixture of different things
2. **chutzpah:** nerve; boldness
3. **methamphetamine:** a stimulant drug
4. **iPod:** a brand of portable digital music player
5. **MP3:** related to a format used to store music or video files on computers

response. "Hi," ditto. It is strange to be among so many people and hear so little. Except that each one is hearing so much.

Yes, I might as well own up. I'm one of them. I witnessed the glazed New York looks through my own glazed pupils, my white wires peeping out of my ears. I joined the cult a few years ago: the sect of the little white box worshippers.

Every now and again I go to church—those huge, luminous[1] Apple[2] stores, pews in the rear, the clerics[3] in their monastic[4] uniforms all bustling around or sitting behind the "Genius Bars," like priests waiting to hear confessions.

Others began, as I did, with a Walkman—and then a kind of clunkier MP3 player. But the sleekness of the iPod won me over. Unlike other models it gave me my entire music collection to rearrange as I saw fit—on the fly, in my pocket.

What was once an occasional musical diversion became a compulsive obsession. Now I have my iTunes in my iMac for my iPod in my iWorld. It's Narcissus[5] heaven: we've finally put the "i" into Me.

And, like all addictive cults, it is spreading. There are now 22 million iPod owners in the United States, and Apple is becoming a mass-market company for the first time.

Walk through any airport in the United States these days and you will see person after person gliding through the social ether as if on autopilot. Get on a subway and you are surrounded by a bunch of Stepford[6] commuters staring into mid-space as if anaesthetized[7] by technology. Do not ask, do not tell, do not overhear, do not observe. Just tune in and tune out.

It would not be so worrying if it were not part of something even bigger. Americans are beginning to narrow their lives.

You get your news from your favorite blogs[8], the ones that will not challenge your view of the world. You tune into a satellite radio service that also aims directly at a small market—for new age fanatics, liberal talk, or Christian rock. Television is all cable. Culture is all subculture. Your cell phones can receive e-mail feeds of your favorite blogger's latest thoughts—seconds after he has posted them—get sports scores for your team or stock quotes of your portfolio.

Technology has given us a universe entirely for ourselves—where the serendipity[9] of meeting a new stranger, hearing a piece of music we would never

1. **luminous:** giving off light
2. **Apple:** the company that makes iPods
3. **clerics:** members of the clergy, people ordained to perform religious services
4. **monastic:** related to a community of monks
5. **Narcissus:** character from Greek mythology who was in love with himself
6. **Stepford:** related to the zombie-like women in the 1975 film *The Stepford Wives*
7. **anaesthetized:** made incapable of feeling sensations
8. **blogs:** Web sites that offer commentary or personal opinions about a subject or diary-like entries
9. **serendipity:** a fortunate discovery by accident

choose for ourselves, or an opinion that might force us to change our mind about something are all effectively banished.

Atomization[1] by little white boxes and cell phones. Society without the social. Others who are chosen—not met at random. Human beings have never lived like this before. Yes, we have always had homes, retreats, or places where we went to relax, unwind, or shut out the world.

But we did not walk around the world like hermit crabs with our isolation surgically attached.

Music was once the preserve of the living room or the concert hall. It was sometimes solitary but it was primarily a shared experience, something that brought people together, gave them the comfort of knowing that others too understood the pleasure of a Brahms[2] symphony or that Beatles[3] album.

But music is as atomized now as living is. And it is secret. That bloke[4] next to you on the bus could be listening to heavy metal or a Gregorian[5] chant. You will never know. And so, bit by bit, you will never really know him. And by his white wires, he is indicating he does not really want to know you.

What do we get from this? The awareness of more music, more often. The chance to slip away for a while from everydayness, to give our lives its own soundtrack, to still the monotony of the commute, to listen more closely and carefully to music that can lift you up and keep you going.

We become masters of our own interests, more connected to people like us over the Internet, more instantly in touch with anything we want, need, or think we want and think we need. Ever tried a Stairmaster[6] in silence? But what are we missing? That hilarious shard of an overheard conversation that stays with you all day; the child whose chatter on the pavement takes you back to your early memories; birdsong; weather; accents; the laughter of others. And those thoughts that come not by filling your head with selected diversion, but by allowing your mind to wander aimlessly through the regular background noise of human and mechanical life.

External stimulation can crowd out the interior mind. Even the boredom that we flee has its uses. We are forced to find our own means to overcome it.

And so we enrich our life from within, rather than from white wires. It is hard to give up, though, isn't it?

Not so long ago I was on a trip and realized I had left my iPod behind. Panic. But then something else. I noticed the rhythms of others again, the sound of the airplane, the opinions of the taxi driver, the small social cues that had

1. **atomization:** breaking something into tiny particles or fragments
2. **Brahms:** a German composer of Romantic music
3. **Beatles:** a popular English rock/pop band

4. **bloke:** man; fellow
5. **Gregorian:** related to a particular group of Catholic monks
6. **Stairmaster:** a piece of exercise equipment

been obscured before. I noticed how others related to each other. And I felt just a little bit connected again and a little more aware.

Try it. There's a world out there. And it has a soundtrack all its own.*

1. What is the thesis of this essay?

_____

2. List three reasons the author provides in support of his thesis.

a. _____

b. _____

c. _____

3. List two concessions the author makes.

a. _____

b. _____

4. Does the author provide any logical evidence to support his thesis?

_____

_____

5. Give an example of emotional evidence the author provides to support his thesis.

_____

6. Did the author convince you to agree with his thesis? Why or why not?

_____

*Source: Andrew Sullivan, "Society Is Dead, We Have Retreated into the iWorld," *Times Online*, February 20, 2005, www.timesonline.co.uk. Reprinted by permission.

In Summary: Steps in Writing Argumentative Essays

1. **Consider your readers.** An analysis of your readers will affect all of the other decisions you will make as you plan and write your essay.

2. **Write a persuasive main idea statement that takes your audience into consideration.** Write a reasonable, assertive thesis statement that clearly expresses what you want your readers to do or to believe.

3. **Match your supporting reasons to your readers' priorities and goals.** Include only those reasons that are relevant to your readers.

4. **Incorporate concessions.** Anticipate and acknowledge the opposing viewpoints and then go on to refute them.

5. **Determine the best order for your reasons.** Decide whether you should arrange your reasons from most important to least important or vice versa. Include transitional words to help the readers follow you from one point to the next.

6. **Develop each reason with either logical or emotional evidence.** Use your analysis of your readers to decide which facts, statistics, expert testimony, examples, or emotional appeals will be most effective.

CHAPTER 17 REVIEW

To review the main points in this chapter, write a brief response to each of the following questions.

1. What does it mean to *argue* a certain position?

2. How is the focus of argumentative writing different from that of other modes of development?

3. What is the very first step in planning an argumentative essay?

4. What are some characteristics of an argumentative thesis statement?

5. What are concessions?

6. What are some transitional words and phrases that signal the end of a concession and the beginning of a writer's argument?

7. Why should writers of argumentative essays use language that is sensitive to their readers?

8. What is the most common pattern for arranging reasons in an argumentative essay?

9. What are some common argumentative transitional words and phrases?

10. What are the two kinds of evidence that you can offer in an argumentative essay? Describe each kind.

11. What are logical fallacies? Why should you avoid using them when you write?

Topic Ideas for Argumentative Essays

Exercises 17.1 and 17.2 include topic ideas that you may want to develop into argumentative essays. Here are some additional ideas:

- Something that should be banned
- Something that should be changed
- A controversial issue
- A book that everyone should read
- Something that is overrated (or underrated)
- Something that is not taught in schools but should be
- Something that is worth saving
- Something that is more harmful than people think
- National health care
- Beauty pageants
- Smoking in public places
- Immigration
- Capital punishment
- Curfews for teenagers
- Same-sex marriage
- Mandatory attendance in college courses
- Tax reform

- Athletes' use of performance-enhancing drugs such as steroids
- Animal rights
- Environmental protection
- Media violence
- Speed limits
- Funding for space exploration

WebWork

Go to the Cable News Network (CNN) Web site at **www.cnn.com**. Explore the site and then write down five different topics that would be suitable for an argumentative essay. Choose one of these topics and determine an appropriate audience. Plan for an essay by writing down a persuasive thesis statement, relevant reasons, and opposing arguments.

Online Study Center For more information and exercises, go to the Online Study Center at **http://www.college.hmco.com/pic/dolphinwriterthree**.

18 Combining Modes of Development

> ## GOALS FOR CHAPTER 18
>
> ▶ Write an essay that is developed with at least two modes.
>
> ▶ Recognize different modes of development in longer passages and essays.

In Chapters 8 through 17 of this text, you examined each of the major modes of development by itself. Although these modes can be used in isolation, they are very often combined to develop one main idea. For example, read the following passage.

There must be an instinct about when the end is near, and one day in May, 1997, we all found ourselves gathered at my parents' home, in Orange County, California. I walked into the house they had lived in for thirty-five years, and my weeping sister said, "He's saying goodbye to everyone." A hospice nurse said to me, "This is when it all happens." I didn't know what she meant, but I soon would.

I walked into the bedroom where he lay, his mind alert but his body failing. He said, almost buoyantly[1], "I'm ready now." I understood that his intensifying rage of the last few years had been against death, and now his resistance was abating[2]. I stood at the end of the bed, and we looked into each other's eyes for a long, unbroken time. At last he said, "You did everything I wanted to do."

I said, "I did it because of you." It was the truth. Looking back, I'm sure that we both had different interpretations of what I meant.

I sat on the edge of the bed. Another silence fell over us. Then he said, "I wish I could cry, I wish I could cry."

At first, I took this as a comment on his plight but am forever thankful that I pushed on. "What do you want to cry about?" I finally said.

"For all the love I received and couldn't return."

1. **buoyantly:** cheerfully   2. **abating:** decreasing

He had kept this secret, his desire to love his family, from me and from my mother his whole life. It was as though an early misstep had kept us forever out of stride. Now, two days from his death, our pace was aligning, and we were able to speak.

I sometimes think of our relationship graphically[1], as a bell curve[2]. In my infancy, we were perfectly close. Then the gap widened to accommodate our differences and indifference. **In the final days of his life, we again became perfectly close.**

My father's death has a thousand endings. I continue to absorb its messages and meanings. He stripped death of its spooky morbidity[3] and made it tangible[4] and passionate. He prepared me in some way for my own death. He showed me the responsibility of the living to the dying. But the most enduring thought was expressed by my sister. Afterward, she told me she had learned something from all this. I asked her what it was. She said, "Nobody should have to die alone."*

To develop the idea in the thesis statement, which is highlighted with bold print, this author chose two modes of development: narration and cause/effect. He tells the story about his father's death. Then he goes on to explain the effects of this event in the last paragraph.

The previous passage uses first one mode and then another to organize and develop the thesis statement. In other essays that combine two or more modes of development, you might want to use one mode to provide the structure for the entire essay while using another mode to provide layers of development. For example, read the following passage.

─────────────   **Diagnosis: Muscle-Bound**   ─────────────

By Lisa Sanders, M.D.

1. Symptoms

The young teacher paced between the rows of teenagers. It was his second day on the job, and he was nervous. His heart was pounding. His tie felt unbelievably tight. Suddenly, it was hard to breathe. Really hard. He could feel sweat beading coolly on his face. He glanced at the clock. Could he make it to the end of the period? Finally, the bell rang—class was over.

1. **graphically:** in graphs or pictures
2. **bell curve:** a line that goes up and down to form the shape of a bell
3. **morbidity:** gruesomeness
4. **tangible:** possible to understand

*Source: Excerpted from Steve Martin, "The Death of My Father," *The New Yorker,* June 17 and 24, 2002, p. 87.

The hallway to the nurse's office seemed to stretch out into the distance. He could feel himself go through the motion of breathing, but the air did not seem to make it to his lungs. "I cannot breathe," he croaked, leaning against the door of the medical office. The school nurse led him to a bed. He could hear her asking questions, trying to get more information, but it was hard to speak. She removed his tie, then placed a mask over his mouth and nose. The cool rush of oxygen brought some relief from the sense of drowning on dry land. The next thing he remembered was being loaded into an ambulance.

At the hospital, doctors diagnosed a massive pulmonary embolism, which occurs when part of a blood clot breaks off and is carried through the circulatory system into the vessels of the lungs. In this patient, it was a very large clot, which prevented most of the circulating blood from reaching his lungs, where the oxygen he breathed could be exchanged. He was started on blood thinners and admitted to the I.C.U.[1] As soon as he was stable, the doctors turned their attention to the clot itself. Where did it come from? Why did it form? They needed to find out because another assault like that could kill him.

Our lives depend on our ability to form blood clots. But like so much in the body, context is everything. In the right place, at the right time, a blood clot can save your life by preventing uncontrolled bleeding. In another setting, that same clot can kill. Clots normally form at the site of injury to a blood vessel. They can also form when blood stops moving; that is why anything that causes prolonged immobility, like traveling or being stuck in bed, increases the risk of a clot. Certain drugs—estrogen and other steroid hormones—can also increase the risk. Some people have a genetic abnormality[2] that makes their blood coagulate[3] too readily. Finding the cause of a clot is crucial to estimating the risk of another.

2. Investigation

So the patient's doctors looked. They found nothing in his legs—the most common source of pathological[4] blood clots. CT scans[5] of his chest, abdomen, and pelvis likewise showed nothing. He had not traveled recently, had not been sick. He took no medicines. His doctors sent off studies of his blood to look for any evidence that his blood was too eager to clot. Normal. They could find no reason for this otherwise healthy young man to have developed a clot.

1. **I.C.U.:** intensive care unit, a location within a hospital where patients are closely monitored
2. **genetic abnormality:** a hereditary condition that affects an individual's genetic code, or DNA
3. **coagulate:** harden
4. **pathological:** related to or caused by disease
5. **CT scan:** an abbreviation for a specialized type of medical test ("computerized axial tomography")

It is difficult to be a patient with an illness that cannot be explained. It is even harder when a diagnostic uncertainty leads to an unacceptable therapeutic certainty: in this case, the patient was told that he would have to take warfarin, an anticlotting drug, for the rest of his life. He was twenty-three years old and liked playing sports. He played baseball and basketball in high school and rugby in college. But when you cannot clot, these games become dangerous. The drug would protect him from another pulmonary embolus, but in return he would have to avoid anything that could cause bleeding.

The patient hoped for an alternative and found Dr. Thomas Duffy, a hematologist[1] at Yale University with a reputation as a great diagnostician[2]—the kind of doctor that other doctors turn to when they are stumped. Perhaps the doctor could figure out what caused his devastating pulmonary embolus and help him get off warfarin.

Duffy is a tall, fit man in his sixties with a preference for bow ties and a precise, thoughtful manner of speaking. He listened to the patient's story, then asked for a few more details. What kind of physical activity had he been doing in the weeks before the clot? He lifted weights every other day and either ran or swam the days between. Had he taken any performance-enhancing drugs? Yes, but not for years.

Duffy considered the possibilities. The usual suspects had already been ruled out; whatever caused this clot was going to be uncommon. Could a clot have formed inside one of his organs—his heart, his liver, his spleen—and traveled to his lungs from there? The scans the patient had would not have shown that. A myxoma, a rare type of tumor that grows in heart muscle, can cause a clot within the heart itself. Could he have such a tumor? An uncommon blood disease called paroxysmal nocturnal hemoglobinuria can cause blood clots in the liver, the spleen, or beneath the skin. Did he have this rarity? The physical exam might give some clues.

When the patient undressed for the exam, Duffy was immediately struck by the highly developed muscles of his upper body. "He looked like one of those young men in a men's fitness magazine," he told me later. Otherwise his exam showed nothing abnormal.

Then Duffy remembered a physical-exam maneuver he learned years ago when he was a medical student. He straightened the patient's arm and held it parallel to the floor. Carefully placing a finger over the pulse at the young man's wrist, he moved the arm behind the patient. Then he asked the patient to tilt his head up and face the opposite direction. The pulse disappeared. When the patient

---

1. **hematologist:** a physician who specializes in study of the blood

2. **diagnostician:** a physician who identifies diseases

looked forward again, the pulse returned. He repeated the maneuver. Again, the pulse disappeared when the patient turned his head. Immediately Duffy suspected what had caused the clot.

3. Resolution

The vessels that carry the blood from the heart to and from the shoulders and arms travel through a narrow space under the clavicle[1] and above the top of the rib cage. The presence of hypertrophied[2] muscles of the shoulder or neck, or in some cases an extra rib, can make this small opening even tighter. This problem, known as thoracic outlet syndrome, is most commonly seen in young athletes who use their upper extremities extensively—baseball pitchers or weight lifters—or in workers who use their arms above the level of their shoulders, like painters, wallpaper hangers, or teachers who write on a blackboard. When these patients put their arm in certain positions, the extra muscle or bone constricts the space between the two structures and cuts off the flow through the vessels like a kink in a garden hose. Blood cannot get into the arm, so the pulse disappears. And blood cannot get out of the arm, so it pools and can clot. When the arm is moved and the vessel reopens, the blood flows once more, but if a clot has formed, it can break loose and travel to the lungs.

Duffy ordered additional tests to make sure there was no other explanation for the clot. He then referred the patient to a surgeon who had experience with an unusual and difficult surgery: the removal of the first rib to widen the narrow opening. Nine months later, during the summer, the patient had the surgery. Three months after that he was able to stop taking warfarin. That was four years ago. The patient continues to teach, play sports, and lift weights without difficulty.

"Seeing that extraordinary musculature reminded me of this unusual anatomical abnormality, and the test, of course, I learned many years ago," Duffy recalled when I spoke to him recently. I had never heard of the old-fashioned arm maneuver. This and other physical-exam techniques are part of a disappearing tradition in medicine—replaced more or (in this case) less successfully with a variety of high-tech imaging techniques. Yet had a doctor not done this simple test, the patient's abnormality may not have been picked up, and he would have been stuck taking medicine he didn't need and missing out on the sports he loved.*

1. **clavicle:** a bone that extends from above the rib cage to the shoulder

2. **hypertrophied:** enlarged

*Source: Lisa Sanders, "Muscle-Bound," *New York Times,* February 25, 2007, www.nytimes.com.
© 2007, Lisa Sanders, M.D. Reprinted by permission.

This essay uses several modes of development. Narration organizes the whole essay, and description, cause/effect, definition, and illustration are all used to develop the details.

Some Common Combinations

While there are many different combinations of the various modes, some combinations, such as the following, tend to occur more frequently than others.

Narration and Description. When you tell a story, it is natural to include details about the people, places, and things involved. Narration is often combined with cause/effect, too. As you saw in the example passage about the death of Steve Martin's father, it is natural to explain the effects of a particular experience.

Comparison/Contrast and Description, Illustration, or Narration. You learned in Chapter 14 that comparisons are often developed with descriptive details or examples. Narration, too, can be used to help readers understand similarities or differences. For example, for the thesis statement *My two trips abroad to France and to Africa were very different; however, both left me with lasting experiences,* you could tell stories about your experiences in each place and explain how those in one place differed from those experienced in the other.

Definition and Illustration. As you saw in Chapter 16, illustration is often used to develop a definition. However, many of the other modes are also useful for explaining what a term means. To develop the thesis statement *Civil disobedience, a technique for protesting unjust laws or policies, has often been an effective technique for bringing about change in societies,* for example, you could give examples of specific acts of civil disobedience in history.

Division and Description. As you divide something into its parts, it is natural to provide descriptive details about each part. If you want to help readers understand the different parts of an automobile assembly line, for example, it would make sense to divide it into its different segments and then describe what you would see and hear in each segment.

Argument and Effects. Providing reasons in support of an argument often involves explaining the consequences of something. For example, if you argued that

Congress should increase funding for space exploration, you would need to explain the beneficial effects of expanding the country's space program. Likewise, putting forth the argument that *Players in all amateur and professional sports should be more harshly penalized for using performance-enhancing drugs such as steroids* would involve explaining the effects of using these kinds of drugs.

Writing an Essay Using a Combination of Modes

When you write an essay that combines two or more modes, you begin by evaluating your thesis statement and selecting the modes that are most appropriate for explaining this idea. Then you follow the guidelines of the modes you have chosen to generate, organize, and develop your points.

Evaluating Your Thesis Statement and Selecting Appropriate Modes

After you have written your thesis statement, study it to determine all of the possible ways that you could develop it. Some thesis statements will clearly indicate which methods to use. For example, if your thesis statement is *Although completing my college degree was one of the most difficult things I have ever done, the struggle was worth it in the end,* you would need to tell stories about the difficulties and then explain the effects of getting the degree.

However, many thesis statements will not suggest any one particular mode of development. For example, if your thesis statement is *My role model is bicycle-racing champion Lance Armstrong,* you could provide reasons, or you could describe the qualities about him that you admire, or you could give examples of admirable things he has accomplished, or you could tell one or more stories about him. You could even compare him with other admirable people with whom readers would be familiar. There are many possibilities.

Other thesis statements will clearly require at least one particular primary mode of development, but they will allow you to choose from various secondary modes of development. For example, if your thesis statement is *Congress should invest more money in mass transportation options for American citizens,* you will obviously choose argument as your primary mode of development, and your reasons will give the paragraph its overall structure. However, how will you develop each reason? You could use cause/effect, explaining the consequences of either people's continuing to rely upon private vehicles and/or building more mass-transit systems. Or you could compare America's current automobile-dominated culture with the mass transit–based culture of other countries.

EXERCISE 18.1   **Selecting Appropriate Modes of Development**

Read each of the following thesis statements. On the blanks provided, briefly explain which modes would best develop each statement.

1. Getting married and remaining single both have their advantages and disadvantages.

   _____

   _____

   _____

2. You can learn to better resolve interpersonal conflicts with family members, friends, neighbors, and coworkers.

   _____

   _____

   _____

3. Many investors tend to fall into one of three categories.

   _____

   _____

   _____

4. All American students should learn to speak Spanish.

   _____

   _____

   _____

5. As Ambrose Bierce put it, love is "a temporary insanity curable by marriage or by removal of the patient from the influences under which he incurred the disorder."

   _____

   _____

   _____

Organizing a Combination Essay and Using Transitions

When you use more than one mode of development, it is particularly important to organize and outline your ideas before writing to avoid confusing your readers. A thesis statement such as *My role model is bicycle-racing champion Lance Armstrong* could result in a very disorganized essay if you do not first spend some time finding the best order for all of your ideas. First, determine which mode will provide the structure for the entire first paragraph or section that will come first. Outline the paragraph's main points using that pattern. For example, you might choose to develop the first point about Lance Armstrong by describing his admirable qualities. Description, then, would be your primary organizational mode, and the beginnings of your informal outline might look like this:

1. Refusal to give up
2. Positive attitude
3. Generosity

This outline indicates that the overall paragraph will be organized according to the three Armstrong traits that you admire.

Next, decide on secondary modes to organize and develop your layers of development. Then expand your outline by adding details related to these other modes:

1. Refusal to give up
   – Tell story about his battle against cancer
2. Positive attitude
   – Tell story about how he trained and resumed winning
3. Generosity
   – Give examples of the charitable work he does

As you write, do not forget to include transitional words that help readers follow you from one point to the next.

EXERCISE 18.2   **Organizing Essays Developed with Different Modes**

On your own paper, prewrite to generate ideas and then complete each of the following thesis statements by filling in the blank(s). Then, on the other blanks provided, identify the modes of development that you would use, and prepare an informal outline by listing the points and details you would include in an appropriate order.

1. I expected _____ to be _____, but it was actually

_____.

Modes of development: _____

Outline:

_____

_____

_____

_____

2. _____ is one person who triumphed over great adversity.

Modes of development: _____

Outline:

_____

_____

_____

_____

3. If you want to succeed in life, you must _____.

Modes of development: _____

Outline:

_____

_____

_____

_____

EXERCISE 18.3 **Recognizing Transitions in an Essay Developed with Different Modes**

Circle all of the transitional words in the following passage.

A Hispanic World of Difference

By Raul A. Reyes

Growing up, I looked forward every Friday to *The Brady Bunch*[1] and its idealized depiction of a typical American family. I liked the firm, yet kind, parents, Mike and Carol. I empathized with Jan, a fellow middle child. I giggled at the

1. *The Brady Bunch:* a 1970s television comedy series

wisecracking housekeeper, Alice. Although my enjoyment of the television show was tempered by the realization that there was no room on its trademark grid of smiling faces for a brown face like mine, I loved the Bradys nonetheless.

In contrast, I often thought my own *familia* was a drag. My Dad wouldn't let us eat grapes or lettuce because he was boycotting them in support of Cesar Chavez's[1] efforts on behalf of underpaid field workers. Mom served rice and beans—which I didn't like—at most meals. And my aunts insisted on speaking to me and my brothers in Spanish, in a vain attempt to make us bilingual. I didn't appreciate their efforts. I didn't want to be called *mi'jo*[2]. I just wanted to be like other kids.

However, when I watched TV or movies or read the newspaper, I had a distinct feeling of being different in a not-so-good way. Back then, I rarely saw Latin people on television, with the exception of Desi Arnaz (on *I Love Lucy* reruns) and Charo (on *The Love Boat*[3]). In films, Hispanic characters were usually maids, prostitutes, or scary drug dealers. On the news, whenever Mexicans were mentioned, it was in connection with illegal immigration or gangs. Sometimes I wondered whether other people thought we were all lowlifes or spoke with an accent.

Every year, when Hispanic Heritage Month rolls around (September 15 to October 15), I think back to my culturally conflicted childhood. I grew up in Southern California in a diverse community where I never felt like a "minority." At school, I studied alongside white, Asian, and other Hispanic kids, so ethnicity usually was not an issue. It was only when I looked beyond my home and my community that ambivalence[4] took root and threatened the self-esteem my parents had worked so hard to nurture. While Dad and Mom encouraged me to be proud of my background, a disconnect persisted between what I was told at home and what I saw in the real world.

Nowadays, the world has changed, and the Hispanic influence in this country is booming, wrapped up in economic power, political influence, and pop-culture accolades[5].

- **Population:** According to the U.S. Census Bureau, we've become the nation's largest minority group, 39 million strong. From 1990 through 2000, in fact, the increase in the Hispanic population was a whopping 58 percent.
- **Immigration:** Latino immigrants to the U.S.A. are estimated at 400,000 annually, the largest flow in U.S. history.

1. **Cesar Chavez:** Mexican-American labor leader and activist
2. *mi'jo*: Spanish slang for "my son"
3. *I Love Lucy* and *The Love Boat:* two television comedy series
4. **ambivalence:** state of having opposing feelings or attitudes
5. **accolades:** praise or awards

- **Economy:** Latino purchasing power also is on the rise. The 2000 Census reported a median Hispanic income of $33,000, the highest ever. Corporations have rushed to embrace the burgeoning[1] Hispanic market.
- **Pop culture:** Entertainers and athletes (think J. Lo and A-Rod) have become household names and, more than that, role models and icons[2] for children of all races.

Most importantly, though, Hispanics have made historic headway in American politics. A new generation of political players has emerged, including New Mexico Governor Bill Richardson, [Attorney General] Alberto Gonzales, and Representatives Linda and Loretta Sanchez, D-Calif., the first sisters ever to serve in Congress. During the 2004 presidential campaign, President Bush and Democratic contender John Kerry dueled over who would do more for Hispanics, the voting bloc[3] that might determine the next occupant of *La Casa Blanca*[4]. Both parties mounted outreach efforts aimed at Latinos: "Viva Bush" and "Unidos Con Kerry." Bush cozied up to Hispanics with his guest-worker proposal for immigrants, while earlier in 2004, the Democrats aired the first-ever Spanish rebuttal[5] to the State of the Union address. Both sides spent record amounts on Spanish-language advertising.

So after being overlooked for so long, suddenly it's hip to be Hispanic. As a kid, I resolved my identity issues right at our dining-room table. On Sunday evenings, my relatives—teachers, nurses, and social workers—would gather for my mother's delicious enchiladas and chile rellenos[6]. They told stories about the old days, before they all attended college, back when they lived in *el barrio*[7].

Aunt Emma liked to remind everyone that she was the first Latina on her college tennis team. Aunt Lola told me how my Grandpa escaped the Mexican Revolution, chased by Pancho Villa[8], and started over in Texas. Dad would play his Vikki Carr records, and if it was someone's birthday, we celebrated with a piñata[9]. On such nights, surrounded by living proof of Latino achievements, I learned to appreciate my cultural inheritance. In our own way, I realized, we were as all-American as Los Bradys.*

1. **burgeoning:** growing and flourishing
2. **icons:** objects of attention and devotion; idols
3. **bloc:** groups united for a common purpose
4. *La Casa Blanca:* the White House
5. **rebuttal:** presentation of opposing evidence or arguments
6. **enchiladas and chile rellenos:** two Mexican dishes
7. *el barrio:* urban area of a Spanish-speaking country
8. **Pancho Villa:** a famous general of the Mexican Revolution in the early twentieth century
9. **piñata:** a container filled with candy or toys, meant to be broken open with sticks by blindfolded players

Source: Adapted from Raul A. Reyes, "A Hispanic World of Difference," *USA Today*, September 21, 2004, p. 23A. Reprinted by permission of Raul A. Reyes.

EXERCISE 18.4   Writing a Combination Essay That Includes Transitions

Choose one of the thesis statements and outlines that you prepared in Exercise 18.2. Then write the essay, including transitional words that indicate how the details are related.

Developing the Details in a Combination Essay

Once you have selected the modes that you will use to develop your thesis statement, you will follow the specific guidelines for those modes to provide the necessary details. For example, if you use illustration to develop your main idea, remember the principles of writing effective illustration. If you use narration, remember that set of principles, and so on.

EXERCISE 18.5   Recognizing Modes of Development in Essays

Read each of the following essays. Then answer the questions that follow by writing your responses on the blanks provided.

The Next Generation

By Rachel K. Sobel

1   If I had wanted to make a lot of money, I would have gone straight into investment banking. If I were enamored[1] solely of science, then I would have chosen a biology PhD. But I decided to apply to medical school. I felt a calling, a desire to be engaged in the special healing bond between a doctor and a patient.

2   At the same time I would have been blind not to notice a weakening of that bond and the ugly cynicism[2] seeping into my chosen profession. The summer before I left for medical school, I read of walkouts by doctors in several states, induced by high malpractice insurance premiums and concerns about frequent lawsuits. I also heard about the rise of "boutique medicine" aimed at rich patients. Friends who had started med school a few years ahead of me already gave off a sense of aloofness[3] and fatigue. When did this cynicism start, I wondered? And how do I maintain the sense of idealism I set out with?

1. **enamored:** in love with
2. **cynicism:** negativity or pessimism
3. **aloofness:** reserved; emotionally distant

3　　My first two years, spent mostly in the classroom, nourished that idealism. To learn about the diseases that I would soon treat energized me. Even more important, I was surrounded by classmates who fueled each other's passion. Some taught science to disadvantaged students; others held health fairs for Hispanic and Asian children. On the last evening of our smoking-cessation[1] group for the homeless, I felt a rush of hope in the room, for the participants who had thrown out their lighters and cigarettes—and for my classmates and our future in medicine.

4　　But this year, my third, has brought a loss of some innocence. As I trained on the hospital wards, I was surrounded by unhappy, jaded[2] residents—med school graduates doing their first stints[3] as working doctors. These residents were my teachers, and they griped about the "bitchbox" or pager that they had to wear and about bothersome patients, such as "High-Maintenance Mom." Cynicism certainly catches on. I was stunned how quickly I had started to change. Just a few months in, I rejoiced with one young doctor when our frail, demented[4] patient was finally transferred to a nursing home. We celebrated not because we had helped him—though we did, a little—but because we were relieved that he was finally off our hands. Another classmate ruled out a specialty she had long considered, because the patients were too needy. "Too needy?" she said. "I can't believe I am thinking this way, but they were just too draining."

5　　But as much as cynicism is contagious, so are compassion, optimism, and hope. One professor required us to include in our case presentations what our patients like to do for fun. He understood that while wading through a sea of data about a patient, it was easy to dehumanize care. The woman with Marfan syndrome[5] and a serious heart problem, it turns out, had been an avid hoops player. The man with cocaine-induced chest pain—he's a serious stamp collector.

6　　One resident showed me that even while being bogged down with paperwork and beeping pagers, taking a few minutes to do what's not "required" is still possible—and can make a real difference. In the clip of a busy day, he found time to counsel a homeless patient, a former lawyer who was diagnosed with alcohol-induced heart disease, about the very serious cardiac consequences of his addiction. "I always thought alcohol was bad for my liver," the patient said, somewhat surprised. "I didn't know it could damage my heart." The patient was discharged, newly informed and newly hopeful, holding a list of local sobriety[6] programs.

1. **cessation:** stopping
2. **jaded:** negative and unfeeling
3. **stints:** periods of time
4. **demented:** mentally ill
5. **Marfan syndrome:** a connective tissue disorder characterized by unusually long limbs

6. **sobriety:** related to refraining from the consumption of alcohol or drugs

7　Fellow students have reminded me, as well, that we possess strong medicine— not the drugs we can give to patients but our words, the timbre[1] of our voice, and the touch of our hands. A few months ago my classmate Julie, who was transferring her patient's care to me, brought me to his bedside to introduce us. A pungent[2] sour odor wafted through the air. There was a pink tray by his side to catch his frequent vomiting. The thin, white-bearded patient greeted her like a close relative: "Julie, my darling, I've been waiting for you."

8　The man, recently diagnosed with end-stage lung cancer, was troubled. His wife had suddenly stopped coming to visit him in the hospital. He worried that she was too scared to see him go, that she could smell the aroma of death in the air. "Do I smell like death, Julie?" he asked, patting his lips after hocking[3] up a small concoction of phlegm and blood. Julie placed her hand on his bony shoulder, bent over toward his straggly beard, and took several deep whiffs. "Absolutely not. Don't you worry one more minute about that." He smiled, looking relieved, and then he thanked her. And I smiled too, to thank Julie for helping to restore my faith in this extraordinary relationship.*

1. What sentence states the thesis of this essay? Where is it located?

_____

_____

2. What mode provides the structure for the first half of the essay (paragraphs 1–4)?

_____

3. What mode provides the structure for the second half of the essay (paragraphs 5–8)?

_____

4. What modes organize the layers of development in this essay?

_____

_____

5. Give an example from your own observation or personal experience to illustrate the author's thesis statement.

_____

1. **timbre:** quality of sound　　　　3. **hocking:** coughing
2. **pungent:** sharp or biting

*Source: Rachel K. Sobel, "The Next Generation," *U.S. News and World Report*, Jan. 31/Feb. 7, 2005, p. 54. Copyright © 2005 *U.S. News and World Report*, L.P. Reprinted with permission.

Why People Love Dogs

By Jon Katz

1 My friend and fellow dog lover Edie, an occupational therapist in Massachusetts, has been looking for a mate for nearly 10 years. She finally thought she'd found one in Jeff, a nice guy, generous and funny, who teaches high school. They dated for several months, and just as there was talk about a future, it occurred to Edie that Jeff hadn't really bonded with her yellow Lab, Sophie. In fact, as she thought more about it, she wasn't sure Jeff was a dog guy at all.

2 She confronted him about this at dinner one night, and he confessed, in some anguish, that he didn't love Sophie, didn't love dogs in general, never had.

3 They broke up the next week. More accurately, she dumped him. "What can I say?" Edie told me, somewhat defensively. "Sophie has been there for me, day in and day out, for years. I can't say the same of men. She's my girl, my baby. Sooner or later, it would have ended."

4 Having just spent two months on a book tour talking to dog lovers across the country, I can testify that this story isn't unusual. The lesson Edie gleaned, she says, was that she should have asked about Sophie first, not last.

5 In America, we love our dogs. A lot. So much that we rarely wonder why anymore.

6 This, perhaps, is why God created academics. John Archer, a psychologist at the University of Central Lancashire, has been puzzling for some time over why people love their pets. In evolutionary terms, love for dogs and other pets "poses a problem," he writes. Being attached to animals is not, strictly speaking, necessary for human health and welfare. True, studies show that people with pets live a bit longer and have better blood pressure than benighted[1] nonowners, but in the literal sense, we don't really need all those dogs and cats to survive.

7 Archer's alternative Darwinian[2] theory: Pets manipulate the same instincts and responses that have evolved to facilitate human relationships, "primarily (but not exclusively) those between parent and child." No wonder Edie ditched Jeff. She was about to marry the evil stepfather, somebody who wasn't crazy about her true child.

8 Or, to look at it from the opposite direction, Archer suggests, "consider the possibility that pets are, in evolutionary terms, manipulating human responses, that they are the equivalent of social parasites." Social parasites inject themselves into the social systems of other species and thrive there. Dogs are masters at that. They show a range of emotions—love, anxiety, curiosity—and thus trick us into thinking they possess the full range of human feelings. They dance with joy when we come home, put their heads on our knees and stare longingly into our eyes. Ah, we think, at last, the love and loyalty we so richly deserve and so

1. **benighted:** ignorant; unenlightened

2. **Darwinian:** related to Darwin's theory of evolution by natural selection

rarely receive. Over thousands of years of living with humans, dogs have become wily[1] and transfixing[2] sidekicks with the particularly appealing characteristic of being unable to speak. We are therefore free to fill in the blanks with what we need to hear. (What the dog may really be telling us, much of the time, is "Feed me.") As Archer dryly puts it, "Continuing features of the interaction with the pet prove satisfying for the owner." It's a good deal for the pets, too, since we respond by spending lavishly on organic treats and high-quality health care.

9   Psychologist Brian Hare of Harvard has also studied the human–animal bond and reports that dogs are astonishingly skilled at reading humans' patterns of social behavior, especially behaviors related to food and care. They figure out our moods and what makes us happy, what moves us. Then they act accordingly, and we tell ourselves that they're crazy about us. "It appears that dogs have evolved specialized skills for reading human social and communicative behavior," Hare concludes, which is why dogs live so much better than moles.

10   These are interesting theories. Raccoons and squirrels don't show recognizable human emotions, nor do they trigger our nurturing ("She's my baby") impulses. So, they don't (usually) move into our houses, get their photos taken with Santa, or even get names. Thousands of rescue workers aren't standing by to move them lovingly from one home to another.

11   If the dog's love is just an evolutionary trick, does that diminish it? I don't think so. Dogs have figured out how to insinuate[3] themselves into human society in ways that benefit us both. We get affection and attention. They get the same, plus food, shelter, and protection. To grasp this exchange doesn't trivialize our love, it explains it.

12   I'm enveloped by dog love, myself. Izzy, a border collie who spent the first four years of his life running along a small square of fencing on a nearby farm, is lying under my desk at the moment, his head resting on my boot. Rose, my working dog, is curled into a tight ball in the crate to my left. Emma, the newcomer who spent six years inside the same fence as Izzy, prefers the newly reupholstered antique chair. Plagued with health problems, she likes to be near the wood stove in the winter.

13   When I stir to make tea, answer the door, or stretch my legs, all three dogs move with me. I see them peering out from behind the kitchen table or pantry door, awaiting instructions, as border collies do. If I return to the computer, they resume their previous positions, with stealth and agility. If I analyzed it coldly, I would admit that they're probably alert to see if an outdoor romp is in the offing[4], or some sheepherding, or some beef jerky. But I'd rather think they can't bear to let me out of their sight.*

---

1. **wily:** clever in a sneaky or deceitful way
2. **transfixing:** amazing
3. **insinuate:** insert; subtly become a part of
4. **in the offing:** coming soon; likely

*Source: From *Slate,* February 12, 2007. As seen online at http://www.slate.com/id/215864. Reprinted by permission.

6. In your own words, state the main point of this essay.

_____

_____

7. What mode of development provides structure for paragraphs 1–4?

_____

8. What is the dominant mode of development in paragraphs 6–9?

_____

9. What mode of development organizes the details in paragraphs 12 and 13?

_____

10. Do you yourself (or someone you know) feel "dog love"? Provide examples from your own observations or personal experiences to illustrate the effects of this feeling.

_____

Confusing "Character" with "Temperament"

By Sydney J. Harris

Two of the words that we use about people I think we tend to use carelessly, and often interchangeably. These words are _character_ and _temperament_.

As we grow older, we should learn that these are two quite different things. Character is something you forge for yourself; temperament is something you are born with and can only slightly modify. Some people have easy temperaments and weak characters; others have difficult temperaments and strong characters.

We are all prone to confuse the two in assessing people we associate with. Those with easy temperaments and weak characters are more likable than admirable; those with difficult temperaments and strong characters are more admirable than likable.

Of course, the optimum[1] for a person is to possess both an easy temperament and a strong character, but this is a rare combination, and few of us are that lucky. The people who get things done tend to be prickly, and the people we enjoy being with tend to be accepting, and there seems to be no way to get around this. Obviously, there are many combinations of character and temperament, in varying degrees, so that this is only a rough generalization—but I think it is one worth remembering when we make personal judgments.

1. **optimum:** most favorable situation

The core in the mystery of what we call personality resides in the individual mix between character and temperament. The most successful personalities are those who achieve the best balance between the strict demands of character and the lenient[1] tolerance of temperament. This balance is the supreme test of genuine leadership, separating the savior from the fanatic.

The human Jesus is, to my mind, the ultimate paradigm[2] of such psychic equilibrium[3]. He was absolutely hard on himself and absolutely tender toward others. He maintained the highest criteria of conduct for himself but was not priggish[4] or censorious[5] or self-righteous about those who were weaker and frailer. Most persons of strength cannot accept or tolerate weakness in others. They are blind to the virtues they do not possess themselves and are fiercely judgmental on one scale of values alone. Jesus was unique, even among religious leaders, in combining the utmost of principle with the utmost of compassion for those unable to meet his standards.

We need to understand temperament better than we do and to recognize its symbiotic[6] relationship to character. There are some things people can do to change and some things they cannot do—character can be *formed,* but temperament is *given.* And the strong who cannot bend are just as much to be pitied as the weak who cannot be firm.*

11. In your own words, state the main point of this essay.

_____

_____

12. What three modes of development does the author use to develop his main point?

_____

13. Give an example from your own observation or personal experience to illustrate one of the author's generalizations about character, temperament, or the mix of the two.

_____

1. **lenient:** not harsh or strict
2. **paradigm:** model or ideal example
3. **equilibrium:** state of balance
4. **priggish:** conforming in an arrogant or smug manner

5. **censorious:** highly critical
6. **symbiotic:** mutually beneficial or dependent

*Source: "Confusing 'Character' with 'Temperament'" from *Clearing the Ground* by Sydney J. Harris. Copyright © 1982, 1983, 1985, 1986, by *The Chicago-Sun Times,* Field Newspaper Syndicate, News-America Syndicate and Sydney J. Harris. Reprinted by permission of Houghton Mifflin. All rights reserved.

In Summary: Steps in Combining Modes

1. **Evaluate your main idea and decide on appropriate modes of development.** Choose one or more modes for developing your thesis statement and then prewrite to generate ideas.

2. **Organize your ideas.** Follow the guidelines for the specific modes you have chosen to create an outline. You may want to use one mode for the structure of the entire essay and the other mode to develop the details.

3. **As you write, develop your details according to the specific guidelines for each mode.** Include transitional words to help the reader understand the relationships among the details.

To review the main points in this chapter, write a brief response to each of the following questions.

1. How are modes of development often combined to expand one main idea?

2. What are some common combinations of modes of development?

3. Which mode of development is often used to develop a definition?

4. Which mode of development is often used to develop an argument?

5. How should you decide which modes of development are suitable for an essay?

Topic Ideas for Combining Modes

Here are some topic ideas that you could develop into paragraphs or essays using a combination of modes:

- An important discovery or invention

- An interesting work of art

- What makes your city or town interesting

- A particular food that you enjoy

- A trip that you took
- Friendship
- Learning
- Someone who left the world a better place
- Then versus now
- An excellent product or service
- A needed change
- An important group or organization
- A new fad or trend
- An important relationship

WebWork

Go to the Guide to Grammar and Writing Web site at **http://grammar.ccc.commnet .edu/grammar/composition/definition.htm#TQM** and read the essay "What Is a Yankee?" How many different modes of development are used in this essay?

(Online Study Center)   For more information and exercises, go to the Online Study Center at **http://www.college.hmco.com/pic/ dolphinwriterthree**.

Using Source Material to Improve Your Essays

GOALS FOR CHAPTER 19

▶ Define the term *source material* and describe the benefits of including it in your writing.

▶ Explain how the first three steps of the writing process can help writers determine the need for source material.

▶ List the three main types of sources and explain how to find each type.

▶ Explain how to determine a source's credibility.

▶ Write a summary.

▶ Describe three different note-taking systems.

▶ Define the term *plagiarism* and explain how intentional and unintentional plagiarism occurs.

▶ Explain the difference between direct quotations and paraphrases.

▶ Paraphrase passages.

▶ Write a paragraph that integrates source material using the MLA style of documentation.

▶ Prepare a works-cited list.

▶ Summarize the guidelines for formatting a paper with MLA documentation.

Determining the Need for Source Material

As you write essays of your own, you will often need to find and include information from other sources. This information, which is known as **source material,** can take the form of facts, statistics, examples, expert testimony, or the

387

observations of others. It can come from books, newspapers, magazines, Web sites, or other kinds of sources. Source material will help develop or prove your ideas and opinions on a subject. Because it adds additional support, it will help you make a more convincing case. Read, for example, the following paragraph about work in America and Europe.

> Americans work more and take fewer vacations than Europeans do, and there are some logical explanations for the difference. Of course, neither is better than the other because working too much and working too little have advantages and disadvantages. Fortunately, though, some signs indicate that moderation is occurring on both sides of the Atlantic.

Now compare that paragraph with the following version that includes source material to further develop and prove the main idea.

> Americans work more and take fewer vacations than Europeans do. Americans now work 20 percent more hours than they did in 1970, and the French, for example, are working 24 percent fewer. With holidays and vacations factored in, the average American works 34.5 hours per week, while the average French or German employee works only 28 hours per week. There are some logical explanations for the difference. According to historians, Europeans reacted to the 1970s oil shocks and economic downturn by trying to spread the work evenly among workers. Meanwhile, in the United States, businesses restructured and laid off many employees, leaving those who remained to work harder and longer. Of course, neither is better than the other because working too much and working too little have advantages and disadvantages. In particular, according to a report by the thirty-nation Organization for Economic Cooperation and Development, Americans produce more and get richer than Europeans by putting in longer hours, but they are also more obsessed with possessions and more stressed out than Europeans are. Fortunately, though, some signs indicate that moderation is occurring on both sides of the Atlantic. In Germany and France, companies are increasing work hours, and in the United States, there is new interest in taking more time off.*

Which version of the paragraph is more convincing? The second paragraph, of course, is more convincing because it provides specific facts and statistics to develop the author's points.

Source: Adapted from "Too Much Work—and Play," no author credited, *USA Today,* July 13, 2004, p. 14A.

When you are deciding whether or not you need information from other sources to support your ideas, you can use the first three steps of the writing process as both guides and steppingstones. In Step One, the prewriting stage, for example, as you generate ideas for your composition, you will probably get a sense of not only what you *do* know about a topic but also what you *do not* know and need to find out. At this stage of the process, after you have decided upon a tentative main idea statement, you can probably jot down a list of information that you will have to acquire through research. You can turn this into a "shopping list" to take to the library or to a computer and then check off each item once you have found it.

In Step 2 of the writing process, when you are organizing your ideas, do not forget to account for source material in your outline. Under the appropriate outline heading, list the facts or other kinds of information that you plan to use in that particular paragraph or section. And think again about each point that you want to make so that you can decide if any additional source material might help you make that point clearer for your readers.

Finally, in Step 3, take a careful look at the paragraphs you have written. Are there ideas that could be made clearer or supported more strongly with facts, statistics, examples, observations, or expert opinions? Evaluate your layers of development, especially in shorter paragraphs, and decide whether you should find more information to bolster your point.

To find source material, you will have to conduct research, usually in a library or on the Internet. This chapter will help you develop your skills in researching, managing information, and incorporating source materials into your own writing.

EXERCISE 19.1   Determining the Need for Source Material

Read each of the following paragraphs. Then, on the blanks that follow each one, list two or three specific facts, statistics, examples, or other kinds of source material that would provide support for the author's ideas. For example, for the first paragraph, you might write *Amount of calcium in a glass of milk.*

1. Are you drinking enough milk? Research is showing that milk is great for your health. It provides a powerful cocktail of essential nutrients, such as calcium. It prevents diseases like osteoporosis, which is responsible for many fractures every year. In addition, some evidence indicates that drinking milk

can help adults lose weight. In one study, obese adults who ate more dairy products lost more weight than people who ate fewer dairy products.*

_____

_____

_____

_____

2. Infections contracted in hospitals can be catastrophic. Every year, many patients in the United States die from a hospital infection. These infections also
add a lot to medical costs. Yet the solution can be as simple as seeing that patients wash their hands with medicated soap or a disinfectant alcohol rub.
According to Elaine Larson, a Columbia University School of Nursing expert
on health-care hygiene, "Improved hand washing can significantly reduce
rates of infection."[†]

_____

_____

_____

3. If you are looking for love online at a match-making Web site such as Match
.com, eHarmony.com, or Smokefreesingles.com, you will have to write a personal ad to describe yourself and set yourself apart from the competition. Experts, however, say that most personal ads use the same vague words. If you
need some help with creating a cleverly written, detailed profile, you can now
hire a professional. One brand-new company interviews clients and asks them
questions about themselves. Then someone writes a profile that can be posted
on most dating Web sites.[‡]

_____

_____

_____

_____

Source: Adapted from Claudia Kalb, "Got (Enough) Milk?" *Newsweek,* Jan. 24, 2005, p. 58.
[†]*Source:* Adapted from Christine Gorman, "Wash Those Hands!" *Time,* March 29, 2004, p. 81.
[‡]*Source:* Adapted from Melanie D. G. Kaplan, "Personals Training," *USA Weekend,* Jan. 21–23, 2005,
p. 20.

EXERCISE 19.2 **Evaluating an Essay for Needed Source Material**

Select one of the essays that you wrote for this class. Read through it, and underline or highlight statements that could be strengthened with the addition of source material. In the margin beside each underlined or highlighted statement, write a specific fact, statistic, example, or other material that could be added to lend more development or support.

Types of Sources

The three main types of source material are printed sources found in the library, online or electronic sources, and nonprint sources.

Library Sources

When you are searching for information about a topic, the library is the obvious place to go. The two main types of library sources are books and periodicals.

Books. There are usually two main types of books in libraries. The general collection, which contains works of fiction as well as nonfiction books like biographies, includes all of the books that can be checked out by those with a library card. In most college libraries, these books will be organized according to the Library of Congress subject headings system, which assigns a letter and number (the call number) to each book so that you can locate it on the shelves. The library's card catalog—which will consist of either printed cards organized in drawers or an electronic database searchable by computer—allows you to look up books by subject, author, or title and then write down the call numbers of the books that you want to examine.

The other type of book is the reference work, which provides factual information about a wide variety of topics. Reference works include general and specialized encyclopedias, statistical sources, dictionaries, and many other books that usually cannot be checked out. They, too, are arranged by call number, and they are usually shelved in a particular section of the library.

EXERCISE 19.3   **Using the Library's Card Catalog to Locate Books**

Choose one of the following subjects: music, the environment, or computers. Then go to your college or community library and use the card catalog to locate two general collection books and one reference book on this subject. Record the title, author, and call number of each of these three books.

Periodicals. The periodicals include magazines, journals, and newspapers that are published periodically—such as every day, once a month, or twice a year. They contain articles on a variety of different subjects. To find articles about your topic, you locate that topic in a printed index such as *The Reader's Guide to Periodical Literature*. Alternately, you can use one of many different computerized indexes that allow you to search by subject, author, or title.

Spend some time familiarizing yourself with the locations and the methods of retrieval for the different types of sources in your library. Then, when you need information, you will know where and how to find it.

EXERCISE 19.4   **Obtaining a Periodical Article**

Go to your college or community library and use its printed or computerized index to locate one magazine article and one newspaper article about the subject that you selected for Exercise 19.3. Find articles that are six months to a year old. Next, record each article's author, title, and date. Then write down the library's procedures for obtaining copies of these articles.

Online Sources

The Internet offers a wealth of information on just about any topic you can name. By using a search engine such as Google or Yahoo!, you can type in a search term, and you will see lists of Web sites that may offer information about it. You can also use a search engine to access the specific Web sites of organizations, government agencies, and businesses.

In addition, you can find many publications online. For example, newspapers like the *New York Times* and *USA Today* post their content online every day. Magazines like *Time, Newsweek,* and *U.S. News and World Report,* also post some or all of their articles online. You can access these sites by typing in a

specific URL, or Web site address, such as www.usatoday.com or www.nytimes
.com into your Internet browser program, or you can find them by using a
search engine.

You can also subscribe to electronic libraries or databases that allow you to
search for information from a wide variety of electronic texts. Some of these,
such as Highbeam Research, require you to pay an annual fee for access to the
content. Other databases, especially those available through your local or campus library, may provide access to the same kind of information at no charge.

EXERCISE 19.5   **Searching the Internet for Information**

Use an Internet search engine such as Google (www.google.com) or Yahoo! (www
.yahoo.com) to find three Web sites that offer information about the topic that you
selected for Exercises 19.3 and 19.4. Record the URL of each of these three Web sites.

Nonprint Sources

The library and the Internet are the obvious places to go when you need information. However, do not overlook a third valuable resource: nonprint sources.

People who are experts on the subject you are researching are an especially
useful source of information. You can set up an interview with one of these individuals and then prepare a list of questions to ask the person. With your inter-
viewee's permission, tape-record your interview so that you will be able to
extract direct quotations to use in your paper to support your ideas.

Television shows, radio programs, and films are other good nonprint resources. Often you can obtain a transcript of a television or radio program by
contacting the station or network that aired the program.

Do not overlook works of art, either. You may find it useful to use a painting, sculpture, photograph, or musical composition as a source.

EXERCISE 19.6   **Considering Nonprint Sources**

Write down two or three potential nonprint sources of information about the topic
that you researched for Exercises 19.3, 19.4, and 19.5. Think of specific individuals
you could interview for information. Also, consider what TV programs, radio programs, or films might be useful.

Evaluating the Credibility of Sources

The first step in strengthening your research skills is to learn where information is located and how to access it. However, once you find it, you must then evaluate the information to make sure that it is *credible,* or believable and trustworthy. If you do not use credible sources, then you will weaken your support for your own ideas. Information posted on Internet Web sites, in particular, should be carefully examined for its worthiness and accuracy. The following are some questions to ask yourself when you are considering a source's credibility.

1. **Is the information current and up-to-date?** When was the book or article published? When was the Web site posted or updated? You will want to include only the latest information, so avoid facts and statistics that seem too old.

2. **Who wrote or posted the information?** Is an author identified? What are the author's credentials? Does he or she seem qualified to be considered an authority on the topic? If not, the information may not be credible. Be careful when using Internet Web sites, in particular, since anyone can create a Web site and post information or opinions on it.

3. **Do the ideas and information agree with those in material that you have found in other reputable sources?** Beware of outlandish claims that are contrary to everything else you have read about a topic.

4. **How objective does the information seem?** Does the author provide information about his or her sources, and are those sources reputable? If the author seeks to persuade you, could that person have manipulated the facts or data to support his or her position? Could the information actually be a form of advertising?

EXERCISE 19.7 **Evaluating Source Credibility**

For each of the sources that you found for Exercises 19.3, 19.4, 19.5, and 19.6, answer the questions in the previous list to evaluate its credibility. Decide whether each source is credible based upon your answers to the questions.

Writing a Summary

Summarizing is an important skill that you will use for incorporating source material when developing the ideas in your paragraphs and essays. In particular, you will use summaries of other sources to support your ideas in research projects such as term papers.

When you summarize a reading selection, you briefly restate, in your own words, its most important ideas. A summary usually focuses on the most general points, which include the overall main idea and some of the major supporting details. As a result, a summary is much shorter than the original material. A paragraph can usually be summarized in a sentence or two, and an entire article can often be summarized in a paragraph.

To write a summary, follow the next three steps.

1. Using active reading techniques, read and reread the original material until you understand it.
2. Identify the main idea and major supporting points. In particular, underline all of the topic sentences. You might also want to create an outline or map that diagrams the general and specific relationships among sentences (in a paragraph) or paragraphs (in an article or chapter).
3. Using your own words, write sentences that state the author's main idea along with the most important major details. Your paraphrase should be accurate; it should not add anything that did not appear in the original or omit anything important that is contained in the original. It should also be objective. In other words, do not offer your own reactions or opinions; just restate the author's points without commenting on them. If you use a phrase from the original, enclose it in quotation marks to indicate that it is the author's words, not yours.

For an example of a summary, first read the following passage from an original source and then read the summary.

Original Source:

According to the research firm Mintel International, eleven new home antibacterial products appeared on the market in 2004, more than twice the number [that appeared] in 2003. The makers of antibacterial products are fond of the word *germs*. It is purposefully vague. Do they mean bacteria? Viruses? Both? Neither? The idea is simply to suggest contamination. These products are as much about cooties as they are about viruses or bacteria.

However, the fantasy of a germ-free home is not only absurd, but it is also largely pointless. The few hundred bacteria on a countertop, doorknob, or spoon pose no threat. The bacteria that cause food poisoning, the only significant rational bacterial worry in the average home, need to multiply into the thousands or millions before they can overwhelm your immune system and cause symptoms.

Not surprisingly, a study by Dr. Elaine Larson at the Columbia School of Nursing called into question the usefulness of antibacterial products for the home. In New York, 224 households, each with at least one preschooler, were randomly assigned to two groups. One group used antibacterial cleaning, laundry, and hand-washing products. The other used ordinary products.

For forty-eight weeks, the groups were monitored for seven symptoms of colds, flu, and food poisoning, and found to be essentially the same. According to research conducted by University of Arizona microbiologist Dr. Charles Gerba, an active adult touches an average of 300 surfaces every thirty minutes. You cannot win at this. You will become obsessive-compulsive. Just wash your hands with soap and water a few times a day, and leave it at that.*

Summary:

According to Mary Roach, author of the *New York Times* article "Germs, Germs Everywhere," the antibacterial product industry is booming in spite of the fact that these products do not do much good. Advertisements for these products promise that they will kill "germs," but the bacteria in the average home are not really dangerous. One study found that the use of antibacterial products does not seem to prevent colds, flu, or food poisoning. Another study found that since adults touch so many surfaces, no one could be able to wipe them all clean. Therefore, the author recommends that people simply wash their hands several times a day and forget about trying to sterilize their homes.

Note that this summary provides only the author's main points and leaves out specific supporting details. It is also objective because it provides only the author's ideas and not the reader's reactions to or opinions about them.

EXERCISE 19.8   **Summarizing a Chapter, Article, or Passage**

Select a chapter from a book, a brief article, or a Web site passage that you found when you completed Exercises 19.3, 19.4, and 19.5. Then write a summary of this chapter, article, or passage.

Note-Taking Methods

If you do not use an organized system to keep up with the source material you collect during research, you run the risk of not being able to find what you need

Source: Mary Roach, "Germs, Germs Everywhere," *New York Times,* Nov. 9, 2004, www.nytimes .com.

when you begin composing. Therefore, as you search for facts, quotations, and other material to incorporate into your writing, you will need to develop a way to collect and manage the information that you find. There are several methods for taking notes, each with its advantages and disadvantages.

The Photocopy/Highlight Method

Many students photocopy or print copies of entire articles, and then they underline or highlight the information that they plan to use to develop a paragraph or essay. The advantages of this method include

- *Time.* It takes less time to print pages or run copies than to write down the information that you need.

- *Convenience.* Having the entire source available later during the composition stage can be beneficial, for you may need to refer to it again.

- *Accuracy.* Because you have access to the original sentence or passage, you are less likely to make a mistake when using the information to develop the ideas in your own paper.

However, this is perhaps the most disorganized of the three note-taking methods because each time that you need a particular fact or detail, you will have to shuffle through a pile of articles in search of that piece of information. Thus, searching for that information might slow down your composition process.

The Note Card Method

This method involves writing specific facts, quotations, and other kinds of information on note cards and then labeling each card by the topic or by the corresponding section of the composition's outline. Although it is a much more organized method than photocopying because the cards can be shuffled to follow the order of your outline, it can be more time-consuming. It also requires the careful transfer of information in order to prevent inaccuracies.

A Combination Method

You may want to consider using a system that combines the photocopy/highlight and note card methods so that you will obtain the advantages of both of these methods. To combine them, follow these steps:

1. Photocopy or print the passage, the page, or the entire article that contains the information you will need to include in your own paragraph or essay.

2. Underline or highlight the specific facts or details that you need.

3. With scissors, cut out this specific passage and paste it to a note card.

4. On the note card, write the topic of the information or—even better—write down the section of the outline to which the information corresponds. Also, do not forget to include bibliographic information (author, title, publication, publication date, page numbers, and so on) for the original source.

5. Before you begin writing, follow the topics of your outline to put your note cards into the order you will need for your paper.

EXERCISE 19.9   **Using the Combination Note-Taking Method**

Use the combination note-taking method to take notes on one of the sources that you found for Exercise 19.3, 19.4, 19.5, or 19.6.

Writing a First Draft Using an Outline and Notes

After you have completed your research, you will be ready to write a first draft of your composition. However, do not make the mistake of simply stringing together all of the information that you found in your sources and then deciding that your paper is complete. Instead, think of source material as *layers of development,* which you learned about in Chapter 4 of this text. A layer of development provides more specific information about a general idea in the sentence that came before it. In compositions that do not include source material, these layers often take the form of specific details or examples from the writer's observations and experiences. In compositions that do include source materials, layers of development can also be in the form of data or statistics, expert opinion, specific facts, or direct quotations.

If source material is used as layers of development, then it stands to reason that the writer still needs to complete all of the steps in the writing process in order to complete a composition containing information from other sources. From generating ideas and an outline to writing a rough draft, the steps for writing a paper that includes source material are the same as those for writing any other kind of composition. The difference, however, is that as the writer is composing the paragraphs of the body in an essay with source material, he or she keeps the stack of note cards containing source material close at hand. Then, during composition, information from the cards is integrated with the other material to develop each paragraph.

Another way to understand how source material should be used in a composition is to remember that every sentence in a paper functions in one of three ways. A sentence states a writer's idea or observation, states an idea or information obtained from another source, or offers the writer's reaction to that information from another source. The paper's thesis statement and topic sentences should be of the first type. In addition, some of the development for topic sentences should be of the first type. However, development of topic sentences can also be of the second or third type.

> **EXERCISE 19.10** **Distinguishing Source Material from the Writer's Ideas**

In the following essay, use a highlighting marker to color all of the sentences that provide facts, statistics, or statements from another source. When you are finished, notice how each paragraph is composed of a blend of source material (colored sentences) and the writer's ideas or reactions (uncolored sentences).

Gas Guzzlers' Shock Therapy

My fellow Americans, drop the fantasy that we'll return to cheap gasoline and pump it for as long as our withered hands can steer an SUV. As the prophet saith, the end is nigh[1]. Demand for oil is running high—in fact, we're gobbling up the stuff. But world production grew by only 0.6 percent a year for the past five years. At some point, supplies will shrink, not grow.

Am I crying wolf? If so, I'm in the company of some pretty big guns in the oil biz—geologists, merchant bankers, analysts, and petroleum engineers. They note that the major companies aren't building new U.S. refineries, investing in drilling, or enlarging the tanker fleet—suggesting that they don't expect much new oil to appear. They also point out that Saudi reserves, which the world depends on to fill every energy gap, remain a state secret; outsiders wonder how big they really are.

Princeton geology professor emeritus[2] Kenneth Deffeyes, who [wrote] a book [published] in 2005 called *Beyond Oil,* waggishly[3] names an Armageddon[4] date: "World oil production will reach its ultimate peak on Thanksgiving Day 2005," he says. Then the long, slow decline begins (for a fuller discussion, see oilpeak.com).

Terrorism is catching the blame for pushing up oil prices. In fact, "the war has very little to do with it," says energy consultant Philip Verleger. Prices are rising under the pressure of soaring demand for gasoline. Markets are catching on to the tightening of supplies, even if civilians aren't.

1. **nigh:** near
2. **emeritus:** retired but retaining honorary status
3. **waggishly:** jokingly or with wit
4. **Armageddon:** the end of the world

None of this means lines at the gas pumps or gas holding firm at $2 a gallon. Oil prices are cyclical, says oil analyst Matt Conlan at Weeden & Co. They'll peak, then drop, bottom out, and rise again. But each cycle will start and end at a higher price.

As you might expect, a campful of critics call this "peak oil" theory nuts. They expect new finds or technologies to keep the black stuff flowing. And maybe they're right. But what if they're wrong? A permanent shrinkage in supplies would so severely damage today's oil-based economy that it makes no sense to wait and see. We need energy options, just in case. If shortages don't develop, we'd still be ahead of the game, with more diverse and cheaper sources of energy for future growth.

What might we turn to? The easiest would be efficient diesel cars, Deffeyes says. They use oil, but are capable of getting more than 90 miles to the gallon. Two little problems: diesels smell bad and pollute the air. But they also can run on a mixture that includes soybean oil, which smells more like salad.

Greenies[1] are eying "hybrid" cars. They run on gasoline but store electrical energy when you step on the brakes. At slower speeds, the cars run on electricity alone (and no, you don't have to plug them in). Consumers Union clocked them at 36 to 51 miles per gallon. The 2004 Toyota Prius hatchback costs up to $1,850 more than conventional models, with some dealers charging over the sticker price. If you drive 15,000 miles a year at an average price of $1.55 a gallon, it takes less than six years to make up that extra cost, says Jim Kliesch of the American Council for an Energy-Efficient Economy. Buyers also [got] a $1,500 write-off[2] on their federal taxes [in 2004]. Some states offer write-offs, too.

Wind technology has already shown its worth. If long-armed windmills were driving electric utilities, there'd be more oil for transportation: planes, trucks, and cars.

What's more, we have an enormous untapped resource—namely, conservation. Conservation, in the form of superefficient energy use, is the fastest-growing and cheapest "source" of energy in the United States. When California's energy prices soared in 2002, the state cut its usage by 14 percent (adjusted for economic growth)—avoiding the need for hundreds of new power plants. Some 40 percent of the nation's energy needs since 1975 have been met purely through using energy more intelligently, says Amory Lovins of the Rocky Mountain Institute, which tackles sustainable[3]-energy projects.

[President] Bush[4] has spectacularly backed off efficiency programs, says the ACEEE. He tried to reduce the new energy-conservation standards for air conditioners. His proposed 2004 budget all but wiped out spending to improve efficiency (Congress restored some of the cuts). The 2005 budget [chopped] again. Required new-appliance standards haven't been issued.

1. **Greenies:** people who advocate protection of the natural environment
2. **write-off:** deduction
3. **sustainable:** capable of being continued
4. **Bush:** George W. Bush, forty-third president of the United States

Tying our future to oil is a dangerous game. Dependency on crude[1] is one of the things that enmeshes[2] us in the explosive conflict of the Middle East at a cost of thousands of lives. I wish that Iraq's only export [was] nuts and dates. We'll be engaged in that part of the world until oil doesn't matter anyway.*

What Is Plagiarism?

As you prepare to incorporate source material as layers of development in your composition, you will need to understand what the term *plagiarism* means. Plagiarism is the intentional or unintentional use of someone else's ideas or words without giving proper credit to that individual and/or clearly acknowledging the original source.

Intentional plagiarism, the most blatant form, occurs when a writer knowingly transfers someone else's sentences or paragraphs into his or her own paper without providing any information about where the material came from. Word processing and the Internet allow writers to copy and paste others' words into their documents, so computers have made it easier for people to plagiarize.

However, a writer can also be guilty of unintentional plagiarism. This occurs when he or she does not properly indicate the point at which borrowed material begins or ends or when he or she fails to provide source information. For example, if a writer does not express someone else's thoughts in his or her own words and ends up using too much of the wording of the original source, plagiarism can result. Likewise, a writer who forgets to acknowledge a source will be inadvertently plagiarizing.

What are the consequences of plagiarism? The practice of using someone else's words as your own is illegal and unethical. It is a lot like lying; you may not go to jail for telling a lie or plagiarizing a passage, but you will cast serious doubt upon your own character and credibility if you commit either one of these moral transgressions. Plagiarizing will undermine your own ideas and arguments because if you are found to have "stolen" the ideas of others, readers will view you as an untrustworthy source of information. What is more, most academic institutions are now imposing serious penalties for students who cheat by plagiarizing, so make sure that you always give credit where credit is due.

In the next section, you will learn how to properly acknowledge other writers and sources—and avoid plagiarism—by using a common system of documentation known as MLA style.

1. **crude:** petroleum in its natural, unrefined state

2. **enmeshes:** entangles or involves

Source: Adapted from Jane Bryant Quinn, "Gas Guzzlers' Shock Therapy," *Newsweek*, Aug. 16, 2004. © Newsweek, Inc. All rights reserved. Reprinted by permission.

Integrating Source Material

To properly integrate source material into your essays, you will first need to decide whether to use a direct quotation or a paraphrase. Then you will appropriately document each direct quotation or paraphrase with a citation in the text along with a corresponding entry on a works-cited page.

Direct Quotations and Paraphrases

When you incorporate source material into your own writing, you can use either direct quotations or paraphrases. A *direct quotation* provides the exact wording of the original source, so it is enclosed in quotation marks:

> Jeffery Sheler writes, "Prayer has become familiar terrain in modern America. It is woven into the daily rhythms of life, its ethos[1] embedded in the public and private experiences of millions. Indeed, a recent Roper poll found that nearly half of all Americans said that they pray or meditate every day."*

A *paraphrase* rewords the information in the original source, so it is not enclosed in quotation marks:

> According to Jeffery Sheler, praying is a regular part of modern American life, both public and private. As a matter of fact, half of our country's citizens claim to pray or meditate on a daily basis.

Is it better to use more direct quotations or more paraphrases when you integrate source material? In general, it is actually better to use more paraphrases for two reasons:

1. **Paraphrasing allows you to include only the essential information.** Although it is true that you can remove parts of quotations and indicate the omission with ellipsis dots (. . .), a paraphrase allows you to incorporate only the pertinent facts or ideas into your work, without including any unnecessary words.

2. **Paraphrases are usually easier to read.** Because paraphrases are in the same wording and style as the rest of your paper, they tend to flow better with the rest of the text. Plus, readers do not have to do the extra mental work required to shift from your voice to a different voice, as they do when they read direct quotations.

1. **ethos:** disposition, character, or values of a particular person or group

Source: Jeffery L. Sheler, "The Power of Prayer," *U.S. News and World Report,* Dec. 20, 2004, pp. 52–53.

EXERCISE 19.11   **Paraphrasing Source Material**

The following passages are directly quoted from various sources. On the blanks provided, write a paraphrase of each passage. Be careful to avoid plagiarism by not including too much of the wording of the original source. However, take care not to change the meaning of the original source as you are expressing the idea in your own words.

1. "A recent experiment showed that when Princeton University students were asked to evaluate two highly qualified candidates for an engineering job— one with more education, the other with more work experience—they picked the more educated candidate 75 percent of the time. But when the candidates were designated as male or female, and the educated candidate bore a female name, suddenly she was preferred only 48 percent of the time." (Natalie Angier and Kenneth Chang, "Gray Matter and the Sexes: Still a Scientific Gray Area," *New York Times,* Jan. 24, 2004, www.nytimes.com.)

_____

_____

_____

_____

_____

_____

2. "Researchers have designed a drug that targets and destroys the blood vessels that feed fat cells. The fat cells die and those extra pounds melt away—but only, so far, in rodents. In one experiment, mice that had doubled in size on a high-fat diet were back to normal weight in just a month, no matter what they ate." (David Bjerklie, "Starve a Fat Cell," *Time,* May 24, 2004, p. 87.)

_____

_____

_____

_____

3. "Once psychologist Robert Maurer decided to lose weight, he did not eschew[1] all carbs or max out his credit card by purchasing the exhortations[2] of a pricey personal trainer. Instead, he decided to throw out the first French fry on his

1. eschew: avoid or shun   **2. exhortations:** strong advice or urging

plate. Eventually, it became two, then three French fries, or a tiny bit of whatever other food he was eating. In this way, Maurer lost 45 pounds in 18 months and became a living example of the premise of his book, *One Small Step Can Change Your Life: The Kaizen Way.*" (Deirdre Donahue, "How to Reach the Summit of Life Success," *USA Today,* Jan. 24, 2005, p. 6D.)

_____

_____

_____

_____

_____

_____

_____

4. "Recent studies show that a lot of self-esteem is not always such a good thing. In fact, it can actually be harmful. Criminals and juvenile delinquents, for instance, often regard themselves very highly. According to a study done by Nicholas Emler at the London School of Economics, a young person with overabundant self-esteem is more likely than someone with average or low self-esteem to be a racist and to engage in physically risky activities, such as reckless and/or drunk driving." (Adapted from Patricia Marx, "Can You Have Too Much Self-Esteem?" O magazine, May 2004, p. 249.)

_____

_____

_____

_____

_____

_____

5. "For all of my adult life, informed people have lived in continual anxiety about an exploding world population and the inevitable resulting mass starvation and environmental degradation. In the 1960s, experts like Paul Ehrlich predicted that famines in the 1970s would cause hundreds of millions of people to starve to death and argued for compulsory[1] population control if

1. **compulsory:** required

voluntary methods failed. A global think tank[1] called the Club of Rome predicted a world population of 14 billion in the year 2030, with no end in sight. Instead, fertility rates fell steadily. By the end of the century, they were about half what they were in 1950, with the result that many now expect world population to peak at 9 billion or so. (It is estimated to be about 6 billion today.) And mass starvation never occurred either. Instead, per capita[2] food production increased through the end of the century. Because of increased agricultural efficiency and better seeds, grain production increased as much as 600 percent per acre." (Adapted from Michael Crichton, "Let's Stop Scaring Ourselves," *Parade,* Dec. 5, 2004, pp. 6–7.)

_____

_____

_____

_____

_____

_____

_____

_____

Documenting Sources

Earlier in this section, you learned how to incorporate direct quotations and paraphrases from other sources. Now you are ready to learn how to properly acknowledge—or document—the source material that you include in your writing in support of your ideas. There are several different systems of documentation, including MLA (Modern Language Association) style, APA (American Psychological Association) style, and the Chicago Manual of Style system. In this text, we will focus on MLA style, the system used most often for papers in the humanities.

MLA style has two main components: (1) citations in the text, enclosed in parentheses, that provide the author's name and the page number (for print sources) of the original source, along with (2) a works-cited list that provides

1. **think tank:** a group that engages in research and problem solving

2. **per capita:** per unit of population

complete bibliographic information for all of the sources cited in the paper. The following examples provide typical citations for direct quotations and paraphrases.

Direct Quotation:

"Carbophobia, the most recent in the centurylong series of food fads to wash over the American table, seems to have finally crested, though not before sweeping away entire bakeries and pasta companies in its path, panicking potato breeders into redesigning the spud, crumbling whole doughnut empires, and, at least to my way of thinking, ruining an untold number of meals" (Pollan 74). (from Michael Pollan, "Our National Eating Disorder," *New York Times,* Oct. 17, 2004, p. 74.)

Partial Quotation:

While other cultures have been eating the same way for generations, America, in contrast, is prone to "applecart-toppling nutritional swings," overnight dietary changes that can be brought about by a scientific study or even just a "lone crackpot with a medical degree" (Pollan 74). (from Michael Pollan, "Our National Eating Disorder," *New York Times,* Oct. 17, 2004, p. 74.)

Paraphrase:

According to the Sierra Club Web site, several victories for the environment occurred in 2004. In particular, President George Bush in November 2004 signed a bill that created more than 750,000 acres of wilderness land in eastern Nevada (Valtin). (from Tom Valtin, "Reasons to Be Cheerful," *The Planet* newsletter, Jan./Feb. 2005, http://www.sierraclub.org/planet/200501/reasons.asp.)

To distinguish source material from your own ideas, make sure to clearly identify source material at both its beginning and its end. In the case of a direct quotation, a quotation mark will indicate the beginning of the material, and a closing quotation mark followed by a parenthetical citation will indicate the end. Paraphrases are often introduced with the author's name to indicate where the source material begins. In that case, the author's name is not repeated in the citation.

According to Michael Pollan, while other cultures have been eating the same way for generations, America, in contrast, is prone to "applecart-toppling nutritional swings," overnight dietary changes that can be brought about by a scientific study or even just a "lone crackpot with a medical degree" (74).

Other common ways to introduce source material include using statements such as *John Smith claims that . . . , Barbara Stock said . . . ,* or *Jack Nelson writes. . . .*

For more information about integrating source material into your writing, see *A Guide for Writing Research Papers Based on MLA Documentation* at http://www.ccc.commnet.edu/mla/index.shtml.

EXERCISE 19.12 **Writing a Paragraph That Includes Documented Source Material**

Write a paragraph about some limited aspect of the topic that you researched as you completed Exercises 19.3, 19.4, 19.5, and 19.6. Include layers of development in the form of source material (direct quotations or paraphrases) from at least two of the sources that you found. Make sure that you properly document the source material.

EXERCISE 19.13 **Evaluating Passages for Plagiarism**

Read the material from the original source, and then evaluate the way in which it has been integrated into the following student's essay. Is the source material appropriately quoted or paraphrased? Is it properly documented? On the blanks provided, write *Correct* if the source material has been integrated correctly. Write *Plagiarism* if it has not been integrated correctly, and explain *why* it is an example of plagiarism.

1. **Original Source:** "In the United States, children recognize logos[1] by 18 months, according to Boston College economist Juliet Schor, and by [age] two, many ask for products by brand name. Some parents report that Baby's first word was not 'mama' or 'dada' but 'Coke'—which makes sense considering that 26 percent of kids two and under have a TV in their room and the average American child sees some 40,000 commercials a year. That in turn helps explain why the United States, with 4.5 percent of the world's population, buys 45 percent of the global toy production. American kids get an average of 70 new toys a year." (Katy Kelly and Linda Kulman, "Kid Power," *U.S. News and World Report,* Sept. 13, 2004, p. 46.)

Integrated Source Material: Modern American parents are spoiling their children. Although our country makes up only 4.5 percent of Earth's population, we purchase 45 percent of the toys that are manufactured all over the world. That is because the average American child is getting seventy new toys every year. A fourth of toddlers even have televisions in their rooms! Not surprisingly, they are watching thousands of commercials and clamoring for the specific brands that they see advertised.

---

1. **logos:** company names or symbols designed for easy recognition

2. **Original Passage:** "Of the fifteen previous presidents who have been elected and then re-elected, not one had a more successful second term than his first, according to presidential historian Robert Dallek. For seven, the second term was catastrophic: felled by assassination or illness, or mired[1] in corruption and controversy. Even George Washington in his second term was bitterly criticized by the Jeffersonians, struggled to avoid war with Great Britain, and sent in the militia to crush tax protesters in western Pennsylvania. His secretary of state, a lifelong friend, was forced to resign under a cloud." (Susan Page, "History Not Kind to Presidents in Second Term," *USA Today*, Jan. 21, 2005, p. 8A.)

Integrated Source Material: Most of America's presidents have tried to win a second term in office, and George W. Bush was no exception. In 2004, he became only the sixteenth president in our country's history to win re-election. In his second inaugural address, he spoke of his optimism and ambitions for his remaining years in office. However, the fifteen presidents who were re-elected for second terms before him all had better first terms than second terms, including George Washington. Seven of them were either killed or forced to deal with catastrophes like illness or scandals (Page 8A).

_____

_____

3. **Original Passage:** "Ronald Reagan used to insist that he was religious even though, as president, he hardly ever entered a church. It turns out he was in good company. Those Americans who tell pollsters they worship faithfully? Many of them are lying. John G. Stackhouse, Jr., a professor of theology and culture, wrote recently in *American Outlook* magazine, 'Beginning [in] the 1990s, a series of sociological studies has shown that many more Americans tell pollsters that they attend church regularly than can be found in church when teams actually count.' In fact, he says, actual churchgoing may be at little more than half the professed[2] rate." (Jonathan Rauch, "Let It Be," *The Atlantic Monthly*, May 2003, p. 34.)

Integrated Source Material: Americans claim to be religious; however, Jonathan Rauch says that they are not always truthful when they report how often they attend church services. Beginning in the 1990s, a series of sociological studies has shown that many more Americans say that they attend church regularly than can be found when teams actually go to the churches to count heads. In fact, churchgoing actually may be at about 50 percent of the professed rate (34).

_____

---

1. **mired:** stuck   2. **professed:** declared or claimed

4. Original Source: "Health-care premiums are rising at unsustainable[1] rates. Some economists estimate that unnecessary tests and procedures, ordered by doctors to build a record just in case there is a lawsuit, cost more than $100 billion a year—enough to provide health insurance for the 40 million Americans who have no coverage. In our culture of legal fear, the candor[2] vital to improving care is a casualty[3]. Because doctors do not feel safe talking about mistakes, they are unable to learn from them—or even offer an honest apology. The villain, I believe, is our legal system, which has become a free-for-all. Most victims of error get nothing, while others win lottery-like jury awards even when the doctor did nothing wrong." (Philip K. Howard, "Yes, It's a Mess—But Here's How to Fix It," *Time,* June 1, 2003, p. 43.)

Integrated Source Material: To reform America's health-care system, we will have to reform our country's legal system. According to Philip K. Howard, two of health care's biggest problems—$100 billion spent on unnecessary tests every year and a climate of fear that prevents doctors from learning from their mistakes—are the fault of our country's legal system. Howard calls the current legal system a "free-for-all" that fails to compensate many of the real victims while awarding huge sums to people who do not deserve them (43).

Preparing the Works-Cited List

A works-cited list is the second element (in addition to citations within the text) of MLA style. This list, which appears at the end of a paper, includes an entry for each source that was cited in the text. Each entry includes specific details about the source placed in a particular order. These entries are arranged in alphabetical order. The following are examples of typical entries.

Book

With one author: Joseph J. Ellis. <u>American Sphinx</u>. New York: Knopf, 1997.

With two or more authors: Rose, Sharon, and Neil Schlager. <u>How Things Are Made: From Automobiles to Zippers</u>. New York: Black Dog and Leventhal, 1995.

1. **unsustainable:** not capable of being continued
2. **candor:** honesty
3. **casualty:** one harmed by some circumstance

Encyclopedia

"Consumerism." <u>Merriam-Webster's Collegiate Encyclopedia</u>. 2000.

Magazine Article

Jeffery L. Sheler. "The Power of Prayer." <u>U.S. News and World Report</u>
    20 Dec. 2004: 52.

Journal Article

Grant, B. F., and D. A. Dawson. "Alcohol and Drug Use, Abuse, and De-
    pendence Among Welfare Recipients." <u>American Journal of Public
    Health</u> 86 (1996): 1450–1454.

Newspaper Article

Hamill, Pete. "The Death of Shame." <u>New York Daily News</u> 11 May
    2003: 41.

Web Site

<u>Firearms and Crime Statistics</u>. 2004. U.S. Department of Justice, Bureau of
    Justice Statistics. <http://www.ojp.usdoj.gov/bjs/guns.htm>.

Interview

Rodriguez, Jose. Telephone Interview. 12 Nov. 2004.

For complete information about formatting works-cited entries for different
kinds of sources, see *A Guide for Writing Research Papers Based on MLA Documentation* at http://www.ccc.commnet.edu/mla/index.shtml. Click on "Citing
Sources" for samples.

 **EXERCISE 19.14**   **Preparing a Works-Cited List**

Prepare a works-cited list for the sources that you found when you completed Exercises 19.3, 19.4, 19.5, and 19.6.

Formatting a Paper with MLA Documentation

A paper that includes MLA documentation should be typed or printed from a
computer on white $8\frac{1}{2} \times 11$-inch paper. Double-space the text, and set all four
margins—upper, lower, left, and right—at one inch. In the upper right-hand
corner of each page, half an inch from the top, type your last name and the page
number.

In the top left corner of the first page, include your name, your instructor's
name, the course, and the date. Double-space this information. On the line below

this header, center your title. Begin the first sentence of your paper on the line below the title.

Begin your works-cited list on a new page, but number it consecutively with the rest of the pages of the paper. Type the title *Works Cited* in the center at the top of the page. Double-space all entries on this page, and do not insert any extra space between them.

Sample Documented Essay

The following is a sample essay documented in MLA style.

Smith 1

Peter Smith

Dr. Charles Abernathy

English 101

1 May 2008

The Case Against Zoos

Many different kinds of zoos exist, from the elaborate, natural habitat–type zoos to the small roadside menageries with animals in cages. Zoos continue to defend their existence with two arguments. First of all, they claim to preserve species, especially animals that are endangered. Secondly, they claim to educate the public about wildlife. In fact, they fall short on both claims. Consequently, wild animals are much better off in the wild, not in zoos.

Zoos claim that their major goal is to protect species against extinction. However, most of the animals housed in zoos are not endangered, and if zoos were successful in achieving this aim, the numbers in species facing extinction would be improving. But they are not. According to one academic and activist, seven out of ten biologists recently polled by the American Museum of Natural History believe that species are becoming extinct faster today than they ever have throughout our planet's history (Best). In truth, most zoos do not focus their research on how to protect wild animal populations. Instead, they concentrate on finding ways to breed animals in captivity so that they can continue to exist.

Even worse, zoos are not only failing to protect wild populations, but they are also damaging the animals already in their care. Although many zoos do make an attempt to provide for animals' needs, most zoo enclosures are too small to accommodate the creatures' natural hunting, feeding, and mating behaviors. Instead, animals are closely confined and have few opportunities for physical exercise or mental stimulation. As a result, many of them begin to exhibit abnormal, self-destructive behaviors that have come to be known as "zoochosis." These are the psychological problems, says Dr. Steve Best, that include "pacing, head-bobbing, rocking, walking in circles, compulsive licking, bar-biting, and even self-mutilation." These are not just signs of boredom; they are symptoms of severe psychological distress. These animals are depressed and neurotic.

According to Oxford University researchers Dr. Georgia Mason and Dr. Ros Clubb, some polar bears in zoos spend 25 percent of their time pacing up and down, and 65 percent of infant polar bears in captivity die. In fact, these scientists say that polar bears, lions, tigers, cheetahs, and other carnivores fare so poorly in captivity that zoos should stop keeping these animals if they cannot significantly increase the size of their habitats (Derr A26).

Even worse, this suffering is for nothing, for zoos do not really educate people, as they claim. Most zoo visitors spend only a few minutes at each exhibit, and they want to be entertained rather than educated. One curator at the National Zoo in Washington, DC, spent five summers tracking 700 people as they wandered through the zoo and the Reptile House. He found that the average visitor spent just a total of fourteen minutes at the Reptile House, which includes eighty-five different exhibits. This curator noticed that "it did not matter what was on display. . . . People [were] treating the exhibits like wallpaper." Furthermore, he concluded that zoos are kidding themselves if they really believe that showing animals behind glass walls teaches anything (Booth D1). If people really want to learn about animals, they are more likely to go to the Internet or turn their televisions to stations like The Discovery Channel or Animal Planet. These days, many people are actually able to travel to places where they can go hiking and see creatures in their natural habitats. Keeping animals in captivity for educational purposes is no longer necessary.

Clearly, zoos are part of the problem rather than the solution to that problem. If we really want to protect animals and conserve species, we should stop patronizing zoos and spend our money instead to support groups like the International Primate Protection League, the Born Free Foundation, the African Wildlife Foundation, and other organizations working to preserve habitats.

Smith 3

Works Cited

Best, Steven. <u>Zoos and the End of Nature</u>. 2005. 21 Apr. 2007.

    <http://www.drstevebest.org/papers/vegenvani/zoos/php>.

Booth, William. "Naked Ape Zoo Attraction." <u>Washington Post</u> 14 Mar.

    1991: D1.

Derr, Mark. "Big Beasts, Tight Space and a Call for Change." <u>New York</u>

    <u>Times</u> 2 Oct. 2003: A26.

CHAPTER 19 REVIEW

To review the main points in this chapter, write a brief response to each of the following questions.

1. What is source material, and what forms can it take?
2. What is the function of source material?
3. What steps of the writing process can help writers determine the need for source material?
4. What are three main types of source material?
5. What are the two types of books in libraries?
6. How are books in libraries arranged?
7. What are periodicals?
8. What are some of the different kinds of online sources?
9. Give some examples of nonprint sources.
10. What is source credibility, and why is it important?
11. What does it mean to summarize a reading selection?
12. Describe three different kinds of note-taking methods.

CHAPTER 19 REVIEW

13. What are the functions of sentences in a paper?

14. What is plagiarism?

15. What is the difference between a direct quotation and a paraphrase?

16. Why is it better to use more paraphrases than direct quotations?

17. What is a system of documentation, and which one is most often used for papers in the humanities?

18. What are the two main components of MLA style?

19. What does an MLA citation usually include?

20. What is a works-cited list, and where in a paper does it appear?

21. What are some of the formatting guidelines for a paper that uses MLA documentation?

Topic Ideas for Essays That Include Source Material

- A current event
- A solution for a particular social problem
- The causes or effects of a particular historical event (such as a battle, a social movement, or a natural disaster)
- An analysis of a work of literature such as a novel or a poem
- A biography
- A worthy cause
- An ethical issue such as stem-cell research or the death penalty
- A good or bad government or institutional policy

WebWork

For more information about using MLA style to document source material, visit the Purdue University Online Writing Lab at **http://owl.english.purdue.edu/owl/resource/557/01/**.

Review the information in Houghton Mifflin's "Internet Research Guide" at **http://college.hmco.com/english/resources/research_guide/1e/students/tutorials/part6.html** and complete the practice activity to generate Internet citations.

Online Study Center   For more information and exercises, go to the Online Study Center at **http://www.college.hmco.com/pic/dolphinwriterthree**.

Reading Selections

El Viejo

By Lillian Diaz-Imbelli

1 For as far back as I can remember, my grandfather always seemed larger than life. My earliest memory of him was of the summer I visited Puerto Rico before he and Abuela returned to New York to live closer to all of us. For the last few years, they were living in San Turce where they ran a small bodega just minutes from their home. I was only four at the time and remember feeling so small amidst all the canned and boxed goods. Despite this, I looked forward to bringing Abuelo his café con leche at or around noon. Abuela would prepare it with a calculated efficiency that I marveled at. I looked on in awe, fully convinced that I could never master such a complicated task and my heart ached to be able to do something so grand—especially for him.

2 Abuela would measure each spoonful of coffee and stir it into boiling water in an awaiting pot. As she blended the two elements together, the air would be transformed and filled with a fragrance so intense it seemed to possess the powers of a magical potion. I could readily imagine its effectiveness in any tale: one sip and surely you would be cast under its spell, willing to do anything for just one more taste. What followed confirmed my thoughts. This brew was first poured into a cloth funnel to separate the coffee grounds. Abuela would then blend the dark liquid into the simmering milk, which was always heated to perfection. Goldilocks would have emphatically approved. For it was: "Not too hot, not too cold, but just right!" The final step was adding the secret ingredient. Abuela would use a large soup spoon to add sugar to the completed café con leche. Scoop after scoop—unos, dos, nueve, cinco—(1, 2, 9, 5)—confounding my youthful counting abilities, was added until she deemed it perfect and then she would add one more spoonful for good measure. Abuelo's café had to be as sweet as he.

3 As much as I loved this ritual, the best part for me was the privilege of bringing it to Abuelo down the street. It was always a mystery to me how Abuelo and Abuela coordinated this exchange, for there was no phone, but as Abuela ushered me out and watched as I made my little pilgrimage to my Abuelo, he was always waiting at the door of the bodega. He would greet me with open arms and announce to all who were there that "La Nena" had arrived. He always seemed so proud and I always felt so important. Because of this, I was always rewarded with the special treat of walking behind the counter, sliding the glass doors aside, and reaching in to retrieve a Chicklet or Bazooka. Every picture that summer shows me with a wad of gum safely tucked into the side of my

Source: Lillian Diaz-Imbelli, "El Viejo," from *Horizons*, Houghton Mifflin Company 2004, pp. 55–61. Reprinted by permission. Lillian Diaz-Imbelli is a writer living in NYC.

mouth, each one a touching reminder of how much Abuelo cared.

4   For the rest of the afternoon, I would wander around the bodega among the domino-playing men dressed in their guayaberas and straw hats, smoking their cigars, filling the air with an intoxicating aroma that seemed uniquely theirs. They were passionate in their playing and my Abuelo was the star. After all, the bodega was his. More of a meeting place than a store, it commanded their respect. It was a haven, which offered them a refuge from a world filled with responsibility. As a reflection of their gratitude and reverence, they called him "El Viejo," the old one; the wise one. To me he was that and more, he was Abuelo.

5   When the day came to its inevitable end, we would walk home together hand in hand. His hands seemed huge, but gentle just the same as they enveloped mine so competently and lovingly. Each visible contrast juxtaposed the less evident ways that they complemented each other: his hands were large and confident, mine were small and innocent; his were the hands of one who worked hard, mine were delicately new; his were dark and sun kissed, mine were unblemished and pale. It was not until many years later that I would become aware of the differences in our complexions though. Color is not a natural concern of a child until an insensitive adult brings it to their attention. My innocence was lost at Abuelo's expense.

6   It happened one summer in the mid-sixties, when the Bronx was just beginning to burn. Building after building succumbed to flames set by some who thought it was their only way to escape lives that held little hope for change. Displaced they could readily join the ranks of those migrating north on the number 6 train. When Abuelo and Abuela arrived in New York from Puerto Rico, they had settled in the South Bronx, where they had lived years before—a place that had always seemed familiar and safe. We lived in the Bronx too, but it was where the number 6 Lexington Avenue line emerged from the tunnel. Always a metaphor for the aspirations all families wished to attain, one ascended from the depths of darkness and left the South Bronx behind, delivered into the light to beginnings filled with hope. As the fires raged, Mami was concerned that the situation on Brook Avenue (an appellation that belied its current reality: a smoldering urban wasteland) warranted exploring the possibilities of moving my grandparents closer to us.

7   Although my mother's characteristic tendency was to remain anonymous whenever and wherever possible, it was superseded by her genuine concern for her parents' well-being. As a result, she and I entered a local realty office to inquire about the possibilities of available apartments. I was only about seven or eight at the time, but I could sense my mother's apprehension as we entered. Nevertheless, I was truly excited about the possibility that Abuelo and Abuela could live within walking distance of us and not a train ride away. The real estate agent greeted us with her saccharine smile and quickly ushered us to a desk in the back, proceeding to ask Mami numerous questions. I remember her smelling of mothballs. To a child, all her queries seemed too personal to be asked and I was certainly surprised to find my normally guarded and very private mother answering so willingly. Not surprising, I found myself adopting my mother's customary role and tried to disappear into the background, slowly inching myself toward the door. Just as I

reached it, I heard the woman ask my mother, "So, honey, what color *are* your parents?"

8   My heart was racing and no longer seemed a part of me. Its pounding seemed to fill the air and I was certain that the moth-ball lady could hear it. Tears swelled in my eyes as I blurted out what was assuredly my most passionate, heartfelt protestation to an adult. Bolting through the door, I cried, "They're purple!" My family, like all Latino families, was a rainbow of colors referring to one another affectionately as Blanca, Negrita, Rubia, Morena-cousins, aunts, friends. We were all different, but it never seemed to matter, until the summer the Bronx began to burn.

9   Abuelo and Abuela never did move up-town. As sirens blared perpetually outside the windows of their development, their home was a place where I frequently sought solace and comfort. When the life of a teenager was too much to bear, I was always La Nena there and their home was my sanctuary. Abuela would effortlessly create delectable meals that seemed to appear as if by magic. The only hint to the evolution of these meals was the enticing smells and distinct sounds that would fill the air in the small apartment. First, we would be treated to the aromas of clove upon clove of garlic sizzling in oil, then to the unique fragrance of the soffrito, which was then added to the pan. A scent that to this day can soothe my most frazzled nerves. Slowly and lovingly she would work wonders, as Abuelo and I watched a baseball game, boxing, or wrestling match on TV.

10   Abuelo would fully involve himself in whatever he was watching: television to him was never a spectator sport. For every punch or body slam in the ring that we would witness, Abuelo had executed two with perfect results. If the athlete in question didn't suc-ceed as well as he had, Abuelo would let him know in no uncertain terms—assailing him with a barrage of insults that left no doubt in my mind who the victor was. When there were no sports on TV, we would then watch American adventure movies. John Wayne was his favorite. Abuelo never fully grasped the English language, but that never deterred him from enjoying his favorite western. He would habitually ask, "¿Quien son los malos? Who are the bad guys?" Once that was established, he followed the storyline effortlessly. No couch potato. He was as fully engaged in each of the Duke's adventures as in a Mantle homerun or a Floyd Patterson knockout. All that mattered to him was that the good guys emerged victorious and that he was along for the ride.

11   This left us both with hearty appetites that were always slaked in Abuela's kitchen. Dinner was almost ritualistic. Abuelo's plate would be heaped to its full capacity with arroz, habichuelas, chulettas, and plantanos. He would consume his meal with such gusto that, although I was always satisfied at table, I sometimes wondered if his meal was some-what different, as special as he. Each swallow lauded Abuela's mastery in the kitchen, but could never convince her that the meal was perfect; she was always certain the habichue-las were too salty, the meat was too dry and she most assuredly hadn't made enough. When Abuelo was finished eating, he would drink ice cold water from a jelly jar kept in the fridge. The meal's end would be ushered in by the steaming cup of café con leche that Abuela always made him. For as long as I can remember, Abuelo would save the last sip of his coffee, the one filled with sugar, just for me. He would carefully pour it into the saucer and hand it to me. A gesture of

love like the sacramental wine at mass. The spontaneity of the gesture and the warmth of his smile were soon taken for granted. I grew to expect this gift and he never disappointed me.

12   From the time that I was a little girl, Abuelo was always my hero. Over the years, I could always visualize Abuelo's heroism in Puerto Rico as he valiantly battled a flying cucaracha, or captured an errant iguana as I bathed in a tub on the patio. In New York, he could always be counted on to slay El Cuco, whether it was hidden under the bed, in the closet, or most ominously of all, inside the imagination of this scared little girl. He prevailed and offered comfort. He was also the one to run to when teeth needed to be painlessly extracted so that they could be left for the tooth fairy, or when a chain needed meticulous patience to be unraveled. Whatever the task, he was willing and able. While he labored over each task, he was lost to it. When it was finished, however, he emerged from his reverie triumphant. Once again, he was the victorious hero rescuing a family member from the perils of quotidian catastrophes. Because of this, it was particularly heartbreaking to find his advancing age making him vulnerable to merciless thugs—the bad guys. On the streets, they were not as recognizable as on TV, waiting for the opportunity to prey on those less capable of defending themselves.

13   The first time that this happened, Abuelo was helping out at a nephew's bodega. When a young man, a child in Abuelo's eyes, came in and pointed a gun at Abuelo, he indignantly smacked it away from his face, before handing over the money. He was angry, but still in control. For a moment, he was still John Wayne. A few years later, he was pushed

into a hidden vestibule, and another child demanded money from him. Frightened by the anger, rage, and fear in this child's eyes, he felt defeated for the first time in his life. He sat sullenly for days afterward, overcome by the burden of his advancing years; no longer the one in control. In the real world, the good guys didn't always win!

14   Children grow up and away, never finding the time for those who always seemed to have more hours than there are in a day just for them. Obligatory calls and infrequent visits are made sporadically, keeping, however tenuous, one's connection alive. Before one can fathom how, more years have passed than intended and are gone forever. By the time I was finished with college, marrying, and began raising a family, Abuelo was being ravaged by dementia, cancer, and tuberculosis: a disease that is still very much a reality in the inner city.

15   On one of my last visits to Abuelo in his home, I remember with heartwrenching awareness his struggle to finish his meal, a meal which was now being consumed merely for sustenance. No longer bringing him the customary joy it once did. Nevertheless, as he labored to bring his café con leche to his lips, he paused, aware that there was still just a drop left. His hand trembled as he extended the cup toward me—a sacramental offering. Unhesitatingly, I accepted and drank from it, unaware that it would be for the last time.

16   From that moment on, the decline was swift and relentless. Soon, after one too many falls, Abuelo had to be placed in a nursing home. As he was being examined for admittance to the home, Abuelo struggled valiantly to overcome his pain and stand tall, wanting so much, once again, to be in control. When the doctor attending him called out his vital

statistics to the awaiting nurse, I was dumbfounded. At 5′3″, my grandfather had always seemed larger than life. He was a giant among ordinary men. To me he still is, for genuine worth is not measured in physical stature, but in the greatness of deeds. I will always look up to him and remember him lovingly and faithfully: always El Viejo, siempre mi Abuelo. ■

Mode and Skill Check

1. What is the thesis statement of this selection?

_____

2. What is the predominant mode(s) that the author uses to organize the details in this selection?

_____

3. What are some of the descriptive details that make the story so vivid?

_____

Questions for Writing and Discussion

1. What do you consider the major theme of this essay? Why do you think so?

2. Diaz-Imbelli describes food and mealtime in detail in this essay. What role does food play in your culture? Is it similar to the role that the author describes in hers or different? Discuss.

3. Do you have or have you ever had someone in your life who played a similar role to that of the grandfather in this essay? Describe this person, using vivid and descriptive language.

4. What examples does Diaz-Imbelli use to illustrate why her grandfather was her hero? Do you think his actions were truly heroic or just heroic in her eyes?

5. Does Diaz-Imbelli effectively paint a portrait of her childhood in the Bronx? How?

The Guardian

By Reggie Jones as told to Liz Welch

1   Many of my childhood friends from Newark got into drugs and are in prison now. I was seconds away from that life. Instead, I joined the Marines and taught myself to box. I went on to win the Golden Gloves, the national championships two years in a row, and a bronze medal in the Pan American Games. At the 1972 Olympics, I pummeled the Soviet Valery Tregubov, but the judges gave him the decision. Millions of people, including Howard Cosell, thought I should have won. I got letters from all over the world and an invitation to the White House from President Nixon.

2   In 1978, I moved back to Newark; I was done with boxing, sick of its politics. I really wanted to help people. So I went to college and got a job working in social services. For the first time, I saw how desperately some people lived: rodent- and bug-infested homes, filthy kids with uncombed hair. But it wasn't until I started working for New Jersey's Division of Youth and Family Services that hell really started.

3   I've been a caseworker for D.Y.F.S. for 18 years now. When I heard about Faheem Williams's death, my heart sank. Every time a kid dies, people at D.Y.F.S. start jumping. They're so worried about covering themselves that they forget that a child is dead. The caseworker didn't kill the child, but we get blamed. That makes me angry. The Child Welfare League of America says the limit should be 17 families. Once, I had 114 kids. Still, when something happens to a kid, it comes down on you.

4   You're supposed to see each kid once a month, but if you're worried, you'll go twice a week to protect the kid and yourself. If a kid winds up with a broken femur, your supervisor wants to know why you didn't prevent it. It's an impossible task. Cases keep coming like an assembly line that's moving too fast, except they are not automobile parts or cans of peas. They are children.

5   When someone calls to report abuse, the case gets time-coded—immediate, 24 hours or 72 hours—and then someone from intake, an elite unit of D.Y.F.S., goes to investigate. I used to go alone, which can be dangerous. People have threatened to kill me; my tires have been slashed. So I drive by the house first to decide if I'll park in front or a few blocks away.

6   I sit down and I talk to my people. If a mother is on drugs, then I want to place her in the right program. If she doesn't want to cooperate, then I have to move the kid, which is a lot of paperwork. But if you leave the kid, then there will be worse problems— the mother won't send the kid to school or get the kid his immunizations. There's a whole lot you have to think about. I get to the point with some of my clients where I will open the refrigerator to see if there is food, and when they don't have it, I go buy some. Then I go back and holler and scream because it makes me so mad. I tell them: "You are grown. Why do I have to talk to you like this?"

7   I've had a lot of heartbreaking cases, but Jeremy stood out. This five-year-old boy was bowlegged with protruding kneecaps,

Source: Reggie Jones as told to Liz Welch, "The Guardian," *New York Times Magazine*, February 2, 2003. © 2003, Liz Welch. Reprinted by permission.

a bloated abdomen, and swollen joints from rickets. He was in the hospital, but his mother rarely came to see him. She had two other children and was being investigated by D.Y.F.S. I started visiting every day. He never said much, but his eyes would light up. Sometimes I didn't want to go. I was too tired, but I knew Jeremy was waiting, so I'd force myself. One day, I brought a teddy bear, and he hugged it to his chest as if it were the first gift he ever received. The nurses teased me, calling me his dad, but I didn't mind. On Thanksgiving, I came early, but Jeremy had a high fever and was with his doctors. When I returned that evening, his bed was empty. "We lost him," a nurse said. I cried as if I had lost one of my own.

8   I was married to my first wife for 14 years; we have three children, 21 to 28 years old. She used to complain that I was never home, and she was right. At one point, she even asked me if I was having an affair. She just couldn't understand that I was committed to this job and that I couldn't turn my back on these kids.

9   I remarried last July. My new wife is still getting used to my schedule. If I see a fire reported on the evening news, I jump into my car to make sure my clients are unharmed. I'm a social worker, but since my weekdays are packed with paperwork, I spend my weekends doing social work. I've bought my clients food, TVs, clothing. Once, I even paid a $500 gas-and-electric bill. I'm not supposed to do any of this, so I don't report it. If I did, my supervisor would ask, "Why isn't the parent doing that?" Then you have this whole new mountain of paperwork to do. I bet 99 percent of D.Y.F.S. workers do the same—not to hide abuse or neglect but because they care.

10   My friends and family have told me to leave so many times. They say, "You cannot save the world." But for some reason, I think I can. When it gets to be too much, I go fishing. I don't even care if I catch a fish. It just feels good to be alone and surrounded by water. Even then, I'll sometimes start thinking about a family, wondering how they are.

■

Mode and Skill Check

1. What is the thesis statement of this selection?

_____

2. What is the predominant mode(s) that the author uses to organize the details in this selection?

_____

3. Identify the steps that Jones goes through in the daily execution of his job as a D.Y.F.S. worker.

_____

Questions for Writing and Discussion

1. List several inferences that you can make about Jones after reading this selection. How do you think he differs, if at all, from his coworkers at D.Y.F.S.?

2. Discuss the effects that being a D.Y.F.S. case worker has had on Jones.

3. In your opinion, do you think Jones is an effective case worker, or do you think he crosses the line when dealing with his clients? Why do you feel the way that you do?

4. Do you think that you would be able to do the job that Jones describes in this selection? Why or why not? Write a brief essay discussing your feelings about taking on a job like this.

5. What effect do you think Jones's upbringing in Newark had on his decision to become a D.Y.F.S. case worker?

Motivate! Then Fail! New Year's Resolutions

By Dave Barry

1 Why make New Year's resolutions? Because you can be a better person. I bet you know somebody who seems to be perfect—somebody who always looks terrific; somebody who manages to devote plenty of time to both family and career; somebody whose house is spotless, whose children are well behaved, and whose dog does not smell as if it sleeps on a bed of decomposing raccoons. You wonder how that person "does it all," don't you? Well, stop wondering and do something! Start right now! Get up off the sofa, put on some active sportswear, and kill that person with a crowbar!

2 No, seriously, you need to make some New Year's resolutions so that you can become a better you—a more-attractive you, an organized you, a you that is . . . well, less like you.

3 At this point, you are saying: "Dave, I would love nothing better than to be less like myself, but every year I make the same New Year's resolution, which is that I will lose weight, and currently my thighs are the diameter of the trans-Alaska pipeline."

4 Don't feel bad! Many people have trouble sticking to their resolutions, and there is a simple scientific explanation for this. In 1987, a team of psychologists conducted a

Source: Dave Barry, "Wait 'Til Next Year," originally published in *Miami Herald,* January 4, 1998. Reprinted by permission.

study in which they monitored the New Year's resolutions of 275 people. After one week, the psychologists found that 92 percent of the people were keeping their resolutions; after two weeks, we have no idea what happened, because the psychologists had quit monitoring.

5   "We just lost our motivation," they reported. "Also, we found ourselves eating Twinkies by the case."

6   So we see that keeping resolutions can be difficult. But you CAN do it, if you follow these practical tips:

1. Be Realistic

7 Many people give up because they "set their sights too high." In making a New Year's resolution, pick a goal that you can reasonably expect to attain, as we see in these examples:

Unrealistic Goal: "In the next month, I will lose 25 pounds."

Realistic Goal: "Over the next year, taking it an ounce or two at a time, I will gain 25 pounds, and my face will bloat like a military life raft."

Unrealistic Goal: "I will learn to speak Chinese."

Realistic Goal: "I will order some Chinese food."

Unrealistic Goal: "I will read a good book."

Realistic Goal: "I will examine the outsides of some good books, then waddle over to the part of the bookstore where they sell pastries."

Unrealistic Goal: "I will do volunteer work for a worthy cause."

Realistic Goal: "I will give myself a hearty scratching."

2. Think Positive

8 To succeed, you must believe in yourself. Write this motivational statement in large letters on a piece of paper and tape it someplace where you will see it often, such as on the inside of your eyeglasses: "I can do it, and I will do it! Starting next year!"

3. Learn from Your Mistakes

9 Let's say that, like millions of weight-conscious Americans, you think you eat sensibly: Your diet consists almost exclusively of mineral water and low-calorie, low-fat foods. And yet you're still gaining weight. Why? I'll tell you why: You're drinking water with minerals in it. Minerals are among the heaviest substances in the universe, second only to guests on the Jerry Springer show. Think about it: The Appalachian Mountains and most major appliances are essentially big wads of minerals, and you're putting those things into your body. No wonder you're gaining weight!

10   FACT: The word *Perrier* is French for "balloon butt."

11   I have run out of room here, thank God, so let me say in closing that I wish you the best of luck with your New Year's resolutions, and I will do my best to keep my own resolution, which is to give you, every single week, the most useful, informative, and accurate columns I possibly can. Starting next year. ■

Mode and Skill Check

1. What is the thesis statement of this selection?

_____

2. What is the predominant mode(s) that the author uses to organize the details in this selection?

_____

3. According to Dave Barry, what are three steps to follow to keep a resolution?

_____

Questions for Writing and Discussion

1. Do you make resolutions? Do you usually achieve them?

2. Why do you think that so many people do not keep their resolutions?

3. Do Barry's practical tips—be realistic, think positively, and learn from your mistakes—have validity as ways to achieve resolutions, or are they included merely to be humorous?

4. Write a brief summary of this selection—without using humor—highlighting Barry's key points.

5. What can you infer about how Barry feels about New Year's resolutions?

Bad Connections

By Christine Rosen

1 In the sixteenth century, Venetian and French glassmakers perfected a technique of coating glass with an alloy of silver to produce an effective mirror. Mirrors soon proliferated in public spaces and private homes, and owning a pocket or hand mirror became a marker of status. The mirror, you might say, was an early personal technology—ingenious, portable, effective—and like all such technologies, it changed its users. By giving us, for the first time, a readily available image of ourselves that matched what others saw, it encouraged self-consciousness and introspection and, as some worried, excesses of vanity.

2 By the nineteenth century, it was the machines of the Industrial Revolution—the power loom, the motor, the turbine—that

Source: Christine Rosen, "Bad Connections," _New York Times Magazine_, March 20, 2005. © 2005, Christine Rosen. Reprinted by permission.

prompted concern about the effects of technology on the person. Karl Marx argued that factory work alienated the worker from what he was toiling to produce, transforming him into "a cripple, a monster." Men were forced to become more like machines: efficient, tireless, and soulless.

3   Today's personal technologies, particularly the cellphone and the digital video recorder, have not provoked similar worries. They are marvels of individual choice, convenience, and innovation; they represent the democratization of the power of the machine. Our technologies are more intuitive, more facile, and more responsive than ever before. In a rebuke to Marx, we have not become the alienated slaves of the machine; we have made the machines more like us and in the process toppled decades of criticism about the dangerous and potentially enervating effects of our technologies.

4   Or have we? The cellphone, a device we have lived with for more than a decade, offers a good example of a popular technology's unforeseen side effects. More than one billion are in use around the world, and when asked, their owners say they love their phones for the safety and convenience they provide. People also report that they are courteous in their use of their phones. One opinion survey found that "98 percent of Americans say they move away from others when talking on a wireless phone in public" and that "86 percent say they 'never' or 'rarely' speak on wireless phones" when conducting transactions with clerks or bank tellers. Clearly, there exists a gulf between our reported cellphone behavior and our actual behavior.

5   Cellphone users—that is to say, most of us—are both instigators and victims of this form of conversational panhandling, and it has had a cumulatively negative effect on so-cial space. As the sociologist Erving Goffman observed in another context, there is something deeply disturbing about people who are "out of contact" in social situations because they are blatantly refusing to adhere to the norms of their immediate environment. Placing a cellphone call in public instantly transforms the strangers around you into unwilling listeners who must cede to your use of the public space, a decidedly undemocratic effect for so democratic a technology. Listeners don't always passively accept this situation: in recent years, people have been pepper-sprayed in movie theaters, ejected from concert halls, and deliberately rammed with cars as a result of rude behavior on their cellphones.

6   Recently, when hackers gained access to Paris Hilton's T-Mobile Sidekick, news organizations had no trouble finding pictures of her talking and typing into the device to illustrate their stories; Hilton, like most wireless users, spends a great deal of time in public engaged in private communications. Why? The cellphone, like the mirror, also offers a great deal of gratification to our egos. By making us available to anyone at any time, it serves as a "publicization of emotional fulfillment," as the French sociologist Chantal de Gournay has argued. Answering the phone and entering into conversation immediately informs everyone around us that we are in demand by someone, somewhere. Like a security blanket, the cellphone and other wireless devices serve as a form of connection when we are alone—walking down the street, standing in line—and connection is our contemporary currency.

7   So is control, and enthusiasts of DVRs like TiVo ecstatically praise the amount of it the device gives them: they can skip commercials, record hundreds of hours of their

favorite shows, pause live television, and be pleasantly surprised by recommendations, based on stored preferences, of other programs they might like to watch. In one TiVo subscriber survey, 98 percent of TiVo owners reported that they "couldn't live without" the device.

8 Fewer Americans will in the years to come. According to Forrester Research, 41 percent of American homes will have a DVR within the next five years. Given that the only two things we do more than watch television are sleep and work, the DVR is, it seems, a perfect technological solution for controlling viewing habits. Yet, as a recent study by Next Research found, DVR users end up watching five to six hours more television per week than they did before they owned the device. Rather than freeing them to watch less television by eliminating waste, the DVR encourages them to watch greater amounts of television by making it a thoroughly personalized experience.

9 The near future promises even more of these ego-casting technologies, which offer us greater control and encourage the individualized pursuit of personal taste. Soon we'll carry cellphones that double as credit cards, toll passes, televisions, and personal video cameras. At home, we'll merge the functions of these many technologies into a single streamlined machine that will respond to the sound of our voice, like the multimodal browser being developed by I.B.M. and Opera. This expansion of choice and control will foster the already prevalent expectation that we can and should be able to have anything we want on demand.

10 This is not a world without costs. Having our every whim satisfied at the touch of a button might encourage a childish expectation of instant gratification and could breed intoler-

ance for the kinds of music, film, and literature that require patience to enjoy fully. As we use these technologies to increase the pace and quantity of our experiences, we might find that the quality of our pursuits declines. Nevertheless, whatever ambivalence we might feel toward these technologies, we end up buying and using them anyway, not only because they make life more convenient but also because everyone else uses them and so we must as well. The traveling businessman without a cellphone will not have a business for long.

11 Although there is no obvious political solution to the unintended problems created by our personal technologies—we wouldn't want the government taxing our TiVo use—there are possibilities for nonpartisan agreement about changing our use of them. Conservatives like to complain about the content of popular culture and yet champion an unregulated market that thrives on creating and supplying new wants. Liberals herald the power of individual choice yet fret about the decline of community and the power corporations often exercise over our politics and culture. Both might agree, then, that it is a good thing if parents discourage children from watching too much television. Both might find something beneficial in private entities enforcing civility in discrete spaces, like restaurants and theaters that ban cellphones, and an increase in public transportation providers who offer cell-free spaces, like the "quiet car" that Amtrak offers.

12 As a society, we need to approach our personal technologies with a greater awareness of how the pursuit of personal convenience can contribute to collective ills. When it comes to abortion or Social Security, we avidly debate the claims of individual freedom against other goods. Why shouldn't we

do the same with our private technologies? In the end, it does matter if we watch six more hours of television every week, and it does affect our broader quality of life if hollering into our cellphones makes our daily commute a living hell for our fellow citizens on the bus or a danger to other drivers on the road. Rather than turning on, tuning in, and dropping out, we might perhaps do better, individually and socially, to occasionally simply turn our machines off. ■

Mode and Skill Check

1. What is the thesis statement of this selection?

_____

2. What is the predominant mode(s) that the author uses to organize the details in this selection?

_____

3. On a separate sheet of paper, draw a diagram of the major causes and effects discussed in this essay.

Questions for Writing and Discussion

1. How much time do you spend in public engaged in private conversations either on your cellphone or on other devices? Do you think that you spend more or less time than your friends do engaged in private conversations in public? Compare their cellphone use with yours.

2. Why do you think that people who have DVR technology spend more time watching television than people without the technology do?

3. Is there any type of technology that you have mixed feelings about yet still use? For instance, do you consider your cellphone a nuisance but feel that you must have one in order to get along in society?

4. Describe, in writing, the type of etiquette that should be employed when one uses a cellphone or some other type of technology in public.

5. If you had to give up one form of technology that you currently use—for example, your cellphone, e-mail, and so on—which would it be, and why would you choose that form?

Experts Schmexperts

By Robert Lipsyte

1   Though it's only been a few months since we learned from experts that being overweight is OK, I've already lost 12 pounds. The day the report was announced I gave up hamburgers, cookies, bread, and beer. Those are my favorite food groups, so portion control on everything else has been easy.

2   I had already given up wine. Actually, that was some years ago, when we learned from experts that red wine was good for your heart. I was a serious devotee of Beaujolais back then. I knew how to let it breathe, then sniff it and roll it around on my tongue. But I gave away my best bottles as gifts and never replaced them.

3   Please don't think of me as a contrarian because I don't jump on the bandwagon when experts come down from their government or academic mountains with a fresh set of commandments that contradicts the last set of commandments. Don't assume I'm complaining about the effort involved in absorbing another wave of expertise. Actually, my only real concern is that I'll end up ignoring all expertise, that I'll become so cynical I won't believe in anything.

4   It's easy to dismiss everything, assume the experts are either honestly wrong or dishonestly lying, paid off by special interests. I don't assume either. I think we have to pick and choose what we believe because most experts—who are probably right half the time—are acting out of self-interest.

5   If most of the expert wisdom is already out there, what's left for the current crop of experts? The only chance for the new guys—the "nexperts"—is to make room for themselves by knocking some old expert wisdom off the shelf.

6   Sometimes, the latest expert wisdom is interesting but doesn't have much to do with our everyday lives. For example, the recent information that Pluto might not be a real planet after all. All my life I've struggled to remember the planets in our solar system and their order from the sun. And now we hear that Pluto might be just another minor object, perhaps to be replaced as a bona fide planet by the newly discovered Sedna. I think astronomer nexperts are merely trying to replace an older generation. Pluto and Sedna are just starry gossip to me. (Think of Brad Pitt and Angelina Jolie replacing Ben Affleck and anyone named Jennifer.)

7   On the other hand, nexpert wisdom can cut close to home. When Tom Ridge was the Homeland Security chief, he would heighten our anxiety by raising the color-coded threat alerts. Now that he's out of the job and a nexpert, he says there was often only flimsy evidence to raise the levels, with which he disagreed at the time. That's pretty tricky nexpertism, Tom. It's also troubling. It makes me wonder whether the government was using the threat levels as a diversion, a kind of color code to the weapons-of-mass-destruction distraction.

Source: Robert Lipsyte, "Experts Schmexperts," from http://usatoday.com/printededition/news/20050718/oplede18 .art.htm. Robert Lipsyte is the author of such young adult novels as "The Contender" and "Raiders Night." His website is robertlipsyte.com.

8   Most nexpert wisdom doesn't have such ramifications. Take water. Please. When I was growing up, the experts told us not to drink water during heavy exercise because our stomachs would explode. When I was grown, we were told to "hydrate" constantly so our brains wouldn't implode. The regimen of eight glasses a day coincided with nexpert information that expensive bottled spring water was better than free tap water. Now we're told to cut back on water during exercise. I hope there's nothing wrong with all that spring water.

9   Though many nexperts are older theorists who have worked their way onto the look-at-me lane on the information highway, two of the most interesting have pushed their way on with new books.

10   One is *Freakonomics* by economist Steven Levitt, co-written with Stephen Dubner. This bestseller has gotten attention for nexpert revisionism, especially the theory that *Roe v. Wade,* by making it easier to abort unwanted children, is the main cause for the drop in crime over the past decade. The previous hypothesis had to do with improved police procedures.

11   The other smart young nexpert is Steven Johnson. His recent book, *Everything Bad Is Good for You,* is summed up in his subtitle— *How Today's Popular Culture Is Actually Making Us Smarter.* He writes that the current spate of video games and TV shows, because they are more complex and demanding than what they have replaced, is creating a more skilled audience. Would the audience be even more intelligent and competent if it were reading books and discussing them? Too late, that's from several generations of experts ago.

12   There's simply no stopping the oncoming waves of nexperts with their ever-changing pronouncements on chocolate, prostate cancer treatment, music, warfare, clothing, the future of humanity. My tendency to discount the nexperts scares me. I don't want to start disbelieving everything new and then everything period. I will become paralyzed as a person and as a citizen. The old line "A pox on both their houses" might sound fair and balanced, but it is really hopeless and dangerous. I want to find some way to integrate the new into the old, hang on to what's worthwhile and add to it.

13   So I'm going to lose weight, eat chocolate, drink tap water, and listen to only rap music that promotes world peace. I will believe that Pluto is a planet. At least until the nexperts disprove Galileo and declare that the sun really does revolve around the Earth. Which is flat. ∎

Mode and Skill Check

1. What is the thesis statement of this selection?

_____

2. What is the predominant mode(s) that the author uses to organize the details in this selection?

_____

3. Identify three or four of the examples the author uses to support his main point.

_____

Questions for Writing and Discussion

1. Have you ever learned about something from an "expert" and then incorporated the belief into your own lifestyle? If so, what did you do, and why did you do it? What effect on your lifestyle did the change have?

2. Do you agree or disagree with the author that "most experts . . . are acting out of self-interest"? Why do you feel as you do?

3. Do some research and find out exactly what experts now say about Pluto. Based on what you have read, do you think that Pluto is a planet or a minor constellation in the solar system? Why? Use evidence from your research to support your thesis.

4. What "expert" advice were you given as a child (for example, do not swim for two hours after eating) that you now know to be untrue? Describe your experience in an essay.

5. Do you believe everything that experts tell you, or are you skeptical about what they say much of the time? Write an essay describing how critical you are when assessing advice or information from experts.

Just Walk On By

By Brent Staples

1   My first victim was a woman—white, well dressed, probably in her early twenties. I came upon her late one evening on a deserted street in Hyde Park, a relatively affluent neighborhood in an otherwise mean, impoverished section of Chicago. As I swung onto the avenue behind her, there seemed to be a discreet, uninflammatory distance between us. Not so. She cast back a worried glance. To her, the youngish black man—a broad six feet two inches with a beard and billowing hair, both hands shoved into the pockets of a bulky military jacket—seemed menacingly close. After a few more quick glimpses, she picked up her pace and was soon running in earnest. Within seconds she disappeared into a cross street.

2   That was more than a decade ago. I was 22 years old, a graduate student newly arrived at the University of Chicago. It was in the echo of that terrified woman's footfalls that I first began to know the unwieldy inheritance I had come into—the ability to alter public space in ugly ways. It was clear that she thought herself the quarry of a mugger, a rapist, or worse. Suffering a bout of insomnia, however, I was stalking sleep, not defenseless wayfarers. As a softy who is scarcely able to

Source: Brent Staples, "Just Walk On By," *Harper's,* December 1986. Reprinted by permission of the author in Kirszner/Mandell, The Blair Reader 5/e, Prentice Hall, 2005, pp. 497–500.

take a knife to a raw chicken—let alone hold it to a person's throat—I was surprised, embarrassed, and dismayed all at once. Her flight made me feel like an accomplice in tyranny. It also made it clear that I was undistinguishable from the muggers who occasionally seeped into the area from the surrounding ghetto. That first encounter, and those that followed, signified that a vast, unnerving gulf lay between nighttime pedestrians—particularly women—and me. And I soon gathered that being perceived as dangerous is a hazard in itself. I only needed to turn a corner into a dicey situation, or crowd some frightened, armed person in a foyer somewhere, or make an errant move after being pulled over by a policeman. Where fear and weapons meet—and they often do in urban America—there is always the possibility of death.

3   In that first year, my first away from my hometown, I was to become thoroughly familiar with the language of fear. At dark, shadowy intersections in Chicago, I could cross in front of a car stopped at a traffic light and elicit the *thunk, thunk, thunk, thunk* of the driver—black, white, male, or female—hammering down the door locks. On less traveled streets after dark, I grew accustomed to but never comfortable with people who crossed to the other side of the street rather than pass me. Then there were the standard unpleasantries with police, doormen, bouncers, cab drivers, and others whose business it is to screen out troublesome individuals *before* there is any nastiness.

4   I moved to New York nearly two years ago and I have remained an avid night walker. In central Manhattan, the near-constant crowd cover minimizes tense one-on-one street encounters. Elsewhere—visiting friends in SoHo, where sidewalks are narrow and tightly spaced buildings shut out the sky—things can get very taut indeed.

5   Black men have a firm place in New York mugging literature. Norman Podhoretz in his famed (or infamous) 1963 essay, "My Negro Problem—And Ours," recalls growing up in terror of black males; they "were tougher than we were, more ruthless," he writes—and as an adult on the Upper West Side of Manhattan, he continues, he cannot constrain his nervousness when he meets black men on certain streets. Similarly, a decade later, the essayist and novelist Edward Hoagland extols a New York where once "Negro bitterness bore down mainly on other Negroes." Where some see mere panhandlers, Hoagland sees "a mugger who is clearly screwing up his nerve to do more than just *ask* for money." But Hoagland has "the New Yorker's quickhunch posture for broken-field maneuvering," and the bad guy swerves away.

6   I often witness that "hunch posture," from women after dark on the warrenlike streets of Brooklyn where I live. They seem to set their faces on neutral and, with their purse straps strung across their chests bandolier style, they forge ahead as though bracing themselves against being tackled. I understand, of course, that the danger they perceive is not a hallucination. Women are particularly vulnerable to street violence, and young black males are drastically overrepresented among the perpetrators of that violence. Yet these truths are no solace against the kind of alienation that comes of being ever the suspect, against being set apart, a fearsome entity with whom pedestrians avoid making eye contact.

7   It is not altogether clear to me how I reached the ripe old age of 22 without being conscious of the lethality nighttime pedestrians attributed to me. Perhaps it was because in Chester, Pennsylvania, the small, angry industrial town where I came of age in the 1960s, I was scarcely noticeable against a

backdrop of gang warfare, street knifings, and murders. I grew up one of the good boys, had perhaps a half-dozen fist fights. In retrospect, my shyness of combat has clear sources.

8   Many things go into the making of a young thug. One of those things is the consummation of the male romance with the power to intimidate. An infant discovers that random flailings send the baby bottle flying out of the crib and crashing to the floor. Delighted, the joyful babe repeats those motions again and again, seeking to duplicate the feat. Just so, I recall the points at which some of my boyhood friends were finally seduced by the perception of themselves as tough guys. When a mark cowered and surrendered his money without resistance, myth and reality merged—and paid off. It is, after all, only manly to embrace the power to frighten and intimidate. We, as men, are not supposed to give an inch of our lane on the highway; we are to seize the fighter's edge in work and in play and even in love; we are to be valiant in the face of hostile forces.

9   Unfortunately, poor and powerless young men seem to take all this nonsense literally. As a boy, I saw countless tough guys locked away; I have since buried several, too. They were babies, really—a teenage cousin, a brother of 22, a childhood friend in his mid-twenties—all gone down in episodes of bravado played out in the streets. I came to doubt the virtues of intimidation early on. I chose, perhaps even unconsciously, to remain a shadow—timid, but a survivor.

10   The fearsomeness mistakenly attributed to me in public places often has a perilous flavor. The most frightening of these confusions occurred in the late 1970s and early 1980s when I worked as a journalist in Chicago. One day, rushing into the office of a magazine I was writing for with a deadline story in hand, I was mistaken for a burglar. The office

manager called security and, with an ad hoc posse, pursued me through the labyrinthine halls, nearly to my editor's door. I had no way of proving who I was. I could only move briskly toward the company of someone who knew me.

11   Another time I was on assignment for a local paper and killing time before an interview. I entered a jewelry store on the city's affluent Near North Side. The proprietor excused herself and returned with an enormous red Doberman pinscher straining at the end of a leash. She stood, the dog extended toward me, silent to my questions, her eyes bulging nearly out of her head. I took a cursory look around, nodded, and bade her good night. Relatively speaking, however, I never fared as badly as another black male journalist. He went to nearby Waukegan, Illinois, a couple of summers ago to work on a story about a murderer who was born there. Mistaking the reporter for the killer, police hauled him from his car at gunpoint and but for his press credentials would probably have tried to book him. Such episodes are not uncommon. Black men trade tales like this all the time.

12   In "My Negro Problem—And Ours," Podhoretz writes that the hatred he feels for blacks makes itself known to him through a variety of avenues—one being his discomfort with that "special brand of paranoid touchiness" to which he says blacks are prone. No doubt he is speaking here of black men. In time, I learned to smother the rage I felt at so often being taken for a criminal. Not to do so would surely have led to madness—via that special "paranoid touchiness" that so annoyed Podhoretz at the time he wrote the essay.

13   I began to take precautions to make myself less threatening. I move about with care, particularly late in the evening. I give a wide

berth to nervous people on subway platforms during the wee hours, particularly when I have exchanged business clothes for jeans. If I happen to be entering a building behind some people who appear skittish, I may walk by, letting them clear the lobby before I return, so as not to seem to be following them. I have been calm and extremely congenial on those rare occasions when I have been pulled over by the police.

14   And on late-evening constitutionals along streets less traveled by, I employ what has proved to be an excellent tension-reducing measure: I whistle melodies from Beethoven and Vivaldi and the more popular classical composers. Even steely New Yorkers hunching toward nighttime destinations seem to relax, and occasionally they even join in the tune. Virtually everybody seems to sense that a mugger would not be warbling bright, sunny selections from Vivaldi's *Four Seasons*. It is my equivalent of the cowbell that hikers wear when they know they are in bear country. ■

Mode and Skill Check

1. What is the thesis statement of this selection?

2. What is the predominant mode(s) that the author uses to organize the details in this selection?

3. In his conclusion, Staples identifies all of the things that he does to disarm people whom he might make nervous by his presence. Are his methods effective? To what does he compare these methods? Is this comparison effective as a conclusion?

Questions for Writing and Discussion

1. Why does Staples walk at night? What effect has his presence had on those around him? Why?

2. What is Staples's purpose in referencing Norman Podhoretz's 1963 essay? Is this reference effective? What can you infer about how Staples feels about the opinions Podhoretz includes in the essay?

3. Why did it take Staples until the age of twenty-two to realize the effect he had on other people?

4. Discuss the different reactions that Staples gets to his presence and the inherent danger in being stereotyped as a thug or dangerous person by others.

5. How would you describe Staples's attitude toward peoples' reactions to him?

Life and Romance in 160 Characters or Less

By Yuki Noguchi

1 Andrew Weigle can fully express himself in several dozen characters or less.

2 That's the amount of space he gets on his Motorola Razr phone to compose text messages, which he sends mostly to friends and, on at least one occasion, to a girlfriend to break up.

3 "It was easier to say, 'Look, things just aren't working out'" over the text message, said Weigle, 23, who lives in Falls Church. "I'm not the most verbal person when it comes to expressing emotions," he admitted, but with text messaging, "I can put it out there and feel like I'm not *saying* it. I find there's a little more freedom to say what you're feeling."

4 A generation ago, those kinds of missives came in handwritten form, taking days or weeks to arrive. Then e-mail made communication much quicker but still allowed time and space for reflection.

5 Now, text messaging—like its older cousin, instant messaging—is giving rise to a new, electronic written culture that is truncating all of that. A text message sent via mobile phone is usually confined to 160 characters or less and takes several seconds to send. To accommodate this short form, language is acquiring acronyms—"H8" (hate), "iluvu" (I love you), and "ruok" (are you okay)—that allow text messages and other instant messages to relay information about life's mundane details as well as its emotional brambles.

6 About 7.3 billion text messages are sent within the United States every month, up from 2.9 billion a month a year ago, according to CTIA, the wireless industry's trade group. After Hurricane Katrina knocked out or overloaded communications systems, one of the only ways to reach lost relatives and friends was through text messaging, which transmits in sturdy little bursts of data that can often make it through even when voice lines are snarled.

7 Compared with an ink-and-paper letter, messages may seem disposable. The relative inconvenience of typing out words using a numeric keypad—the letter "c," for example, requires three presses of the "2" button— and the brevity of the message may seem a hostile environment for heartfelt discussion. But the discipline of having to distill thoughts into short bulletins, then waiting to receive the response, allows users to pour more meaning into the writing, some text-message users say.

8 "There is something different about communications that are mediated by a piece of technology; it is easier to talk about difficult subjects, and that is both good and bad,"

Source: Yuki Noguchi, "Life and Romance in 160 Characters or Less," *Washington Post,* from http://www.washingtonpost.com/wpdyn/content/article/2005/12/28/AR2005122801430.html. © 2005, *Washington Post,* reprinted with permission.

said Amanda Lenhart, senior researcher at the Pew Internet and American Life Project, who has interviewed many teenagers about how they use technology. "You don't see the person's upper lip tremble. You don't hear [the person's] voice quiver. You don't get those external, non-textual cues," so delicate subjects might be easier to broach, if also sometimes easier to misunderstand, she said.

9   Text-based intimacy went on display during a recent Bon Jovi concert at the MCI Center, when Sprint Nextel Corporation invited the audience to send in text messages, which then scrolled across a gigantic screen behind the stage, including proclamations of love, birthday shout-outs, and even several marriage proposals.

10   Robert Helsel III and his two sisters high-fived when their text message to their baby brother lit up the screen: "Todd helsel here in our harts."

11   "In June 2002 our little brother was killed in a car accident," said Helsel, an Elkton resident. Todd was 18 and a week shy of his high school graduation. "We grew up on Bon Jovi. We've always been huge fans; we always wanted to see Bon Jovi before we died," Helsel said over the din of the crowd. Seeing Todd's name appear over the stage was a kind of fulfillment of that, he said. "It was like closure. It just made it feel like he was right there with us."

12   The brevity of a text message gives it a certain poetic beauty, said Washington resident Erik Lung, 34. As in enigmatic haiku, there is lots of space for reading between lines, particularly in an early-stage romance.

13   "You can send a quick little message saying you're thinking of her," the operations research analyst said. Then "you start paying attention not only to what the message says, but you care about the response time."

There's a meta-message: The shorter the response time, the more she cares.

14   Text messages also feel more personal because the cell phone is always physically close, Lung said—a feature that works for and against him. He recently got into an argument with a friend, for example, who sent angry messages in all capital letters, berating him for ignoring her. "She started insulting me over text message . . . and it was not a good scene. It annoyed the hell out of me," he said. "Text messaging will catch you no matter where you are."

15   Messaging alters language and composition style, said Tom Keeney, director of messaging for T-Mobile USA. Slang has gotten more detailed and sophisticated, making it possible to say more on a tiny canvas, much like poetry, he said. "It's almost like letters gave way to postcards. It was a way to say something on the go."

16   Text messaging became popular in the United States about three years ago, coinciding with the first television season of *American Idol,* which allowed viewers to vote for contestants by sending messages to the show. Now, almost a third of the country's 200 million cellular phone subscribers use text messaging regularly for social or business purposes.

17   In a recent survey, more than 60 percent of U.S. adults used text messages to tell others they missed or loved them, according to a survey by Tegic Communications, a company that makes predictive-spelling software used on most U.S. cell phones. In the same survey, 27 percent said they used them to flirt, 7 percent to ask someone for a date, and 2 percent to break up. Two percent proposed marriage via text.

18   In Europe and Asia, where text-messaging started earlier, emotional messaging is more

common, according to Tegic. Among Germans, 70 percent said, "I love you" or "I miss you" over text; 13 percent of Italians and 12 percent of Chinese subscribers admitted to breaking up over text.

19 Alexandria resident John Mallory said he has developed emotional attachments to some old text messages but occasionally must erase them to make room for new ones. "It says, 'Your mailbox is 90 percent full,'" said Mallory, 24, opening his phone to read an old message. "I am in a constant battle to pick which ones to save."

20 But the saved messages can come back to bite. "I have had a friend in particular whose girlfriend was going through his phone and saw flirtatious text messages to an ex-girlfriend," he said. And that was a deal breaker. ■

Mode and Skill Check

1. What is the thesis statement of this selection?

_____

2. What is the predominant mode(s) that the author uses to organize the details in this selection?

_____

3. According to the author, what are some negative effects of text messaging's growing popularity?

_____

Questions for Writing and Discussion

1. How, if at all, has your life changed since you got the ability to text message? Write an essay comparing and contrasting the "before and after" of your text messaging.

2. Do you think that it is easier to talk about difficult subjects through text messaging? Why or why not?

3. Have you ever ended a relationship via text message? If so, describe what happened. If not, would you ever consider breaking up via text message? Why or why not?

4. What are the advantages of having text messaging capabilities? Discuss your thoughts in a brief essay or with a classmate.

5. With the advent of new technologies—text messaging, e-mail, and so on—do you think that the days of writing letters are completely over? If so, do you think this is a negative development? Why or why not?

Becoming American

By Dinesh D'Souza

1   Critics of America, both at home and abroad, have an easy explanation for why the American idea is so captivating, and why immigrants want to come here. The reason, they say, is money. America represents "the bitch goddess of success." That is why poor people reach out for the American idea: they want to touch some of that lucre. As for immigrants, they allegedly flock to the United States for the sole purpose of getting rich. This view, which represents the appeal of America as the appeal of the almighty dollar, is disseminated on Arab streets and in multicultural textbooks taught in U.S. schools. It is a way of demeaning the United States by associating it with what is selfish, base, and crass: an unquenchable appetite for gain.

2   It is not hard to see why this view of America has gained a wide currency. When people in foreign countries turn on American TV shows, they are stupefied by the lavish displays of affluence: the sumptuous homes, the bejeweled women, the fountains and pools, and so on. Whether reruns of *Dallas* and *Dynasty* are true to the American experience is irrelevant here; the point is that this is how the United States appears to outsiders who have not had the chance to come here. And even for those who do, it is hard to deny that America represents the chance to live better, even to become fantastically wealthy. For instance, there are several people of Indian descent on the *Forbes* 400 list. And over the years I have heard many Indians now living in the United States say, "We want to live an Indian lifestyle, but at an American standard of living."

3   If this seems like a crass motive for immigration, it must be evaluated in the context of the harsh fate that poor people endure in much of the Third World. The lives of many of these people are defined by an ongoing struggle to exist. It is not that they don't work hard. On the contrary, they labor incessantly and endure hardships that are almost unimaginable to people in the West. In the villages of Asia and Africa, for example, a common sight is a farmer beating a pickax into the ground, women wobbling under heavy loads, children carrying stones. These people are performing very hard labor, but they are getting nowhere. The best they can hope for is to survive for another day. Their clothes are tattered, their teeth are rotted, and disease and death constantly loom over their horizon. For the poor of the Third World, life is characterized by squalor, indignity, and brevity.

4   I emphasize the plight of the poor, but I recognize, of course, that there are substantial middle classes even in the underdeveloped world. For these people basic survival may not be an issue, but still, they endure hardships that make everyday life a strain. One problem is that the basic infrastructure of the Third World is abysmal: the roads are not properly paved, the water is not safe to drink, pollution in the cities has reached hazardous levels, public transportation is overcrowded and unreliable, and there is a two-year waiting period to get a telephone. Government

Source: from Dinesh D'Souza, *What's So Great About America* (Washington, DC: Regnery Publishing, 2002). Excerpted in Kirszner and Mandell: *The Blair Reader,* 5th ed. Prentice Hall, 2005. Reprinted by permission of the author.

officials, who are very poorly paid, are inevitably corrupt, which means that you must pay bribes on a regular basis to get things done. Most important, there are limited prospects for the children's future.

5   In America, the immigrant immediately recognizes, things are different. The newcomer who sees America for the first time typically experiences emotions that alternate between wonder and delight. Here is a country where *everything works:* the roads are clean and paper smooth, the highway signs are clear and accurate, the public toilets function properly, when you pick up the telephone you get a dial tone, you can even buy things from the store and then take them back. For the Third World visitor, the American supermarket is a thing to behold: endless aisles of every imaginable product, fifty different types of cereal, multiple flavors of ice cream. The place is full of countless unappreciated inventions: quilted toilet paper, fabric softener, cordless telephones, disposable diapers, roll-on luggage, deodorant. Most countries even today do not have these benefits: deodorant, for example, is unavailable in much of the Third World and unused in much of Europe.

6   What the immigrant cannot help noticing is that America is a country where the poor live comparatively well. This fact was dramatized in the 1980s, when CBS television broadcast an anti-Reagan documentary, "People Like Us," which was intended to show the miseries of the poor during an American recession. The Soviet Union also broadcast the documentary, with a view to embarrassing the Reagan administration. But by the testimony of former Soviet leaders, it had the opposite effect. Ordinary people across the Soviet Union saw that the poorest Americans have television sets and microwave ovens and cars. They arrived at the same perception of America that I witnessed in a friend of mine from Bombay who has been unsuccessfully trying to move to the United States for nearly a decade. Finally I asked him, "Why are you so eager to come to America?" He replied, "Because I really want to live in a country where the poor people are fat."

7   The point is that the United States is a country where the ordinary guy has a good life. This is what distinguishes America from so many other countries. Everywhere in the world, the rich person lives well. Indeed, a good case can be made that if you are rich, you live better in countries other than America. The reason is that you enjoy the pleasures of aristocracy. This is the pleasure of being treated as a superior person. Its gratification derives from subservience: in India, for example, the wealthy enjoy the satisfaction of seeing innumerable servants and toadies grovel before them and attend to their every need.

8   In the United States the social ethic is egalitarian, and this is unaffected by the inequalities of wealth in the country. Tocqueville noticed this egalitarianism a century and a half ago, but it is, if anything, more prevalent today. For all his riches, Bill Gates could not approach a homeless person and say, "Here's a $100 bill. I'll give it to you if you kiss my feet." Most likely the homeless guy would tell Gates to go to hell! The American view is that the rich guy may have more money, but he isn't in any fundamental sense better than you are. The American janitor or waiter sees himself as performing a service, but he doesn't see himself as inferior to those he serves. And neither do the customers see him that way: they are generally happy to show him respect and appreciation on a plane of equality. America is the only country in the world where we call the waiter "Sir," as if he were a knight.

9   The moral triumph of America is that it has extended the benefits of comfort and affluence, traditionally enjoyed by very few, to a large segment of society. Very few people in America have to wonder where their next meal is coming from. Even sick people who don't have proper insurance can receive medical care at hospital emergency rooms. The poorest American girls are not humiliated by having to wear torn clothes. Every child is given an education, and most have the chance to go on to college. The common man can expect to live long enough and have free time to play with his grandchildren.

10   Ordinary Americans enjoy not only security and dignity, but also comforts that other societies reserve for the elite. We now live in a country where construction workers regularly pay $4 for a nonfat latte, where maids drive very nice cars, where plumbers take their families on vacation to Europe. As Irving Kristol once observed, there is virtually no restaurant in America to which a CEO can go to lunch with the absolute assurance that he will not find his secretary also dining there. Given the standard of living of the ordinary American, it is no wonder that socialist or revolutionary schemes have never found a wide constituency in the United States. As sociologist Werner Sombart observed, all socialist utopias in America have come to grief on roast beef and apple pie.*

11   Thus it is entirely understandable that people would associate the idea of America with a better life. For them, money is not an end in itself; money is the means to a longer, healthier, and fuller life. Money allows them to purchase a level of security, dignity, and comfort that they could not have hoped to enjoy in their native countries. Money also frees up time for family life, community involvement, and spiritual pursuits: thus it produces not just material, but also moral, gains. All of this is true, and yet in my view it offers an incomplete picture of why America is so appealing to so many. Let me illustrate with the example of my own life.

12   Not long ago, I asked myself: what would my life have been like if I had never come to the United States, if I had stayed in India? Materially, my life has improved, but not in a fundamental sense. I grew up in a middle-class family in Bombay. My father was a chemical engineer; my mother, an office secretary. I was raised without great luxury, but neither did I lack for anything. My standard of living in America is higher, but it is not a radical difference. My life has changed far more dramatically in other ways.

13   If I had remained in India, I would probably have lived my entire existence within a one-mile radius of where I was born. I would undoubtedly have married a woman of my identical religious, socioeconomic, and cultural background. I would almost certainly have become a medical doctor, an engineer, or a software programmer. I would have socialized within my ethnic community and had cordial relations, but few friends, outside that group. I would have a whole set of opinions that could be predicted in advance; indeed, they would not be very different from what my father believed, or his father before him. In sum, my destiny would to a large degree have been given to me.

14   This is not to say that I would have no choice; I would have choice, but within nar-

---

*Werner Sombart, *Why Is There No Socialism in the United States?* (White Plains, NY: International Arts and Sciences Press, 1976), pp. 109–110.

rowly confined parameters. Let me illustrate with the example of my sister, who got married several years ago. My parents began the process by conducting a comprehensive survey of all the eligible families in our neighborhood. First they examined primary criteria, such as religion, socioeconomic position, and educational background. Then my parents investigated subtler issues: the social reputation of the family, reports of a lunatic uncle, the character of the son, and so on. Finally my parents were down to a dozen or so eligible families, and they were invited to our house for dinner with suspicious regularity. My sister was, in the words of Milton Friedman, "free to choose." My sister knew about, and accepted, the arrangement; she is now happily married with two children. I am not quarreling with the outcome, but clearly my sister's destiny was, to a considerable extent, choreographed by my parents.

15 By coming to America, I have seen my life break free of these traditional confines. I came to Arizona as an exchange student, but a year later I was enrolled at Dartmouth College. There I fell in with a group of students who were actively involved in politics; soon I had switched my major from economics to English literature. My reading included books like Plutarch's *Moralia*; Hamilton, Madison, and Jay's *Federalist Papers*; and Evelyn Waugh's *Brideshead Revisited*. They transported me to places a long way from home and implanted in my mind ideas that I had never previously considered. By the time I graduated, I decided that I should become a writer, which is something you can do in this country. America permits many strange careers: this is a place where you can become, say, a comedian. I would not like to go to my father and tell him that I was thinking of

becoming a comedian. I do not think he would have found it funny.

16 Soon after graduation I became the managing editor of a policy magazine and began to write freelance articles in the *Washington Post*. Someone in the Reagan White House was apparently impressed by my work, because I was called in for an interview and promptly hired as a senior domestic policy analyst. I found it strange to be working at the White House, because at the time I was not a United States citizen. I am sure that such a thing would not happen in India or anywhere else in the world. But Reagan and his people didn't seem to mind; for them, ideology counted more than nationality. I also met my future wife in the Reagan administration, where she was at the time a White House intern. (She has since deleted it from her résumé.) My wife was born in Louisiana and grew up in San Diego; her ancestry is English, French, Scotch-Irish, German, and American Indian.

17 I notice that Americans marry in a rather peculiar way: by falling in love. You may think that I am being ironic, or putting you on, so let me hasten to inform you that in many parts of the world, romantic love is considered a mild form of insanity. Consider a typical situation: Anjali is in love with Arjun. She considers Arjun the best-looking man in the world, the most intelligent, virtually without fault, a paragon of humanity! But everybody else can see that Arjun is none of these things. What, then, persuades Anjali that Arjun possesses qualities that are nowhere in evidence? There is only one explanation: Anjali is deeply deluded. It does not follow that her romantic impulses should be ruthlessly crushed. But, in the view of many people and many traditions around the world,

they should be steered and directed and prevented from ruining Anjali's life. This is the job of parents and the community, to help Anjali see beyond her delusions and to make decisions that are based on practical considerations and common sense.

18   If there is a single phrase that encapsulates life in the Third World, it is that "birth is destiny." I remember an incident years ago when my grandfather called in my brother, my sister, and me, and asked us if we knew how lucky we were. We asked him why he felt this way: was it because we were intelligent, or had lots of friends, or were blessed with a loving family? Each time he shook his head and said, "No." Finally we pressed him: why did he consider us so lucky? Then he revealed the answer: "Because you are Brahmins!"

19   The Brahmin, who is the highest ranking in the Hindu caste system, is traditionally a member of the priestly class. As a matter of fact, my family had nothing to do with the priesthood. Nor are we Hindu: my ancestors converted to Christianity many generations ago. Even so, my grandfather's point was that before we converted, hundreds of years ago, our family used to be Brahmins. How he knew this remains a mystery. But he was serious in his insistence that nothing that the three of us achieved in life could possibly mean more than the fact that we were Brahmins.

20   This may seem like an extreme example, revealing my grandfather to be a very narrow fellow indeed, but the broader point is that traditional cultures attach a great deal of importance to data such as what tribe you come from, whether you are male or female, and whether you are the eldest son. Your destiny and your happiness hinge on these things. If you are a Bengali, you can count on other Bengalis to help you, and on others to discriminate against you; if you are female, then certain forms of society and several professions are closed to you; and if you are the eldest son, you inherit the family house and your siblings are expected to follow your direction. What this means is that once your tribe, caste, sex, and family position have been established at birth, your life takes a course that is largely determined for you.

21   In America, by contrast, you get to write the script of your own life. When your parents say to you, "What do you want to be when you grow up?" the question is open-ended; it is you who supply the answer. Your parents can advise you: "Have you considered law school?" "Why not become the first doctor in the family?" It is considered very improper, however, for them to try and force your decision. Indeed, American parents typically send their teenage children away to college, where they live on their own and learn independence. This is part of the process of forming your mind and choosing a field of interest for yourself and developing your identity. It is not uncommon in the United States for two brothers who come from the same gene pool and were raised in similar circumstances to do quite different things: the eldest becomes a gas station attendant, the younger moves up to be vice president at Oracle; the eldest marries his high-school sweetheart and raises four kids, the youngest refuses to settle down, or comes out of the closet as a homosexual; one is the Methodist that he was raised to be, the other becomes a Christian Scientist or a Buddhist. What to be, where to live, whom to love, whom to marry, what to believe, what religion to practice—these are all decisions that Americans make for themselves.

22   In most parts of the world your identity and your fate are to a large extent handed to you; in America, you determine them for yourself. In America your destiny is not prescribed; it is constructed. Your life is like a blank sheet of paper, and you are the artist. This notion of you being the architect of your own destiny is the incredibly powerful idea that is behind the worldwide appeal of America. Young people especially find irresistible the prospect of being in the driver's seat, of authoring the narrative of their own lives. So too the immigrant discovers that America permits him to break free of the constraints that have held him captive so that the future becomes a landscape of his own choosing. ■

Mode and Skill Check

1. What is the thesis statement of this selection?

_____

2. What is the predominant mode(s) that the author uses to organize the details of this selection?

_____

3. List all the comparisons that the author makes between the United States and the rest of the world.

_____

Questions for Writing and Discussion

1. According to D'Souza, what is the one thing that distinguishes the United States from other countries?

2. What is the difference between the rich in America and the rich in other parts of the world? What examples does D'Souza use to illustrate this point?

3. What does D'Souza call America's "moral triumph"? What examples does he use to support his claim?

4. How has D'Souza's life changed since he came to the United States? Discuss what his life would have been like had he stayed in India.

5. According to D'Souza, what makes the United States an appealing place to immigrate to?

Working with Difficult People

By Constance Faye Mudore

1 Friction on the job is a fact of life. With the right know-how, it doesn't have to get the better of you.

2 Travis waited tables on weekends at a popular restaurant. He had worked there for more than a year and liked the job. But his feelings toward work changed after Helene, an assistant manager, was hired. This was because Helene often exploded at Travis in front of customers.

3 He complained to the manager, who only made excuses for Helene. Travis wondered how much longer he could work with such a difficult person.

4 Difficult people are the folks who frustrate and dampen the spirits of the people who work with them. While we can all be difficult at times, difficult people are seen as problems by most of the people around them most of the time. Worst of all, they tend to be reluctant to change their ways.

5 The good news is that there are ways to cope with difficult people. But make no mistake. Coping has nothing to do with changing someone else. The only person's behavior you can change is your own. It also has nothing to do with winning or losing battles with others. Coping requires that you learn ways to help you and the difficult person function together at work as effectively as possible.

6 What follows is a guide to dealing with three difficult personality types you're likely to meet on the job: Helen Hostile, Walter Whiner, and Corey Clam.

Rx for Hostiles

7 Helen Hostile gets her way at work by bullying others. Hostiles usually have strong opinions about how others "should" behave. When they sense a lack of confidence in others, they attack. When their targets run from them, they become even more aggressive.

8 Dr. Robert Bramson, a business management consultant and author of *Coping with Difficult People in Business and in Life,* says, "The first rule of coping with anyone aggressive is that you stand up to that person." But, Bramson emphasizes, you must stand up to them without fighting.

9 Why? Hostiles are good at fighting. If you become aggressive toward them, they'll probably become even more aggressive toward you. You are likely to lose. And even if you do win a particular battle, by becoming aggressive yourself, you damage your own reputation at work.

10 How do you stand up for yourself without fighting? Bramson suggests that you give Hostiles time to run down. Then, get their attention and state your opinions firmly.

11 Travis says, "I figured I had nothing to lose since I was ready to quit anyway. So the next time she blew up at me—which was the next time I worked with her—I let her vent a little. I was nervous, but I looked her in the eye and said, 'Helene, you have the right to discuss my work. But you don't have the right to humiliate me.'"

Source: Constance Faye Mudore, "Working with Difficult People," *Career World,* February/March 2001, pp. 16–19. Reprinted by permission.

12 "She looked at me like she'd never seen me before and walked away. I've worked with her since then. She still explodes, but not at me."

The Silent Treatment

13 Corey Clam volunteers little information, typically answering questions with one word, if he responds at all. A clam's most comfortable response to new information or potential conflict is to shut down.

14 Take Laura. She needed Corey's approval to begin a plan to train employees more effectively. She scheduled a meeting with him and enthusiastically laid out her ideas. At the conclusion, she expected him to comment. He said nothing. Confused, she asked. "Do you need more information?" He said no and indicated that he had another appointment.

15 Laura felt like she had had the wind knocked out of her. She didn't know how to interpret his silence. But if her plan was to proceed, she had to draw him out.

16 How do you get clams to tell you what they think? Ask open-ended questions. These are questions that can't be answered with one word. Instead of asking, "Do you need more information?" Laura should have asked, "What's your reaction to what I'm proposing?"

17 It's also important to give clams time to answer. This might mean you have to get comfortable with long silences. At such times, Bramson suggests "friendly, silent staring," preferably focusing your eyes on the clam's chin. (Direct eye contact can be threatening to clams.) Friendly staring communicates that you're expecting the clam to start speaking at any moment.

18 If the clam still doesn't talk, comment on what's happening by saying, "I'm notic-ing that you're not commenting. What does that mean?" If none of this works, let the clam know that you will make another appointment to discuss the issue.

19 Laura went back to see her boss and got him to open up. She says, "Corey liked my plan. When I left his office after our first meeting, I was sure that his silence meant he hated it. I'm glad I checked out that assumption."

Warning: Whiners at Work

20 Walter Whiner is another difficult person on the work scene. Whiners complain about problems on the job, but don't do anything to improve things. They tend to believe that it is someone else's responsibility to "fix it."

21 The employees at the bank where Walter works avoid him when he starts complaining about the bank being mismanaged. Missy, who works there after school, says, "I groan inside when Walter comes over to talk to me. I know I'm in for a long monologue of gripes. Sometimes, he even blames me. To top it off, he never tries any of the things I suggest."

22 How to cope? Listen to what whiners have to say, Bramson says, but put a time limit on it. This allows them to let off steam, but doesn't lock you into having to listen indefinitely. Let them know that you heard what they said by restating their complaints. Don't agree or apologize for any of the things they may be dumping on you as "your fault." And try to get them to problem solve.

23 Here's what Missy did. "The next time Walter came over, I listened to what he said for several minutes. He was complaining about the office manager because she gets to work late every day.

24 "I let him know that I could tell he was frustrated with the manager. But I also let

him know that the manager was always available when I needed help. I asked him to think about whether there was anything he could do about the situation and to get back to me. Then I told him I had some work to finish before I left for the day. He went back to his cubicle. Walter still complains a lot, but I don't feel so helpless in dealing with him."

Wishing Doesn't Work

25 Wishing that a difficult person were different is a waste of time. It's only by developing our own interpersonal and problem-solving skills that we can cope with them. Viewed positively, difficult people are some of the best teachers we will ever have. ■

Mode and Skill Check

1. What is the thesis statement of this selection?

2. What is the predominant mode(s) that the author uses to organize the details in this selection?

3. Into what three categories does the author divide difficult personality types in this selection? In your own words, describe these three difficult personality types.

Questions for Writing and Discussion

1. The author begins this selection with the statement "Friction on the job is a fact of life." Do you agree? If so, what kind of friction do you encounter at your job?

2. Write a brief essay discussing the difficult types of people with whom you have worked, putting them into categories so that their personality types are clear to your readers.

3. What effect does working with difficult people have on your quality of life at work?

4. What coping mechanisms do you use to deal with the difficult people at your workplace and in your life in general? How effective are your skills?

5. Pick one of the difficult types of coworkers listed in this selection and discuss how you would deal with this person.

Why Literature Matters

By Dana Gioia

1 In 1780 Massachusetts patriot John Adams wrote to his wife, Abigail, outlining his vision of how American culture might evolve. "I must study politics and war," he prophesied, so "that our sons may have liberty to study mathematics and philosophy." They will add to their studies geography, navigation, commerce, and agriculture, he continued, so that *their* children may enjoy the "right to study painting, poetry, music . . ."

2 Adam's bold prophecy proved correct. By the mid-twentieth century, America boasted internationally preeminent traditions in literature, art, music, dance, theater, and cinema.

3 But a strange thing has happened in the American arts during the past quarter century. While income rose to unforeseen levels, college attendance ballooned, and access to information increased enormously, the interest young Americans showed in the arts—and especially literature—actually diminished.

4 According to the 2002 Survey of Public Participation in the Arts, a population study designed and commissioned by the National Endowment for the Arts (and executed by the U.S. Bureau of the Census), arts participation by Americans has declined for eight of the nine major forms that are measured. (Only jazz has shown a tiny increase—thank you, Ken Burns.) The declines have been most severe among younger adults (ages 18–24). The most worrisome finding in the 2002 study, however, is the declining percentage of Americans, especially young adults, reading literature.

5 That individuals at a time of crucial intellectual and emotional development bypass the joys and challenges of literature is a troubling trend. If it were true that they substituted histories, biographies, or political works for literature, one might not worry. But book reading of any kind is falling as well.

6 That such a longstanding and fundamental cultural activity should slip so swiftly, especially among young adults, signifies deep transformations in contemporary life. To call attention to the trend, the Arts Endowment issued the reading portion of the Survey as a separate report, "Reading at Risk: A Survey of Literary Reading in America."

7 The decline in reading has consequences that go beyond literature. The significance of reading has become a persistent theme in the business world. The February issue of *Wired* magazine, for example, sketches a new set of mental skills and habits proper to the twenty-first century, aptitudes decidedly literary in character: not "linear, logical, analytical talents," author Daniel Pink states, but "the ability to create artistic and emotional beauty, to detect patterns and opportunities, to craft a satisfying narrative." When asked what kind of talents they like to see in management positions, business leaders consistently set imagination, creativity, and higher-order thinking at the top.

8 Ironically, the value of reading and the intellectual faculties that it inculcates appear[s] most clearly as active and engaged literacy declines. There is now a growing awareness of the consequences of nonreading to the workplace. In 2001 the National Association of Manufacturers polled its members on skill deficiencies among employees. Among hourly

Source: Dana Gioia, "Why Literature Matters," *Boston Sunday Globe,* April 10, 2005, C12. Reprinted by permission of The National Endowment For the Arts.

workers, poor reading skills ranked second, and 38 percent of employers complained that local schools inadequately taught reading comprehension.

9   Corporate America makes similar complaints about a skill intimately related to reading—writing. Last year, the College Board reported that corporations spend some $3.1 billion a year on remedial writing instruction for employees, adding that they "express a fair degree of dissatisfaction with the writing of recent college graduates." If the twenty-first-century American economy requires innovation and creativity, solid reading skills and the imaginative growth fostered by literary reading are central elements in that program.

10   The decline of reading is also taking its toll in the civic sphere. In a 2000 survey of college seniors from the top 55 colleges, the Roper Organization found that 81 percent could not earn a grade of C on a high school–level history test. A 2003 study of 15- to 26-year-olds' civic knowledge by the National Conference of State Legislatures concluded, "Young people do not understand the ideals of citizenship . . . and their appreciation and support of American democracy is limited."

11   It is probably no surprise that declining rates of literary reading coincide with declining levels of historical and political awareness among young people. One of the surprising findings of "Reading at Risk" was that literary readers are markedly more civically engaged than nonreaders, scoring two to four times more likely to perform charity work, visit a museum, or attend a sporting event. One reason for their higher social and cultural interactions may lie in the kind of civic and historical knowledge that comes with literary reading.

12   Unlike the passive activities of watching television and DVDs or surfing the Web, read-

ing is actually a highly active enterprise. Reading requires sustained and focused attention as well as active use of memory and imagination. Literary reading also enhances and enlarges our humility by helping us imagine and understand lives quite different from our own.

13   Indeed, we sometimes underestimate how large a role literature has played in the evolution of our national identity, especially in that literature often has served to introduce young people to events from the past and principles of civil society and governance. Just as more ancient Greeks learned about moral and political conduct from the epics of Homer than from the dialogues of Plato, so the most important work in the abolitionist movement was the novel *Uncle Tom's Cabin*.

14   Likewise our notions of American populism come more from Walt Whitman's poetic vision than from any political tracts. Today when people recall the Depression, the images that most come to mind are the travails of John Steinbeck's Joad family from *The Grapes of Wrath*. Without a literary inheritance, the historical past is impoverished.

15   In focusing on the social advantages of a literary education, however, we should not overlook the personal impact. Every day authors receive letters from readers that say, "Your book changed my life." History reveals case after case of famous people whose lives were transformed by literature. When the great Victorian thinker John Stuart Mill suffered a crippling depression in late-adolescence, the poetry of Wordsworth restored his optimism and self-confidence—a "medicine for my state of mind," he called it.

16   A few decades later, W. E. B. DuBois found a different tonic in literature, an escape from the indignities of Jim Crow into a world of equality. "I sit with Shakespeare and he winces not," DuBois observed. "Across the

color line I move arm in arm with Balzac and Dumas, where smiling men and welcoming women glide in gilded halls." Literature is a catalyst for education and culture.

17   The evidence of literature's importance to civic, personal, and economic health is too strong to ignore. The decline of literary reading foreshadows serious long-term social and economic problems, and it is time to bring literature and the other arts into discussions of public policy. Libraries, schools, and public agencies do noble work, but addressing the reading issue will require the leadership of politicians and the business community as well.

18   Literature now competes with an enormous array of electronic media. While no single activity is responsible for the decline in reading, the cumulative presence and availability of electronic alternatives increasingly have drawn Americans away from reading.

19   Reading is not a timeless, universal capability. Advanced literacy is a specific intellectual skill and social habit that depends on a great many educational, cultural, and economic factors. As more Americans lose this capability, our nation becomes less informed, active, and independent-minded. These are not the qualities that a free, innovative, or productive society can afford to lose. ■

Mode and Skill Check

1. What is the thesis statement of this selection?

_____

2. What is the predominant mode(s) that the author uses to organize the details in this selection?

_____

3. Describe the consequences that the decline in reading has had on Americans, according to Gioia.

_____

Questions for Writing and Discussion

1. Do you think that literature and reading are important? Why or why not? Write an essay discussing and defending your view on the topic.

2. Gioia outlines several negative effects that a lack of interest in literature and reading has on society. Which of these do you feel is the most serious? Why? Either discuss your opinion with a classmate or write an essay about your feelings.

3. Is there a book that changed your life? If so, what was it, and how did it affect you? Write an essay discussing the book and its effect on you.

4. Do you prefer to read or watch television? Why do you prefer one activity over the other?

5. Do you think that having a knowledge of the great works of literature can be a benefit to you? Why or why not?

Handbook

Parts of Speech

Every word in every sentence you write functions as a particular part of speech. A word can be different parts of speech depending on its *context,* that is, the other words around it. For example, the word *left* can be a noun, verb, adjective, or adverb:

> Turn **left** at the stop sign. (adverb)
> She writes with her **left** hand. (adjective)
> I **left** her a message. (verb)
> I live in the first house on the **left.** (noun)

In each sentence, the context determines the part of speech of this particular word.

Nouns

A **noun** is a word that names a person, place, thing, or idea: *doctor, building, fruit, hate.* Nouns are either common or proper. *Common nouns* refer to general people, places, or things: *girl, pharmacy, car. Proper nouns* name one specific person, place, thing, or idea, so they are capitalized:

> George Washington
> Zion National Park
> Volvo

Collective nouns are those that refer to a group of people or things (*team, class, crowd, group, company, audience, family, jury, gang, faculty*).

To identify nouns in a sentence, ask yourself if a word names a person, place, thing, or idea.

common noun   *common noun*
Cashews are crunchy **nuts.**

   proper noun   *common noun*
Nelson Mandela is my **hero.**

Also, look for the words *a, an,* and *the,* which often appear in front of nouns.

common noun   *common noun*
The *dog*   ate **a**   *treat.*

proper noun   *common noun*
A *Ferrari* is **a** fast *car.*

NOTE: Adjectives, such as the word *fast* in the previous sentence, will often separate *a, an,* or *the* from the noun.

Nouns can be individual words, or they can be phrases. For example, read the following sentences:

Cooking dinner is the chore I hate most.
He wants **to go to Ireland.**

These phrases function as nouns. In the first sentence, the phrase *cooking dinner* is a noun phrase that functions as the subject of the sentence. In the second example, *to go to Ireland* is a noun phrase that functions as the direct object.

EXERCISE 1

Circle all of the nouns in each of the following sentences.

1. The boys found a nest of baby birds.
2. Throwing a frisbee is one of my favorite hobbies.
3. Everest is the tallest mountain in the world.
4. Her daughter has curly blonde hair.
5. Failing the test made Joe very upset.
6. *The Amityville Horror* was a frightening film.
7. The beach is a relaxing place for vacations.
8. Our class had to write summaries of that article.

9. Playing the piano develops children's mathematical reasoning.

10. The highway was congested with traffic.

For practice in identifying nouns in sentences, go to http://www.college .hmco.com/pic/dolphinwriterthree.

Pronouns

A **pronoun** is a word that is used in place of a noun. For example, if you write one sentence that says, "John left the theater," the next sentence you write could substitute a pronoun instead of repeating the name *John*: "*He* did not like the movie." *He* is the pronoun used in place of the name *John*.

There are different kinds of pronouns. One kind refers to one or more specific people or things:

I	you	she	they
me	yourself	her	them
myself	yourselves	herself	themselves
it	we	he	their
itself	us	him	
	ourselves	himself	

She took **him** to see **them**.
He did **it himself.**

I, he, she, it, we, you, and *they* are the **personal pronouns.**

Other pronouns are called *indefinite* because they do not refer to any particular person, place, or thing:

all	both	many	someone
any	everybody	one	something
anybody	everyone	no one	several
anyone	everything	nothing	some
anything	few	somebody	

Everybody is sure what will happen.
He longs to tell **someone** her secret.

Another kind of pronoun points out specific things by referring to a certain noun. These are called **demonstrative pronouns.**

> this
> that
> these
> those

> **Those** are the nicest shoes I have ever seen.
> **That** is my house.

NOTE: The pronouns *this, that, these,* and *those* also function as adjectives when they precede and point out a particular noun. For example, in the sentence "These boots belong to Susan," the word *these* is an adjective that answers the question *Which boots?* For more on adjectives, see the Parts of Speech section of this Handbook.

Some pronouns introduce questions:

> who   what
> whom   whose
> which

> **Which** car is yours?
> **Who** is coming to the movies with us?

And finally, still other pronouns introduce dependent clauses, which you will learn more about in the Subordination section of this Handbook. These are the **relative pronouns:**

> that   whose
> what   whoever
> which   whichever
> who   whatever
> whom

> He is the one **who** loves to fish.
> Her flight, **which** leaves at 7:00 a.m., will last two hours.

EXERCISE 2

Circle all of the pronouns in the following sentences.

1. She followed him home.

2. I told her to do it herself.

3. Did you make this cake by yourself?

4. Nobody knew the answer.

5. Anybody can win the grand prize.

6. From whom did we receive these flowers?

7. Who brought you here?

8. That is the new show we told her about.

9. Make sure someone writes down the phone number.

10. Everyone should study the material and memorize it.

For practice identifying pronouns in sentences, go to http://www.college .hmco.com/pic/dolphinwriterthree.

Adjectives

Adjectives modify (describe or limit) either nouns or pronouns. They tell *how many, what kind,* or *which one.*

> **four** dogs
> **blue** shirt
> **those** trees
> a **snowy** evening
> **few** participants

Some adjectives introduce questions:

> **Which** one is the wrong answer?
> **Whose** coat is this?

An adjective can appear before or after the noun or pronoun that it modifies:

> I will have **another** slice of **juicy** steak.
> She is a woman **possessed.**
> He is **strong** and **rugged.**

One special class of adjectives includes the words *a, an,* and *the,* which are called *articles.* These words precede and point out specific people, places, or things.

> She ate **a** piece of candy.
> Tell me **the** story again.
> She drank **an** ounce of medicine to relieve **the** coughing.

Like nouns, adjectives can be individual words, or they can be phrases:

He made the decision **to go to Paris.**
Trying to skip, she tripped and fell.

Circle all of the adjectives in each of the following sentences.

1. Tonya likes to take long, relaxing baths.
2. Changing a light bulb is an easy task.
3. He enjoys fried seafood very much.
4. Fearing the worst, she slowly opened the front door.
5. Please give me some good news.
6. Poisonous snakes often have pointed heads.
7. I am a big fan.
8. Can you pick up three ripe, red tomatoes at the produce stand?
9. You seem worried.
10. Elvis Presley had dark hair.

For practice identifying adjectives in sentences, go to http://www.college.hmco.com/pic/dolphinwriterthree.

Most adjectives have two additional forms. One of them, the **comparative** form, is used to compare two things. The other, the **superlative** form, is used to compare three or more things.

Adjective	*Comparative*	*Superlative*
pretty	prettier	prettiest
young	younger	youngest
smart	smarter	smartest
dull	duller	dullest
hungry	hungrier	hungriest

You usually add -*er* to the end of many adjectives to form the comparative form. You add -*est* to the end to form the superlative form. However, some adjectives stay the same and add the word *more* to form the comparative and *most* to form the superlative.

Adjective	Comparative	Superlative
grateful	more grateful	most grateful
foolish	more foolish	most foolish
determined	more determined	most determined
gorgeous	more gorgeous	most gorgeous

Still other adjectives are irregular and change forms altogether.

Adjective	Comparative	Superlative
good	better	best
bad	worse	worst
little	less	least
much, many, some	more	most
far	farther	farthest

Verbs

Verbs express either the *action* or *state of being* of the sentence's subject.

The girl **dove** into the pool. (action verb)
They **read** the directions. (action verb)
I **am** a mother. (being verb)
He **was** thirty years old. (being verb)

Verbs that indicate a state of being are the forms of **to be:**

am
is
are
was
were
be
been
being

Verbs can be in the *present tense*, expressing that the time of the action or state of being is occurring now:

> He **likes** to eat hamburgers.
> They **are** excited about the new neighborhood.
> She **teaches** high school English.

Verbs can also be in the *past tense*, expressing that the action or state of being occurred in the past:

> He **liked** to eat hot dogs.
> They **were** excited about the new neighborhood.
> She **taught** high school English.

Sometimes we indicate past tense by adding *-d* or *-ed* to the end of the verb. For other words (such as *break/broke* and *fly/flew*), the form of the verb changes.

To express a verb's tense, one or more helping (or auxiliary) verbs are added to create verb phrases:

is	were	will
are	has	shall
am	had	could
be	have	would
was	might	

> She **has spoken** to him twice.
> We **might be going** to Puerto Rico.
> They **will have been** in Madrid for six months this June.

EXERCISE 4

Circle the verb or verb phrase in each of the following sentences.

1. I am leaving at five tomorrow.

2. They are angry.

3. Kurt lost his way.

4. I am concerned about the outcome.

5. Maria should be arriving soon.

6. Chen has chosen accounting for his major.

7. He has served on the board for two years.

8. I walked three miles yesterday.

9. Tai will be calling you later this evening.

10. We invested our money wisely.

For practice identifying verbs in sentences, go to http://www.college.hmco
.com/pic/dolphinwriterthree.

Adverbs

Adverbs modify verbs, adjectives, and other adverbs by telling *when, where, how,*
or *to what degree* an action occurred. Many adverbs end in *-ly (certainly, hun-
grily, really),* but not all of them do. Adverbs can appear anywhere in a sentence.

> She **unhappily** does her homework. (does it *how?*)
> The rooster crowed **loudly.** (crowed *how?*)
> We are having a party **tomorrow.** (are having a party *when?*)
> We should go **home.** (go *where?*)
> They were **very** surprised. (surprised *to what degree?*)

Adverbs can be phrases as well as individual words.

> We threw her **into the pool.** (threw her *where?*)
> I want your answer **by next week.** (want it *when?*)

NOTE: Answers to the question *What?* are direct objects, not adverbs.

>   *direct object adverb*
> She stubbed her *toe* **on the bed post.**

The question *Stubbed what?* is answered by *toe,* which is the direct object. The
question *Stubbed where?* is answered by *on the bed post,* which is the adverb.
For more on direct objects, see The Basic Sentence section of this Handbook.

EXERCISE 5

Circle all of the adverbs in each of the following sentences.

1. She finished her homework early.

2. The doctor will see you on Wednesday.

3. The snake slithered through the grass slowly.

4. I picked up the mail from the post office.

5. We cheered on our team loudly and enthusiastically.

6. Clearly, you work hard.

7. I will let you know by Monday.

8. Fortunately, the plane landed safely.

9. Excitedly, we began the new project.

10. Patty passed the note to him.

For practice identifying adverbs in sentences, go to http://www.college
.hmco.com/pic/dolphinwriterthree.

Conjunctive adverbs show the close relationship between complete sentences or independent clauses, often joined by a semicolon. Conjunctive adverbs help you show relationships such as the following:

Comparison: likewise, similarly, nevertheless
Addition: furthermore, moreover, additionally, also, further
Contrast: similarly, however, instead, nonetheless, otherwise, although
Time: meanwhile, finally, next, then, still
Result: accordingly, hence, consequently, therefore

Like adjectives, some adverbs can have comparative and superlative forms. Usually, you add the word *more* to form the comparative and *most* to form the superlative.

Adverb	*Comparative*	*Superlative*
bravely	more bravely	most bravely
quick	more quickly	most quickly
rudely	more rudely	most rudely

Of all the people I spoke to, Ellen behaved **most rudely.**
This shrub grows **more quickly** than that shrub does.

Prepositions

Prepositions are words or groups of words that show how a noun or pronoun, called an *object of the preposition,* is related to the rest of the sentence. Many prepositions show position or time orientation:

about	before	but	into	over
above	behind	by	like	past

across	below	despite	near	through
after	beneath	down	of	to
against	beside	during	off	toward
along	between	except	on	under
among	beyond	for	onto	underneath
around	in	unlike	until	up
from	on	upon	at	with
without	out	outside		

Others are phrases:

according to	ahead of	along with
as far as	as well as	aside from
because of	in back of	in case of
in front of	in spite of	instead of
on account of	together with	with respect to

A **prepositional phrase** consists of a preposition, its object (which is always a noun or a pronoun), and the object's modifiers. For example, look at this prepositional phrase:

preposition   *object*

behind the short bush

    modifiers

In sentences, prepositional phrases can function as either adjectives or adverbs.

Adverb: The plate broke **into a million pieces.** (broke *how?*)
Adjective: The man **with the red coat** is my father. (*which* man?)

EXERCISE 6

In the following sentences, circle the prepositions and underline the objects of prepositions.

1. Marci went to the ballet on Tuesday.

2. She is not from Thailand.

3. Before today, we had no knowledge of the problem.

4. Until now, she had never completed anything.

5. In spite of my warnings, the dog bit her on the leg.

6. That joke went over my head.

7. Between you and me, this makes no sense.

8. Look for the index in the back of the book.

9. What is a little gossip among friends?

10. The restroom is the first door down the hall on your left.

For practice identifying prepositions in sentences, go to http://www.college .hmco.com/pic/dolphinwriterthree.

Conjunctions

Conjunctions connect and show relationships between words, phrases, or clauses. The seven **coordinating conjunctions** that can link any type of elements together are

and	yet
but	so
or	for
nor	

not this **but** that (words)
for love **or** for money (phrases)
We are out of mustard, **so** we cannot have hotdogs. (clauses)

Some conjunctions come in pairs; they are called the **correlative conjunctions.**

both/and	not/but
neither/nor	whether/or
either/or	not only/but also

Both the parents **and** the children look forward to summer vacation.
Either you are with us, **or** you are against us.

Other conjunctions link dependent clauses to independent clauses. A *clause* is a group of words with a subject and a verb. An *independent clause* can stand alone as a complete sentence, but a *dependent clause* cannot. The following list contains conjunctions that begin dependent clauses and show the relationship between dependent and independent clauses. These are called **subordinating conjunctions.**

after	because	provided	where
although	before	since	whereas

as	but that	so that	wherever
as if	if	until	while
as long as	in order that	when	notwithstanding
as soon as	whenever		

*subordinating
conjunction*

While I waited, she ran some errands.

dependent clause   independent clause

*subordinating
conjunction*

We cancelled the outdoor party **because** it was snowing.

independent clause   dependent clause

NOTE: You probably noticed that some of the words in the list of conjunctions can also be prepositions. To tell them apart, determine whether the word is part of a phrase or a clause.

She finished **before** dinner. (preposition)
She finished **before** we ate breakfast. (conjunction)

EXERCISE 7

Circle all of the conjunctions in each of the following sentences.

1. Whenever I go to the store, I always forget something.

2. After lunch, Chris took a nap, and Yolanda went for a jog.

3. I will help you as long as you help yourself first.

4. I wanted to shop, but you changed my mind.

5. Because Diane takes many business trips, she prefers staying home on the weekends.

6. Pat will make chicken and broccoli in an Asian sauce for dinner.

7. Either he goes, or I do.

8. We do not have a lot of money, yet we manage to take a vacation every year.

9. He does not ski, nor does he surf.

10. She loves her job, so she does not mind working long hours.

For practice identifying conjunctions in sentences, go to http://www.college
.hmco.com/pic/dolphinwriterthree.

Interjections

Interjections are words or phrases that express emotion or surprise.

>**Oh,** you scared me.
>**Darn!** We lost again.
>**Hey!** He looks great.

Because of their informality, interjections are rarely appropriate in academic and
professional writing.

For practice identifying different parts of speech in sentences, go to http://
www.college.hmco.com/pic/dolphinwriterthree.

The Basic Sentence

Now that you have reviewed the eight parts of speech, you can begin to see how
words are put together to form sentences. Once you learn about basic sentences,
you can begin to understand how to make your own sentences interesting, sophisticated, and grammatically correct.

A **simple sentence** is defined as one independent clause only. An independent clause is a group of words that can stand alone as a separate sentence because it contains both a subject (a noun or pronoun that causes the action or is
in some state of being) and a verb. A simple sentence can also contain other
parts of speech, such as adverbs or prepositions, but it includes just one subject-
verb relationship.

>**Key Terms**
>
>**Simple sentence** = one independent clause.
>**Independent clause** = a group of words that can stand alone as a separate sentence;
>it contains a subject and a verb.
>**Subject** = a noun or a pronoun that causes the action or is in some state of being.
>**Verb*** = a word that shows action or expresses a state of being

*Verbs are covered in more detail later in this section of the Handbook.

subject verb

We   ate   soup.

     subject   verb

The candidate spoke from the podium.

Subjects

The **subject** of a sentence is always a noun or a pronoun. Therefore, when you are trying to identify the subject, find all of the nouns and pronouns first. Next, find the verb, the word or words that express action or a state of being. (Verbs are discussed in detail later.) Then ask yourself *Who or what is performing the action or expressing some state of being?* For example, look at the following sentence:

She yelled her greeting across the field.

There are two nouns and one pronoun in this sentence.

pronoun   noun   noun

She yelled her **greeting** across the **field.**

Thus, the subject of the sentence is either *she, greeting,* or *field.* Now, what is the action being performed? The past-tense verb in this sentence is *yelled.* Who is doing this calling? It is *she,* so *she* is the subject of the sentence.

Can you identify the subjects in the following sentences?

The microwave broke yesterday.
English is my favorite subject.
I cannot find my clarinet.

In the preceding sentences, the subjects are *microwave, English,* and *I.*

Locations of Subjects

You have probably noticed that subjects often appear at or near the beginning of sentences. However, they can also follow the verb:

    verb   subject

Here   is   an   **apple.** (In this sentence, *here* is an adverb, not the subject.)

      verb   subject

In the car sat the **dog.**

In questions, too, the subject may follow the verb or part of the verb.

verb   *subject*   *verb*

Can   **you**   go with us tomorrow?

To determine the subject in a question, you can mentally rearrange the sentence so that it is a statement:

subject   *verb*

You   can go with us tomorrow.

Now it is easier to see that the subject is *you*.

In sentences that make commands or requests, the subject often is not stated. Instead, it is implied:

Go get my raincoat.
Please come to my party.

The subject of both these sentences is *you*. Although the word does not appear in either sentence, it is understood that the person to whom the sentence is directed is to perform the action.

EXERCISE 8

Circle the subject in each of the following sentences. If the subject is implied, write the implied subject beside the sentence.

1. Annie is my best friend.

2. *General Hospital* is a long-running afternoon soap opera.

3. You should have dinner ready at 6:00 p.m.

4. Does the library rent DVDs?

5. Please wipe your feet.

6. Alex baby-sits my children.

7. What did he think of my latest article?

8. The light bulb in the lamp broke.

9. Here is my donation.

10. Be polite!

For practice identifying the subjects of sentences, go to http://www.college .hmco.com/pic/dolphinwriterthree.

Simple and Complete Subjects

So far, you have been identifying just the simple subject of a sentence. The **simple subject** is a single noun or pronoun. A **complete subject,** on the other hand, is the subject along with all of its modifiers (the articles and adjectives that limit or describe it).

> **Our fabulous trip** included a trip to Disney World.

In this sentence, *trip* is the simple subject, and *our fabulous trip* is the complete subject.

> **A desire to save lives** led him to become a paramedic.

In this sentence, *desire* is the simple subject, and *a desire to save lives* is the complete subject.

Do not forget that a noun phrase can be the subject of a sentence:

> **Exploring the South Pole** was an incredible achievement.

To review noun phrases, see the Parts of Speech section of this Handbook.

EXERCISE 9

Circle the complete subject in each of the following sentences.

1. The playful puppies wrestled in the backyard.
2. My beautiful mother has blonde hair.
3. Performing ballet has been one of her dreams.
4. Do you hear that funny noise?
5. Writing a novel was my long-term goal.
6. Becoming a chef was Fran's greatest achievement.
7. A groomed dog looks neat and clean.
8. Her spoiled son cries a lot.
9. Cooking a great meal makes me happy.
10. Your oldest sister is quite gorgeous.

For practice identifying complete subjects in sentences, go to http://www.college.hmco.com/pic/dolphinwriterthree.

Compound Subjects

A **compound subject** is defined as two or more subjects joined by the word *and,* *or,* or *nor.*

> *subject*   *subject*
>
> The **dentist** and his **wife** are going to Barcelona.

> *subject* *subject*
>
> **Francisco** or **I** will pick you up.

> *subject*   *subject*
>
> Neither the **cat** nor the **dog** can swim.

EXERCISE 10

Circle all of the compound subjects in the following sentences.

1. In that section are videos and DVDs.
2. Neither the dog nor the cat ate its food.
3. Did you or Luisa wash the dishes?
4. On his shelf are trophies and awards.
5. Seeing the Eiffel Tower and visiting museums are two things to do in Paris.
6. Where are Rob and Sarah going to college next fall?
7. Bowling and snowboarding are his favorite hobbies.
8. Either Julio or Akilah will unlock the door.
9. Schools, banks, and the post office are often closed on holidays.
10. Answering the phone and making photocopies are two of Farid's responsibilities.

For practice identifying compound subjects in sentences, go to http://www.college.hmco.com/pic/dolphinwriterthree.

Subjects Versus Objects of Prepositions

Often, it can be easy to confuse a subject with the object of a preposition. The object of a preposition cannot be the subject of a sentence, so you might want to identify all prepositional phrases before you decide what the subject is.

One of the girls in the class is on the gymnastics team.

The nouns in this sentence are *one*, *girls*, *class*, and *team*. To identify the ones that are objects of prepositions, draw parentheses around all of the prepositional phrases.

> One of the girls in the class is on the gymnastics team.

Now it is much easier to see that *one* is the simple subject of the sentence. Refer back to pages 460–461 for a list of the prepositions.

EXERCISE 11

In each of the following sentences, put parentheses around all of the prepositional phrases and then circle the simple subject.

1. Driving to Philadelphia took four hours.
2. Dancing in high heels is dangerous.
3. Three of his sisters go to the university.
4. Several of the ushers were related to the groom.
5. The man with the big dog walks along my street on the weekend.
6. Flying to Bermuda during the hurricane was scary.
7. On the back of the book is a photograph of the author.
8. In the trunk was a set of golf clubs.
9. I clapped with glee at the puppet show.
10. In an instant, the whole plate of cookies vanished.

> *For practice identifying subjects among prepositional phrases, go to* http://www.college.hmco.com/pic/dolphinwriterthree.

Other Elements of Simple Sentences

As mentioned earlier, a simple sentence must contain both a subject and a verb. It can also include a direct object, an indirect object, modifiers, and appositives.

Verbs

A **verb** is defined as a word or a phrase that expresses action or a state of being. Verbs are discussed in detail in the next section of this Handbook. Note, however, that verbs—like subjects—can be **compound**.

They **ate** a picnic lunch and **played** Frisbee.

In this sentence, the subject, *They,* is performing two actions, so there are two verbs.

EXERCISE 12

Circle all of the verbs and verb phrases in the following sentences. Watch for compound verbs, and make sure that you circle both verbs.

1. My house is very small.

2. We talked and watched the Super Bowl last week.

3. Dianne dances with a famous troupe.

4. Rose sings in her church choir and plays the piano.

5. What is the right answer?

6. I walked to his house from my office.

7. This is the right way to handle the situation.

8. Her children fight and argue much of the time.

9. The dolphins jumped and frolicked in the surf.

10. Consider the consequences of your actions.

For practice identifying verbs in sentences, go to http://www.college.hmco.com/pic/dolphinwriterthree.

Direct Objects

A simple sentence may or may not include a direct object. A **direct object** is a noun or pronoun that answers the question *whom?* or *what?* for an action verb.

verb direct object
He lost his **watch.**   (lost *what?*)

To find the direct object in a sentence, you will need to locate the verb first.

She wrote the letter with tears in her eyes.

In this sentence, the verb is *wrote*. Now ask the question *wrote what?* The answer is *letter*, which is the direct object.

We thanked her for the generosity.

In this sentence, the verb is *thanked*. When you ask the question *thanked whom?* the answer is *her*, which is the direct object.

Direct objects can be compound, just as subjects and verbs can.

       direct object   direct object

He sings **jazz** and **opera.**

        direct object   direct object

She set the **package** and the **keys** on the table.

EXERCISE 13

Circle the direct object(s) in each of the following sentences.

1. You read that poem beautifully.
2. She sings pop and hip-hop.
3. Connie loves television.
4. The lawyer read the testimony.
5. I studied biology in high school.
6. Henry enjoys movies and plays.
7. The church collected funds for its renovation.
8. Please mail this package.
9. Isabel sent an e-mail to Charlie.
10. Check your dog for fleas.

For practice identifying direct objects in sentences, go to http://www.college .hmco.com/pic/dolphinwriterthree.

Indirect Objects

A simple sentence may or may not include an indirect object. An **indirect object** answers the question *to whom, for whom, to what,* or *for what?* for an action verb.

> *indirect object*
>
> He gave his **friend** a present.   (gave *to whom?*)

To find the indirect object, locate the verb first.

> My brother gave me his car.

In this sentence, the verb is *gave.* To find the direct object, you ask *gave what?* The answer is *car.* To find the indirect object, ask *gave to whom?* The answer is *me,* which is the indirect object.

Like direct objects, indirect objects can be compound:

> *indirect object*   *indirect object*
>
> My grandfather left his **children** and his **grandchildren** all of his money.

EXERCISE 14

Circle the indirect object(s) in each of the following sentences.

1. I bought my sister show tickets.
2. Jose wrote Andrea a poem.
3. Molly gave me the phone number.
4. Michelle prepared Roberto and Barry dinner.
5. I gave him some books.
6. The nurse handed the patient a bandage.
7. Please give me and Patty your address before the end of the day.
8. They sent the secretary a bouquet.
9. We found the dog a home.
10. Jim left the waiter twenty dollars.

For practice identifying indirect objects in sentences, go to http://www.college.hmco.com/pic/dolphinwriterthree.

Modifiers

A simple sentence may include **modifiers,** which are adjectives or adverbs. You learned in the section about parts of speech that adjectives, which modify nouns or pronouns, can be single words or phrases:

adjective

She stopped speaking to her **disloyal** friend.   [*Disloyal* describes the noun *friend.*]

adjective

The cast **of the play** took a bow.   [The prepositional phrase *of the play* answers the question *which cast?*]

Adverbs, which modify verbs, adjectives, or other adverbs, can also be single words or phrases:

adverb

He speaks **quickly.**   [The adverb *quickly* answers the question *speaks how?*]

adverb

She studied **until dinner.**   [The prepositional phrase *until dinner* answers the question *studied when?*]

adverb

He was **very** tired.   [*Very* is an adverb that modifies the adjective *tired.*]

For more on adjectives and adverbs, see The Basic Sentence section of this Handbook.

EXERCISE 15

Circle the adjectives and underline the adverbs in the following sentences.

1. A soft rain fell this morning.

2. The efficient assistant types fast.

3. The frazzled father fell asleep in the chair.

4. Quickly, I ran through the dark parking lot.

5. This computer works well.

6. Fortunately, I can attend the glamorous ball.

7. A good student studies every evening.

8. Three conscientious members attended the board meeting and listened carefully.

9. Was that bus the very last one?

10. The daily newspaper includes extremely important articles on gardening.

For practice identifying adjectives and adverbs in sentences, go to http://www.college.hmco.com/pic/dolphinwriterthree.

Appositives

Simple sentences might include appositives. An **appositive** is a noun or a noun phrase that follows a noun or a pronoun and renames it.

> *appositive*
> Our neighbor, **Mr. Franklin,** rides a moped. (*Mr. Franklin* renames *neighbor.*)

An appositive phrase includes the appositive and all of its modifiers:

> *appositive phrase*
> John, **the worst player on our team,** scored the winning basket.

In this sentence, *player* is the appositive that renames *John,* and the other words in the phrase modify the word *player.*

EXERCISE 16

Circle the appositive or appositive phrase in each of the following sentences.

1. Bon Jovi, my favorite band, was performing at the concert.

2. Jack Kerouac, a member of the Beat Generation, wrote many stories.

3. Two of my friends, Melissa and George, exercise daily.

4. *What Not to Wear,* a makeover show, is one of my favorites.

5. September 11, the anniversary of the terrorist attacks, is a sad day.

6. Pinot Grigio, a white wine, has become very popular.

7. My favorite movie, *King Kong,* starred Faye Wray.

8. Mr. Espinoza, my English teacher, has published a novel.

9. Tilapia, a type of fish, is delicious.

10. Do you, an avid reader, recommend joining a book club?

For practice identifying appositives in sentences, go to http://www.college.hmco.com/pic/dolphinwriterthree.

Avoiding Sentence Fragments

To be complete, a sentence must contain a subject and a verb. When either is lacking, a sentence fragment results. Notice how both of the following examples lack subjects:

> Made her sad.
> Found my keys in the car.

Adding subjects, though, will make them complete:

> *subject*
> The romantic **movie** made her sad.

subject
> **I** found my keys in the car.

The following examples lack verbs:

> Only one of the dishes.
> Mr. Kaplan, my favorite neighbor.

Adding verbs will make them complete:

> *verb*
> Only one of the dishes **broke.**

> *verb*
> Mr. Kaplan, my favorite neighbor, **is moving.**

For information about avoiding other types of sentence fragments, see pages 486, 494, and 540.

For practice identifying sentence fragments, go to http://www.college.hmco.com/pic/dolphinwriterthree.

Verbs

In the previous sections of this Handbook, you learned that a verb is the word (or words) in a sentence that expresses the subject's action or state of being. In this section, you will examine in more detail the various features of verbs. Knowing how to use verbs correctly will strengthen your writing significantly.

Action Verbs and Linking Verbs

There are two kinds of verbs, action verbs and linking verbs. **Action verbs** express action of some kind.

> She **thought** about the book.
> He **studied** night and day.
> They **swam** in the ocean.

Linking verbs express some state of being:

am	appear
is	seem
are	become
was	grow
were	remain

> I **am** amazed. (*amazed* describes *I*)
> That man **is** a sales representative. (*sales representative* renames *man*)
> They **appear** elated after the trip to Chile. (*elated* describes *they*)

NOTE: The verbs *am, is, are, was,* and *were* can also be helping verbs that are part of action verbs. Helping verbs are discussed later in this section.
Or linking verbs can relate to the senses:

look	sound
smell	feel
taste	

> Her meatloaf **smells** wonderful.
> I **feel** grouchy.
> The chocolate cake **tastes** like heaven.

EXERCISE 17

In each of the following sentences, circle the verb and write on the blank whether it is an *action verb* or a *linking verb*.

_____   **1.** She drinks hot tea every night.

_____   **2.** Janet is happy about the new baby.

_____   **3.** That hairstyle looks beautiful on her.

_____   **4.** I feel like a winner!

_____   **5.** David walks to school every day.

_____   **6.** Florence studies every night.

_____   **7.** I am interested in the story.

_____   **8.** She enters many competitions.

_____   **9.** Marisol becomes more restless every second.

_____   **10.** Stuart teaches seventh grade science.

For practice identifying action verbs and linking verbs in sentences, go to http://www.college.hmco.com/pic/dolphinwriterthree.

Verb Tense

Verbs always express time, which is called **tense.** Two of the basic tenses, or simple tenses, are present tense and past tense. (The other is future tense, which is discussed later in this section.) **Present-tense verbs** indicate that the action or state of being is occurring now or is ongoing.

> I **am** tired.
> They **adore** each other.
> He **wants** to begin a new life.
> She **cooks** dinner on Mondays.

The form of a present-tense verb often changes based on whether the subject is *singular* (meaning that it refers to just one person or thing) or *plural* (referring to more than one thing).

Singular	*Plural*
I ask	we ask
you ask	you ask
he, she, it asks	they ask

Notice that the singular form that goes with *he, she,* and *it* has an -*s* on the end. The other forms do not. This is the case with many verbs that are *regular,* that is, conform to predictable patterns. The following are a few more regular verbs that add an -*s* to certain forms.

> I stop, he stops
> You ride, she rides
> I speak, it speaks

Past-tense verbs indicate that the action or state of being happened completely in the past.

> I **was** tired.
> They **adored** each other.
> He **wanted** to start a new life.
> She **cooked** dinner on Mondays.

To form the past tense of regular verbs, you add -*ed*, -*d*, or -*ied*, depending on how the base form ends. The following are some examples.

Base Form	*Past Tense*
wink	winked
learn	learned
start	started
stop	stopped
rub	rubbed

When the base form of the word ends in a consonant, you will usually add -*ed* to form the past tense. Sometimes forming the past tense requires doubling the final consonant of the verb and then adding -*ed*, as you saw in the last two examples in the preceding list.

Base Form	*Past Tense*
like	liked
hope	hoped
change	changed
file	filed

For regular verbs that end in -*e*, you will usually add just a -*d*, as you saw in the preceding examples.

Base Form	*Past Tense*
cry	cried
carry	carried
satisfy	satisfied

For regular verbs that end in -*y*, you will usually drop the -*y* and add -*ied*, as shown in the preceding examples.

EXERCISE 18

In each of the following sentences, write on the blank the correct form of the verb contained in parentheses.

1. Yesterday, Lane _____ about you. (*ask*)

2. When she lived there, she _____ the house. (*clean*)

3. Every time he brings up the subject, she _____ it. (*change*)

4. Paul throws the ball, and his dog _____ it. (*fetch*)

5. They _____ the two numbers while she waited. (*multiply*)

6. At last year's show, I _____ for a good turnout. (*hope*)

7. The frog _____ into the pond when we startled it. (*hop*)

8. Every day, we _____ our teeth. (*brush*)

9. Last night, I _____ the potatoes. (*roast*)

10. At this moment, he _____ water. (*need*)

For practice using the correct forms of past-tense and present-tense verbs, go to http://www.college.hmco.com/pic/dolphinwriterthree.

Helping Verbs

Past and present are two of the basic tenses. A third basic tense is the **future tense,** which indicates that the action or state of being will occur in the future. To indicate the future tense, as well as more specific types of the other two simple tenses, helping verbs are added to the main verb. The **helping verbs** are

is	be	may	would
am	can	might	has
are	could	must	have
was	do	shall	
were	does	should	
been	did	will	

The following lists show examples of verbs in the present, past, and future tenses.

Base Form (Present Tense)	Past Tense	Future Tense
like	liked	will like
hope	hoped	will hope
change	changed	will change
file	filed	will file
cry	cried	will cry
carry	carried	will carry
satisfy	satisfied	will satisfy

Different combinations of helping verbs and main verbs allow speakers of English to indicate different times and qualities of verbs. In particular, some of these helping verbs allow us to express twelve different verb tenses, which are summarized in the following table.

Present	I work
	He works
	They work
Past	I worked
	He worked
	They worked
Future	I **will** work
	He **will** work
	They **will** work
Present Perfect	I **have** worked
	He **has** worked
	They **have** worked
Past Perfect	I **had** worked
	He **had** worked
	They **had** worked
Future Perfect	I **will have** worked
	He **will have** worked
	They **will have** worked
Present Progressive	I **am** working
	He **is** working
	They **are** working

Past Progressive	I **was** working
	He **was** working
	They **were** working
Future Progressive	I **will be** working
	He **will be** working
	They **will be** working
Present Perfect Progressive	I **have been** working
	He **has been** working
	They **have been** working
Past Perfect Progressive	I **had been** working
	He **had been** working
	They **had been** working
Future Perfect Progressive	I **will have been** working
	He **will have been** working
	They **will have been** working

Other helping verbs express different qualities of the action (such as ability, possibility, or necessity) or are used to form questions.

> She **can work** tomorrow.
> They **do** not **work** as hard as she does.
> **Do** you **work** on Tuesdays?
> He **could be** at work.
> You **should have been working.**
> **May** I **work** with you?

The main verb combined with its helping verb or verbs is called a **verb phrase**.

EXERCISE 19

Circle the verb phrases in the following sentences.

1. She has been investing money for years.

2. Will he be applying for that job?

3. She will help you with the project.

4. Are you leaving tomorrow?

5. I can carry your groceries.

6. You have qualified for the loan.

7. Should we talk about this issue later on today?

8. Did Javier achieve his goal?

9. Frances is causing problems.

10. Shall we dance?

For practice identifying verb phrases in sentences, go to http://www.college .hmco.com/pic/dolphinwriterthree.

Irregular Verbs

So far, you have focused only on regular verbs, the verbs that change forms according to predictable patterns. However, there is another category of verbs called *irregular verbs*. **Irregular verbs** are those verbs that change form in different tenses and when forming the *past participle*, the form of the verb that is used with the helping verbs *has*, *have*, and *had*. Whereas the past-participle form of regular verbs is usually the same as the past-tense form (he *worked*, he has *worked*), the past-participle form of irregular verbs is different from the past-tense form (it *flew*, it has *flown*). The following list includes many common irregular verbs.

Base Form	Present Tense	Past Tense	Past Participle
arise	arises	arose	arisen
be	is	was/were	been
bear	bears	bore	borne
begin	begins	began	begun
bite	bites	bit	bitten/bit
blow	blows	blew	blown
break	breaks	broke	broken
bring	brings	brought	brought
buy	buys	bought	bought
catch	catches	caught	caught
choose	chooses	chose	chosen
come	comes	came	come
creep	creeps	crept	crept
dive	dives	dived/dove	dived
do	does	did	done
draw	draws	drew	drawn
dream	dreams	dreamed/dreamt	dreamt

Base Form	Present Tense	Past Tense	Past Participle
drink	drinks	drank	drunk
drive	drives	drove	driven
eat	eats	ate	eaten
fall	falls	fell	fallen
fight	fights	fought	fought
fly	flies	flew	flown
forget	forgets	forgot	forgotten
forgive	forgives	forgave	forgiven
freeze	freezes	froze	frozen
get	gets	got	got/gotten
give	gives	gave	given
go	goes	went	gone
grow	grows	grew	grown
hang	hangs	hung	hung
hide	hides	hid	hidden
know	knows	knew	known
lay	lays	laid	laid
lead	leads	led	led
lie	lies	lay	lain
light	lights	lit	lit
lose	loses	lost	lost
prove	proves	proved	proved/proven
ride	rides	rode	ridden
ring	rings	rang	rung
rise	rises	rose	risen
run	runs	ran	run
see	sees	saw	seen
seek	seeks	sought	sought
set	sets	set	set
shake	shakes	shook	shaken
sing	sings	sang	sung
sink	sinks	sank	sunk
sit	sits	sat	sat
speak	speaks	spoke	spoken
spring	springs	sprang	sprung
steal	steals	stole	stolen
sting	stings	stung	stung
strike	strikes	struck	struck
swear	swears	swore	sworn
swim	swims	swam	swum
swing	swings	swung	swung
take	takes	took	taken

Base Form	Present Tense	Past Tense	Past Participle
tear	tears	tore	torn
throw	throws	threw	thrown
wake	wakes	woke/waked	woken/waked/woke
wear	wears	wore	worn
write	writes	wrote	written

EXERCISE 20

In each of the following sentences, write on the blank the correct form of the verb contained in parentheses.

1. Have you _____ this blouse before? (*tear*)

2. The students have _____ their test. (*take*)

3. I _____ her a month ago. (*forgive*)

4. The staff has already _____ home. (*go*)

5. After they finished dinner, Shawn _____ out the candles. (*blow*)

6. In the last game of the season, Harry finally _____ a touchdown. (*make*)

7. I have been _____ to participate. (*choose*)

8. The dog _____ the cake that fell on the floor. (*eat*)

9. She _____ the bat and missed the ball. (*swing*)

10. Pete _____ a pole with his car yesterday. (*strike*)

For practice using the correct forms of irregular verbs, go to **http://www .college.hmco.com/pic/dolphinwriterthree.**

Verbals

As you are learning to identify verbs in sentences, you will need to watch for words called **verbals** that look like verbs but function as other parts of speech in sentences. There are three kinds of verbals: *infinitives, gerunds,* and *participles.*

An **infinitive** is composed of the word *to* plus the base form of the verb. Infinitives often act as nouns in sentences:

He wanted **to drive.** (The infinitive *to drive* is a direct object that answers the question *wanted what?*)

To write was her only goal. (*To write* is the subject of the sentence.)

Infinitive phrases include the infinitive and its modifiers, objects, and/or complements.

> He wanted **to drive all day long.**
> **To write a best-selling novel** was her only goal.

A **gerund,** which is a verb form with -*ing* on the end, functions as a noun.

> **Losing** was not easy. (*Losing* is the subject of this sentence.)
> He loved **swimming.** (*Swimming* is the direct object.)

A gerund phrase includes the gerund and its modifiers, objects, and/or complements.

> **Losing the race** was not easy.
> He loved **swimming in the pool.**

Participles are verb forms that end in -*ed* or -*ing*. They function as adjectives in sentences.

> **Dancing,** he fell and broke his leg. (*Dancing* is an adjective that describes *he.*)
> I caught her **stealing.** (*Stealing* is an adjective that describes *her.*)
> He was a fugitive **hunted** in three states. (*Hunted* is an adjective that modifies *fugitive.*)

As you see in the third example, a participle phrase consists of a participle and its modifiers, objects, and/or complements. Modifiers in participle phrases can be prepositional phrases:

> **Dancing on the slippery floor,** he fell and broke his leg.
> I caught her **stealing a pack of gum.**

EXERCISE 21

In each of the following sentences, circle the verbal and then write on the blank whether it is an *infinitive*, a *gerund,* or a *participle.*

_____ **1.** The girl dancing in the middle is my daughter.

_____ **2.** Skating is my hobby.

_____ **3.** To attend camp is Dee's dream.

_____ **4.** He wanted to help.

_____ **5.** He was a lawyer desired by every major firm in Chicago.

_____ **6.** Singing well is a goal of mine.

_____ **7.** Diving can be dangerous.

_____ **8.** A driver following another car too closely often runs into it.

_____ **9.** She wants to learn Arabic.

_____ **10.** They are working on memorizing all of the irregular verbs.

For practice identifying verbals in sentences, go to http://www.college .hmco.com/pic/dolphinwriterthree.

Avoiding Sentence Fragments

Verbals cannot stand alone. They must be attached to an independent clause; otherwise, they are sentence fragments. For example, read the following sentences.

> *sentence fragment*
>
> **Dancing and singing songs.** The performers put on a show.

> *sentence fragment*
>
> He set a goal. **To complete his master's degree.**

Both of these sets of an independent clause and a fragment must be combined to eliminate the fragments.

For information about avoiding other kinds of sentence fragments, see pages 475, 494, and 540 of this Handbook.

For practice recognizing sentence fragments, go to http://www.college.hmco .com/pic/dolphinwriterthree.

Writing Better Sentences

You can write better, more interesting sentences of your own by paying more attention to your choice of verbs. In particular, avoid using too many passive-voice verbs, choose strong verbs instead of weak ones, and make sure that the tenses of your verbs are consistent.

Passive Versus Active Voice. We can write sentences in either of two basic ways. The first uses **active voice,** in which the subject of the sentence is the performer of the action.

> *subject   verb direct object*
>
> Jim   pruned the hedge.

The active voice, which shows the subject performing an action, is clear and direct. In **passive-voice** sentences, on the other hand, the *receiver* of the action (the direct object in the active voice sentence), instead of the performer, is the subject. The performer of the action, Jim, is now the object of the preposition.

subject	verb	object of preposition
The hedge	was pruned	by Jim.

In this version, the reader has to wait until the end of the sentence to find out who performed the action. This type of sentence is less interesting and less energetic than an active-voice sentence. It also tends to include unnecessary words.

However, the passive voice is appropriate in some sentences. If you do not know who the performer of the action is, passive voice permits you to leave out that information:

The dishwasher was turned off sometime during dinner.

In addition, if you want to omit the subject to conceal who was responsible for an action, then passive voice may be appropriate:

Mistakes were definitely made.

The point is that the passive voice should be used intentionally rather than accidentally. In most instances, if the subject is known, the active voice is the better, more interesting choice.

EXERCISE 22

On the blanks provided, rewrite each of the following sentences, changing the passive voice to the active voice.

1. All of the hamburgers were eaten by the children.

_____

2. The radio was listened to by Allegra.

_____

3. The test was taken by all of the students.

_____

4. The spaghetti was served by Marie.

_____

5. Damage was done by the hurricane.

_____

6. The birthday party was enjoyed by my friends.

_____

7. The chocolate pudding was eaten by the adults.

_____

8. The TV show _American Idol_ is watched by my family.

_____

9. The portrait was painted by me.

_____

10. The house was designed by Victor.

_____

For practice rewriting passive-voice sentences, go to http://www.college
.hmco.com/pic/dolphinwriterthree.

Strong Verbs Versus Weak Verbs. Clear, interesting writing always includes strong action verbs. The more descriptive the verb, the sharper the image it produces in the reader's mind. Compare these next two sets of examples:

Weak: At our tag sale, we **will have** free baked goods.
Strong: At our tag sale, we **will give away** free baked goods.

Weak: He **comes** in every morning.
Strong: He **saunters** in every morning.

In the second sentence of the first set of examples, a more action-oriented verb brings more vitality to the sentence. In the second sentence of the second set of examples, a more specific verb conveys more information about _how_ the subject moves.

As you write, you may tend to choose weaker verbs because they are the first ones that occur to you. Using _to be_ and _to have_ verbs, in particular, often drains the life from a sentence.

Weak: He **was** all over the room.
Strong: He **paced** the room.

Weak: He **has** a great love for beagles.
Strong: He **adores** beagles.

Notice how the second sentence of each pair conveys the same information as the first sentence but does so with more action and energy. Beware, too, of writing too many sentences that begin with the words *there is/are* or *it is.* Although this wording can sometimes be an appropriate way to begin a sentence, the sentence will automatically include a weak *to be* verb. Notice how each of the following revisions improves the sentence.

Weak: There are many reasons why I am against the idea.
Strong: I oppose the idea for many reasons.

Weak: It is important that we stop spending so much time on the computer.
Strong: We must stop spending so much time on the computer.

When you see sentences in your own writing that begin with *there is/are* or *it is,* try to rewrite them to eliminate those words and substitute stronger verbs.

As you are evaluating the strength of your verbs, be aware that the best verb choice can be lurking elsewhere in the sentence as another part of speech:

We **have been having** quite a few calls of complaint.

This sentence relies on a weak *to have* verb. But notice the word *calls,* which is functioning as the direct object, as well as the word *complaint,* which is hiding in a prepositional phrase at the very end of the sentence. Another form of either one of these words would be a better verb for this sentence, which needs a little rewriting:

People **are calling** often to complain.
Callers **are complaining** often.

Now look at the sentence that follows. Which word in this sentence would actually be better as a verb form?

We will have a short meeting to get prepared.

If you said that a form of the word *meeting* should be the verb, you are right. We could rewrite this sentence to read *We will meet briefly to get prepared.*

Also, ask yourself if you are overusing adjectives and adverbs instead of using strong verbs. For example, read the next sentence.

He walked quickly into the room.

The adverb *quickly* tells how he walked, but you could replace the phrase *walked quickly* with one strong verb, such as *strode, jogged,* or *trotted.* Here is another example:

Her eyes were very pretty and shiny in the sunlight.

You could substitute strong verbs for the weak verb *was* and the adjectives *pretty* and *shiny:*

Her eyes shone and sparkled in the sunlight.

EXERCISE 23

On the blanks provided, rewrite each of the following sentences to include a stronger verb.

1. There was a strange noise coming from the basement.

_____

2. I am very fond of Dawn.

_____

3. We took a plane ride to Paris.

_____

4. There were crocodiles floating in the river.

_____

5. There are a lot of things that we will discuss at the parent-teacher meeting.

_____

6. Mary Anne laughed hard and very loudly when she saw that hilarious movie.

_____

7. It is important that you listen to your parents.

_____

8. He was dishonest when he talked to me.

_____

9. The moon looked bright and glowing in the night sky.

_____

10. There are many reasons for Baker to agree to this plan.

_____

For practice rewriting sentences to include stronger verbs, go to http://www.college.hmco.com/pic/dolphinwriterthree.

Consistency in Verb Tense. As you write, you will want to make sure that you use verb tenses consistently. Mixing past and present tenses inappropriately can confuse readers. Note the shift in verb tense in the following sentence:

    present tense   *past tense*

We **shop** at Food Emporium, and I **bought** tomatoes.

The first verb, *shop,* should be in the past tense, *shopped.* We may shift tenses like this in casual conversation, but we should not write this way. If you start out in the past tense, remain in the past tense throughout the sentence and/or paragraph. If you start out in the present tense, remain in the present tense.

EXERCISE 24

In each of the following sentences, underline the two verbs. Then correct the second verb so that its tense matches that of the first verb. Write the corrected verb form on the blank following the sentence.

1. Last night, we went to the movies, but Sandy stays home. _____

2. We arrived home, and the doorbell rings. _____

3. Every morning, Marguerite puts on a dress and slipped on some shoes. _____

4. During the lecture, Tory took notes, but Joseph doodles in his notebook. _____

5. Gabriela plays the piano, and I danced. _____

6. Alicia invested in the stock market, but Morgan wastes his extra money on clothes. _____

7. Last year, we cleaned out the garage and donate many items to charity. _____

8. Every Christmas, she decorates the house and made cookies for all of her neighbors. _____

9. Every time you try something new, you gave up too soon. _____

10. We left for work at the same time, but Lynn gets there first. _____

For practice correcting errors in verb tense consistency, go to http://www.college.hmco.com/pic/dolphinwriterthree.

Modifiers: Adjectives and Adverbs

In previous sections of this Handbook, you learned that **modifiers** are either adjectives or adverbs. In this section, you will explore both kinds of modifiers in more detail.

Adjectives

Adjectives are words that describe or limit nouns. They tell *how many*, *what kind*, or *which one*.

blue pants	(*what kind?*)
fourth verse	(*which one?*)
that man	(*which one?*)
five students	(*how many?*)
several reasons	(*how many?*)

The **articles**—*a*, *an*, and *the*—are special kinds of adjectives that point out nouns.

the door
a dog
an angel

Adjectives can come before the noun, or they can follow the verb in a sentence with a linking verb.

She looks **gorgeous.**
He is **short, slim,** and **attractive.**

 **EXERCISE 25**

Circle the adjectives in each of the following sentences.

1. Tex wore a big black hat.

2. The squealing children sledded down the hill.

3. A loud, noisy fire engine roared past us.

4. Were the grammatical errors corrected?

5. Was that gold ring expensive?

6. The principal looks young and vivacious.

7. Mrs. Perry is a cheerful woman.

8. The yellow motorcycle won the race.

9. Mr. Diamond is a math whiz.

10. The white poodle barks a lot.

For practice identifying adjectives in sentences, go to http://www.college.hmco.com/pic/dolphinwriterthree.

Phrases That Function as Adjectives. Adjectives can be single words, or they can be phrases. Prepositional phrases, which you learned about in the section on parts of speech, can function as adjectives:

the man **in the window**	(the phrase describes *man*)
fudge **with marshmallows**	(the phrase describes *fudge*)
the shoe **on the floor**	(the phrase describes *shoe*)

Participle phrases also function as adjectives in sentences. A participle is a verb form that ends in *-ed* or *-ing*.

Skipping slowly, the child headed for the swing.
The hamburger **topped with cheese and onions** was delicious.
The cat **hissing its head off** belongs to me.

Notice that a phrase that functions as an adjective can come either before or after the noun it modifies.

EXERCISE 26

Circle the phrases that function as adjectives in each of the following sentences.

1. The audience in the auditorium was silent.

2. The woman next to me was cheering.

3. Running quickly, the lacrosse players took the field.

4. That sundae topped with hot fudge and whipped cream is mine.

5. The child lost in the woods was rescued.

6. Singing joyfully, the choir sounded wonderful.

7. The man in the back of the room is Fred's dad.

8. The people sitting in the front row had the best view.

9. Worried about the test, the students trudged into the classroom.

10. That gerbil running on the exercise wheel is entertaining.

For practice identifying phrases functioning as adjectives, go to **http://www.college.hmco.com/pic/dolphinwriterthree.**

Avoiding Sentence Fragments. Prepositional and participle phrases cannot stand alone; unless they are attached to an independent clause, they are sentence fragments. For example, read the following sentences:

sentence fragment

Dialing the phone slowly. Joe attempted to remember the number.

sentence fragment

She sat beside her ailing husband. **Through the whole day.**

In both examples the sentence (the independent clause) and the phrase must be combined to eliminate the fragment. For information about avoiding other kinds of sentence fragments, see pages 475, 486, and 540 of this Handbook.

For practice recognizing sentence fragments, go to http://www.college.hmco .com/pic/dolphinwriterthree.

Comparative and Superlative Forms of Adjectives. Most adjectives have two additional forms. One of them, the **comparative** form, is used to compare two things. The other, the **superlative** form, is used to compare three or more things.

Adjective	Comparative	Superlative
pretty	prettier	prettiest
young	younger	youngest
smart	smarter	smartest
dull	duller	dullest
hungry	hungrier	hungriest

Therefore, we would say, for example, that the rose is *prettier* than the daisy. But we would say that the rose is the *prettiest* flower in the whole bouquet.

As you can see in the preceding list, we often add *-er* to the end of the adjective to form the comparative form. We add *-est* to the end to form its superlative form. However, some adjectives keep the same spelling and add the word *more* to form the comparative and *most* to form the superlative.

Adjective	Comparative	Superlative
grateful	more grateful	most grateful
foolish	more foolish	most foolish
determined	more determined	most determined
gorgeous	more gorgeous	most gorgeous

Still other adjectives are irregular and change forms altogether.

Adjective	Comparative	Superlative
good	better	best
bad	worse	worst
little	less	least

| much, many, some | more | most |
| far | farther | farther |

EXERCISE 27

On the blank in each sentence, write the correct form of the adjective contained in parentheses.

1. He is _____ than she is. (*foolish*)

2. I am the _____ person in the world. (*happy*)

3. We have the _____ free time of all of our friends. (*little*)

4. Of all of the contestants, Kellie seemed _____. (*intelligent*)

5. Which of the five kittens is _____? (*cute*)

6. You are the _____ person I have ever met. (*honest*)

7. We own the _____ house in town. (*good*)

8. Which of the two options is _____? (*bad*)

9. That is the _____ thing I have ever done. (*bad*)

10. Bill Gates is the _____ man in America. (*wealthy*)

For practice using the correct forms of adjectives in sentences, go to **http:// www.college.hmco.com/pic/dolphinwriterthree.**

Punctuating Adjectives. When you use more than one adjective to describe a noun, you may need to separate the adjectives with a comma:

It was a **cold, windy** day.
The **thin, bare** tree swayed in the wind.

However, no comma is necessary in this sentence:

Let us get some **delicious Chinese** food.

To decide whether or not to include a comma, you mentally insert the word *and* between the two adjectives. If the sentence still makes sense, you will need to add a comma:

It was a cold **and** windy day.
The thin **and** bare tree swayed in the wind.

Both of these sentences require a comma between the two adjectives.

You can also try to reverse the two adjectives. If the sentence still makes sense, insert a comma:

It was a windy, cold day.

Notice that the adjectives in the earlier sentence cannot be reversed. You would not write this:

Let us get some **Chinese delicious** food.

Thus, no comma is added.

EXERCISE 28

In each of the following sentences, circle the adjectives (but not the articles) and add a comma between them if necessary. If no comma is necessary, write *No comma needed* beside the sentence.

1. The plane rose into the cloudless night sky.

2. My family needs a reliable honest babysitter.

3. There is nothing like a good hot cup of coffee.

4. I bought a light blue cashmere sweater.

5. The skinny funny-looking dog was finally adopted.

6. The bright red bird disappeared in the woods.

7. Our final essay exam was very easy.

8. The patients liked the optimistic competent nurse.

9. She looked cool calm and composed.

10. The tall ornate Byzantine church has a huge spire.

For practice punctuating adjectives in sentences, go to **http://www.college .hmco.com/pic/dolphinwriterthree.**

Adverbs

Adverbs are words that describe or limit verbs, adjectives, or other adverbs. They tell *where*, *when*, *how*, and *to what degree*.

Please put it **there.**   (put *where?*)
They will call **tomorrow.**   (will call *when?*)

She cried **loudly.**   (cried *how?*)
It is **very** lovely.   (lovely *to what degree?*)

Many adverbs end in *-ly (gracefully, terribly, poorly),* but others do not *(soon, later, so, here).*

Adverbs can appear anywhere in a sentence:

Recently, I saw Jack.
He is **usually** late.
I picked up the crumbs **carefully.**

EXERCISE 29

Circle the adverbs in each sentence.

1. Usually you are on time.

2. Sadly, Mike left Saturday.

3. They will arrive tomorrow.

4. I will be there later.

5. Taylor honked the horn repeatedly.

6. We meet too infrequently.

7. Pam is terribly sick.

8. They are an extremely diverse group of people.

9. Put that very large box here.

10. She works out regularly.

For practice identifying adverbs in sentences, go to http://www.college .hmco.com/pic/dolphinwriterthree.

Phrases That Function as Adverbs. Adverbs, like adjectives, can be single words, or they can be prepositional phrases, which you learned about in the section on parts of speech.

The meeting begins **at five o'clock.**   (begins *when?*)
He raced **around the track.**   (raced *where?*)
She jumped **with glee.**   (jumped *how?*)

EXERCISE 30

Circle the phrases that function as adverbs in each of the following sentences.

1. My socks are under the bed.

2. Dea takes violin lessons on Thursdays.

3. We went to the grocery store.

4. The campground is next to the river.

5. The audience clapped with enthusiasm.

6. Marisa attends a writing workshop every week.

7. He eats too fast.

8. I went to the museum.

9. On Saturdays we go to the sailing school.

10. She pursues her goals with determination.

For practice identifying phrases functioning as adverbs, go to **http://www .college.hmco.com/pic/dolphinwriterthree.**

Comparative and Superlative Forms of Adverbs. Like adjectives, some adverbs can have comparative and superlative forms. Usually we add the word *more* to form the comparative and *most* to form the superlative.

Adverb	*Comparative*	*Superlative*
bravely	more bravely	most bravely
quickly	more quickly	most quickly
rudely	more rudely	most rudely

Of all the people I spoke with, Ellen behaved **most rudely.**
This shrub grows **more quickly** than that shrub does.

Avoiding Double Negatives. Certain adverbs that express the negative should not be used together in the same sentence. These words include

no	never
not	hardly
none	barely
nothing	scarcely

Notice how double negatives are corrected in the following sentences.

Double negative: I have **hardly never** been on time.
Corrections: I have hardly ever been on time.
                     I have never been on time.

Double negative: There is **not no** jelly for the sandwich.
Corrections: There is not any jelly for the sandwich.
                     There is no jelly for the sandwich.

Using Adjectives and Adverbs Correctly

Certain adjectives and adverbs are easily confused if you are unsure which is which. The words *good* and *well, bad* and *badly,* and *real* and *really* are the three pairs that are most often misused in sentences.

The adverbs in these pairs are *well, badly,* and *really.* The last two are easy enough to remember because they both end in *-ly,* like many other adverbs.

You read **well** last night.   (**not** you read *good*)
He sings **badly.**   (**not** he sings *bad*)
She is **really** exhausted.   (**not** she is *real* exhausted)

The adjectives are *good, bad,* and *real.* They all describe nouns, but they are often misused with linking verbs:

He feels **bad** about that.   (**not** he feels *badly*)
The chicken smells **good.**   (**not** the chicken smells *well*)

Notice how the meaning changes in the following sentences depending on whether you use an adjective or an adverb:

He smells bad.
He smells badly.

In the first sentence, the adjective *bad,* which follows a linking verb, communicates that the subject is the source of a foul odor. In the second sentence, the word *smells* is an action verb, and the word *badly* is an adverb. Therefore, the sentence indicates that the subject's nose is not functioning properly.

EXERCISE 31

Rewrite each of the following sentences to correct adverb errors. Check for the correct use of comparative and superlative forms, double negatives, and adjectives incorrectly used as adverbs. If the sentence needs no correction, write *No correction needed.*

1. You dance good.

_____

2. There is not nothing to do.

_____

3. Maxine is real beautiful.

_____

4. He acts bad when his parents are not around.

_____

5. Jan cooks poor.

_____

6. The party went well.

_____

7. There is hardly any sugar in the bowl.

_____

8. That is not no way to talk to your mother!

_____

9. He sings very bad.

_____

10. Many animals can see good in the dark.

_____

For practice correcting adverb and adjective errors, go to http://www.college.hmco.com/pic/dolphinwriterthree.

Avoiding Dangling and Misplaced Modifiers

In a sentence an adjective modifier must be placed next to the word it describes. If a modifier is not next to the word it describes, it is called a **misplaced modifier:**

>Debbie saw a turtle **driving down the street.**

In this sentence, the phrase *driving down the street* modifies *turtle* because that is the closest word to the phrase. Therefore, this sentence is saying that the turtle was driving down the street. Actually, though, it was Debbie who was doing the driving. To correct this sentence, rewrite it so that the modifier is next to the word that it modifies.

>**Driving down the street,** Debbie saw a turtle.

Misplaced modifiers can be phrases or single words. The word *only,* for example, is commonly misplaced:

>When he reached for a cookie, he **only** found crumbs.

In this sentence, the word *only* is modifying the verb, but it should be modifying the word *crumbs.* Therefore, it needs to be moved:

>When he reached for a cookie, he found **only** crumbs.

Dangling Modifiers. If the word the modifier is supposed to be describing is not in the sentence at all, the error is called a **dangling modifier.**

>**Working hard for two weeks,** the project was finally finished.
>**At four years old,** my grandfather began my reading instruction.

In the first sentence, the modifier *working hard for two weeks* is incorrectly describing *project.* It is not the project that worked hard but rather the person or people who completed it. In the second sentence, the modifier *at four years old* is incorrectly describing *grandfather.* It is not the grandfather who was four years old but rather the speaker of the sentence. To correct these errors, rewrite the sentences to add the missing information:

>Working hard for two weeks, **the group** finally finished the project.
>At four years old, **I** began reading instruction with my grandfather.

EXERCISE 32

Underline each dangling or misplaced modifier in the following sentences. If a sentence does not contain a dangling or misplaced modifier, write C for "Correct" beside it.

1. Overripe and mushy, Tom did not eat the banana.

2. Huffing and puffing, the piano was hard to push up the hill.

3. Cecilia found her twenty-dollar bill lying on the floor.

4. The children flying overhead saw a flock of geese.

5. Bleeding heavily, stitches were needed.

6. Distracted by his ringing cell phone, the driver ran the stop sign.

7. Topped with butter and jam, Bob ate the biscuit.

8. Flying home from Florida, a snowstorm hit.

9. My brother, locked out of his house, had to call a locksmith.

10. As the wife of a soldier, periods of living alone are common.

Writing Better Sentences

There are three ways to improve your writing by using adjectives and adverbs.

1. Use them to add descriptive detail.
2. Do not overuse them.
3. Do not substitute them for strong verbs.

Adjectives and adverbs help create mental images in your readers' minds. Notice the difference between the two examples in the following sets of sentences:

Our living room was cool.

Our air-conditioned, chilly living room was cool and quite inviting on a hot summer day.

The leaves fell down to earth.

The red, yellow, and gold leaves fell gently to earth.

The second sentence of each pair, which includes more adjectives and adverbs, provides more descriptive details that help readers form a sharper mental picture.

Especially when you are describing an object, a person, or a place, make sure that you are adding adjectives and adverbs to bring your description to life.

However, beware of overusing adjectives and adverbs. You do not want to load your sentences with too many of them, for an excess can slow the pace of your sentences and bog down your ideas with unnecessary information.

Too many modifiers:	The young lady was very lovely looking and very desirable to young men her own age.
Revision:	The men desired the lovely young lady.
Too many modifiers:	He quickly threw the ball hard, fast, and with a lot of power to first base.
Revision:	He threw the ball hard and fast to first base.

Check to make sure that each adjective or adverb offers essential information and that your modifiers are not simply repeating each other.

If you have a tendency to use too many modifiers, you may also be using adjectives and adverbs to convey meaning that could be more effectively delivered by your verbs.

Too many adjectives:	We went for miles and miles down the long, lonely stretch of deserted highway.
Revision:	The lonely highway **stretched** for miles before us.
Too many adjectives:	He was in the deep snow, struggling to walk.
Revision:	He **trudged** through deep snow.

EXERCISE 33

Rewrite each of the following sentences to add modifiers, eliminate modifiers, or strengthen verbs as appropriate.

1. He is an enthusiastic pitcher and batter, full of energy.

_____

2. Their children are smart, intelligent, brilliant, and always demonstrating the ability to get high grades.

_____

3. He shook his head *no* from side to side, with an expression of disapproval pulling down the corners of his mouth.

_____

4. The big, bright, golden sun went down, going out of sight and disappearing in a blaze of color.

---

5. Carmel and I are in admiration of the person wearing the gold medal.

For practice revising sentences to improve the use of adjectives and adverbs, go to http://www.college.hmco.com/pic/dolphinwriterthree.

Subject-Verb Agreement

The Basics of Subject-Verb Agreement

Earlier in this Handbook, you learned that a basic sentence contains both a subject and a verb. This subject and verb must agree in number; that is, if the subject is singular (one person, place, thing, or idea), then the verb in the sentence must also be in its singular form. If the subject is plural (more than one person, place, thing, or idea), then the verb in the sentence must also be in its plural form.

> *singular singular*
> The **alarm   buzzes** at seven.

> *plural plural*
> The **alarms buzz** at seven.

The third-person singular forms of regular verbs (see page 458) end in -*s*.

> She reads.
> The flag waves.
> The audience applauds.

Irregular verbs (such as *to be* and *to have*) have different singular and plural forms.

> I **am**.
> They **are**.

> He **has**.
> We **have**.

EXERCISE 34

In each of the following sentences, underline the simple subject. Then circle the verb that agrees with that subject.

  1. Her dogs (whine, whines) constantly.

  2. The computer (crash, crashes) regularly.

  3. The members (meets, meet) once a month.

  4. I (run, runs) with my dogs every afternoon.

  5. (Do, does) you mow on weekends?

  6. Rai (bake, bakes) bread every Tuesday.

  7. Squirrels (eat, eats) some of the birdseed in the feeder.

  8. Architects and builders (works, work) together.

  9. My father (relax, relaxes) during his daily train ride.

 10. The curtains (need, needs) cleaning.

For practice making subjects and verbs agree, go to http://www.college.hmco .com/pic/dolphinwriterthree.

Trickier Subject-Verb Agreement Situations

Basic subject-verb agreement is relatively straightforward. However, you will need to write sentences that will present you with trickier subject-verb agreement situations. They might be tricky because the subject is more difficult to find, or they may be tricky because you are not sure whether the subject is singular or plural. The remainder of this section covers the kinds of sentences that will make choosing the correct verb a little more challenging.

Intervening Prepositional Phrases. Sometimes a prepositional phrase will separate the subject and the verb of a sentence, causing confusion about what the subject of the sentence really is. As you learned earlier, the object of a preposition cannot be the subject of a sentence. Therefore, before you attempt to determine the right verb, you may want to physically or mentally cross out the prepositional phrase or phrases that intervene between the subject and the verb.

One of the boys **plays** catch every day.

In this example, it might be tempting to conclude that *boys* is the subject of the sentence. However, *boys* is the object of the preposition, and *one* is actually the subject. If you use the plural form of the verb (*play*) to make it agree with *boys*, then your sentence will contain a subject-verb agreement error. The singular subject *one* must be matched with the singular verb *plays*.

Cross out the intervening prepositional phrases in the following sentences and then decide whether or not the verbs agree.

People with a good sense of humor **is** exactly what we need.
The wrinkles in her face **makes** her look wise.
Men in tuxedoes **are** very handsome.

In the first sentence, the subject is *people* (not *sense* or *humor*, which are the objects of prepositions). The subject is plural and the verb *is* is singular, so the sentence contains a subject-verb agreement error. The verb should be *are*. In the second sentence, *wrinkles* is the subject, and *face* is the object of the preposition. The singular verb *makes* does not agree with the plural subject, so it should be changed to *make*. In the last sentence, both the subject (*men*) and the verb (*are*) are plural, so the sentence is correct.

EXERCISE 35

In each of the following sentences, draw parentheses around prepositional phrases that intervene between the subject and the verb. Then circle the verb that agrees with the subject.

1. Students at this school (takes, take) many standardized tests.

2. These jugs of water (is, are) not free.

3. The value of these stocks (has, have) decreased.

4. The children in this class (play, plays) well together.

5. The sound of frogs (keep, keeps) her awake at night.

6. The men in the choir (perform, performs) tonight.

7. The reasons for his decision (is, are) mysterious.

8. A platoon of soldiers (becomes, become) very close-knit.

9. This basket of apples (weigh, weighs) ten pounds.

10. His belief in miracles never (decrease, decreases).

For practice making subjects and verbs agree in sentences with intervening prepositional phrases, go to http://www.college.hmco.com/pic/dolphinwriter three.

Inverted Word Order. Another type of sentence that makes the subject more difficult to discern is one with inverted word order. In a sentence with inverted word order, the subject comes *after* the verb. In sentences that begin with *there* or *here,* for example, the subject follows the verb:

> verb   subject

Here **are** two *sandwiches* for your lunch.

The subject of this sentence is the plural *sandwiches.* The word *here* is an adverb, and the word *lunch* is the object of a preposition. Therefore, if you were to write *Here **is** two sandwiches for your lunch,* the sentence would be incorrect.

In questions, too, inverted word order can make determining the subject more challenging:

> verb   subject

Where **are** my *socks?*

In this sentence, the verb (*are*) must agree with the plural subject *socks. Where* is an adverb. Therefore, writing *Where is my socks?* would be incorrect.

Finally, there are other cases of inverted word order:

> verb   subject

In the cooler **were** two *sodas* on ice.

In the cooler and *on ice* are prepositional phrases, so cross them out. Then you can see that *sodas* (plural) is the subject, so the verb must be plural, too.

★ EXERCISE 36

In each of the following sentences, underline the subject and then circle the verb contained in parentheses that agrees with that subject.

1. There (is, are) strange noises coming from my car's engine.

2. On my table (is, are) a ring.

3. Under the couch (is, are) two pairs of shoes.

4. Here (comes, come) the sun.

5. Where (is, are) my papers?

6. (Is, Are) there a problem?

7. In the dirt (was, were) a footprint.

8. In my refrigerator (was, were) two cans of soda.

9. On the roof (perches, perch) two blackbirds.

10. There (goes, go) my friends.

For practice making subjects and verbs agree in sentences with inverted word order, go to http://www.college.hmco.com/pic/dolphinwriterthree.

Indefinite Pronouns. In the remaining tricky sentences, the subject is not necessarily difficult to find, but you may wonder whether some of the indefinite pronouns used as subjects are singular or plural. As you learned in the section about parts of speech, indefinite pronouns do not refer to any particular person, place, or thing.

> **Everybody** loves cake.
> **Anybody** can come.

The meaning of an indefinite pronoun becomes more specific when a prepositional phrase is added.

> **One** *of my friends* won the blue ribbon.
> **No one** *in the class* is prepared for the lecture.

However, each indefinite pronoun is either singular or plural, regardless of the phrase that modifies it. The singular indefinite pronouns are

one	nobody	nothing	each
anyone	anybody	anything	either
someone	somebody	something	neither
everyone	everybody	everything	

   singular   *singular*

Each *of my children* **loves** me in a different way.

   singular   *singular*

Everyone *in Richmond* **wants** a ticket.

The plural indefinite pronouns include

both	many
few	several

plural　　　　*plural*
Both of my arms **were** fractured.

plural　　　　　*plural*
Several of his assertions **are** good ones.

But perhaps the trickiest of the indefinite pronouns are the ones that can be either singular or plural, depending on the noun or pronoun to which they refer. These pronouns are

all	most
any	none
more	some

Notice the differences in the following examples:

singular　*singular*
Most of the *pie*　　　**is** gone.

plural　*plural*
Most of my *friends* **know** how to paint.

singular　　*singular*
All of the *book*　　　**is** dull.

plural　　*plural*
All of her *relatives*　**plan** to attend the party.

EXERCISE 37

In each of the following sentences, circle the verb that agrees with the subject.

1. Each of us (is, are) happy to have friends.

2. Everyone (needs, need) sleep.

3. Most of the children (ride, rides) the bus.

4. One of the players (is, are) injured.

5. None of our neighbors (shops, shop) at that store.

6. Several of the dogs (has, have) fleas.

7. Most of the bread (is, are) moldy.

8. Both of her brothers (join, joins) the swim team every year.

9. All of the forest (are, is) on fire.

10. Some of the participants still (owe, owes) money.

For practice choosing verbs that agree with indefinite pronoun subjects, go to http://www.college.hmco.com/pic/dolphinwriterthree.

Compound Subjects. You have learned that a compound subject consists of two or more subjects joined by a coordinating or correlative conjunction (*and, or, either/or, neither/nor*). This conjunction determines whether you use the singular form of the verb or the plural form of the verb. If the word *and* joins the two subjects, they are plural, and you use the plural form of the verb:

The stars *and* the moon **are** twinkling tonight.
My son *and* I **love** to surf.

However, if the subjects are joined by *or, either/or,* or *neither/nor,* the verb agrees with the subject that is closest to the verb.

    singular subject   plural subject
The **nanny** *or*   the **children** always **eat** the pizza.

      singular subject   plural subject
Either **Michael** *or*   his **brothers clean** the yard every day.

       plural subject   singular subject
Neither the **monkeys** *nor* the **elephant is** in this particular show.

EXERCISE 38

In each of the following sentences, circle the verb that agrees with the subject.

1. Either the point guard or the forward (get, gets) the ball.

2. Neither walking nor driving (is, are) an option for us.

3. My sister and brothers (attend, attends) day camp.

4. Cut flowers or a potted plant (cheer, cheers) up a hospital patient.

5. Neither this sweater nor those jackets (fit, fits) me.

6. Either a tiger or two lions (performs, perform) in the show.

7. Connie or her sons (mow, mows) their elderly neighbor's lawn each week.

8. Abbie and Ben (visit, visits) their cousins in Texas every spring.

9. Neither the team members nor the coach (is, are) willing to give up.

10. The reporters or the editor (find, finds) stories to cover in the newspaper.

For practice choosing verbs that agree with compound subjects, go to http://www.college.hmco.com/pic/dolphinwriterthree.

Singular Nouns That End in -s. Some nouns end in *-s* as do plural nouns, but they are nevertheless considered singular because they refer to a single thing. The following list includes some examples of these words.

physics   series
news   politics
economics   measles

The news **is** not positive.
The series **starts** tonight on NBC.

Collective Nouns. Collective nouns are those that refer to a group of people or things (*team, class, crowd, group, company, audience, family, jury, gang, faculty*). If the subject of the sentence is a collective noun and the group is acting together as one unit, then use a singular verb:

The squad **practices** every evening.
The audience always **snickers** at that joke.
The family **dines** together every evening.

However, if the members of the group are acting individually, use a plural verb:

The family **go** to different parts of the house after dinner.

Sums of money and measurements are also considered to be singular when they are one unit.

Ten dollars for a gourmet lunch **is** expensive.
Fourteen miles **is** the length of the path.

Titles and Other Proper Nouns. Titles of poems, novels, short stories, plays, films, and other works are always considered to be singular.

Tom Sawyer **is** Mark Twain's best book.
The Jetsons **is** my favorite cartoon.

A proper noun, such as the name of a person, place, or thing, is also considered singular.

> Wendy's **is** open until ten o'clock.
> The southeastern United States **lies** in the tornado's path.
> Disney **is** releasing the feature film this summer.

EXERCISE 39

In each of the following sentences, circle the verb that agrees with the subject.

1. Politics (interest, interests) me.
2. The Tony Awards (is, are) a big event for Broadway actors and actresses.
3. The team (refuse, refuses) to skip practice.
4. McDonald's (is, are) still open.
5. Two tons (are, is) the weight of that truck.
6. The company constantly (updates, update) the information.
7. The class (take, takes) a short break at 1:00 p.m.
8. The series (has, have) been canceled.
9. Diabetes (is, are) a serious illness.
10. *Pride and Prejudice* (were, was) written by Jane Austen.

For practice making verbs agree with singular nouns that end in -s, collective nouns, and proper nouns, go to www.college.hmco.com/pic/hmcollegewriting seriesthree_1e.

Pronouns and Pronoun Agreement

In this Handbook's section about parts of speech, you learned that a pronoun is a word that is used in place of a noun. In this section, you will learn how to choose the correct pronouns for your sentences.

Pronoun Case

The **case** of a pronoun refers to its function in a sentence. A pronoun that functions as a subject or refers back to the subject (its complement) is in the **subjective case.** The subjective, or subject, pronouns are

I	we
he	they
she	who
you	whoever
it	

In the following sentences, the subjective pronouns are functioning as subjects:

You and **I** should have dinner.
We hope to win the prize.
Who is at the door?

Subjective pronouns can also follow the words *than* or *as* in a comparison:

You are smarter than **I.** (The verb *am* is implied after the subject *I.*)

We are as capable at tennis as **they.** (The verb *are* is implied after the subject *they.*)

We do not always speak this way, though, so you may hear someone say, "You are stronger than *me.*" However, this usage is incorrect in writing.

In the next set of examples, the pronouns are referring to the subject, so they, too, are subjective:

We players are having a fund drive.
The rest of us—Ann, Jin, and **I**—will gather the newspapers.

The **objective pronouns** function as direct objects, indirect objects, or objects of prepositions, or they refer back to objects. The objective, or object, pronouns are

me	us
him	you
her	them
it	whom, whomever

direct object
I saw **her** at the gym this morning.

indirect object

The child gave **me** a big wave.

object of preposition

Give the new jacket to **him**.

object of preposition

To **whom** did you send the e-mail message?

refers to direct object

They sent **us** boys to the auditorium.

Therefore, if you figure out the part of speech of a pronoun, you can determine whether you should use the subjective or objective case. For example, look at the following sentence. What function does the pronoun in question serve?

Mr. Meyer and (I, me) presented the information to the class.

This sentence has a compound subject, and the pronoun is the second half of that subject. Thus, we must choose the subjective case pronoun, *I*. Now read another example:

For (he, him) and (I, me), this is a wonderful day.

In this sentence, the two pronouns are objects of the preposition *for*. Therefore, we must use the objective case pronouns, *him* and *me*. Here is one final example:

(We, Us) students want to go home now.

In this sentence, the pronoun refers to the subject *students*, so it must be the subjective *we*. If you pretend that the word *students* is not there, you can see that *We want to go home now* is correct.

Of all of these pronouns, *who* and *whom* tend to be two of the most confusing. The difference between these two words is discussed later in this Handbook.

 **EXERCISE 40**

In each of the following sentences, circle the correct pronoun contained in parentheses.

1. He and (I, me) play hockey together.

2. Lisa and (I, me) are best friends.

3. The argument between Chris and (I, me) flared up suddenly.

4. (We, Us) jury members need to come to a consensus.

5. (She, Her) and (I, me) are always late to the meeting.

6. The cat scratched (me, I).

7. I asked (her, she) for ten dollars.

8. The business trip was a necessity for (she, her) and (I, me).

9. Peter sent (me, I) a case of wine.

10. They made (us, we) promise to call soon.

The **possessive pronouns** indicate possession, or ownership. The possessive pronouns are

my	our
mine	ours
your	your
yours	yours
his	their
her	theirs
hers	
its	

Julie has finished writing **her** paper.
Hernando gave me **his** granola bar, and I gave him **my** pear.

For practice choosing the correct pronoun case, go to http://www.college
.hmco.com/pic/dolphinwriterthree.

Pronoun Consistency

When you write, you take a certain **point of view,** or perspective. In the *first-person* point of view, you use the pronouns *I* and *we* because you describe the events from your own perspective. In the *second-person* point of view, you use the pronoun *you* because you are usually directing the reader to do something. In instructions, for example, you would write "you do this" and "you do that." In the *third-person* point of view, you use *he, she, they,* and *it,* and you avoid the first- and second-person pronouns.

If you start out using one point of view, remain consistently within that point of view, and do not shift from one to another. Notice how the point of view changes in the following sentences.

first person   *second person*

When **I** applied for my passport, **you** had to stand in line for hours.

first person   *first person*

Although **we** dislike getting winded, **we** signed up for a class at the gym
    second person

because **you** have to take it.

second person   *first person*

You do not want to feed the cat until **we** find out if it has a home.

To remain consistent, change the *you* to *I* in the first sentence and the *you* to *we* in the second sentence. In the third sentence, you can change the *you* to *we* or the *we* to *you*.

EXERCISE 41

In each of the following sentences, cross out the pronoun that is inconsistent, and write the correct pronoun above it.

1. They know she is a vegetarian, so you do not serve her meat.

2. We are going to the gym because you need the exercise.

3. If you know that smoking is bad for you, one should kick the habit.

4. We like swimming in Florida's rivers, but you have to watch out for snakes.

5. Many people do not speak a second language, but you would benefit in many ways if you became bilingual.

For practice revising inconsistent pronouns, go to http://www.college.hmco .com/pic/dolphinwriterthree.

Clear Pronoun Reference

Another pronoun problem is unclear reference. A pronoun always refers to a noun or another pronoun, and this word is called an **antecedent.** If a pronoun's antecedent is not clear, confusion can result.

Bob told his father that **he** had acted like a jerk.

In this sentence, does the pronoun *he* refer to Bob or to his father? Is Bob criticizing his father's behavior, or is Bob assessing his own actions? Because there are two possible antecedents for the pronoun *he*, the meaning of this sentence is in question. To correct it, you would probably have to rewrite the sentence:

Bob said to his father, "I acted like a jerk."

The following is another sentence that contains an unclear reference.

> The girl on the bicycle ran into a tree, but **it** was barely damaged.

In this sentence, the pronoun *it* could refer to the bicycle or to the tree. To correct the unclear reference, rewrite the sentence.

> The girl ran into the tree, but her bicycle was barely damaged.

Possessive pronouns also can be unclear:

> She let her daughter wear **her** mink coat to the opera.

Does the coat belong to the mother or the daughter? The pronoun *her* does not make the meaning clear. Here is one way to correct the problem:

> She wore her mother's mink coat to the opera.

Be aware, too, of including a pronoun that has no antecedent at all:

> I took my car to be fixed, and **they** said that I need a new starter.

Who is *they* in this sentence? Readers can assume that this pronoun refers to the mechanics who examined the car, but readers cannot be sure. To correct the unclear reference, rewrite the sentence, eliminating the unclear pronoun altogether if necessary:

> I took my car to be fixed, and the mechanics said that I need a new starter.

✦ EXERCISE 42

Rewrite each of the following sentences to eliminate unclear pronoun reference.

1. Ricardo told his neighbor that his door was broken.

_____

2. The car hit the wall, but it was damaged only a little.

_____

3. She told her boss to take her car.

_____

4. I wanted to get my computer repaired, but they said it could not be fixed.

_____

5. Barbara told her daughter that she needed to do her homework.

_____

6. Joe took his son to the shoe store so that he could buy a pair of cleats.

_____

7. Simon told his brother that his car needed gas.

_____

8. Calvin dropped the vase on the floor, but it did not break.

_____

9. Janice wanted to make a dentist appointment, but they said none were available.

_____

_____

10. I pulled up to the drive-through window, but they said that they were closed.

_____

_____

For practice eliminating unclear pronoun reference, go to http://www.college.hmco.com/pic/dolphinwriterthree.

Pronoun Agreement

A pronoun must agree with, or match, the gender and the number of its antecedent. **Gender** refers to whether the antecedent is masculine (*he/him/his*), feminine (*she/her/her*), or neutral (*it/it/its*). In the following sentences, notice how the gender of the pronoun matches the gender of the italicized antecedent.

His *wife* gave **her** vow.
The *man* driving the car said that **he** was exhausted.
The *horse* bruised **its** leg when **it** tried to jump over the brook.

Number refers to whether the antecedent is singular or plural. If the antecedent is singular, use a singular pronoun, and if the antecedent is plural, use a plural pronoun.

    singular   *singular*
The *professor* dropped **his** pencil.

plural   *plural*

The *men* are packing **their** bags right now.

singular   *singular*

Her *hair* has lost **its** sheen.

Basic pronoun agreement is relatively straightforward. However, you will need to write sentences that will present you with trickier pronoun-agreement situations. They are usually tricky because you are not sure whether the antecedent is singular or plural. The remainder of this section covers the kinds of sentences that make choosing the correct pronoun a little more challenging.

Indefinite Pronouns. Earlier in this Handbook, you learned that the indefinite pronouns can make subject-verb agreement tricky. When an indefinite pronoun is an antecedent, choosing the pronoun that agrees with it is more challenging. However, you can apply what you learned about indefinite pronouns and subject-verb agreement to pronoun-antecedent agreement.

Most of the indefinite pronouns are singular:

one	nobody	nothing	each
anyone	anybody	anything	either
someone	somebody	something	neither
everyone	everybody	everything	

Therefore, you will use a singular pronoun to match an antecedent that is one of the indefinite pronouns in the preceding list. When you know the gender of the antecedent, choose the appropriate singular pronoun:

Each of the men broke **his** promise.
Neither of the boys knows where **he** stands.

To avoid gender bias when the gender of the indefinite pronoun is either unknown or mixed, writers often use the phrases *he or she* and *his or her*:

Everyone thinks that **he or she** would love to win lots of money.
One of the students forgot to write **his or her** address on the application.

In spoken conversation, you will often hear (and say), "Each of the men broke *their* promise" and "Everybody paid *their* dues on time." However, both of these sentences contain pronoun-agreement errors, so this usage is incorrect in formal writing. If you think that writing *he or she* and *his or her* is cumbersome, then rewrite the sentence with a plural subject. Then you can use *they* or *their* as the pronoun:

All *people* think **they** would love to win lots of money.

The indefinite pronouns that are plural include

both   many
few   several

Use plural pronouns with these subjects:

Both of the ladies wore **their** red coats.
Few remembered what **they** were supposed to bring to the dinner.

Finally, remember that some indefinite pronouns can be singular or plural, depending on the noun or pronoun to which they refer. These pronouns are

all   most
any   none
more   some

Most of the *books* are missing **their** spines.
Most of the *soil* had lost **its** ability to absorb water.

 **EXERCISE 43**

In each of the following sentences, underline the antecedent. Then circle the pronoun that agrees with that antecedent.

1. Each of the children brought (his or her, their) favorite stuffed animal to the show.

2. Everybody washes (his or her, their) car on Saturday.

3. Neither of the men located (his, their) basketball.

4. Everyone assumes that (he or she, they) will win.

5. Most of them believe that (he or she is, they are) good athletes.

6. Her cat has lost (her, its) collar.

7. She placed (its, her) airline tickets in the folder.

8. One of the members of the men's track team thanked (his, their) spouse at the awards ceremony.

9. Each of my sisters got (her, their) hair cut.

10. Everybody in our neighborhood keeps (his or her, their) yard looking nice.

For practice making pronouns agree with indefinite pronoun antecedents, go to http://www.college.hmco.com/pic/dolphinwriterthree.

Compound Subjects. As with subject-verb agreement, if the word *and* joins two antecedents, they are plural, and you use the plural form of the pronoun.

Troy *and* the rest of the team brought in presents for **their** coach.
The man *and* the woman looked at **their** schedules.

However, if the antecedents are joined by *or, either/or,* or *neither/nor,* the pronoun agrees with the antecedent that is closest to it.

       plural antecedent   singular antecedent singular pronoun
Neither the **dogs**   *nor* the   **cat**   would stop **its** crying.

Collective Nouns. Collective nouns are those that refer to a group of people or things (*team, class, crowd, group, company, audience, family, jury, gang, faculty*). If the antecedent is a collective noun and the group is acting together as one unit, then use a singular pronoun:

The *flock* fixed **its** attention on the group of photographers.

However, if the members of the group are acting individually, use a plural pronoun:

The *flock* scattered in different directions to save **their** own hides.

EXERCISE 44

In each of the following sentences, underline the antecedent(s). Then circle the pronoun that agrees with that antecedent.

1. The board will announce (its, their) decision tomorrow.

2. Annette and the other girls brought flowers for (her, their) teacher.

3. Congress will begin (its, their) new session on Monday.

4. The boy and his sister do not know (his, their) cousins.

5. The girls and their mother would not agree to cut (her, their) hair.

6. The audience clapped to express (its, their) approval.

7. The workers and their employer have pledged (his, their) loyalty to one another.

8. Neither the dance team nor the cheerleaders practice (its, their) routines on Saturdays.

9. The committee has many items on (its, their) agenda.

10. That species is known for (its, their) ability to hunt and gather.

For practice making pronouns agree with compound subjects and collective nouns, go to http://www.college.hmco.com/pic/dolphinwriterthree.

Coordination

The Compound Sentence

In previous sections of this Handbook, you worked on mastering the simple sentence, an independent clause with only one subject-verb relationship. In this section, you will focus on the compound sentence, which has two or more subject-verb relationships. Learning to use compound sentences correctly will help you elevate the complexity and sophistication of your writing.

Compound Elements

In previous chapters, as you learned about the elements of the basic sentence, you encountered various kinds of compound elements. As you recall, *compound* means more than one. Thus, subjects are compound if there are two or more nouns or pronouns performing an action or existing in some state of being:

> *subject   subject verb*
> **Jack** and his **uncle**   *ride* snowmobiles every Saturday.

A verb is compound if the subject is performing more than one action:

> *subject verb   verb*
> *She* **polished** the silver and **vacuumed** the floor.

Likewise, direct objects, indirect objects, antecedents of pronouns, and other elements can be compound.

In the next sections, you will see how sentences can be compound, and you will learn to distinguish compound sentences from compound elements in a simple sentence.

EXERCISE 45

In each of the following sentences, circle each of the two words that form a compound element. Then, on the blank, identify the elements as *CS* (compound subject) or *CV* (compound verb).

_____ **1.** The dogs barked and whined at the cat outside.

_____ **2.** My boyfriend and I are soul mates.

_____ **3.** Fish and gerbils make interesting pets.

_____ **4.** We ate and talked at the dinner.

_____ **5.** Mark writes poetry and performs it at the theater.

_____ **6.** George buys and renovates houses.

_____ **7.** Kim and Steve have not seen each other in a long time.

_____ **8.** The security guard locked the building and went home.

_____ **9.** My sister and mother live next door to one another.

_____ **10.** Museums and art galleries are my favorite places to go.

For practice identifying compound elements in sentences, go to http://www.college.hmco.com/pic/dolphinwriterthree.

Three Kinds of Compound Sentences

Compound sentences contain at least two different subject-verb relationships:

subject   verb   subject   verb

Ratings *were* low, so the **network** *canceled* the show.

subject verb   subject verb

He *proposed* to her; **she**   *said* no.

subject verb   subject verb

She   *hates* hip-hop music; however, **she**   *went* to the concert anyway.

A group of words that can stand alone as a complete sentence because it contains a subject and a verb is called an **independent clause.** A compound sentence contains at least two independent clauses.

EXERCISE 46

In each of the following compound sentences, circle the subjects and underline the verbs.

1. Raj specializes in corporate law, but he also handles estate planning.

2. We went sky diving; they went fishing.

3. I curled my hair; it looked nice.

4. The refrigerator died, for it was old and dilapidated.

5. Andrew pruned the trees; some branches needed trimming.

6. We misplaced the keys, so we looked for them.

7. James traveled to New York City; he brought back many souvenirs.

8. She quit her job, but she found another one the next day.

9. The plates are in the cupboard, and the silverware is in the drawer.

10. I need your phone number; it is not in the phone book.

For practice identifying subjects and verbs in compound sentences, go to http://www.college.hmco.com/pic/dolphinwriterthree.

Because there are two separate independent clauses, a compound sentence could be written as two complete sentences that could each stand alone:

Ratings were low. The network canceled the show.
He proposed to her. She said no.
She hates hip-hop music. However, she went to the concert anyway.

However, the two independent clauses are combined to form one longer compound sentence because there is some relationship between the two clauses. In the first example, for instance, the first event is the *cause* of the second event, so they can be linked together with a coordinating conjunction (*so*) to indicate this relationship. We could separate these two independent clauses and write them as two simple sentences, but linking them together increases the sophistication of the writing. It also prevents readers from having to determine on their own whether or how the two clauses are related.

There are three ways to form compound sentences. You can join independent clauses with a comma and a coordinating conjunction, with a semicolon followed by a conjunctive adverb and a comma, or with a semicolon only.

Independent Clauses Joined by a Coordinating Conjunction

The first way to form a compound sentence is to join two independent clauses with a coordinating conjunction. You already know that the conjunctions *and, or, for, but, so, nor,* and *yet* link together words or phrases. These connecting words are known as the *coordinating conjunctions* because they join coordinate, or equal, elements. Two coordinate independent clauses can also be joined with these conjunctions:

subject   verb   subject   verb

We *stopped* at the bakery, **and** then we   *went* to the bank.

subject verb   subject   verb

I   *want* to own a dog, **but** I   *know* nothing about animals.

subject   verb   subject   verb

You *can spend* your gift certificate now, **or** you *can save* it for something better.

Each of the coordinating conjunctions indicates a certain type of relationship.

Addition:	*and*
Cause or effect:	*for, so*
Contrast:	*but, yet*
Choice or alternative:	*or, nor*

EXERCISE 47

On the blank in each of the following sentences, insert the word *and, or, for, but, so, nor,* or *yet* to indicate the relationship between the two independent clauses.

1. The time for the movie is inconvenient, _____ I cannot go.

2. Judy rides her bike every day, _____ she is very toned.

3. Patrick loves hockey, _____ his sister prefers baseball.

4. We have been to Bermuda, _____ we have also been to Belize.

5. He will not come to the meeting, _____ will he join the organization.

6. Either you are a leader, _____ you are a follower.

7. I cannot attend the party, _____ I will be there in spirit.

8. We were forced to cancel the game, _____ it was far too wet to play.

9. I will help you with grammar exercises, ____ I cannot help you with math.

10. Would you like a cup of coffee, ____ would you like tea?

For practice using coordinating conjunctions to indicate relationships, go to http://www.college.hmco.com/pic/dolphinwriterthree.

When you join two independent clauses with a coordinating conjunction, notice that you add a comma *before* (and not after) the conjunction.

Incorrect: The day is rainy and, the streets are wet.
Correct: The day is rainy, and the streets are wet.

EXERCISE 48

On the blanks provided, write compound sentences that are correctly punctuated.

1. _____ and _____.

2. _____ so _____.

3. _____ but _____.

4. _____ or _____.

5. _____ for _____.

6. _____ nor _____.

7. _____ yet _____.

For practice writing and punctuating compound sentences with coordinating conjunctions, go to http://www.college.hmco.com/pic/dolphinwriterthree.

Independent Clauses Joined by a Semicolon and Conjunctive Adverb

The second way to join two independent clauses involves adding a semicolon and a conjunctive adverb or a transitional expression (both followed by a comma). Some of the most common **conjunctive adverbs** and transitional expressions are

also	moreover
as a result	nevertheless
consequently	next

finally	now
furthermore	on the other hand
hence	otherwise
however	similarly
in addition	soon
indeed	still
in fact	then
instead	therefore
likewise	thus
meanwhile	

He is very smart; **in fact,** he graduated valedictorian of his class.

The rain was very heavy; **as a result,** the basement flooded.

She has a law degree; **however,** she does not work as an attorney.

Like coordinating conjunctions, conjunctive adverbs signal different relationships between the two independent clauses. The adverbs *as a result, consequently, therefore,* and *thus* all indicate a cause/effect relationship. The adverbs *however, instead, nevertheless,* and *on the other hand* signal contrast. The adverbs *finally, next,* and *soon* indicate a time-order relationship.

Your choice of a conjunctive adverb matters, for you can change the meaning of a sentence by changing just the conjunctive adverb:

They married without knowing each other; **later,** they divorced.

In this sentence, the word *later* indicates only a time-order relationship between the two clauses. Notice how the meaning changes in the next compound sentence:

They married without knowing each other; **consequently,** they divorced.

In this sentence, the word *consequently* suggests that their marrying without knowing each other was the *cause* of the breakup.

EXERCISE 49

On the blank in each of the following sentences, insert one of the conjunctive adverbs or transitional expressions in the list on pages 526–527 to indicate the relationship between the two independent clauses.

1. She wants to be a chef; _____, she is going to cooking school.

2. We were not able to go to the party; _____, we missed a good time.

3. You are really busy; _____, we should find time to chat briefly.

4. This house is too expensive; _____, it needs a lot of repairs.

5. Please come with me; _____, I will have to go by myself.

6. The dance party at the elementary school is tonight; _____, our middle school is having a bingo party.

7. You could start classes this summer; _____, you could wait until next semester.

8. Running daily is good for your muscles; _____, it can help lower your blood pressure.

9. My property increased in value; _____, it is worth almost three times the original price.

10. Dede does not practice her violin consistently; _____, she does not yet play well.

For practice using conjunctive adverbs after semicolons connecting independent clauses to indicate relationships, go to http://www.college.hmco.com/pic/dolphinwriterthree.

When you join independent clauses with a semicolon and a conjunctive adverb, notice that you add a semicolon *before* the conjunctive adverb and a comma *after* it:

Incorrect: The painting is unusual, nevertheless, I like it.
Correct: The painting is unusual; **nevertheless,** I like it.

Do not make the mistake of using a comma in place of the semicolon, or you will create an error called a *comma splice*, which is discussed later in this section.

Independent Clauses Joined by a Semicolon

The third way to form a compound sentence is to join independent clauses with just a semicolon:

We have to leave now; it is time for dinner.
He did not want to seem rude; he fibbed about liking her new house.

Notice that when a semicolon joins independent clauses, the second clause begins with a lowercase letter.

Before you link two independent clauses, make sure that the two ideas they express are closely related. One sentence may show a cause and the other an effect. The two ideas may be contrasting. There could be a time relationship, and so on. Then consider whether you should provide a conjunctive adverb that more explicitly explains the relationship. Your reader may or may not discern the relationship you mean to suggest, so providing an adverb will remove the guesswork:

> He did not want to seem rude; **therefore,** he fibbed about liking her new house.

By adding the conjunctive adverb *therefore,* you now make the relationship between the two clauses more clear.

Distinguishing Compound Elements from Compound Sentences

At the beginning of this section, you reviewed compound elements such as compound subjects, compound verbs, and compound direct objects. Now that you know how to write compound sentences, you can practice distinguishing them from a basic, or simple, sentence with a compound element. Knowing the difference will ensure that you punctuate your sentences correctly.

Notice the difference between the following sentences:

> *subject verb*   *verb*
>
> The **day** *started* out rainy but then *cleared*.

> *subject verb*   *subject verb*
>
> The **day** *started* out rainy, but then the **sky** *cleared*.

Should the first sentence have a comma after the word *rainy* and before the coordinating conjunction *but*? No, it should not; the first sentence is not a compound sentence. It contains a compound verb: the subject is *day,* and the two verbs are *started* and *cleared.* Because the sentence does not contain two different subject-verb relationships, we do not add a comma before the conjunction.

EXERCISE 50

For each of the following sentences, write CS on the blank if the sentence is compound. Write CE on the blank if the sentence contains a compound element but is not a compound sentence. Then add missing punctuation as needed.

_____ **1.** Jacques practiced every day and played beautifully at the concert.

_____ **2.** They like that restaurant and eat there every week.

_____ **3.** Ming rehearsed but still forgot her lines during the performance.

_____ **4.** She asked the questions and I answered them.

_____ **5.** The judge pounded her gavel and the trial began.

_____ **6.** He plants daffodils but not tulips.

_____ **7.** It could be the right phone number but I doubt it.

_____ **8.** Roy either watches television or reads in the evenings.

_____ **9.** My husband drove and I read the directions.

_____ **10.** Either you will make the team or you will not make the team.

For practice distinguishing and punctuating compound sentences and compound elements, go to http://www.college.hmco.com/pic/dolphinwriterthree.

Avoiding Comma Splices and Run-ons in Compound Sentences

Now that you have learned how to write the three different kinds of compound sentences, you can learn to recognize two serious errors—the comma splice and the run-on sentence—that occur when compound sentences are not correctly punctuated.

The Comma Splice

A **comma splice** occurs when a comma is used in the place where a semicolon should be:

> He is holding a full house, he definitely has the winning hand.
> She made the salad, meanwhile, he got the drinks.

In both of these sentences, only a comma separates the two independent clauses. A comma is appropriate if the clauses are joined with a coordinating conjunction; however, neither of these two includes a coordinating conjunction. In the first sentence, the comma must be replaced with a semicolon:

> He is holding a full house; he definitely has the winning hand.

In the second example, which includes the conjunctive adverb *meanwhile,* the first comma must be replaced with a semicolon:

> She made the salad; meanwhile, he got the drinks.

You can also correct a comma splice by replacing the incorrect comma with a period and creating two separate sentences. However, the comma error is usually an indication that the two independent clauses are related, so it is often more appropriate to link them in some type of compound sentence.

EXERCISE 51

On the blank before each of the following sentences, write *CS* if the sentence contains a comma splice and *Correct* if it is correct. In those sentences you have labeled *CS*, circle the commas that must be changed to semicolons.

_____ **1.** The mower is broken, it will not start.

_____ **2.** The book was interesting, but I did not finish it.

_____ **3.** The time to choose is now, so you should make your decision.

_____ **4.** The car is warmed up, let's leave.

_____ **5.** *Survivor* is my favorite TV show, is it yours?

_____ **6.** The snow is starting, get the shovels.

_____ **7.** I buy my holiday cards in January, that is the best time to get good deals.

_____ **8.** The baby needs a diaper change, for her diaper is wet.

_____ **9.** We need to buy eggs, and you need cereal.

_____ **10.** The washing machine is broken, it is shaking.

For practice identifying and correcting comma splices, go to http://www .college.hmco.com/pic/dolphinwriterthree.

The Run-on Sentence

A **run-on sentence,** which is also known as a *fused* sentence, occurs when there is no punctuation at all between two independent clauses:

We could go sailing we could go skiing.
She would love to visit Madrid she does not have a valid passport.
Lasagna is his favorite food he eats it often.

These three sentences each contain two independent clauses that are run together without any punctuation.

We can correct them one of three ways. First of all, we could simply add a semicolon between the two independent clauses:

We could go sailing; we could go skiing.
She would love to visit Madrid; she does not have a valid passport.
Lasagna is his favorite food; he eats it often.

Or we could add a comma and an appropriate coordinating conjunction:

We could go sailing, **or** we could go skiing.
She would love to visit Madrid, **but** she does not have a valid passport.
Lasagna is his favorite food, **so** he eats it often.

A third way to correct a run-on sentence is to add a semicolon and an appropriate conjunctive adverb or transitional expression followed by a comma:

We could go sailing; **on the other hand,** we could go skiing.
She would love to visit Madrid; **however,** she does not have a valid passport.
Lasagna is his favorite food; **therefore,** he eats it often.

For a list of conjunctive adverbs, see pages 526–527.

EXERCISE 52

For each of the following run-on sentences, write three different corrections on the blanks provided. Make sure that you add the necessary punctuation to your corrected sentences.

1. She asked for a raise her boss agreed to her request.

_____

_____

_____

2. Kyle hates the dentist he agreed to go.

_____

_____

_____

3. Jaime's computer crashed he needs to buy a new one.

_____

_____

_____

4. She needs a facial she needs a haircut.

_____

_____

_____

5. They lost their way in the woods they were rescued.

_____

_____

_____

For practice identifying and correcting run-on sentences, go to **http://www .college.hmco.com/pic/dolphinwriterthree.**

Subordination

The Complex Sentence

In the previous section, you learned about the compound sentence, which links related ideas together to make their relationships clearer to readers. This section discusses how to increase the clarity and sophistication of your writing by creating complex sentences, which are combinations of dependent and independent clauses.

Dependent Clauses

As you recall from previous sections of this Handbook, an *independent clause* is a group of words that can stand alone as a separate sentence because it contains both a subject and a verb, along with their modifiers and objects. Likewise, a **dependent clause** is a group of words that contains both a subject and a verb and their modifiers and objects. However, a dependent clause cannot stand alone; in order to make sense, it must be attached to an independent clause. Therefore, a dependent clause *depends* upon an independent clause to complete its meaning. Notice how the following dependent clauses express thoughts that are incomplete.

> Because she did not practice
> When you get to the coffee shop
> Unless you plan to be present

However, when these dependent clauses are added to independent clauses, their meaning becomes complete and clear:

> *dependent clause*   *independent clause*
> *Because she did not practice,* her playing sounded terrible at the recital.

> *dependent clause*   *independent clause*
> *When you get to the coffee shop,* call me.

> *independent clause*   *dependent clause*
> I will not count on you *unless you plan to be present.*

Combining one or more dependent clauses with an independent clause creates a **complex sentence.** A **compound-complex sentence** contains two or more independent clauses and one or more dependent clauses.

Subordinating Conjunctions

When you learned about compound sentences, you saw that their independent clauses are linked together with coordinating conjunctions. These conjunctions indicate that both clauses are *coordinate,* or equal. The clauses in a complex sentence, however, are not equal. One of them is dependent on, or subordinate to, the other. Thus, they are linked together with **subordinating conjunctions,** words that indicate this subordinate relationship. By adding one of the following words or phrases to the beginning of a clause, you make it dependent, or subordinate.

after	though
although	unless
as	until
because	what
before	when
even if	whenever
even though	where
how	whereas
if	whether
in order that	whichever
since	while

Notice how adding one of these words to an independent clause instantly creates a dependent clause that requires the addition of an independent clause to complete its meaning:

Independent clause:	We lost the game.
Dependent clause:	**After** we lost the game
Dependent clause:	**Even though** we lost the game
Dependent clause:	**When** we lost the game

These subordinating conjunctions not only point out which idea is subordinate but also indicate the relationship (time order, cause/effect, compare/contrast, and so on) between the two ideas.

EXERCISE 53

In each of the following complex sentences, circle the subordinating conjunction and underline the entire dependent clause.

1. When Jim leaves, I will let you know.

2. Because you were late, we need to reschedule.

3. Marlene left because she had to be somewhere else.

4. Beth will come unless her kids are home.

5. When you feel hungry, we will get some lunch.

6. Whenever you go to New York, think of me.

7. We should go skiing even though it is warm.

8. We should not begin the game until everyone arrives.

9. They will have dessert after they wash the dishes.

10. If you decide to go with us, let Ted know.

For practice recognizing subordinating conjunctions and dependent clauses in complex sentences, go to http://www.college.hmco.com/pic/dolphinwriter **three.**

Punctuating Dependent Clauses

When a dependent clause that begins with a subordinating conjunction starts a sentence, the dependent clause is followed by a comma:

> *dependent clause*   *independent clause*
> *Because she suffers from allergies,* she cannot own a rabbit.

> *dependent clause*   *independent clause*
> *Since she came to work here,* the office is more disorganized.

If the dependent clause *follows* the independent clause, you usually do not need a comma.

> *independent clause*   *dependent clause*
> She cannot own a rabbit *because she suffers from allergies.*

> *independent clause*   *dependent clause*
> The office is more disorganized *since she came to work here.*

EXERCISE 54

In each of the following sentences, underline the dependent clause and add a comma to the sentence if one is needed. If no comma is needed, write the word *Correct* beside the sentence.

1. Javier did not renew his driver's license until it expired.

2. Even though she left early he was able to see her.

3. The ground is really soggy because we have had so much rain.

4. Although we lost the big game we were still proud of ourselves.

5. Unless the situation changes I will be here tomorrow.

6. I will wait for you if you want.

7. Wherever he goes he takes a bottle of water.

8. They will not go if you have already seen the movie.

9. Let Taylor know when you plan to leave.

10. It has been two weeks since we last got together.

For practice punctuating dependent clauses, go to http://www.college.hmco.com/pic/dolphinwriterthree.

Relative Clauses

The **relative clause** is a type of dependent clause that begins with a relative pronoun such as *that, which, who,* or *whom.*

> Children **who eat well** benefit from a balanced diet.
> The vase **that fell and broke** was very rare.

This type of clause functions in a sentence as an adjective:

> The file **that he looked at** is missing. (The dependent clause is an adjective that answers the question *which file?*)
>
> Her paper, **which she wrote in a day**, earned a C. (The clause is an adjective that modifies the word *paper.*)

EXERCISE 55

In each of the following sentences, underline the relative clause.

1. The person whom I miss most is my husband.

2. The yellow cat, which belonged to my neighbor, hid in the bushes.

3. The car that I bought was in bad shape.

4. Mr. and Mrs. Mauras, who live on my street, have one daughter.

5. The shrub that I just planted is starting to bloom.

6. The person whom you should contact is the office manager.

7. The house that has the biggest backyard costs the most.

8. My brother, who snowboards, is very athletic.

9. Our refrigerator, which broke last week, will cost $100 to repair.

10. The brownies that she made were delicious.

For practice recognizing relative clauses in sentences, go to http://www.college.hmco.com/pic/dolphinwriterthree.

Punctuating Relative Clauses

You may have noticed by now that some of the sample sentences in this section have included commas around relative clauses, and some have not. Whether a relative clause is separated from the rest of the sentence by commas depends on whether the clause is essential or nonessential. The nonessential relative clause adds information that is not necessary for the reader to know which person or thing the writer is discussing:

Mr. Ricardo, *who lives in the mansion,* is very wealthy.

In this sentence, the relative clause *who lives in the mansion* is not essential to understand who the subject is. Therefore, the clause is not essential; it could be eliminated without any loss of meaning. As a result, it is separated from the rest of the sentence by placing a comma before and a comma after it.

Sometimes, however, a relative clause contains information that is essential for understanding which person or thing the writer means.

The man *who lives in the mansion* is very wealthy.

In this sentence, we do not know which man the writer means without knowing the information in the relative clause. Therefore, the clause is essential, and it is *not* enclosed within commas.

Using *That, Which, Who,* and *Whom* Correctly

Writers often confuse the relative pronouns *that, which, who,* and *whom.* They cannot be used interchangeably, so you will need to learn to distinguish them from one another.

First of all, the relative pronouns *that* and *which* refer to things and animals, whereas the relative pronouns *who* and *whom* refer to people.

Incorrect: A woman **that** inspires me is Hillary Rodham Clinton.
Correct: A woman **who** inspires me is Hillary Rodham Clinton.

Next you will need to distinguish between *that* and *which. That* begins *essential* relative clauses, whereas *which* begins *nonessential* relative clauses.

essential relative clause

The meal **that I love the most** is chicken and pasta.

nonessential relative clause

I eat chicken and pasta, **which is my favorite dish,** at least once a week.

Therefore, relative clauses beginning with *that* will not be enclosed in commas. Relative clauses beginning with *which* offer information that is not essential, so they are set off with commas from the rest of the sentence.

Finally, learn the difference between *who* and *whom.* In the section about pronouns, you studied the subjective and objective forms of pronouns. The relative pronoun *who* is the subjective form. Therefore, it is the correct pronoun to use when it is immediately followed by a verb:

verb

The person **who** *gets* the most pledges wins the contest.

As you recall from the previous section about punctuating essential and nonessential relative clauses, you will separate any *who* clause that offers nonessential information with commas from the rest of the sentence:

Her friend, *who arrived yesterday,* plans to stay a month.

The relative pronoun *whom* is the objective form. Therefore, it is the appropriate form to use when it is immediately followed by a noun or a pronoun:

noun

The woman **whom** the *judges* chose cried tears of joy. (*Whom* is the direct object of the verb *chose*.)

Use commas before and after a *whom* clause if the information it offers is not essential:

nonessential relative clause

His brother, **whom he loves,** is his best friend.

EXERCISE 56

In each of the following sentences, circle the correct relative pronoun. Use the punctuation in each sentence for clues about the right choice.

1. The writer (who, whom) is most loved in our family is Mark Twain.

2. A television show (which, that) disgusts me is *Fear Factor.*

3. My sister, (who, whom) I see often, lives in Alabama.

4. *King Kong* is the only movie (that, which) frightened her.

5. *King Kong,* (that, which) is an interesting film, frightened her.

6. The repairman (who, whom) called says he will fix the leaky faucet.

7. The letter (that, which) I sent you contains the information you need.

8. The person (who, whom) eats the most hotdogs will win the contest.

9. My daughter, (who, whom) is my best friend, calls me every day.

10. Her guidance counselor, (who, whom) she sees every day, is very caring.

For practice using that, which, who, *and* whom *correctly in sentences, go to* http://www.college.hmco.com/pic/dolphinwriterthree.

EXERCISE 57

Add necessary commas to each of the following sentences. Use the relative pronouns in the sentences as clues. If no commas should be added, write the word *Correct* beside the sentence.

1. The story that he loves to hear is *The Little Prince.*

2. *The Little Prince* which is a great book is his favorite.

3. Bettina who is my neighbor is a dancer.

4. The baseball team that is his favorite is the Yankees.

5. His coach was the only one whom he trusted.

6. The deli that I like was supposed to be open.

7. The deli on the corner which was supposed to be open was closed.

8. The letter that was supposed to arrive on Tuesday arrived on Wednesday.

9. People who exercise regularly are in better shape than people who do not.

10. My physical exam which occurred on May 1 revealed no major problems.

For practice punctuating sentences with relative clauses, go to http://www.college.hmco.com/pic/dolphinwriterthree.

Avoiding Sentence Fragments

You learned at the beginning of this section that dependent clauses cannot stand alone. A dependent clause must be attached to an independent clause that completes its meaning. Therefore, if a dependent clause ends with a period, it becomes a type of sentence fragment:

Sentence fragment: Although he loves to exercise.
Sentence fragment: That she plans to revise herself.

In the next sections, you will learn methods for correcting these fragments.

Correcting Dependent Clause Sentence Fragments

Dependent clause sentence fragments are those that begin with a subordinating conjunction and end, incorrectly, with a period:

Sentence fragment: **Even though** he is a minor.
Sentence fragment: **Because** this hotel does not have any rooms.

This type of fragment can be corrected in one of two ways. First of all, you can simply remove the subordinating conjunction, a deletion which would make the clause independent:

He is a minor.
This hotel does not have any rooms.

The second way to correct a dependent clause fragment is to add an independent clause that would complete its meaning. This independent clause is often the sentence that comes immediately before or after the fragment:

Even though he is a minor, he still has an opinion.

I will have to go to a different hotel *because this hotel does not have any rooms.*

Correcting Relative Clause Sentence Fragments

Relative clause sentence fragments are those that begin with a relative pronoun and end, incorrectly, with a period:

Sentence fragment: **Which** I do not understand.
Sentence fragment: **Who** keeps students engaged.

This type of fragment can be corrected in one of two ways. First of all, you can rewrite the fragment to eliminate the relative pronoun and create an independent clause:

I do not understand the homework assignment.
Mrs. Peavey keeps students engaged.

Notice that you will usually have to change the pronoun subject to a noun or make the object a noun in those clauses.

The second way to correct a relative clause fragment is to attach it to the independent clause that completes its meaning. This independent clause is often the sentence that comes immediately before or after the fragment:

I have not done the homework assignment, *which I do not understand.*
Mrs. Peavey is a great teacher *who keeps students engaged.*

EXERCISE 58

On the blanks provided, rewrite each of the following fragments in two different ways so that they are no longer sentence fragments. Add or delete words as necessary to make these fragments complete thoughts.

1. That I played.

_____

_____

2. Even though it was rare.

_____

_____

3. Because she had no time.

_____

_____

4. Who does not know me.

_____

_____

5. Which was sad.

_____

_____

For information about avoiding other types of sentence fragments, see pages 475, 486, and 494.

For practice correcting sentence fragments, go to http://www.college.hmco.com/pic/dolphinwriterthree.

Parallelism

When a sentence contains either a pair or a series of elements, those elements must be **parallel.** That is, the elements must be in the same grammatical form or have the same structure. Parallelism gives sentences balance, which makes them easier to read and understand. So, as you write, you will need to make sure that words, phrases, and clauses are all parallel.

Parallel Words

A pair or a series of words in a sentence should have the same form or be the same part of speech:

Parallel nouns:	**Neighbors, friends, constituents,** please vote.
Parallel adjectives:	Her singing was **beautiful, lilting,** and **melodic.**
Parallel adverbs:	He dances **gracefully** and **emotionally.**

Can you find the parallelism error in the following sentence?

She enjoys dancing, singing, and cards.

This sentence contains a series of three direct objects. Although all three are nouns, the first two are gerunds, nouns that are formed by adding *-ing* to a verb. The third item in the series is not a gerund, so the sentence contains an error in parallelism. To correct it, we need to change the form of the third item in the series to a gerund:

She enjoys dancing, singing, and **playing cards.**

If the series takes the form of adverbs, make sure that all of its elements are adverbs. If the series takes the form of adjectives, make sure that all of its elements are adjectives, and so on.

In addition, do not mix single-word elements with phrases:

She enjoys dancing, singing, and **to play cards.**

In this series of direct objects, the first two are gerunds, but the last item is an infinitive phrase. Because all three elements in the series do not have the same form, the sentence contains a parallelism error.

Parallel Phrases

A pair or series of phrases must be parallel as well.

Parallel prepositional phrases:
She looked **in the dresser, under the stove,** and **behind the door.**

Parallel infinitive phrases:
She is determined **to make a lot of money, to get her doctorate,** and **to move to a bigger house.**

Parallel gerund phrases:
Falling down the stairs, getting poison ivy, and **catching the flu** are a few of the things that happened to Sarah this year.

Can you find the parallelism errors in the following sentence?

> To get out of debt, cut up your credit cards, paying cash for your purchases, and patient saving for more expensive items.

This sentence is confusing because it offers a list of things to do to get out of debt, but the three things are presented in three different forms:

> cut up your credit cards (verb phrase)
> paying cash for your purchases (gerund phrase)
> patient saving for more expensive items (noun phrase)

Because of the parallelism errors, this sentence is difficult to comprehend. To correct it, rewrite the sentence so that all three elements are in the same form:

> To get out of debt, **cut** up your credit cards, **pay** cash for your purchases, and patiently **save** for more expensive items. (verb phrases)

> To get out of debt, begin **cutting** up your credit cards, **paying** cash for your purchases, and patiently **saving** for more expensive items. (gerund phrases)

> To get out of debt, you need **the courage** to cut up your credit cards, **the resolve** to pay cash for your purchases, and **the patience** to save for more expensive items. (noun phrases)

> Also, avoid combining a series of phrases with a clause:

> The week before he planned to propose marriage, he rented a boat, ordered flowers, and the restaurant took his reservation.

In what should be a series of three verb phrases, the first two items are verb phrases, but the third item is in the form of an independent clause. To correct the parallelism error, revise the clause to be another verb phrase:

> The week before he planned to propose marriage, he **rented** a boat, **ordered** flowers, and **made** a dinner reservation.

The coordinating conjunctions—especially the words *and, or,* and *but*—will often signal the need for parallel construction of the phrases they join. Also, pay attention to parallelism when you write two words or phrases that are joined with the pairs of correlative conjunctions *either/or, neither/nor, not only/but also, but/and,* and *not/but:*

> The money was *not* **for her** *but* **for him.**
> His obligation was *not only* **to himself** *but also* **to his daughter.**

EXERCISE 59

In each of the following sentences, underline the word or phrase that is preventing parallelism.

1. Bebe is beautiful, smart, and has talent.

2. When I am tired, I like to turn on the television, prop up my feet, and relaxing.

3. Before we leave, turn off the coffee pot, lock the door, and your keys.

4. If you want to lose weight, reduce the amount you eat, exercise every day, and commitment to the goal should be made.

5. Writing a book, getting my degree, and to own a dog are three of my dreams.

6. The ball rolled out of our yard, into the street, and the neighbor's lawn.

7. She feels gratitude toward not only her father and her brother Jim.

8. The boots came not from L. L. Bean, and they did come from Land's End.

9. To achieve more, set goals, work toward them, and refusing to give up.

10. Juan enjoys drawing, painting, and sometimes he sculpts.

For practice recognizing parallelism errors, go to http://www.college.hmco .com/pic/dolphinwriterthree.

Parallel Clauses

Like words and phrases, clauses must be parallel. In pairs and series, both independent and dependent clauses should have the same structure.

Parallelism and Independent Clauses

When pairs or series of independent clauses express parallel ideas, they must be parallel in structure:

> One brother is plump, and the other is slim.

Notice how changing the structure of the second independent clause makes the relationship between the two clauses a little harder to understand:

> One brother is plump, and "slim" best describes the other one.

Not only is this sentence more difficult to understand, but also its lack of balance causes it to sound cumbersome and awkward.

Now read two more compound sentences that lack parallelism and try to determine how the structure changes:

He broke up with his girlfriend, and the rejection was struggled with by her.
Does absence make the heart grow fonder, or out of sight out of mind?

In the first example, the first independent clause is in the active voice, and the second one is in the passive voice. Notice how much easier it is to understand this sentence when the second clause is revised to be in the active voice:

He broke up with his girlfriend, and **she struggled** with his rejection.

In the second example, the second clause is not in the question form of the first clause. To make the clauses parallel, we could write:

Does absence make the heart grow fonder, or **is** a person out of sight out of mind?

The coordinating conjunctions—especially the words *and, or,* and *but*—will often signal the need for parallel construction of the clauses they join. Also, pay attention to parallelism when you write two independent clauses that are joined with pairs of correlative conjunctions such as *either/or, neither/nor,* or *not only/but also.*

Either **we will reach** the summit of the mountain, *or* **we will die** trying.

Not only **can he prepare** gourmet meals, *but* he *also* **can repair** a leaky faucet.

EXERCISE 60

Identify each of the following compound sentences as parallel (P) or not parallel (NP). Write your answers on the blanks provided.

_____ **1.** Either she will have a baby, or working full time will be her choice.

_____ **2.** One sister is wise, and "foolish" is how we think of the other one.

_____ **3.** Either we will go to the beach, or we will go to the lake.

_____ **4.** He hit another vehicle, and damage was done to his car.

_____ **5.** She not only knows Arabic; she knows Spanish.

_____ **6.** Misha needed a new roommate, so she posted a notice on the bulletin board in the college lounge.

_____ **7.** Either we will finance the house for twenty-five years, but we might have to finance it for thirty years.

_____ **8.** One of my sisters is an accordion player, and the other is a piano player.

_____ **9.** Are you a leader, or _follower_ is the word that describes you better?

_____ **10.** Either we will win, or losing will be what happens.

For practice recognizing parallelism errors in compound sentences, go to http://www.college.hmco.com/pic/dolphinwriterthree.

Parallelism and Dependent Clauses

In complex sentences, too, a pair or series of dependent clauses should be parallel in structure:

Parallel relative clauses:
I hope **that** you will come to my party and **that** you will bring me a gift.

Parallel dependent clauses:
When he was born and **where** he lives now are none of our business.

Parallel dependent clauses:
The murder occurred sometime **after** the caterer arrived but **before** he left.

Many errors in parallelism occur when writers unintentionally mix words, phrases, and/or clauses in pairs or series of elements. The following sentence, for example, is not parallel:

        dependent clause   _independent clause_
He told her **that he loved her,** and **she should run away with him.**

In this sentence, the subject (_he_) says two things, so these two things should be expressed with parallel structure. But they are not: one is in the form of a dependent clause, and the other is in the form of an independent clause. To correct this error, we need only remove the comma and add the word _that_ before the independent clause:

He told her **that** he loved her and **that** she should run away with him.

Can you spot the parallelism errors in the following sentences?

She is a talented golfer and who is also good at bowling.
He was angry about the change and because no one had notified him.

Because she lacked experience and displaying a negative attitude, she was not hired for the job.

The first sentence pairs a noun phrase (*a talented golfer*) with a relative clause (*who is also good at bowling*). To correct it, revise so that the sentence contains two noun phrases:

She is a talented **golfer** and a good **bowler.**

The second sentence pairs a prepositional phrase (*about the change*) with a dependent clause (*because no one had notified him*). To correct it, revise the sentence so that it contains either two prepositional phrases or two dependent clauses:

He was angry **about** the change and **about** the lack of notification. (prepositional phrases)

He was angry **because** the change had been made and **because** no one had notified him.

In the third sentence, a dependent clause (*Because she lacked experience*) is paired with a participle phrase (*displaying a negative attitude*). To correct this sentence, rewrite it to include either two dependent clauses or two participle phrases:

Because she lacked experience and **because** she displayed a negative attitude, she was not hired for the job. (dependent clauses)

Lacking experience and **displaying** a negative attitude, she was not hired for the job. (participle phrases)

In addition, you could also revise this sentence to include a compound object of the preposition:

Because of her **lack of experience** and **negative attitude,** she was not hired for the job.

EXERCISE 61

Identify each of the following complex sentences as parallel (P) or not parallel (NP). Write your answers on the blanks provided.

_____ **1.** Because he made a mess and refusing to clean it up, his parents punished him.

_____ **2.** She is a great cook and who is also a black belt in karate.

_____ **3.** The team was happy about the win and that they were eligible for the playoffs.

_____ **4.** I am aware that you want the job and that we will both be applying for it.

_____ **5.** Pasha was thrilled to find the shirt and that it was the perfect color.

_____ **6.** Because the smoke detectors went off and in addition to knowing the escape route, we got out of the building in time.

_____ **7.** She will tell me where we will meet and the time of the meeting.

_____ **8.** Because you want to see that film, and because I do, too, we should see it together.

_____ **9.** You can see the doctor before she goes to lunch or after she returns.

_____ **10.** When the blizzard hit and that there was ice on the runways, the airport closed.

For practice recognizing parallelism errors in dependent clauses, go to http://www.college.hmco.com/pic/dolphinwriterthree.

Combining Sentences

To make the necessary connections for your readers, to reduce wordiness, and to increase the overall sophistication of your writing, you will want to vary the length of your sentences. Earlier in this Handbook, you learned to join two independent clauses together in compound sentences to more clearly indicate the relationship between two ideas. In this section, you will learn how to combine two sentences. Combining sentences involves not simply linking but also _blending_ them together. As you revise and edit your writing, experiment with the six different ways to turn one sentence into an element of another sentence.

Use a Compound Subject or Compound Verb

One way to combine sentences is to create a compound subject or a compound verb to blend one sentence into another. For example, look at these two sets of short sentences:

Jose drives a station wagon. Fred drives one, too.
Jennifer bought coffee. Then she went to the library.

The first set of sentences can be combined by using a compound subject to blend the information in the second sentence into the first sentence:

subject   subject
   Jose and **Fred** drive station wagons.

The second set of sentences can be combined by using a compound verb to blend the information in the second sentence into the first sentence:

         verb   *verb*
   Jennifer **bought** coffee and then **went** to the library.

Note that both of these revised sentences are less wordy.

 **EXERCISE 62**

On the blanks provided, combine each of the following pairs of sentences by using a compound subject or a compound verb.

1. Patricio went to Paris. Jacques went, too.

_____

2. Pablo goes to work at dawn. Jackie goes to work at dawn, too.

_____

3. Marie went to dinner. Then she saw a movie.

_____

4. Erin graduated from college. Afterward, she began her nursing career.

_____

5. Pedro enjoys water sports. Carissa enjoys water sports as well.

_____

6. Carrie is an editor for the company. Kellie is an editor for the company, too.

_____

7. Jisela drove to North Carolina. Then she found a good barbecue restaurant.

_____

8. I fell in love. Then I got married.

_____

9. Jon paid off his credit cards. He cut them all up.

_____

10. The Goldbergs live on this block. The Mulligans live on this block, too.

_____

For practice using a compound subject or compound verb, go to http://www
.college.hmco.com/pic/dolphinwriterthree.

Use a Dependent Clause

Another way to combine sentences is to turn one of the sentences into a dependent clause. For example, look at these sets of sentences:

She did not read the directions. She failed the test.
The artist had already painted the canvas. He realized his mistake.

The first set of sentences can be combined by turning the first independent clause into a dependent clause and attaching it to the second independent clause:

    dependent clause   *independent clause*
Because she did not read the directions, she failed the test.

The second set of sentences can be combined by turning the second sentence into a dependent clause:

    independent clause   *dependent clause*
The artist had already painted the canvas **before he realized his mistake.**

In both new sentences, the information in one of the original sentences becomes an adverb clause for the other original sentence. Notice how the relationship between the two original sentences becomes much clearer when they are combined.

EXERCISE 63

On the blanks provided, combine each of the following pairs of sentences by turning one of them into a dependent clause.

1. It was raining. We canceled the picnic.

_____

2. I asked her about her sister. She gave me all of the details about the wedding.

_____

3. The morning was gloomy. The afternoon was sunny.

_____

4. We did not answer the phone. We were having dinner.

_____

5. Francisco will take the children to the park. He will go when Janet comes home.

_____

6. One lane of the highway was closed for construction. Traffic congestion has dramatically increased.

_____

_____

7. He looked around the kitchen for his keys. She searched the bedroom.

_____

8. Jane had already begun making the omelet. She realized that she was out of cheese.

_____

_____

9. There was a hurricane on Friday. We could not have the barbecue.

_____

10. I will help you. I will stay until the babysitter arrives.

_____

For practice with turning sentences into dependent clauses, go to http://www.college.hmco.com/pic/dolphinwriterthree.

Use a Relative (*Who, Which,* or *That*) Clause

Sentences can also be combined by turning one of them into a relative (adjective) clause. Read the following two sets of sentences:

Some people eat fruits and vegetables often. These people are generally healthy.

The play won a Tony Award. I liked it.

The first set of sentences can be combined by turning the first sentence into a relative clause and blending it into the second sentence:

relative clause

People **who eat fruits and vegetables often** are generally healthy.

The second set of sentences can be combined by turning the second sentence into a relative clause:

relative clause

The play **that I liked** won a Tony Award.

Notice that the relationships are clearer when the sentences are combined.

EXERCISE 64

On the blanks provided, combine each of the following pairs of sentences by turning one of them into a relative clause.

1. Some people exercise regularly. They are healthy.

_____

2. That actor won an Academy Award. He is one of my favorites.

_____

3. The stray dog is a German Shepherd. We adopted it.

_____

4. My cowboy boots are comfortable. They were a gift.

_____

5. Tran plays hockey. He wears number nine on his jersey.

_____

6. The album is very popular. Kwan likes it.

_____

7. The house on the corner is being renovated. It has been empty for years.

_____

8. The spa is in Colorado. The spa is very luxurious.

_____

9. Some people can get badly sunburned. They are people with pale skin.

_____

10. The girl rejected his proposal. He adores her.

_____

For practice with turning sentences into relative clauses, go to http://www
.college.hmco.com/pic/dolphinwriterthree.

Use an Appositive

Sentences can also be combined by turning one of them into an appositive. For
example, read the following sentences:

> Renee delivered an interesting speech. She is the valedictorian.
> The coat was a gift from her parents. It was lime green.

The first set of sentences can be combined by turning the second one into an
appositive and blending it into the first sentence:

> _appositive_
> Renee, **the valedictorian,** delivered an interesting speech.

The second set of sentences can be combined by turning the first one into an
appositive:

> _appositive_
> The coat, **a gift from her parents,** was lime green.

EXERCISE 65

**On the blanks provided, combine each of the following pairs of sentences by turning
one of them into an appositive.**

1. Our neighbor is neat and tidy. He is a very meticulous man.

_____

2. Lance Armstrong has three children. He is a great cyclist.

_____

3. Burton is a tenor. He sang a song from _The Barber of Seville_.

_____

4. The pants are very uncomfortable. They are cotton khakis.

_____

5. Mario made a delicious pasta dish. He is a gourmet chef.

_____

6. The painting is beautiful. It is a Picasso.

_____

7. The dessert is very tasty. It is a kind of custard.

_____

8. Dr. Hendrickson is our principal. He is retiring at the end of the year.

_____

9. Jupiter is our solar system's largest planet. It is the fifth planet from the Sun.

_____

10. My sister is a regional manager with a phone company. She works hard.

_____

For practice with turning sentences into appositives, go to http://www
.college.hmco.com/pic/dolphinwriterthree.

Use a Prepositional Phrase

Yet another way to combine sentences is to turn the information in one of them
into a prepositional phrase. For example, read these sentences:

> The tree had the kite. The kite was stuck.
> She heard her favorite song. The radio was playing it.

The first set of sentences can be combined by turning the first sentence into a
prepositional phrase and blending it into the second sentence:

> *prepositional phrase*
> The kite was stuck **in the tree.**

The second set of sentences can be combined by turning the second sentence
into a prepositional phrase:

> *prepositional phrase*
> She heard her favorite song **on the radio.**

On the blanks provided, combine each of the following pairs of sentences by turning one of them into a prepositional phrase.

1. The mouse was running around. Its location was the kitchen.

_____

2. I saw my favorite band. The Paramount was where it performed.

_____

3. He flew to Nevada. It was raining.

_____

4. She washed the comforter. The bed is where it was.

_____

5. Patricia drove to my house. It was snowing.

_____

6. Marlena took us to the movies. We used her truck.

_____

7. Gene cooked the steaks. He used the grill.

_____

8. I found my gloves. A drawer was where they had been placed.

_____

9. Joaquin picked up the dishwasher. Sears was the place where he got it.

_____

10. Terry rearranged the furniture. He was alone.

_____

For practice with turning sentences into prepositional phrases, go to www.college.hmco.com/pic/hmcollegeseriesthree_1e.

Use a Participle (-*ed* or -*ing*) Phrase

One last way to combine sentences is to turn one of the sentences into a participle phrase. For example, read the following sets of sentences:

> He was a fugitive. He was wanted in three states.
> She crouched down low. She remained hidden from sight.

The first set of sentences can be combined by turning the second sentence into a participle phrase and blending it with the first sentence:

participle phrase

He was a fugitive **wanted in three states.**

The second set of sentences can be combined by turning the first sentence into a participle phrase:

participle phrase

Crouching down low, she remained hidden from sight.

NOTE: When using this method, beware of creating dangling or misplaced modifiers.

EXERCISE 67

On the blanks provided, combine each of the following pairs of sentences by turning one of them into a participle phrase.

1. She is a volunteer. She is collecting money for the American Heart Association.

_____

2. The dog dug in the dirt. She looked for bones.

_____

3. The nurse was exhausted. He often worked double shifts.

_____

4. She drove too slowly. She angered other drivers.

_____

5. Mary is a great teacher. She is wanted for lectures.

_____

6. Bill is the architect. He is designing our city's new arena.

_____

7. Cesar listened to his gut instinct. He rejected the baseball contract.

_____

8. Ivanka searched for answers. She went to the library.

_____

9. Marge is a popular hairstylist. She is booked for weeks in advance.

_____

10. Chet eluded capture. He hid in the basement.

_____

For practice with turning sentences into participle phrases, go to http://www.college.hmco.com/pic/dolphinwriterthree.

Mechanics

Punctuation

Correct punctuation is important in sentences. The proper punctuation marks help readers read more easily, and these marks also prevent confusion and misreading. In this section, you will learn the rules for the major punctuation marks: periods, question marks, exclamation points, commas, semicolons, colons, apostrophes, and quotation marks.

Periods, Question Marks, and Exclamation Points

Periods, question marks, and exclamation points are all types of end punctuation. That is, they indicate that a sentence has ended.

> I cannot see you.
> Where did you go?
> There you are!

Using a period is the most common way to end a sentence. If a sentence does not ask a question or present something in an exclamatory way, such as the first sentence in the preceding group, it ends with a period. The question mark ends a sentence that asks a question, such as *Where are you?* If a sentence is exclamatory in nature, such as the last sentence in the preceding example, it ends with an exclamation point. You probably will not use exclamation points as frequently as you use periods and question marks in your writing, but if you want to emphasize the severity or excitement of a certain sentence, an exclamation point is appropriate.

A period is also used to indicate abbreviations, such as those for Doctor (Dr.), Registered Nurse (R.N.), or Mister (Mr.).

EXERCISE 68

In each of the following sentences, supply the necessary end punctuation marks.

1. Where is Franco

2. Get this bug off my shoulder

3. Do not forget to brush your teeth

4. Mr Byrnes is my father's friend

5. Get out of here now

6. Where do you want to go on vacation, Jim

7. Did you buy a new sweater yesterday

8. Diana finished reading the book

9. Is Kathy a corporal or a sergeant

10. Do not come back here again

For practice punctuating with periods, question marks, and exclamation points, go to http://www.college.hmco.com/pic/dolphinwriterthree.

Commas

Commas often seem to be tricky punctuation marks. However, there are actually only seven rules for comma usage. Memorize these seven rules; then each time you wonder whether or not you should insert a comma, ask yourself if the situation is one of those described here.

Commas separate certain elements in sentences. Use commas to

1. Separate words in a series of three or more words, phrases, or clauses:

> I went to the library and looked through some fiction, nonfiction, and reference books.
>
> The paper blew across the yard, down the street, and into the river.

2. Connect two independent clauses that are joined by a coordinating conjunction (*and, but, for, nor, yet, or, so*).

> I went to the department store, **but** I forgot to buy stockings.

3. Separate introductory elements from a sentence, including dependent clauses:

> Running down the street, I broke the heel of my shoe.
>
> Because she attended every class, she received an award for perfect attendance.

4. Separate an element—such as an appositive, certain relative clauses, or the name of the person being spoken to—that could be removed from the sentence without changing its meaning:

> The play, which is overly long, is difficult to sit through.
> Mrs. Miller, my piano teacher, is very talented.
> I wonder, Elaine, if it is acceptable to take that book without asking.

5. Separate two or more coordinate adjectives:

> This delicate, colorful shirt looks great on you.

6. Separate elements in direct quotations:

> She said, "Yes."

7. Separate phrases that indicate contrast:

> I asked her to hand me a cup, not a bowl.

EXERCISE 69

In each of the following sentences, add commas as necessary.

1. Because you are late I cannot let you in.

2. He decided to learn Spanish French and Portuguese.

3. We were going to eat out but Pedro made dinner instead.

4. This television station which is devoted to home decorating is fun to watch.

5. Jorge the catcher is also a good hitter.

6. Can you help me with my homework Mai?

7. Lexie said "No I did not do it."

8. We decided to drive not fly.

9. Running down the road Joanne tripped on her shoelace.

10. Annie my best friend is very devoted to her husband.

For practice punctuating with commas, go to http://www.college.hmco .com/pic/dolphinwriterthree.

Semicolons

There are only two uses of the semicolon in sentences:

1. To link two independent clauses:

You should give me a ride; I do not have a car.

Greg and Jennifer did not carpool to work; otherwise, she would have been on time.

2. To separate the items in lists that already contain commas:

In attendance at the meeting were Mr. Jones, president; Ms. Anderson, vice president; Mr. Lee, treasurer; and Mrs. Lopez, secretary.

EXERCISE 70

In each of the following sentences, add semicolons as necessary.

1. Sheng read a book I worked on a puzzle.

2. We visited several cities on our trip, including Paris, France Madrid, Spain and Rome, Italy.

3. The members of our band include Roy, the lead singer Stan, the guitarist Angelo, the drummer and Phil, the bass player.

4. Do not forget to use sunscreen a sunburn is painful.

5. The game starts at one o'clock we do not want to miss the kickoff.

For practice punctuating with semicolons, go to http://www.college.hmco .com/pic/dolphinwriterthree.

Apostrophes

Apostrophes have only three uses.

1. They form contractions:

> do not = don't
> have not = haven't
> there is = there's
> you are = you're

2. They indicate possession:

> Mrs. Smith's garden
> the girls' mittens
> my brother-in-law's motorcycle

3. They are used to form plurals of single letters and numerals:

> She earned A's in all of her classes.
>
> When you are rolling dice, two 1's are called *snake eyes* and two 6's are called *boxcars*.

EXERCISE 71

In each of the following sentences, add apostrophes as necessary.

1. I cant go with you.

2. Theres a hole in this bucket.

3. Youre a great dancer.

4. Jerrys children didnt do their homework.

5. Peter got all As and Bs on his report card.

6. Simons sister lives in Pennsylvania.

7. Were having a great time.

8. Its almost time to go home.

9. Cindys luck isnt very good.

10. He got two 3s and two 4s on his standardized test.

For practice punctuating with apostrophes, go to http://www.college.hmco .com/pic/dolphinwriterthree.

Colons

Two of the main uses for colons are listed below.

1. They introduce a list:

> The executive board of the parent-teacher association at my school is composed of the following members: president, vice president, secretary, and treasurer.

2. They introduce some direct quotations:

> Every time I use salt in my cooking, I throw a bit over my right shoulder and say: "Once over the shoulder for good luck."

EXERCISE 72

In each of the following sentences, add colons as necessary.

1. The following people will ride in my car Ming, Jennifer, Carmela, and Carrie.

2. When you go to the grocery store, buy me these things lettuce, salad dressing, potato chips, and bread.

3. Sharon always has this to say "Do not do anything I would not do."

4. Do not forget to add these things to your list return this phone call, finish this memo, and check your e-mail.

5. As you write, you should constantly ask yourself "Should I provide more details to help the reader understand?"

For practice punctuating with colons, go to http://www.college.hmco.com/pic/dolphinwriterthree.

Quotation Marks

Quotation marks have three main uses in sentences. They are used to

1. Indicate that you are using someone else's exact words:

   Someone once said, "Beauty is only skin deep."

2. Indicate an unusual use of a word or reservation:

   I do not agree with Mayor Elliott's position on the energy "program."

   Used in this way, the quotation marks indicate that the writer thinks that "program" is not the correct way to describe the energy situation.

3. Indicate titles of poems, short stories, songs, and articles:

   I recently read the poem "To a Skylark."

EXERCISE 73

In each of the following sentences, add quotation marks as necessary.

1. Dr. McNulty said, You will be fine.

2. Have you read the poem The Raven?

3. The so-called war on drugs has not been very effective.

4. I love the song Night and Day.

5. The hostess said, Your table is ready now.

For practice punctuating with quotation marks, go to http://www.college .hmco.com/pic/dolphinwriterthree.

Capitalization

It is important to use capital letters properly. To make sure that you are capitalizing words correctly, memorize the rules in this section.

The Rules of Capitalization

- The first letter of the first word in every sentence is capitalized:

    *A*fter much thought, we decided to sell our house.

- Whenever the pronoun *I* is used in a sentence, it is capitalized, regardless of its placement in a sentence:

    I wanted to go to dinner, but *I* did not have any way to get to the restaurant.

- Proper nouns—those nouns that name specific people, places, and things— are capitalized, as are family relative titles:

    We went to *A*ruba with *A*unt *R*ose, *U*ncle *E*d, and *J*ack.

- Proper adjectives—adjectives formed from proper nouns—are also capitalized:

    The *L*ebanese businesswoman traveled internationally for work.

- Titles that precede names are capitalized, but those that are not followed by names are not capitalized:

    *P*resident Anwar Sadat, the late *p*resident of Egypt, was a great humanitarian.

- Directions that are names of regions are capitalized; compass points (north, south, east, west) are not capitalized.

    The *S*outhwest is a lovely part of the country to visit, as is *e*astern Utah.

- Capitalize the days of the weeks, the months of the year, and holidays:

    On *F*riday, *D*ecember 31, we will celebrate *N*ew *Y*ear's *E*ve.

■ Capitalize the names of countries, nationalities, and specific languages:

> Despite being *B*elgian and speaking *F*rench, Christian speaks fluent *E*nglish.

■ Capitalize the major words in the titles of books, articles, and songs:

> *The Catcher in the Rye* is a wonderful novel.

■ Capitalize the names of groups such as Jews, African Americans, and Hispanics:

> The Catholics in my town have two churches.

■ Capitalize names of organizations such as the Democratic Party, the National League, and the Association of Teachers:

> The *D*emocratic *P*arty held a fundraiser.

■ Capitalize the names of buildings and businesses such as *S*hea Stadium, Mount Sinai Hospital, and Bloomingdale's:

> The *W*aldorf *A*storia is a luxurious hotel.

■ Capitalize names of school courses such as Anatomy I and English 101:

> My *F*reshman Composition course meets on Wednesdays at three o'clock.

■ Capitalize historical periods such as the Renaissance and the Ice Age, and the names of major conflicts such as the Civil War:

> World War I saw an increase in American casualties.

■ Acronyms—those letters that stand for a longer title—are capitalized:

> The National Rifle Association, or *NRA,* is a strong group in Washington.

EXERCISE 74

In each of the following sentences, circle every word that should begin with a capital letter.

1. have you read the novel *cold mountain?*

2. after her husband, president bill clinton, left office, hillary clinton became a senator.

3. i enjoy reading books about the american revolutionary war.

4. you can pick me up in front of my hotel.

5. in september, florida is quite warm.

6. marlie, john, and david usually do something together on saturday nights.

7. we order chinese take-out food once a week.

8. when marcelle came to our house, he told us stories about his grandparents.

9. i used to go to los angeles often.

10. our representative to congress opposes this legislation.

For more practice capitalizing words correctly, go to http://www.college .hmco.com/pic/dolphinwriterthree.

Spelling

The Importance of Correct Spelling

Before you submit anything you have written to someone else, you will need to check it carefully for spelling errors. Readers tend to judge writing that is marred by misspellings as sloppy, careless, or indicative of a lack of knowledge. In order to avoid these kinds of judgments, make sure you have spelled every word in your paper correctly.

You can check spelling in three main ways:

1. **Look up words in a dictionary.** During the proofreading and editing stage of the writing process, comb your paper carefully for words that might be misspelled. If you have the slightest doubt that a word is correctly spelled, look it up.
2. **Use a computer spell-checker to help you locate misspelled words.** Word processing programs such as Microsoft Word will identify possible misspellings for you and will even suggest the correct spellings. These programs are not foolproof, but they will help you find more errors so that you can remove them from your paper.
3. **Ask others to proofread your papers.** Ask people you know—relatives, friends, coworkers—who are known to be good spellers to read your draft and circle possible misspellings.

Some Spelling Rules

In addition to using one or more of the three methods for locating spelling errors, you can memorize a few rules that will help you improve your spelling.

Forming Plurals. Most words are made plural by adding an *-s* to the end of the word. For example, add an *-s* to *head* to make the plural *heads*. Or add an *-s* to the word *hand* to make the plural *hands*. However, as with many of the rules you have learned so far in this Handbook, there are exceptions to the rules. They are listed as follows:

Nouns that end with -s, -z, -x, -sh, or –ch

To form the plural of a noun that ends in *-s*, *-z*, *-x*, *-sh*, or *-ch*, add *-es*:

pass	pass*es*
buzz	buzz*es*
tax	tax*es*
crash	crash*es*
glitch	glitch*es*

Nouns that end in -o

In most cases, also add *-es* to nouns that end in *o*:

potato	potato*es*
tomato	tomato*es*

There are a few exceptions, such as the word *pianos*.

Words ending in -f or -fe

Words ending in *-f* or *-fe* are made plural in one of three ways. For some, add *-s*, as with other plurals:

belief	belief*s*
chief	chief*s*

Some words ending in *-f* or *-fe* are made plural with *-ves*:

shelf	shel*ves*
elf	el*ves*
life	li*ves*

For words that end in *–ff* or *-ffe*, add *-s*:

staff	staff*s*
gaffe	gaffe*s*
giraffe	giraffe*s*

Words that are the same whether singular or plural

Some words are the same in both their singular and plural forms:

deer   sheep
elk   fish

EXERCISE 75

For each of the following sentences, write on the blank provided the plural form of the boldfaced word.

1. The movers broke six of our **glass.** _____

2. After the heavy rain, the **ditch** overflowed with water. _____

3. We saw three **deer** during our hike. _____

4. Have your **belief** changed? _____

5. The **staff** at both stores are hoping that the stores will be closed on Christmas Eve. _____

Adding Suffixes to Words.

-y words

Change the final *-y* to *-i* and add *-es* to make words ending in *-y* plural or to change verb tense:

supply   suppl*ies*   suppl*ied*
cry   cr*ies*   cr*ied*
empty   empt*ies*   empt*ied*

-e words

When you add certain suffixes to many words that end in *-e*, you will drop that final *-e* before adding the suffix:

bike   bik*ing*
love   lov*able*
obese   obes*ity*

Doubling a final letter

Double the final letter if (1) it is a consonant, (2) its last two letters are a vowel followed by a consonant, (3) it is a one-syllable word or is accented on the last syllable, or (4) the suffix that you want to add starts with a vowel:

hop   hop*ped*   hop*ping*
rub   rub*bed*   rub*bing*
refer   refer*red*   refer*ring*

-*ally* and -*ly* words

A word becomes an adverb when -*ally* or -*ly* is added. If the word ends in -*ic*, add -*ally*, as in *frantically*. Otherwise, add -*ly* to the end of the word, as in *lovely*.

EXERCISE 76

Add -*ing* or -*ed*, as appropriate, to the word in parentheses, and write the correct form of the word on the blank provided in each sentence.

1. We are _____ this TV show. (*tape*)

2. She _____ for the best. (*hope*)

3. He was _____ the sauce. (*stir*)

4. They _____ over the puddle. (*step*)

5. I _____ right away. (*reply*)

Add -*ally* or -*ly*, as appropriate, to the word in parentheses, and write the correct form of the word on the blank provided in each sentence.

6. They have a few differences, but they are _____ the same. (*basic*)

7. _____, the project went well. (*initial*)

8. I _____ question her judgment. (*rare*)

9. He _____ finished the report at midnight. (*final*)

10. _____, we have run out of ice cream. (*tragic*)

ie and *ei* **Words.** Usually, if we say the old rhyme "*I* before *E* except after *C* or when sounding like *A* as in n*ei*ghbor and w*ei*gh," we can figure out how to spell *ie* and *ei* words. Again, there are exceptions to this rule.

ie: science, conscience, species, sufficient

ei: seize, either, weird, height, foreign, leisure, counterfeit, forfeit, neither, sleight

EXERCISE 77

In each of the following sentences, circle every word that is misspelled, and write above it the correct spelling. If there are no misspelled words, write *Correct*.

1. My neice is coming to visit next week.

2. Her assistant is very efficeint.

3. You will recieve the package tomorrow.

4. Niether of us knows what to do.

5. We never seem to have enough leisure time.

6. Her weight has recently increased.

7. When the team was late for the game, it had to forfiet.

8. I am working hard to acheive my goals.

9. Have you taken any foriegn correspondence courses?

10. The government seized all of thier property.

For practice locating spelling errors, go to http://www.college.hmco.com/pic/dolphinwriterthree.

Commonly Confused Words. Here are some commonly confused homonyms (words that sound alike), with their definitions. Study these words to learn the differences in their meanings:

accept   to agree to
except   excluding
(*continued*)

adverse	negative
averse	reluctant
advice	counsel
advise	to give an opinion
affect	to influence
effect	result
allude	to refer to indirectly
elude	to evade
allusion	indirect reference
illusion	false impression
assure	to guarantee
ensure	to guarantee
insure	to cover or underwrite
bare	naked
bear	large animal; to carry
bazaar	festival
bizarre	odd
bored	without interest
board	flat piece of wood; to climb on
breath	mouthful of air
breathe	to take breaths
by	near
buy	to purchase
capitol	building in which a legislature meets
capital	assets; seat of government
cite	to refer to
site	location
sight	ability to see
close	to shut
clothes	apparel
coarse	rough
course	path; unit of study
complement	to balance; to go together
compliment	admiring comment

conscience	moral/ethical principles
conscious	aware
decent	civilized or well mannered
descent	to go down
dissent	to disagree with
defuse	to calm
diffuse	to spread
desert	arid, sandy place
dessert	a sweet served at the end of dinner
devise	to concoct
device	mechanism
disburse	to pay out
disperse	to scatter
dual	twofold
duel	contest between two combatants
dye	to change color
die	to expire
elicit	to draw out
illicit	illegal
envelop	to surround
envelope	cover; packet
fair	balanced
fare	payment for services
farther	beyond (distance)
further	additional
faze	to put off, disturb
phase	stage
fiscal	relating to money
physical	having to do with the body
for	in favor of; intended for
fore	front
four	a number
formally	officially
formerly	previously

| hear | to perceive sound |
| here | at this time; presently |

| hole | gap |
| whole | all together |

incidence	occurrence
incident	event
instance	example

| its | possessive of *it* |
| it's | contraction of *it is* |

| know | to be aware of something |
| no | rejection |

| later | afterward |
| latter | concluding |

| liable | accountable |
| libel | written slander |

| lead | to show the way; a metallic element |
| led | showed the way |

| lightening | lessening a load |
| lightning | electricity related to a storm event |

| lose | to misplace |
| loose | unfastened |

| meat | animal protein |
| meet | to convene or get together |

| miner | someone who works underground in a mine |
| minor | of lesser importance |

| passed | approved or accepted; gone by |
| past | history; what went before |

| patience | endurance or fortitude |
| patients | people under the care of a doctor |

| peace | serenity |
| piece | a segment of something larger |

peak	climax
peek	to steal a look
pique	to arouse interest or ire

personal	private
personnel	group of employees
plain	without adornment
plane	flat surface; aeronautical transportation
populace	public
populous	densely populated
pore	small opening; to study
pour	to dispense
pray	to meditate
prey	quarry or victim
precede	to come before
proceed	to go ahead
presence	attendance
presents	gifts
principal	head of a school
principle	belief
quiet	calm; without sound
quite	to a certain extent
rain	precipitation
reign	rule
rein	strap to hold a horse
raise	to lift up
raze	to tear down
right	correct
rite	ritual
write	to put pen to paper
road	street
rode	traveled
root	origin
rout	disorderly retreat; defeat
route	direction
sale	transaction
sail	part of a boat
scene	location
seen	noticed

stationary	not moving
stationery	writing paper and envelopes
than	a conjunction used to indicate an unequal comparison or difference
then	subsequently
their	belonging to them
there	in that place
they're	contraction of *they are*
threw	tossed
through	during; from beginning to end
to	in the direction of
too	also
two	a number
waist	the midsection of the body
waste	garbage; to use up illogically
weak	without strength
week	seven days
weather	climate; to endure
whether	a conjunction to indicate alternatives
which	a pronoun indicating choice
witch	a woman possessing magical powers
who's	contraction of *who is*
whose	the possessive form of *who*
wood	a piece of lumber
would	past tense of the verb *will*
yore	of old
your	the possessive of *you*
you're	contraction of *you are*

EXERCISE 78

In each of the following sentences, circle the word that fits the context of the sentence.

1. (Who's, Whose) notebook is this?

2. Do not (waste, waist) this opportunity.

3. We will decide in a (week, weak).

4. I always ride my (stationery, stationary) bike.

5. Her (reign, rein, rain) as queen was short-lived.

6. I cannot (accept, except) this gift.

7. This survey should (illicit, elicit) a good response.

8. Try to have some (patients, patience).

9. The manager (dispersed, disbursed) the paychecks.

10. That lie you told should bother your (conscious, conscience).

Abbreviations

In some respects, this might be called the era of abbreviations because writers are used to quick e-mails and instant messages that use shorthand for common phrases such as "be right back" (brb). No doubt more and more written conversation abbreviations will continue to show up, but in writing paragraphs and essays for college, traditional rules for using abbreviations correctly continue to apply.

What to Abbreviate

Check this table to learn what you do need to abbreviate.

Abbreviate	Examples
Titles before and after people's names	Mr., Ms., Mrs., Dr., Jr., Sr., C.P.A., M.D., Ph.D., D.V.M.
Time and date words used before and after a number	200 B.C.E., 554 C.E., A.D. 1776, 200 B.C., 5:00 a.m., 12:00 p.m.
Names of organizations, corporations, and certain countries	UK, USA, FBI, NAACP, NCAA, NSA, UNICEF

What Not to Abbreviate

Do Not Abbreviate	*Examples*
Titles before a person's surname	Professor Aguilar, Reverend Smith, Officer Jones, Sergeant Reyes
Days and months	Friday, Wednesday, August, January
Measurements	three pounds, one inch, six feet
States and countries (except when in a mailing address)	Iowa, California, British Columbia, Canada, Nigeria, New Zealand
Courses	English (not Eng), Chemistry (not Chem)

Numbers

The following are some guidelines for when you need to spell out numbers.

When a number appears at the beginning of a sentence, spell it out:

Eight players showed up for the baseball game.

When a number can be expressed in one or two words, spell it out:

eighteen children
two thousand years

Use a hyphen with numbers between twenty-one and ninety-nine.

She turned **thirty-two** on the same day that her great-great grandmother would have turned two hundred.

Spell out simple fractions:

He cut the recipe by **one-half.**

NOTE: On the other hand, use numerals in your writing in the following situations.

When a number cannot be expressed as one or two words	672 redwoods left
Decimals, percents, whole numbers plus fractions	5.2, 36 percent, $8\frac{1}{2}$
Game scores	7–4
Precise sums of money used with a dollar sign	$2.19
Route or road number	Route 12, Interstate 95
Dates (days and years)	June 25, 1959
Chapters, pages, volumes	chapter 6, page 482, volume 32
Addresses	12 Beacon Street, 174 Elm Avenue

Additional Practice for Multilingual Writers

English differs from other languages in certain aspects of grammar and sentence construction. For writers whose native language is not English, this appendix addresses some of these issues.

Countable and Noncountable Nouns

Many nouns in the English language are **countable.** That is, they refer to things—such as dollars, birds, CDs, and waves—that are separate units. Therefore, they can be counted, and they have both singular and plural forms.

Singular	*Plural*
boat	boats
message	messages
potato chip	potato chips
child	children

Other nouns in English, however, are **noncountable.** They name ideas, emotions, or other things that cannot be divided into separate parts or pieces. Some examples of noncountable nouns follow.

Abstract ideas: honesty, bravery, happiness, patience

Activities: homework, housework, football, surfing, chess, sleeping

Things made up of small particles or grains: oatmeal, salt, sugar, flour, dust

Liquids: blood, soup, paint, coffee, water, milk, gravy, oil

Certain foods: bread, popcorn, butter, cheese, ham, beef, bacon

Gases: air, steam, hydrogen, oxygen, smoke, pollution

Things with individual parts that are thought of as a whole: furniture, garbage, luggage, jewelry, food, clothing, money

Weather and other natural phenomena: snow, rain, thunder, sunshine, fog, gravity

Materials: cotton, glass, concrete, copper, steel, wood

Subjects or fields of study: biology, photography, English, math, computer science

Noncountable nouns do not have a plural form. Adding an *–s* to the noncountable noun *fun,* for example, is not appropriate. *Fun* does not have a plural form, so *funs* would be incorrect.

Some nouns have both a countable and a noncountable meaning. The context determines which meaning is specific, and therefore countable, or more general, and therefore noncountable.

Countable:	She accidentally broke two wine **glasses.**
Noncountable:	The window is made of **glass.**

Countable:	He was charged with two **crimes.**
Noncountable:	**Crime** does not pay.

EXERCISE 1

Write the correct form of the noun in parentheses on the blank.

1. Hannah completed her algebra and English _____. (*homework*)

2. Will the _____ be delivered tomorrow? (*mail*)

3. We served the children _____ of juice. (*glass*)

4. If you do not drink plenty of _____, you will get dehydrated. (*water*)

5. She spread _____ on the two slices of _____. (*butter, bread*)

6. During the storm, we heard loud, rumbling _____. (*thunder*)

7. They showed us several _____. (*photograph*)

8. We brought _____ and _____ to the picnic. (*ham, bean*)

9. There are only two _____ left to play. (*game*)

10. The two boys showed _____ in the face of danger. (*courage*)

Articles

The is a definite article, a kind of adjective that refers to one or more specific things. It is used before singular and plural countable nouns.

> the zoo
> the salesclerk
> the organizations
> the feelings

The can sometimes be used before noncountable nouns if the noun is specifically identified.

> She was surprised by **the** patience that he displayed.
> I was able to find **the** information you need.

A and *an* are indefinite articles that refer to one nonspecific thing. They are used before singular countable nouns.

> a teacher
> a promise
> an ability
> an orange

A and *an* are never used before noncountable nouns.

 **EXERCISE 2**

Circle any article that is used incorrectly. If the use of articles in the sentence is correct, write *Correct* on the blank.

1. She is an employee of the company. _____

2. We are making the progress on our report. _____

3. Both of the job applicants have a computer experience. _____

4. He ordered a salad and a bread. _____

5. That athlete has both the strength and the speed. _____

6. We heard a laughter coming from the kitchen. _____

7. I gave him a help with his math homework. _____

8. She did not have an answer for the question. _____

9. The audience gave the actors the loud applause. _____

10. They are having the fun on their trip. _____

Order of Verbs in Verb Phrases

There are twelve verb tenses, which are listed and illustrated in the following chart.

SIMPLE TENSES indicate a past, present, or future action.	
Present tense	He walks to school every day.
Past tense	He walked to school last year.
Future tense	He will walk to school next year.

PERFECT TENSES indicate that an action was or will be completed before another time or action.	
Present perfect tense	He has walked to school every day for the last three years.
Past perfect tense	He had walked to school once or twice in the past before he started taking the bus.
Future perfect tense	By the time he graduates, he will have walked to school for three years.

PROGRESSIVE TENSES indicate continuing action at a specific time.	
Present progressive tense	He is walking to school right now.
Past progressive tense	He was walking to school at 7:30 yesterday.
Future progressive tense	He will be walking to school at 7:30 tomorrow morning.
Present perfect progressive tense	He has been walking to school for twenty minutes now.
Past perfect progressive tense	He had been walking for twenty minutes when he realized that he did not have his backpack.
Future perfect progressive tense	When the clock strikes eight, he will have been walking for thirty minutes.

As you can see from this chart, different combinations of helping (or auxiliary) verbs and main verbs allow speakers of English to indicate different times and qualities of verbs. The components of verbs must occur in a specific order:

MODAL* + BASE FORM OF VERB
I must write.
He can write.
They must write.

Has/have/had + PAST PARTICIPLE OF VERB
I have written.
He has written.
They had written.

Is/are/was/were + PRESENT PARTICIPLE (–ING FORM) OF VERB
I am writing.
He is writing.
They are writing.

MODAL + has/have + PAST PARTICIPLE OF VERB
I might have written.
He should have written.
They could have written.

MODAL + be + PRESENT PARTICIPLE OF VERB
I could be writing.
He will be writing.
They may be writing.

MODAL + has/have + been + PRESENT PARTICIPLE OF VERB
I will have been writing.
He must have been writing.
They may have been writing.

*The modals are *can, could, may, might, must, will, would, should,* and *shall.*

EXERCISE 3

Fill in the blank with the correct order of the words in parentheses to express the tense.

1. We _____ the schedule. (*changing be will*)

2. Lin _____ the problem. (*have solved must*)

3. I _____ you. (*have should called*)

4. By the time the plumber arrived, the pipe _____ for eight hours. (*leaking been had*)

5. At ten o'clock, they _____ for twelve hours. (*been will working have*)

6. They _____ her a ride. (*given should have*)

7. He _____ next. (*be will performing*)

8. By the time she graduates, she _____ in college for five years. (*have been will*)

9. She _____. (*been acting have must*)

10. I _____ to Mexico this summer. (*be may going*)

For additional practice using verbs and verb tense, see the Parts of Speech section of the Handbook.

Verbs with Gerunds and Infinitives

Some verbs are followed by a gerund (a *verbal,* a verb form that functions as another part of speech in a sentence), and others are followed by an infinitive, another verbal. A **gerund** is the *–ing* form of a verb that acts as a noun in a sentence.

> **Dancing** is great exercise.
> She enjoys **reading** and **traveling.**

The following verbs are usually followed by a gerund:

admit	discuss	finish	practice	resist
avoid	dislike	imagine	put off	risk
consider	enjoy	miss	quit	stop
deny	escape	postpone	recall	suggest

You would not write: *He practiced **to hit** the ball.* Instead, you would write: *He practiced **hitting** the ball.*

An **infinitive** is made up of the word *to* plus the base form of a verb. It most often functions as a noun in a sentence (but can also be an adjective or an adverb). The following infinitives (nouns) are direct objects:

He asked her **to dance.**
She likes **to read.**

The following verbs are usually followed by an infinitive acting as a noun (direct object):

afford	fail	need	refuse
agree	forget	neglect	remember
appear	hesitate	plan	start
begin	hope	prefer	try
continue	intend	pretend	wait
decide	learn	promise	
expect	mean	offer	

You would not write: *She cannot afford **buying** a new car* (gerund phrase). Instead, you would write: *She cannot afford **to buy** a new car.* Notice that gerunds and infinitives can take objects to form gerund or infinitive phrases. When that happens, the whole verbal phrase functions as the sentence element (direct objects in these examples).

> ★ **EXERCISE 4**

Circle the correct word or words in parentheses for each sentence.

1. He just learned (whistling, to whistle).

2. Did she offer (doing, to do) that chore?

3. I remember (giving, to give) him the information.

4. Do not forget (bringing, to bring) your ticket.

5. She hopes (marrying, to marry) him one day.

6. They dislike (riding, to ride) the bus.

7. The dog finally quit (barking, to bark).

8. He decided (applying, to apply) for the position.

9. Have you stopped (smoking, to smoke)?

10. She agreed (joining, to join) the organization.

Verbs with Prepositions

Prepositions are often used with verbs to express certain meanings. For example, notice how the verb *waited* is paired with different prepositions in the following examples:

> I waited **for** an hour.
> I waited **on** the customers.
> I waited **at** the bus stop.
> I waited **in** the waiting room.

These prepositions are not interchangeable, for they express different meanings. Consult a dictionary when you are unsure of the right preposition to use with a particular verb.

EXERCISE 5

Circle the correct preposition in parentheses for each sentence.

1. She argues (with, about) her brother.

2. She and her brother argue (with, about) everything.

3. He agrees (to, with) you.

4. He agreed (to, with) the proposal.

5. I did not want to part (with, from) her.

6. I did not want to part (with, from) my hard-earned money.

7. Did she wait (in, for) them?

8. Did she wait (in, for) the lobby?

9. The employees differ (from, about) one another in their views on the best course of action.

10. They differ (from, about) the best course of action.

The Prepositions *in*, *at*, and *on*

For expressions related to time and place, the prepositions *in*, *at*, and *on* have specific meanings.

Use *in*

- before a month, year, season, century, or time period: *in June, in 2003, in spring, in the nineteenth century, in a week*

- before a city, state, country, or continent: *in Seattle, in California, in France, in South America*

- to mean "into" or "inside of": *in the kitchen, in the lake*

Use *at*

- before an actual clock time: *at five o'clock*

- before a specific place or address: *at the post office, at 1612 Oak Street*

Use *on*

- before a day or date: *on Thursday, on April 5*

- before holidays: *on Thanksgiving, on Labor Day*

- to mean "supported by," "on top of," or "at a certain place": *on the bench, on the table, on Oak Street*

EXERCISE 6

Circle the correct preposition in parentheses for each sentence.

1. My appointment is (in, at, on) Tuesday.

2. The doctor can see you (in, at, on) the morning.

3. They met (in, at, on) 4:30 p.m.

4. The mall is (in, at, on) King Boulevard.

5. The mall is (in, at, on) 2100 King Boulevard.

6. He swam (in, on) the ocean.

7. He sailed (in, on) the lake.

8. Her wedding is (in, at, on) June.

9. Her wedding is (in, at, on) June 4, 2007.

10. We bought these souvenirs (in, at, on) Germany.

Unnecessary Repetition of Subjects

In some languages, some parts of sentences are repeated. Resist in particular the repetition of the subject of a sentence. It is unnecessary to state the subject and then refer with a pronoun to it again, as in the following sentences:

> Mrs. Rodriguez **she** is an excellent teacher.
> Her raise in pay **it** was not enough.
> The employees at the factory **they** work in shifts.

To correct each of these sentences, simply eliminate the boldfaced pronoun.

EXERCISE 7

In each of the following sentences, circle pronouns that unnecessarily repeat the subject. If there are no unnecessary pronouns, write *Correct* on the blank.

1. The room it was empty. _____

2. The nurse she took his temperature. _____

3. Le Mei and he plan to go to medical school. _____

4. Mrs. Davis and her students they enjoyed the performance. _____

5. We stopped to see him, but he was not home. _____

6. The story he wrote it was very interesting. _____

7. The people waiting in line they were getting angry. _____

8. Unlike him, she speaks Spanish. _____

9. The reasons for his decision they made sense. _____

10. She pushed, and she pulled, but she could not move the dresser.
_____

Index

Rhetorical Index

Classification

Division

Comparison/ Contrast

Combination of Rhetorical Modes

double-spacing